The cinema of Pedro Almodóvar

Manchester University Press

Spanish and Latin American Filmmakers

Series editors:
Núria Triana Toribio, University of Kent
Andy Willis, University of Salford

Spanish and Latin American Filmmakers offers a focus on new film-makers; reclaims previously neglected filmmakers; and considers established figures from new and different perspectives. Each volume places its subject in a variety of critical and production contexts.

The series sees filmmakers as more than just auteurs, thus offering an insight into the work and contexts of producers, writers, actors, production companies and studios. The studies in this series take into account the recent changes in Spanish and Latin American film studies, such as the new emphasis on popular cinema, and the influence of cultural studies in the analysis of films and of the film cultures produced within the Spanish-speaking industries.

Already published

The cinema of Pedro Almodóvar

Ana María Sánchez-Arce

Manchester University Press

Published by Manchester University Press
Oxford Road, Manchester M13 9PL

www.manchesteruniversitypress.co.uk

British Library Cataloguing-in-Publication Data
A catalogue record for this book is available from the British Library

ISBN 978 0 7190 7442 4 hardback
ISBN 978 1 5261 6712 5 paperback

First published 2020
Paperback published 2022

Typeset by
Servis Filmsetting Ltd, Stockport, Cheshire

A mis padres, que me educaron en la pasión
por el cine y el silencio a partes iguales.

Contents

Figures

Acknowledgements

I have accumulated many debts as I have worked on this book. I am particularly indebted to Manchester University Press and its staff, who believed in the project and my ability to see it through to publication, even after unavoidable delays due to all sorts of setbacks. Núria Triana Toribio and Andy Willis, series editors for Spanish and Latin American Filmmakers, have also demonstrated infinite patience. The reviewers of the original book proposal made numerous excellent suggestions. The British Academy funded archive research for this book with a small grant. I have also been supported by Sheffield Hallam University's (SHU) Humanities Research Centre (HRC), which has assisted me materially and by allowing me to take periods of leave to write up the bulk of this book. The head of the HRC, Chris Hopkins, has been an unfailing ally.

I would never have thought of writing this book had it not been for the encouragement of Neil Sinyard (University of Hull). I have been able to share my love of cinema with colleagues in the Department of Humanities, who have been a source of strength throughout. The staff at SHU library and film archives (Madrid) have been incredible in tracking down research materials. Many thanks also go to Carmen Ramos Villar (University of Sheffield), and Stuart Green (University of Leeds), who have lent books (I promise to return them!) and talked about all things Spanish with me.

I have been fortunate to find extremely generous and encouraging specialists in Hispanic Studies and film along the way, including José Arroyo (University of Warwick), Fiona Noble (Durham University) and Sarah Wright (Royal Holloway, London). Fiona has given me the most precious gift, time (when she had little herself), as she offered to read sections of this book in its draft form. So has Goran Stanivukovic

(St Mary's University), who not only has kept me sane by talking about film and literature but also offered feedback that made all the difference. José M. Sánchez Rangel, filmmaker and video editor, was there when I needed help identifying old equipment. Other friends (you know who you are) have kept me going with numerous acts of kindness.

My good friend Carmen Ruiz Sánchez has always been there. I can almost hear her saying (like Ignacio writes to Enrique in *La mala educación*), '¡*Pero si la cinefila soy yo!*' My family in Spain have been my magpies, collecting all things Almodóvar. I owe the most to Jonathan Ellis – *il miglior fabbro* – without whose infinite help I may have given up, and to Pablo, who has graciously put up with *mamá* working days, nights, and weekends for a long time. ¡*Gracias!*

Introduction: ~~All about Almodóvar,~~ ~~or how to become a Spanish auteur~~

When I first thought of writing this book, I provisionally titled this introduction 'All about Almodóvar, or how to become a Spanish auteur'. As I sit down to write it, I realise that this title embodies an insurmountable task, for many reasons. An introduction to a book is often a relatively gentle exposition of its main ideas, a tool to help readers decide how to use it. This introduction will do some of this. But as I re-read the provisional title, I realised that I was think-ing of the introduction in terms of a person, of Pedro Almodóvar as someone I was formally introducing to readers. This book was originally conceived to be read by both scholars and students, so perhaps the idea of an 'introduction' as bringing Almodóvar's cinema to new viewers was not as outlandish as it may seem. This is also why I envisaged this volume as being comprehensive, analysing all of Almodóvar's films to date, including a discussion of some of his early short films shot between 1974 and 1978 with a Super-8 camera. These shorts were soundless and Almodóvar used to screen them in Madrid at parties and other happenings, with his own commentary and sound effects.

Unfortunately, only two of these short films – *Muerte en la car-retera* (1976) and *Salomé* (1978) – are available to view at the Madrid *Filmoteca* (Film Archives). A third, slightly later short with sound, *Tráiler para amantes de lo prohibido*, originally screened on Spanish television in 1985 and conceived as a companion piece to and teaser for Almodóvar's feature film *¿Qué he hecho yo para merecer esto?* (What Have I Done to Deserve This?, 1984) is also available at the Biblioteca Nacional (Madrid). For this reason, this volume will concentrate on the feature films and *Tráiler* will be analysed within the chapter devoted to *¿Qué he hecho?* Almodóvar's output is not confined to film.

However, I regret that there is not space in this book to analyse his comics, short stories, and non-fiction writing, as well as his stint as a pop singer and musician, activities that allowed him to rehearse themes and techniques for his films, as well as building his public persona.

Yet, even with an extended introduction, nobody can presume to know or explain *all about* anyone or anything. The subtitle offers some hope of narrowing down the topic, but again I need to add a caveat: this book is not a manual for budding would-be auteurs, nor do I focus particularly on the Almodóvar brand. My bias towards thinking of Almodóvar as an auteur originates in traditional ways of study-ing Spanish cinema and personal experience. As Peter Buse, Núria Triana Toribio, and Andy Willis, state in their introduction to *The Cinema of Álex de la Iglesia*, 'too often in the study of Spanish cinema there is a silent endorsement of the concepts of the auteur and art cinema and not enough acknowledgement that approaches to film that are anchored in authorship are both historically contingent ... and, since the 1970s, increasingly discredited' (2007: 7). I share their ambivalent recognition of the function of the concept of the auteur to 'organise cinema for film critics and teachers of cinema' and also their reservations since 'tied up with the concept of the auteur is a whole set of assumptions about genius and creativity, not to mention gender, which makes the concept of the auteur at best anachronistic if not approached with eyes wide open' (Buse, Triana Toribio, and Willis, 2007: 7–8). In this book, although I seldom use 'Almodóvar' in inverted commas, and only when referring to the way the Almodóvar construct is used in critical analysis, I refer to Almodóvar films or the cinema of Almodóvar with an understanding that the Almodóvar construct hides a team of collaborators, including actors, art directors, cinematographers, composers, editors, designers, producers, and many others who have contributed to the final products. Although I have occasionally mentioned the impact that some of these collabora-tors have on individual films, in particular artists who appeared in his early films, this volume does not do justice to the role played by long-standing collaborators such as Ángel Luis Fernández and José Luis Alcaine (cinematographers), José Salcedo (editor), Alberto Iglesias (composer), Antxón Gómez (art director), Agustín Almodóvar and Esther García (producers), Juan Gatti (graphic designer), and Sonia Grande (costume designer), as well as less frequent collaborators such as Jean Paul Gaultier (costume designer) and many others.

One could say that Almodóvar fits the main requirements to be considered an auteur, including being a director who is also the sole screenwriter for most of his films, who experiments with form and content, and who has a distinctive range of visual styles that develop over his career and set trends. As Marvin D'Lugo and Kathleen Vernon say, 'he has established a cinematic style that other filmmakers imitate (the adjective "Almodovarian" is not only applied to his own work but also to the style of others who appear to be emulating him)' (2013: 4). His particular take on Hollywood melodrama, wonderfully analysed by Núria Triana Toribio (1995), has also generated specific genre terminology, for example, the 'Almodrama', coined by Vicente Molina Foix (Epps, 2005: 271).

Due to his co-ownership (with younger brother Agustín Almodóvar) of the production company El Deseo, S.A. (henceforth El Deseo), Almodóvar also has substantial autonomy in the production process, something that most filmmakers and many auteurs do not. El Deseo was founded in 1985 and has not only produced all of Almodóvar's films since *La ley del deseo* (The Law of Desire, 1987) but also many other films including the internationally acclaimed *El espinazo del diablo* (The Devil's Backbone, del Toro, 2001) and *La vida secreta de las palabras* (The Secret Life of Words, Coixet, 2005). El Deseo placed Almodóvar in an enviable position as a filmmaker in that he was able to take control of all the films he directed. Almodóvar has said that 'with my first five films [before founding El Deseo], I felt I had had five children all by different fathers with whom I was always disagreeing. ... Producers often commit atrocities to the negatives and I wanted to retain my control over them' (Strauss, 2006: 63). His first feature film, *Pepi, Luci, Bom y otras chicas del montón* (Pepi, Luci, Bom, and Other Girls on the Heap, 1980), had been put together in a haphazard way when money became available from businessmen and arts patrons and was finally produced by Pepón Coromina of Figaro Films; nowadays we would say it was partly crowdfunded. *Laberinto de pasiones* (Labyrinth of Passion, 1982) was produced by the Madrid cinema Alphaville, who had seen first hand how popular Almodóvar's first film was. Tesauro, a company that belonged to Hervé Hachuel, produced *Entre tinieblas* (Dark Habits, 1983) as a vehicle for Hachuel's then girlfriend, Cristina Sánchez Pascual, and *¿Qué he hecho?* I discuss the difficulties that arose in *Entre tinieblas* in Chapter 2. The filmmaker's wariness of relinquishing control to producers is fictionalised directly in *Los abrazos rotos* (Broken Embraces, 2009).

In 1983, a new law – the *Real Decreto 3304/1983 de 28 de diciembre, sobre protección* de la *cinematografía* (Law on the Protection of Cinema; Spain, 1984), commonly known as the Miró Law after the name of the General Director of Cinema who introduced it, filmmaker turned politician Pilar Miró – was passed in order to aid the production of quality films, experimental films, children's films, and work by new directors (cf. Triana Toribio, 2003b: 111–21). The emphasis was on quality films and international projection and, as D'Lugo explains:

> the roots of Almodóvar's current version of globalized Spanish pro- duction and marketing can be traced to his brief engagement with the efforts of the first post-Franco Socialist government to stabilize what Pilar Miró in 1984 famously called 'Cine español para el mundo,' [Spanish cinema for the world] an effort by the Ministry of Culture to promote for international markets a broad notion of cinema of quality, the founding principle of which was 'cine de autor' [auteur cinema]. (2006: 79)

The Miró Law made it easier for directors to produce their own films as state help went directly to producers. Once the Almodóvar brothers saw how easily the producer of *Matador* (1986) had managed to obtain one of these grants, they decided that they could do this themselves: 'For *Matador*, the last film I made before the birth of El Deseo, my producer [Andrés Vicente Gómez, Cia Iberoamericana de TV, S.A.] simply went to the Ministry of Culture with a dossier I had pre-prepared myself, asked them for a subsidy and then pre-sold the television rights. ... I was not at all interested in continuing such a non-collaborative relationship' (Almodóvar, quoted in Strauss, 2006: 63). El Deseo S.A. was born.

The Miró Law favoured auteur cinema to the detriment of a more collaborative view of filmmaking. Likewise, media coverage of Almodóvar's cinema has always tended to focus on him as an auteur, a creative genius with a penchant for women's roles, as much of a celebrity as the actors who work with him. I encountered the cinema of Almodóvar in my early teens through news of the international success of *Mujeres al borde de un ataque de nervios* (Women on the Verge of a Nervous Breakdown, 1988), which cemented Almodóvar's reputation in Spain; *Mujeres* had been selected to represent Spain at the Oscars and nominated for the Best Foreign Film award. I was too young to watch even this most tame of Almodóvar's films, so my first encounter was – as for many Spaniards – mediated through the news and cultural programmes on national television, Televisión Española. These focused on the director as the originator and creative source of the work and the actors as celebrities subordinated to him, as seen in the widespread use of the term *chicas Almodóvar* (Almodóvar girls, directly alluding to the interchangeable Bond girls), coined to refer to the women actors who appeared in that film, a term that has continued to be used for women actors who have collaborated with him in subsequent films and which will be indelibly linked in my memory to the famous still of the female cast of *Mujeres* sitting on a sofa on the film set, a composition that is frequently echoed in publicity stills for other films by Almodóvar. This still is particularly powerful because it is linked to another publicity still of Almodóvar himself lying on the very same sofa reading what one can only presume to be the screenplay. There are other stills of the cast with the director, which powerfully suggest an identification of the filmmaker as a performer in his own right, and this performance being as much part of his films' paratextual apparatus as posters, credits, and so on.

Many critics have remarked on the 'overidentification' of Almodóvar with his women characters, but none more eloquently than Paul Julian Smith, who compares Almodóvar's role to the more auteurist or directorial personas or Spanish auteurs from a slightly older generation such as Carlos Saura and locates Spanish critical discomfort with the Almodóvar persona in this divergence from the figure of the creative genius (2014: 100). José Enrique Monterde's review of *Kika* in the Spanish film magazine *Dirigido por ...* is a particularly good example of how some Spanish film critics have used Almodóvar's media savviness and his wider persona to attack Almodóvar himself rather than focusing on his work, although the best known adversary of Almodóvar in film journalism circles is certainly Carlos Boyero, film critic for the Madrid daily *El País*, who regularly writes dismissive reviews containing personal attacks on the filmmaker. Monterde writes thus about Almodóvar:

> As long as Almodóvar believes it necessary to parade his circus, euphemistically known as the 'Almodóvar girls,' and composed of the most famous transsexual in Spain, the ugliest actress (?) in our cinema, etc., he is closer to the antics of a Dipsy, Laa-Laa, Po, and Tinky Winky than to the artistic practices of a reputable film narrator; ... as long as there

continues to be confusion between the films' characters and the clown-
ish paper dolls whose presence there predates the conception of the
film; as long as the obsession of the nouveau riche [director] who not
only writes but produces his films, saturates every corner of the film,
wielding as his trademark the most nauseating concept of 'design'
as he flaunts his association with Sakamoto/Morricone or Gaultier/
Versace ... (quoted in Cerdán and Fernández Labayen, 2013: 143)

Monterde objects to the spectacular persona of Almodóvar, his association with trans individuals and women who do not follow established canons of beauty. He also dismisses Almodóvar as 'nouveau
riche', implying that he may have the means to make films but not
the taste or technical ability to do so successfully. This response is in
line with what sociologist Pierre Bourdieu has identified as stratified
cultural taste according to social class position in *Distinction* (2013
[1984]). Monterde's objections recur in much Spanish criticism of
Almodóvar's cinema that dismisses it as a product for mass consumption with airs of grandeur. In effect, a concept of Almodóvar's cinema
as a commodity prevents it from being considered a legitimate work
of art belonging to what Bourdieu calls 'the field of restricted production' (1993: 115). Monterde's assessment of Almodóvar's work
is therefore directly and indirectly related to Almodóvar's perceived
social class and his lack of formal education in filmmaking. One
could say that Almodóvar's cinema is in fact – despite his marketing
as highbrow outside Spain – perceived as middlebrow in his own
country.

Almodóvar's biographical legend (to borrow Boris Tomashevsky's
term) contributes to interpretations of his work seen above, but also
to much more positive (though equally constructed) views of him as a
Spanish filmmaker inextricably linked to the construction of Spanish
national culture, however much his cinema appropriates and is
repelled by it in equal measure. Almodóvar's biography constantly
frames discussions of his work and is part of his popular persona. In
1992, Smith was already commenting on its repetitious nature (64).
Diane McDaniel analyses the role this biographical legend plays in
the creation of a version of Spain and summarises it thus:

Born between 1949 and 1951, Almodóvar grew up in the remote village
of Calzada de Calatrava where he felt about at home as an 'astronaut
in King Arthur's court.' (This observation of Almodóvar appears with

amazing regularity.) His grandfather made wine; his father was a bookkeeper for a gas station. Enchanted with his mother's stories of Madrid, Almodóvar occupied himself by painting, reading, watching movies until he ended up in Madrid at age 16, 17, or 18 (each is reported as often as the other), without any money, and supported himself by street peddling [I have also read that he stayed at his sister and brother-in-law's]. Soon after, he got a job working for the national telephone company, where he spent 10 years.

Almodóvar arrived in Madrid in time to witness and participate in the extraordinary upheaval called La Movida ... He soon found himself at the center of it all ... His involvement with the theater group Los Goliardos led him to make his first film. In 1969 he started making movies with a Super-8 camera. ... In 1979, on weekends, he began making his first feature film ... in which he got his friends to act. (1994)

McDaniel is not interested in fact-checking. On the contrary, her focus is on how the frequent repetition of these chosen episodes of Almodóvar's life contribute to 'the dual sense of historical fate and ahistorical spontaneity', which in turn played no small part in the transformation of Spain's image post-Franco from 'the isolated third-world country it remained under Franco's long and brutal dictatorship into a vital and vibrant part of the European Union' (1994). Throughout the book, I engage with this narrative of national rebirth, explaining that it is not simply the product of the post-Franco desire to project an image of modernity abroad and at home but also a recycling of eighteenth-century stereotypes about Spain as the Oriental 'other', stereotypes that Almodóvar's cinema embraces and dismantles in equal measure.

As McDaniel explains, Almodóvar's 'oft repeated story represents something more than simply the personal story of one Pedro Almodóvar; it represents a whole new Spain. This is a Spain where the collective past is irrelevant to an individual's present and future' (1994). Almodóvar's success was relayed to Spaniards from the late 1980s as a sign of Spain's restored status. Abroad, his films were seized upon as a sign that Spain had become a democratic, capitalist country, as discussed in Chapter 1. It is important to note how as Spain's narrative of itself has changed through the late 1990s and the twenty-first century, due to its (limited) engagement with the recovery of historical memory and interrogation of its democratic credentials, analyses of Almodóvar's cinema and the director's biographical details available publicly have also changed to accommodate this new story of him/itself. In this sense, this volume is an expected development in the evolving way in which the cinema of Almodóvar is employed to read Spain, whatever 'Spain' may be. It is in its focus on how these films engage with 'Spain', with the narrative of the nation, and its contribution to the study of contemporary Spanish cinema's engagement with the country's twentieth-century traumas that this book's significance lies.

Almodóvar and El Deseo have become adept at harnessing the power of media to promote their films. In fact, as Núria Triana Toribio explains, not only is Almodóvar one of the most media-minded Spanish directors, he also 'set the terms of reference by which other producers/directors operate *vis à vis* marketing' (2008: 262–3). Triana Toribio reclaims the term '*directores mediáticos* (media-minded/media friendly directors)', which had originally been used in a 'somewhat derogatory way to describe the media-friendliness and exposure of certain auteurs (namely Pedro Almodóvar, Alejandro Almenábar and Julio Médem)', attributing it to directors who 'understand the need to treat marketing as an integral part of production, but equally importantly are highly mindful of the commercial usefulness to the Spanish industry of the category of the auteur as key to strategies for "placing the product"' (2008: 260).

Almodóvar is always positioning himself as an auteur, even in the early days when his films were more obviously the result of collaboration with a range of artists working in 1980s Madrid, loosely associated with what has been called *la movida* (I discuss *la movida* particularly in Chapter 1): 'whether they are good or bad, my films are absolutely different from other Spanish films and even from other foreign cinema. ... But if you see all of my films, I'm sure you can differentiate them from the others, you can recognize them' (quoted in Kinder, 1987: 37). At the same time, in these early days at least, his use of pop, camp, and postmodernist aesthetics (which typically undermine notions of authorship, intentionality, and ideas of the artist as a creative genius) were seen as auteurial markers, signs of his experimental range of visual styles, by some. Others, mainly critics in Spain as explained above, saw them instead as evidence of Almodóvar's lack of formal mastery. This book moves beyond these paradigms in arguing that Almodóvar's films are not postmodern but metamodern.

The first film produced by El Deseo, *La ley*, was not as easy to fund as the Almodóvar brothers thought and Almodóvar had to ask for a personal loan. This is probably due to its focus on gay and trans relationships and lives. I discuss this covert censorship in the chapter on *La ley*. Almodóvar was exploring trans issues before queer trans studies emerged fully as is the case now and placing gay sexuality at the centre of his films during one of the most difficult times to do so in the twentieth century: the height of the panic about the Aids epidemic and its negative impact on public opinion on homosexuality. Censorship of LGBTQ+ identities and sexualities is related in subsequent chapters to historical censorship of trauma and the compromises Spanish politicians and society had to agree to during the Transition (1975–1982) that shaped contemporary post-Transition Spain. Readers interested in the shared themes of trans issues, LGBTQ+ concerns, and the deconstruction of masculinity in relation to personal and historical memory may want to concentrate on the chapters on the early films, *Entre tinieblas*, *La ley*, *Tacones lejanos* (High Heels, 1991), *Todo sobre mi madre* (All about My Mother, 1999), *La mala educación* (Bad Education, 2004), *La piel que habito* (The Skin I Live In, 2011), *Los amantes pasajeros* (I'm So Excited!, 2013), *Dolor y gloria* (Pain and Glory, 2019), and, to a lesser extent, *Julieta* (2016). The deconstruction of masculinity is further explored in the chapters on *Matador* and *Carne trémula* (Live Flesh, 1997).

The funding difficulties and reception of *La ley* illustrate the complex relationship that Almodóvar has towards LGBTQ+ activism. On the one hand, he places traditionally marginalised identities centre stage. On the other, 'he has annoyed Spanish gay activists in trying to distance himself from an account of his "gay experience" as if the idea were limiting to everything else Almodóvar was trying to be' (Mira, 2013: 98). As Alberto Mira explains, Almodóvar's desire to draw a line between his private life and public persona is understandable:

> As a gay man growing up during the years when the label was used against homosexuals, he has been suspicious of self-identification. The implication, so distant from classical activist doctrine, is that any labeling [*sic*] of sexual identity ghettoizes the subject. That there are commercial repercussions in such ghettoizing is not irrelevant to this discussion, but neither is it the whole story. (2013: 98–9)

Despite rave reviews in gay publications at the time of release, *La ley* and Almodóvar's cinema more generally have retrospectively been found wanting in relation to positive representations of gay characters or explicit political interventions. Throughout this book, I argue that despite Almodóvar's rejection of gay activist doctrine (just as he rejects political activism more generally) his cinema always engages with these issues without the 'labelling'. It is therefore unreasonable to claim, as Smith does, that 'in its disavowal of AIDS and homophobia' *La ley* refuses to 'deal with the everyday life of lesbians and gays in Spain' (2014: 90). Both Aids and homophobia are present in *La ley* and other films by Almodóvar, just not in the expected way. As Smith goes on to explain:

> Almodóvar seeks to intervene at the more potent and fluid level of fantasy, of the constitution of new cinematic subjects. And his self-producing characters, scornful of fixed gender identity and object choice, have earned him attacks from both the homophobic right, who would enforce silence, and the moralistic left, who would insist on more positive images. (2014: 90)

With *Dolor y gloria*, Almodóvar finally self-identifies as gay, but even this is done indirectly in the film's blurring of the boundaries between autobiography, autofiction and fiction, and in interviews where he discusses being different and how this must have affected his family.

The cinema of Almodóvar does not wear its politics on its sleeve, as also demonstrated by the periodic outcries about the films' portrayals of women and sexual violence against them, something I discuss throughout this book and that Almodóvar has recently sought to address (Smith, 2019). However, the disregard of many of Almodóvar's characters for binary gender structures and heteronormativity speak to a politics of fait accompli: the world portrayed in Almodóvar's cinema is a world constructed upon the unsavoury past and present, not aiming to change the present and future through analysis of the social context but by presenting an (not necessarily utopian) alternative. As Almodóvar said to Marsha Kinder in 1987, '[w]e don't have confidence in the future, but we are constructing a past for ourselves because we don't like the one we had' (1987: 37). I agree with Mark Allinson that:

> [t]hose seeking progressive images of happy homosexuals in Almodóvar's films are the most frequently disappointed, for Almodóvar

is always interested in crisis and imbalance. Gays and lesbians are just as likely to be unhappy as heterosexuals. Almodóvar does not perceive any duty to compensate for decades of repression and invisibility by substituting politically correct 'positive images' of gays and lesbians. (2001: 101)

I would not go as far as to say that gays and lesbians' 'political or social context does not interest Almodóvar' (Allinson, 2001: 101), more that is highlighted through the films' formal elements. The legacy of 'decades of repression and invisibility' is present in Almodóvar's films: as an unseen past that is revealed as an absence of what audiences know to be social reality, in contrast with the fantasy represented; when the fantasy filmic world is disturbed by micro-aggressions and aggressions suffered by LGBTQ+ characters and their responses to those around them; and, finally, in the centrality of trauma to Almodóvar's work, normally represented in the form of absences (ellipses) signified by traces, structural complexity (narrative analepses and flashbacks), and cinematic excess (linked to the poetic or symbolic function of language). There has been an incremental increase in the visibility of this context in Almodóvar's cinema, but as *Dolor y Gloria* brilliantly articulates, the personal cost of repression reverberates in the present, even when the agents of repression are no longer.

The trauma of 'repression and invisibility' is particularly acute within the LGBTQ+ community, and in Spain it is part of a wider repression of the past, including crimes against humanity committed during the Spanish Civil War and subsequent military dictatorship. It is the filmic expression of trauma in its many forms and how it may relate to this original trauma, as well as the role of film narrative in the suppression and re-creation of memory, that I am particularly interested in, without it being the sole focus of the book. Although Almodóvar's interest in collective and historical memory has become more obvious since *Carne trémula* with the first insertion of scenes set in the historical past, Almodóvar has always engaged with the legacy of Spain's past and its repercussions in the present, be it through intertextuality with films of the dictatorship, challenges to traditional ways of thinking, or focus on individual trauma and healing processes. This engagement can already be seen in his first feature film, *Pepi, Luci, Bom*, with its unsympathetic representation of the policeman, parody of traditional clothes, and appropriation of conservative behaviour (the submissive housewife reconfigured as a lesbian masochist). The initial refusal to address the dictatorship directly was a result of the following: rebellion against past repression; elation at the possibilities of self-definition that opened up after Franco's death and the peaceful political Transition of the 1970s and early 1980s (the failed 1981 military coup notwithstanding); disenchantment at the realisation that change would not happen immediately; and, finally, an ambivalent attitude to traditional Spanish culture. However, this book takes the view, in line with Smith's line of thought in *Desire Unlimited*, that:

> the conspicuous frivolity of Almodóvar's cinema is intimately linked to serious concerns which have often gone unnoticed; and that the frequent dismissal of Almodóvar's work as 'zany' or 'kitsch' arises from a disrespect for a register coded as 'feminine' and for those men who identify themselves with women's concerns. ... [F]aced by the horrors of Francoism or (more recently) the po-faced pieties of Socialism, frivolity can be seen in a Spanish context as a political posture whose effects are as potent as they are uncontrollable. (2014: 2)

What in the early days seemed a stance of radical apoliticism was instead very much political, an attempt to undertake social critique via frivolity in line with other artists of *la movida*.

Almodóvar's equivocation about his engagement with contemporary Spanish history, and the way his films were used by successive Spanish governments to market an image of democratic Spain as having moved beyond the past, resulted in an early perception of Almodóvar's aesthetic as 'apolitical', something that critics such as Smith have strenuously contested by always embedding analyses of Almodóvar's films in their socio-political contexts, an inspiring blending of formal and cultural materialist methodology best seen in Smith's prominent monograph *Desire Unlimited: The Cinema of Pedro Almodóvar* (1994), now in its third, updated edition (2014). In recent years, this perception has lessened somewhat, particularly because Almodóvar's later films are more obviously engaged with Spain's past and its effects on the present but also due to the works of critics too numerous to mention in this introduction but whom I cite throughout this book, including Brad Epps and Despina Kakoudaki's edited collection, *All about Almodóvar: A Passion for Cinema* (2009), *A Companion to Pedro Almodóvar*, edited by Marvin D'Lugo and Kathleen M. Vernon (2013), and Julián Daniel

Gutiérrez-Albilla's *Aesthetics, Ethics and Trauma in the Cinema of Pedro Almodóvar* (2017). Although the majority of this book was drafted before this last monograph appeared, I was able to draw on the series of foundational articles on which much of it is based.

Despite this academic work, the narrative about Almodóvar's cinema is still in many quarters one in which apoliticism gives way to engagement. Whereas Almodóvar has become more vocal, I wonder whether the perception of his increasing engagement is also the product of Spain's own narrative about itself and its relationship with the past traumas of the Civil War (1936–1939) and subsequent dictatorship. His early films are not as disengaged as initially made out, and the later films contain cinematic excess that resists interpretation (for example, the night swimmer in *Hable con ella* (Talk to Her, 2002) and the scene of the stag running alongside the train in *Julieta*), reminding us that Almodóvar is employing the poetic function to enhance the films' symbolic planes. This is one of the reasons why, after considering sections for this book (and wanting to keep a chronological order for students' ease), I decided against them. I would like to think of Almodóvar's cinema as a continuum where motifs, images, characters, and style traits recur not necessarily in terms of development but as images or patterns do in poems, accumulating meaning in such a way that they are best considered together.

I am fully aware that my interpretation is likely to be the product of looking at Almodóvar's cinema from the vantage point of the twenty-first century, particularly my own disappointment at the less-than-perfect Transition and the hidden legacies of the Civil War and dictatorship in my country in terms of social attitudes and, more importantly, structural violence (also referred to as social injustice), as established hierarchies of power and narratives of the past were left unchallenged during and after the Transition. My methodology, whilst decidedly blending feminism and formalism, foregrounds texts as products of their socio-historical environment and thus my analysis shows how Almodóvar's engagement with Spanish history and culture follows closely Spain's own engagement with its past. As a postcolonialist, I have on occasion noted issues to do with race and Spain's colonial past and postcolonial present within the films, but unfortunately had no space to develop these further here. However, this issue certainly warrants extended study.

Besides the playfulness and wilful shock tactics present in his early films and also in later work such as *Los amantes*, Almodóvar uses a range of aesthetic techniques to tackle the socio-historical contexts of Spain from the 1980s until the present day, as well as increasingly delving into the traumatic origin of these in the immediate past, including camp, satire, and pop aesthetics. Postmodernist features predominantly used in his cinema include the celebration of popular culture (including blurring high and low cultural styles and references), textual fragmentation (Almodóvar's famous hybrid genres and use of multiple narratives-within-narratives), and disruption of the boundaries between fiction and reality with the result of a heightened sense of artificiality (metacinematic techniques, authors and filmmakers as characters, and breaking of the fourth wall), pastiche, and parody.

These postmodernist traits, in particular the way Almodóvar's cinema draws on popular culture, its conscious artificiality, and its emphasis on textual fragmentation, have led to the continuous dismissal of Almodóvar's work in Spain by many critics. As Josetxo Cerdán and Miguel Fernández Labayen explain, 'the two major critical narratives about Almodóvar' in Spain are 'the artificiality of his visual imagination and the lack in his films of a solid narrative structure. Of course these are problems only if ... film is understood in terms of ... classic dramaturgy' (2013: 136–7). Almodóvar's voracious cinephilia and his love of popular genres, combined with the popularity of his own work, also contrive to edge him out of the safety of art-house cinema in Spain, however much he is considered outside Spain to be the most prominent, living Spanish auteur and representative of Spanish cinema and culture. As Cerdán and Labayen conclude, '[t]he persistent inability on the part of many Spanish critics to appreciate the multiple facets of the Almodóvar oeuvre is the product of a schematic vision that continues to evaluate forms of cultural expression in terms of high versus low and art versus folklore. For them, his films offer an impossible dialectic between visual sophistication and traditionalist populism' (2013: 148). This continues to be so as seen in a recent review of *Dolor y gloria*, which views the lack of transsexuals or body changes as positive (Roldán Usó, 2019).

This book does not, however, espouse the theory that Almodóvar belongs fully within a postmodern tradition. This rejection of the postmodern label is not because his cinema is not experimental enough or because of Almodóvar's courting of the public, as 'the salesman whose resistance to losing the audience's favour is the reason why he dare not take that final step' (Losilla, 2013: 96). I propose a much less elitist argument: Almodóvar has never bought completely into postmodernism, even during the 1980s when he associated himself with it fully. He employs postmodernist techniques, but with a different intent, something that I begin discussing in relation to *Matador*'s reworking of cultural tradition, where postmodern playfulness hides a pointed unravelling (through appropriation) of the 'naturalness' of national traditions and symbols. Sidney Donnell noticed as early as 2001 that Almodóvar 'embrac[es] postmodernism and some aspects of structuralist thought without abandoning story-telling and its ability to help him communicate historical truths' (2001: 64). This divergence can be explained in terms of a balance between modernist and postmodernist frames, as I show in my discussion of *Carne trémula*, where I refer to the voice-over's optimistic tone as pointing to postmodern irony with a modernist intent. As part of this discussion, I introduce the idea that Almodóvar is not, in fact, a postmodern filmmaker but a metamodern one, due to his use of postmodern aesthetics with a different, ethical intent. Metamodernism was coined in 2010 by Timoteus Vermeulen and Robin van den Akker and further theorised in 2017 by van den Akker, Alison Gibbons, and Vermeulen. The more Almodóvar tackles serious socio-political and historical issues, the more he uses postmodern distancing techniques. This is an argument that is developed more fully in the latter part of the book, from the discussion of *Carne trémula* onwards. If indeed Almodóvar is employing postmodernist features with an ethical intent, it would then follow that he was metamodern before metamodernism, but this is a topic for another time.

1

The early films: *Pepi, Luci, Bom y otras chicas del montón* and *Laberinto de pasiones*

Pedro Almodóvar's early films have been viewed outside Spain through his established fame as an auteur. Although these early films had some international distribution at film festivals, they were not widely available until after the success of *Mujeres al borde de un ataque de nervios* (Women on the Verge of a Nervous Breakdown, 1988). To an extent, this is also the case in Spain, where the majority of Spaniards would have encountered these films only years after their releases, when Almodóvar's growing success abroad justified their television premieres. *Pepi, Luci, Bom y otras chicas del montón* (Pepi, Luci, Bom, and Other Girls on the Heap, 1980) was released in 1980 in Spain but was not released in France until 1987 and the USA until 1992. *Laberinto de Pasiones* (Labyrinth of Passion, 1982) was premiered in 1982 but not released until 1990 in the USA and 1993 in the UK. Their reception was coloured by the historical moment in which they were conceived, which was only a few years after the death of dictator General Francisco Franco in 1975, during the period of Transition towards a democratic system. *Pepi, Luci, Bom* and *Laberinto* were seen as examples of an emerging 'modern' Spain, a 'new' Spain that was supposed to have fully embraced pop, punk, rock, and capitalism. Additionally, the films are particularly interesting as early rehearsals of what later would become recognisable traits in Almodóvar's style, including the exploration of desire within and outside the limiting family and social structures of post-Franco Spain, the clash between an old Spain and the new pop culture, the use of a realist style to depict situations that stretch the imagination and moral norms of the time, and the strategic use of surrealism and cinematic excess. They are a reminder of how far Almodóvar's filmmaking has progressed in narrative and visual terms as he learnt his trade by making films. Almodóvar's ability to write stories was more developed than the visual aspects of cinematic language since he had been writing for longer than he had held a camera. His focus on narrative rather than style in the early stages of his career was criticised by other Spanish filmmakers, particularly those who worked, as he did, on experimental Super-8 short films. This was perhaps due to a lack of resources and the fact that he literally learnt how to make films by making them: 'If I have learnt anything, I have done so on the go and with my pants down, in front of the whole world. But since what interested me was fiction and fabulation, I sensed from the very beginning that the script was the main element to start a story' (quoted in Gallero, 1991: 5; my translation). Together with his Super-8 shorts, the early films should be regarded as juvenilia.

Pepi, Luci, Bom is a film about revenge, growing up, and friendship. Pepi (Carmen Maura) is a young woman who lives off her father's handouts until he stops sending money and she has to get a job in marketing. One of her neighbours, a policeman (Félix Rotaeta), realises she is growing cannabis at home and she has to allow him to rape her to ensure his silence. Pepi is determined to get revenge for the loss of her virginity (which she sees as a commodity that has been stolen from her) and lures the policeman's wife, Luci (Eva Siva), to her flat, where it is discovered that she is a masochist. Luci falls for punk teenager Bom (Olvido Gara, also known as Alaska) and the three friends have a great time until Luci is beaten up by her husband, much to her enjoyment, and decides to return to the marital home. Pepi and Bom lose a friend but start a deeper friendship or perhaps a sexual relationship.

Labyrinth of Passion is a parody of romantic comedies with parallel stories and an international intrigue thrown in. Sexilia (Cecilia Roth) and Riza Niro (Imanol Arias) are young people with non-normative sexualities that become 'normalised' when they fall for each other. Sexilia is a nymphomaniac and Riza is a promiscuous homosexual. Riza is also the son of the sultan of Tirana and is in Madrid incognito. His stepmother, Toraya (Helga Liné), is looking for him because she wants him to get her pregnant. Many obstacles are put in the couple's path to happiness and the stories of secondary characters take precedence for much of the film, but in the end it is revealed that both Sexilia's and Riza's 'aberrant' sexual behaviours stem from childhood traumas they sustained at the same time and their love for each other 'cures' them.

The story of how *Pepi, Luci, Bom* was filmed is well known. It has become part of Almodóvar mythology, here recounted by the director himself to Fredric Strauss:

> We shot the film with a crew of almost all first-timers. The camera-men cut off some heads, mine above all during the general erection competition. The shoot was very chaotic and lasted a year and a half, starting in 1979 and ending in 1980. We could only work at weekends and when we had the money. We constantly had to adapt the schedule to our material circumstances – which changed constantly. One day, when we'd completely run out of money and we weren't even sure we could finish the film, I remember thinking I'd appear on screen myself and tell the audience how the film ended. After all, telling a story was what interested me most. (quoted in Strauss, 2006: 12)

This 'chaotic' filming is a testament to the resilience and self-belief of Almodóvar and his collaborators. It also seems to have affected the film itself, which tells the story of how Pepi becomes a writer and director. Pepi is as resourceful as Almodóvar had to be. She, too, is driven by an interest in 'telling a story', the story of her friends' relationship.

As far as narrative is concerned, Almodóvar has a tendency to over-complicate. When he is writing a script, he usually starts with a simple idea and keeps adding characters and plotlines to it. Sometimes a sub-plot becomes the main plot in another film, as is the case with the story of the nurse in *La flor de mi secreto* (The Flower of My Secret, 1995) who becomes the main character in *Todo sobre mi madre* (All about My Mother, 1999). In *Pepi, Luci, Bom*, multiple plots are apparent in, for example, the intermittent scenes about the *flamenco-pop* singer who has come from her village to triumph in Madrid or the backstory of the man who pays for the 'general erections' party and is a closet homosexual. *Laberinto de pasiones* contains even more parallel stories, some of which are as important as the main romantic plot. Marvin D'Lugo talks of how 'in the early films, especially in *Laberinto de pasiones*, a rich choral effect is created by the array of characters' (2006: 21). Even though the main thrust of the film is the love story between Riza and Sexilia, their romance is really a framing device to which the other characters' stories are attached. In narrative terms, Riza's and Sexilia's relationship would be too boring (because it is far too easy for them to fall in love and stay together) to devote more time to it. The parodic psychoanalytic explanation of all their problems is a comic distraction from the fact that these two people do not seem to have that many real problems. Sexilia's photophobia is linked to her father's rejection (which coincided with her being blinded by the sun in a beach scene), her nymphomania to both her father's and young Riza's unavailability during that same scene. The sun could easily be read in historical terms as the dictatorship with its emblematic hymn *Cara al sol* (Facing the Sun) and Sexilia's sexual behaviour as Spain's fear and avoidance of politics. By the same token, Toraya is the nasty stepmother that features prominently in Spanish films and literature, the stand-in for the rule of the absent father (cf. Kinder, 1993: 197–275).

Pepi, Luci, Bom is less of an ensemble film, containing two related stories, Pepi's revenge and Luci and Bom's relationship. The relationship between the three women remains central and we are shown its development from getting to know each other to the break-up between Luci and the other two and the possible budding sexual relationship between Pepi and Bom. This final development is shown mostly in visual terms towards the end of the film, as the two friends spend the night at Pepi's after Luci's disappearance and Pepi cooks an elaborate cod dish for Bom. This is the first of many more significant kitchen and cooking scenes in Almodóvar's filmography. What the characters cook and how they do it is as important as what they say. For instance, Bom comments on how surprised she is that Pepi is making such a complex dish when she was only expecting 'an omelette or something'. This shows how special the relationship between the two women is, but may also be an explicit comment on the women's sexuality since lesbians are commonly known as *tortilleras* (omelette-makers) in Spanish slang. As Pepi shakes the casserole, Bom flirts with her:

PEPI   If you didn't have such weird tastes, you'd soon find a replacement.

BOM   My tastes change as time goes by. When I was small, I used to like women of over 50. Last year I was into 40 somethings. And now I wouldn't say no to a woman of 35. [looking meaningfully at Pepi]

PEPI   If you go on like that, next year you'll be into 10-year-olds.
...

BOM   Give me a kiss. [Pepi kisses her and laughs] Look out.

PEPI   I'll spill it.
BOM   Are you embarrassed?
PEPI   That's why it was a quick one.
BOM   I'll clean it for you later.
PEPI   Clean it now.
BOM   No, later.

After this exchange there is an abrupt cut to an extreme close-up of the bubbling casserole dish, a visual clue as to what may be happening between the two women. The device of cutting to an object that is invested with sexual meaning is typical of Almodóvar, who uses it in other films such as *La ley del deseo* (The Law of Desire, 1987) and *Hable con ella* (Talk to Her, 2002).

Pepi, Luci, Bom was greeted as a new type of filmmaking. In 1980, Almodóvar joked that 'when a film has a flaw it is seen as wrong, but when there are several mistakes, then it is called a new language or style. And *Pepi, Luci, Bom* ... has that' (quoted in Vidal, 1989: 38; my translation). The lack of continuity between many of the shots and the poor lighting, sound, and photography were the product of the haphazard way in which the film was shot and a filmmaker who was still learning his trade. Most Almodóvar critics mention the first scene as an example of this new style. For example, Paul Julian Smith writes that 'the film seemed to make a clean break with existing cinematic forms: when the camera pans shakily over Pepi's building, when successive sequences cheerfully flout continuity, it is as if ... the most basic syntax of cinema (of cinematography and editing) is being invented anew' (2014: 17). Alejandro Varderi goes further to suggest that 'the lengthy shooting process led to compose the scenes using short takes, sometimes filmed months apart, which generates a fragmented reading of the female body' (1996: 76).

Both Smith and Varderi are right, but it is Almodóvar's concern for plot rather than style that creates these innovations. He shows disregard for conventional cinematography and editing, whether on purpose or not is not always clear. This can be seen in this long opening shot, which shows Pepi's neighbours' windows and zooms back to her own, focusing on her marihuana plants, then following the wall to her bedside table and zooming out again to show her. This long take must have been difficult to film and is not particularly well-executed. For example, the plants are out of focus. It is reminiscent of the wonderful opening of *Rear Window* (Hitchcock, 1954), where the camera pans out of Jeff Jeffries' (James Stewart) window to pry at the neighbours' windows only to come back and focus on the main character and his belongings. It pursues a similar narrative strategy to Hitchcock's, placing voyeurism and secrecy at the heart of the film. The establishing shot of the closed windows with their closed curtains and geraniums gives the viewer clues as to where we are (a modest neighbourhood) and provides a direct contrast between Pepi's lifestyle and that of her neighbours. Closed windows are a sign of the privacy and secrecy that had been necessary in Spain if one was to avoid getting into trouble. Pepi's lifestyle is presented, through the open windows and curtains, in direct opposition to these closeted lives. The innocuous geraniums in neighbouring windows are also in opposition to Pepi's own illegal marihuana crop. The first shot could be said to stand in for *la movida* within Spain. The camera is literally on the move, retreating from the anodyne past of fear and secrecy and embracing punk, drug-culture, and openness. This movement keeps the viewer firmly on Pepi's side. Had this been a subjective shot from the policeman's window signifying his spying on Pepi, the sympathies would have been elsewhere.

Almodóvar himself remembers that

> when I shot my first film, I had major problems that forced me to take several shots of the same scene over a whole year. Consequently, at the start of the scene, the actress had short hair; in the next shot, her hair is medium long; and, in the third shot, very long. On noticing this while cutting the film, I thought the audience would howl, because this went against the most basic rule of all, that of the match cut. But no one noticed a thing. Ever. And that was a great lesson for me. It proved that in the end, no one gives a damn about technical errors as long as the film tells an interesting story with a genuine point of view. (quoted in Tirard, 2002: 82–3)

Almodóvar's visual style goes back to the early days of filmmaking, when the 'basic rules' had not been established and audiences went to the cinema for thrills and stories. The photography and editing of *Pepi, Luci, Bom* and other early Almodóvar films can thus be said to be innovative, but not consciously so. A related aspect of this is the comic-influenced credits and intertitles made by artist Ceesepe for the film. These are both a reminder of the pop culture Almodóvar was immersed in at the time and a wink (whether voluntary or not) to the editing of early cinema, where separate shots were often joined together by explanatory titles. This modern treatment of narrative is thus a return to one of the earliest film narrative traditions. The intertitles do not necessarily explain anything that an audience cannot gather by themselves from the film (information such as 'Pepi was hungry for revenge' or 'And the policeman also knew how it felt' is unnecessary), but add a layer of detached humour to the story and even a touch of childishness or amateurishness that befits the film-within-the-film and responds to a more spontaneous-seeming style.

Despite Almodóvar's focus on narrative and character, which are staples of classic narrative cinema, his films frequently jolt viewers out of the illusion of reality that is typical of this type of filmmaking. This contradiction within the films, together with the need to obtain proof of Spain's cultural and political change during the Transition, meant that the less realist aspects of his early films have often been overlooked. Vidal explains that 'people wanted to see *Pepi* ... as a film about customs and manners ...', but the customs of a different type of people, and it is true that it is a mirror to these other people, but it is not an exploration of customs and manners' (1989: 15; my translation). The same can be said of *Laberinto de pasiones*. Taking either of the films (or any of Almodóvar's films) as straight realism should be impossible, given their metacinematic elements and the incredible events and characters that populate them.

For example, Pepi lectures Luci and Bom on the artificiality of all filmmaking, even when it is inspired by reality:

PEPI   As well as being yourselves, you have to act.
BOM   What do you mean?
PEPI   You can't just go like this to the camera. As well as being your-selves, you have to represent your characters, and representation is always artificial.
LUCI   I don't understand.
...
PEPI   So, you're a housewife but you really like to party. So you have to show that. I've seen you being slapped and eating snot without turning a hair.
LUCI   I don't know.
PEPI   And you like it?
LUCI   I love it.
PEPI   We have to show that. You eat snot like it was a slice of bread.

LUCI   That's how I am.

PEPI   Of course. But cinema isn't life, cinema is falsehood. They use a machine to make rain, because real rain can't be photographed. I'm including the scene where Bom pisses on you, just as it happened. Do you remember? It was brilliant. So when she pisses on you, you have to moan with pleasure. ... If we don't do it, people won't believe you're a masochist.

Bom and Luci cannot simply be themselves; they have to 'represent' themselves in a credible way. In case the audience misses this, Pepi adds that 'cinema isn't life, cinema is falsehood' and makes a direct comment on one of the film's previous scenes, 'where Bom pisses on' Luci, implying that the piss, equivalent of rain, will also have to be artificial. The golden shower scene acquires a metacinematic dimension as Pepi's instructions deconstruct it. Did this most memorable scene really happen or are we being shown Pepi's film?

This scene is incredibly complex in relation to the cinematic gaze. Varderi explains that the scene subverts the traditional male gaze predominant in cinema: 'Almodóvar sets down the basis of his aesthetic in altering the place of the cinematic gaze – which subordinates and objectifies femininity to a masculine eye – and by giving women an active role, that is, giving their bodies back to them' (1996: 196–7; my translation). Whilst it is true that women, particularly Pepi and Bom, have an 'active role' in the scene, there is also an extreme close-up of Luci, who plays a typically passive feminine role. Luci is the 'victim' and enjoys it, a recurrent trope in the sexualisation of women in mainstream film and in the pornographic industry. The scene begins with an establishing shot with all three characters in a single frame. Then, in a more painterly composition, Bom's legs form a human frame to the left and top of the shot and Luci's body performs a similar function at the bottom right corner. Pepi is in the background of the action but occupies the centre of the frame. She is a peculiarly active voyeur since she both comes up with the idea, arranges the 'actors' and *mise-en-scène*, and then places herself in the best position to see everything. The budding filmmaker is both Almodóvar's and the spectator's double. While we are given the chance of being the sadist and the victim through shots from Bom's and Luci's perspectives, we never see the scene literally from Pepi's point of view. Pepi derives pleasure from looking at Luci and Bom, just as spectators derive pleasure from looking at Luci and Bom and seeing Pepi's vicarious

1.1   Pepi 'directs' the golden shower (*Pepi, Luci, Bom y otras chicas del montón*, 1980)

enjoyment. Almodóvar is using these discourses to bring home the reality of cinema's perversity, a perversity instigated by filmmaker and audience alike (Figure 1.1).

Pepi's role of director and spectator is clear; in the initial golden shower scene she proposes that Bom urinate on Luci, actively helps out, and tells both Bom and Luci what to do. Her role as director is reinforced by the fact that in the credits she appears alongside a caricature of Almodóvar. Mark Allinson has noted that 'Pepi's obvious sadistic pleasure ... as she watches her friends beat up Juan (the policeman's twin brother) inverts traditional cinematic voyeurism and sadism' (2001: 85). This is also the case in the urination scene, with the addition of inverting the typical gender of film directors. The figure of the director as a voyeur and a raconteur recurs in Almodóvar's work, appearing in films such as *La ley del deseo*, *¡Átame!* (Tie Me Up! Tie Me Down!, 1989), *La mala educación* (Bad Education, 2004), *Los abrazos rotos* (Broken Embraces, 2009), and *Dolor y gloria* (Pain and Glory, 2019). Of all these instances, only Pepi is a woman director, a voyeur and a sadist. The issue of women's enjoyment of pornography and violence involving other women as victims is thorny. As Laura Mulvey explains, women are not immune to scopophilic patriarchal discourses (1997). However, it could also be seen as an extended fantasy where women are perpetrators and victims, just as in the lesbian sado-masochist comic that Pepi gives Luci. Both things are possible.

Pepi, Luci, Bom can be seen as a film-within-a-film without clear boundaries. On the one hand there is Almodóvar's film about the three women; on the other, Pepi's own autobiographical film about her friends. How much of the film is Pepi's own version of events is never clear, but were the whole film to be seen as Pepi's fictionalisation of her life and that of her friends, her starring role in it as the most modern and successful character would be justified. It would also add an extra layer of parody to a film that was filmed, much in the way Pepi proposes to do, at weekends with borrowed cameras and using friends as actors.

During the 1980s there was a political need to represent Spain abroad as a modern European country.[1] Outside Spain it was politically expedient to embrace and foster Spanish democracy, including rejoicing in evidence of a cultural renaissance. The Madrid underground movement, commonly known as *la movida*, was ripe for such political uses. Almodóvar was first seen as a talented member of *la movida* and, by extension, the Spanish cultural renaissance of the 1980s. The importance of *la movida* as a framework for critical interpretation cannot be dismissed, but neither should it become a mythical ur-text that explains the early films away. For *la movida* was not a coherent generation or artistic group. In fact, many of its participants deny that it ever existed (cf. Gallero, 1991). An often-rehearsed definition describes it as a cultural movement based in Madrid in the decade following Franco's death that was characterised mainly by frivolity and radical apoliticism. It never really began in an organised way and the activities seen as part of *la movida* simply stopped, were incorporated into the mainstream, or continued in a less visible way. Even its meaning as a label is debatable. Its most appropriate translation is 'the Madrid scene', but it has come to represent the idea of Spain as a country that is 'moving', going places. The term *movida* was associated with drug use but it became a catch-all word for anything illegal or exciting. As Alberto García Alix states: 'The word *movida* was used for everything. Everyone knew that everyone else was doing things. But it really came from the drug world, from going to get high: I have a *movida* so I'll see you later. Afterwards it began to be employed as an all-purpose word' (quoted in Gallero, 1991: 154; my translation).

Almodóvar's early films have been used as source material for the study of *la movida* and this is the context that frames most critical interpretations of them. This has been aided by the collaborative nature of film and the fact that Almodóvar turned to friends to help him make his early films, for example, to graphic designer Ceesepe for posters and promotion materials, Alaska y Los Pegamoides and Favio MacNamara for music and acting, and the Spanish Gilbert and George, las Costus, for set design and cameos. This has resulted in the work of these artists being immortalised in film, but also to the films themselves being a composite of all of these artists' sensibilities. However, whereas once *la movida* was the important event and Almodóvar merely one of its players, in the twenty-first century the roles have been reversed. Almodóvar is now the main event and the old participants of *la movida* are merely his associates wheeled out in documentaries and international events in an attempt to explain the genesis of Almodóvar's genius.

The artists commonly ascribed as belonging to *la movida* did not share aesthetic or political principles. Most of its participants refused to dwell overtly on Spain's past and made fun of politics, but their frivolous stance frequently had an underlying objective. Comments by Tomás Cuesta, one of the participants in *la movida*, are a good example of these contradictions. *La movida*, he says,

> was the first truly post-Franco generation, where Francoism did not even appear as a referent ... It did not even break with the old situation. It emerged from somewhere else. It was a generation that genuinely had no interest in the past or the struggle for freedom. It was only concerned with having a good time and, above all, creating a parallel society with values that were hated by the lefties who were about to come to power. (quoted in Gallero, 1991: 327; my translation)

These views reflect the common argument that Franco was dead and that young Spaniards had already forgotten. This attitude is a literal take on the *pacto del olvido* (Pact of Oblivion), a formal amnesty signed on 14 October 1977 for all who had committed crimes 'against the rights of people', including those who had opposed Franco but also those guilty of crimes against humanity on behalf of the dictatorship. The term *pacto del olvido* is used popularly to refer to the unwritten part of the amnesty that relegated events leading up to and during the dictatorship to oblivion. Members of *la movida* ignored and poked fun at left-wing aspirations for a cultured, modern Spain by embracing kitsch. This is a flight from ultra-conservative and left-wing politics, but nevertheless a flight that paradoxically took members of *la movida* back to Franco's Spain, the Spain of kitsch and local colour for tourists, a Spain of bullfights and traditional songs.

Cuesta is aware of the paucity of Spanish culture at the time but does not make the link between this and the dictatorship: 'Frivolity was terrorism. It had to be done because culture was then devoid of any transcendence. The best way of attacking it was to use the frivolous, to profane a little the altar of transcendence by placing frivolity above it. The problem arises when that statement becomes commonplace. Then it becomes extremely boring' (quoted in Gallero, 1991: 334; my translation). In this sense, *la movida* represents one of the most devastating critiques of Spanish politics and culture during the Transition, a critique characterised by the absence of direct involvement and criticism of either the present or the past but one that had the potential to make people think along those lines nevertheless.

Whilst frivolity and apoliticism are certainly applicable to most of Almodóvar's declarations until the 1990s, they are not necessarily staples of his filmmaking, even in the early films. As Gwynne Edwards explains, Almodóvar differs from other Spanish filmmakers of the time in that 'instead of questioning those [past] values and exposing them for what they are, [he] presents an entirely different world' (1995: 22). However, the frivolous world present in his early films is politics by the back door. The alternative world presented by Almodóvar is an exaggeration of the way most Spaniards were behaving at the time in terms of politics. Forty years of repression had made people nervous of stating political views and criticising the government openly. Marginalised groups are given centre stage here whereas before they had been hidden, but their attitudes to politics are very much those of the rest of the country at that time. After the pact of oblivion it was practically impossible to refer to the past and thirty years had to pass before overt cultural references to the Civil War and the dictatorship emerged. The early films are therefore not as detached from contemporary politics as they seem; their politics is executed through farce, parody, and the absurd. They are certainly a reaction to post-Civil War left-wing politics, which were seen as serious and self-aggrandising, but also an artistic response to what Teresa Vilarós has called 'the cold turkey of Spanish disenchantment' (1994: title; my translation). Vilarós sees the late 1970s and early

1980s as 'a period of excessive behaviour and exuberance' in response to Franco's death and, with it, the death of a utopian fantasy of radical change to which left-leaning Spaniards were addicted (1994: 220; my translation). Franco had died and some things were beginning to change, but not quickly or radically enough. Almodóvar's early films were an example of this period's politics as absence of politics.

The fact that the films do not carry an overt ideological message does not preclude their ability to address social issues. For instance, the theme of immigration from the countryside into cities like Madrid and Barcelona recurs in Almodóvar's films. This is a response to the mass immigration of poor labourers to industrial towns during the 1960s and 1970s and one that had also been tackled in comedic tones by reactionary popular films during the dictatorship such as *La ciudad no es para mi* (*City Life Is Not for Me*, Lazaga, 1966). Early Almodóvar films do not foreground migration to the cities as much as films such as *¿Qué he hecho yo para merecer esto?* (What Have I Done to Deserve This?, 1984) and *Volver* (2006), but this trope also appears, particularly in *Pepi, Luci, Bom* where one of the parallel stories is that of an Andalusian woman (Kiti Mánver) who has moved to the capital to try to make it as a *flamenco-pop* singer. The humour of this storyline results from her insistence on artistic modernity combined with traditional feminine values of modesty. We first encounter her arguing with her agent, shouting that she does not need an agent to get a job in a brothel. It is not clear whether she is right to jump to conclusions, but her reaction is understandable given the fact that many young girls who left their villages for the cities did end up as prostitutes. Another clue to the film's knowing references to the exodus from countryside to city is Bom's and Luci's first exchange of words: 'Where are you from?' 'Murcia'. This opening question reflects the reality of mass immigration during this period.

The life of the underclass is also briefly seen in Luci's life with her husband and the behaviour of her annoyingly simple friend, Charito. As a girl living off family handouts, it makes sense that Pepi would live in a cheap area. The flat in the new neighbourhood that Luci's husband has bought is presented, as it was at the time, as a wonderful step up, but in reality these flats are just a high-rise development for the better-off working classes and the lower middle class. We never see this flat but we hear about it on at least four occasions. The flat is both a class marker and an intertext to an amazing and troubling film, *Duerme, duerme mi amor* (*Sleep, Sleep My Love*, Regueiro, 1975), where Mario (José Luis López Vázquez) moves to a brand new flat in a new estate and falls in love with his neighbour. Gradually we discover that he keeps his wife sedated in bed and that her existence is kept a secret. Both Mario in *Sleep, Sleep My Love* and the policeman in *Pepi, Luci, Bom* want to keep their wives within the confines of feminine domesticity. As Mario whispers to his drugged wife: 'If you could always be like this. You're a saint when you're asleep.' There is a difference in the treatment of these two men, however. Whereas in the former film there is sympathy for Mario and understanding that his wife may be better off sedated, in Almodóvar's the policeman's point of view is never accepted. The policeman is mocked by Luci for being unable to keep her at home without resorting to the law and seen as ineffectual when she leaves. He even asks police colleagues whether he can make her return by law. This may sound far-fetched to contemporary ears, but it was common practice during the dictatorship for women who left their husbands or who complained about being abused by them to be told to go back to them by the police. The policeman acts as if the dictatorship had not ended.

As Vidal notes, the policeman is more a caricature than a character (1989: 275; my translation), but so are most of the other characters in this comic film. The policeman is the embodiment of the ultra-conservative ideology that ruled Spain for a long time and can still be heard at times. His reaction to the assault on his brother – 'With so much democracy in this country where will it end?' – was frequently heard at the time. His only two interventions as a policeman are to warn Pepi that he has recognised her marihuana plants only to agree to keep quiet if she lets him have sex with her and, later, to search her house with other policemen when he thinks he can get back at her for making his wife 'go astray'.

The most sinister aspect of the policeman is his attitude towards his wife. Whilst he does not hit her until the very end after much goading by Luci, he asserts his authority in the home by not allowing Luci a say in any matter. For example, during his discussion with his brother, he tells Luci: 'Shut up. This is man's business.' This was a typical and acceptable way of behaving during the dictatorship, reflecting the status of married women as legal minors (Domingo, 2007: 35; my translation). Ideological 'education' by the Feminine Section of the Falangist movement and the Catholic Church promoted an ideal woman who was 'self-denying, submissive, pious, pure, with good breeding, home-loving, family-focused'

(Domingo, 2007: 55; my translation). Luci is so indoctrinated into victimhood that she willingly returns to the marital home once her husband becomes the violent man she expected him to be in the first place. Luci, like Spanish society, wants freedom outwardly but is trapped in a sado-masochist relationship for which discourses of femininity that portray women as self-sacrificing home-makers, as silent companions and willing victims of domestic abuse, are key.

Consequently, although Pepi, Luci and Bom seem to share the same space and values for a while, much in the way that *la movida* brought together people from different social classes and backgrounds, this is ultimately an impossible utopia. Luci belongs in another era, not because of her age but because of her indoctrination into Francoist ideals of femininity. Pepi and Bom are quite different women in that they take the initiative more than Luci and combine traditional masculine and feminine roles. Luci is only attracted to them as temporary substitutes for male violence. It could be said that the ending, with Luci going back to her husband, is more true to what was actually happening in Spanish society during the 1970s and 1980s than *la movida* itself, since the vast majority of Spaniards were not part of *la movida*, which they perceived as a collection of bohemian, immoral eccentrics; they stayed at home and continued in much the same way as before the death of Franco, too afraid to let go of their way of life or too conditioned by their upbringing to even question it.

Note

1 Spain joined NATO in 1982 and the EEC in 1986. At the time there were both an acute anti-American feeling and a feeling of inferiority in relation to the rest of Europe.

2

Kicking the habit: *Entre tinieblas*

Entre tinieblas (Dark Habits, 1983) is crucial to understanding Almodóvar's films in relation to his ambivalent attitude towards Spanish popular cinema and traditions. It is particularly indebted to two of the three major genres encouraged under Franco's regime, the 'cinema of folklore' and the 'cinema of priests' (Higginbotham, 1988: 18).[1] These were frequently combined and *Entre tinieblas* belongs to a distinct popular sub-genre, even if it sends many of its genre traits up: the folkloric religious film. *Entre tinieblas* perhaps has been sidelined in Almodóvar scholarship because of these obscure origins and a blind spot about its use of Catholic ritual and iconography. As Paul Julian Smith points out:

> On its release in Britain critics were unanimous in proclaiming that *Entre tinieblas* recycled old jokes about 'naughty nuns', jokes which could only prove shocking and titillating to Spaniards accustomed to Francoist censorship. This somewhat patronizing verdict not only neglected the contributions of music and performance in rendering 'naughtiness' highly serious, it also misread Spanish history. (2014: 39)

Entre tinieblas is not 'shocking and titillating' in the sexualised way the term 'naughty' connotes. These adjectives belong more to the genre of nuns' sexploitation films, a genre to which *Entre tinieblas* is indebted but does not belong. *Entre tinieblas* shares many of the features of nuns' sexploitation films, but it does not fit into this genre. A viewer familiar with sexploitation films would be aware of the cinematic roads that Almodóvar has not taken.

Significantly, there is very little exposure of the female body. The only instance of nudity happens when the Mother Superior (Julieta

Serrano) lingers for a little too long in Yolanda's (Cristina Sánchez Pascual) room as she is getting changed. Yolanda's pointed stare at the Mother Superior (and the viewer who occupies her point of view) kills off any possible eroticism. It would have been easy for Virginia's story or the backstory of Merche (Cecilia Roth) and the Mother Superior to become raunchy tales of sinful goings-on in the convent. Instead, Almodóvar concentrates on a nun who is obsessed with cleaning, another who writes romances, and a third who takes acid.

The Mother Superior is the only nun whose behaviour could be classed as unacceptable but she is ineffectual, her narrative of lesbian romance thwarted by the coldness of her love object, Yolanda. Moreover, in *Entre tinieblas* it is women (not men as is usually the case in nuns' sexploitation films) who finally try to restore order. Smith notes that 'Catalan and Spanish critics were unanimous in claiming that the film was not simply anti-clerical, and was more humorous than scandalous or sacrilegious' (2014: 29). Significantly the film sold extremely well in Italy, another Catholic country where audiences would have been aware of the iconography and film genres employed by Almodóvar, who stretches genre boundaries to create a film that is more tragic than comic.

Reviews of the type mentioned by Smith contain an uninformed and prejudiced view of Spanish audiences as unsophisticated. At the heart of Almodóvar's religious community is a desire to do good and support drug addicts. Therefore, its objectives are similar to those of many pro-Catholic films to which *Entre tinieblas* alludes. The benign nature of the religious order is nevertheless significantly at odds with the role of the Catholic Church in the oppression of women in post-war Spain. Following Franco's victory, the Church had a major role in 're-educating' women who were not toeing the line politically or on a personal level. It was a major agent of repression, dictating how women should dress and behave, actively discouraging women from working, and seeking to convert those who did not believe in God. Those who did not follow the Church's precepts ended up in prison or, if they were there already, were punished severely, including the removal of their children. A good example of the close relationship between the Church and the fascist regime was the addition of nuns to the women's prison staff from August 1939 (cf. Domingo, 2007).

Seeing nuns using hard drugs and planning to become drug mules may be shocking, but extravagance had come to be expected of the Spanish religious film. Religious films during the dictatorship ranged from the repellently indoctrinating such as *Sor Intrépida* (Path to the Kingdom, Gil, 1952) to the utterly bizarre as in *Sor Citroen* (Sister Citroen, Lazaga, 1967). For the most part, they centre on how far the protagonists might go to achieve their pious goals. This could be played for laughs (that is, a young novice or nun scandalises the rest of the community with her loudness and 'modern' ways) or seriously to provide examples of Christian behaviour approved by religious advisers.[2] For example, the main character in *Path to the Kingdom* (Dominique Blanchard) is a famous singer who becomes a nun, records five albums of traditional Spanish songs anonymously in order to save the convent from bankruptcy, leaves for a leper's mission in India, and dies a martyr. Dominique Blanchard bears an uncanny physical resemblance to the Mother Superior in *Entre tinieblas* and her ambition, annoyingly superior manner, and pride in her humility are also precursors of Almodóvar's character.

Sympathies always remained with the transgressive main character and comedy was created mostly at the expense of an old-fashioned nun or by showing how older nuns took to 'modern' ways. A clear example of this is *Sor Ye-Yé* (Fernández, 1967), which tells the story of how a convent is saved by a pop-star turned novice turned pop-star nun who wins a music festival. An earlier instance of the zany folkloric religious film is *La hermana alegría* (Sister Joy, Lucía, 1954). This film is a key intertext for *Entre tinieblas* formally and thematically. It is set in a convent that doubles as an institution for young 'wayward' women, mostly girls who have had a relationship with the 'wrong' man or with any man outside marriage. Sewing, like in *Entre tinieblas*, is used to 're-educate' them and also as an income-generator for the convent. Some of the *mise-en-scène* in *Entre tinieblas*, particularly the internal patio of the convent and its balcony overlooking it, is also reminiscent of *La hermana alegría*. In the latter, the girls look out of the balcony to ogle at the new gardener, who is then found to be exceedingly ugly. In the former, Yolanda sees a tiger out of the window. As Almodóvar admits, the masculine presence in the convent's garden is transformed into a tiger: 'The tiger is almost certainly the only thing that represents men. If there is any masculine presence in this film, it's the tiger' (quoted in Vidal, 1989: 89; my translation). The masculine is thus relegated to tamed nature within the convent. It is an alien being, but one that is immediately associated with the Mother Superior since she touches Yolanda to reassure her but Yolanda seems just as disturbed by the nun's touch as by the presence of the tiger. The symbiotic relationship between the Mother Superior and the tiger is also reinforced, this time in a comic tone, by the film's poster that shows a nun with a tiger's face and the emblem of the religious community (what looks like a sacred heart pierced by syringes) that has been lassoed by a woman in a red evening dress. The heart pierced by syringes recurs in Almodóvar's cinema, most recently in the poster for 'Addiction' in *Dolor y gloria* (Pain and Glory, 2019).

One of the keys to understanding Almodóvar's tone in *Entre tinieblas* can be found in a scene from *La hermana alegría*, where Sister Consolation (Lola Flores) asks her confessor: 'When a person wants to do something for someone else's good, how far can she go?' This is the premise followed by most religious films produced during Franco's dictatorship. *Entre tinieblas* takes this metaphorical question (because in Francoist films the transgressions are not that serious) and literalises it, making his nuns – particularly the Mother Superior – go further than anyone could have imagined at that time (including drug-taking and drug-trafficking) and daring audiences to pass judgment.

Entre tinieblas does not pass moral judgement on its characters' actions. This lack of a moral centre is not reflected in the otherwise excellent English translation of the title, which puns on the word 'habit' as being what the nuns wear and their supposedly 'sinful' behaviour, including having a drugs habit. The original Spanish title – *Entre tinieblas* (among *tenebrae* or in darkness) – reflects the characters' lack of guidance and also the fact that audiences are not given direction as to how to read the film. As Edwards states, '[t]he reference is to the darkness which descended upon the world at the time of Christ's crucifixion, to his feeling of abandonment and, by extension, to men and women in spiritual darkness' (1995: 34). 'Tinieblas' refers to *tenebrae*, the Easter service commemorating this darkness where candles are extinguished one by one. There are variations on this ritual, some of which leave the central candle, which symbolises the light of Christ abandoned by all his disciples. Others leave the church in complete darkness, with the last candle signifying the death of Christ. This is then marked by the bell's toll. Either way the ramifications within the story in relation to Easter, death, and resurrection and allegiance to religious tenets multiply.

Yet these are never tied in to a particular way of thinking. On the contrary, they are floating signifiers, the meaning of which changes within the film itself depending on where individual viewers place themselves. Closure is never offered. A good example of this is the use of religious ritual in the most striking scene of the film, that of Yolanda's arrival in the convent after eluding the police and wandering the streets of Madrid at night. Her arrival in the convent's church coincides with the nuns walking to the altar to take communion. An establishing shot of the priest taking the host is reinforced by the intradiegetic use of a well-known Eucharistic hymn. A reverse shot from the priest's (or the host's) point of view at the altar then shows the nuns singing and going towards him to take communion. The main door of the church is emphasised by the shaft of light filtering from outside, which contrasts with the darkness of the interior. The Mother Superior is first in line when the door bursts open with a loud bang and daylight comes in. She turns away from the altar and looks towards the door. A brief close-up of her illuminated face is quickly followed by a reverse shot of what she sees: Yolanda bathed in blue light as the other nuns keep singing. 'You are the path' is being sung when the camera shifts from the Mother Superior with the altar behind her to Yolanda and the outside world. Immediately the camera angle changes to a high angle from above the altar as we see the Mother Superior walk towards Yolanda and the light. Yolanda is therefore seen as the path that the Mother Superior takes. In other words, the film shifts from darkness to daylight, the Mother Superior from communion with God to a more human (and physical) relationship.

The scene sets up the dynamics of the whole film visually. As Almodóvar explained to Nuria Vidal: 'This scene sums up best the film's religiosity. ... The church contains all the sacred elements, that's why I wanted Yolanda's appearance to take place in the church, as a very clear metaphor. There is a line that goes from Yolanda to the altar, which Julieta follows and is the axis of the film' (1989: 75; my translation). The movement of the Mother Superior away from the altar, from organised religion to Yolanda, is obvious but not what it represents. Visually Yolanda is the light that vanquishes the church's darkness. This identification with light aligns her with the figure of Jesus and its opposite, the anti-Christ.[3] Following traditional ways of thinking Yolanda can be seen as a temptress fittingly dressed in red underneath the shabby raincoat, but she is also identified with the Virgin by the use of blue light. This association is reinforced through later shots of Yolanda in front of a painting of the Virgin where the

Virgin's crown seems to be on Yolanda's head and, towards the end of the film, when Yolanda dresses up to sing in one of the dresses made for the statue of the Virgin of the Forsaken.

The cinematography of *Entre tinieblas*, with its use of *chiaroscuro*, high and low camera angles, and unusual bodily contortions (Merche's arrest or Yolanda's final dance), is indebted to (mostly religious) baroque paintings such as those of Francisco de Zurbarán. Almodóvar has acknowledged this debt: 'When I was working on the film with Ángel Luis Fernández I told him to refer to Sirk in terms of lighting, but also to Zurbarán's chiaroscuros' (quoted in Vidal, 1989: 173). Alejandro Varderi has noted how of all of Almodóvar's films, *Entre tinieblas* has 'the *mise-en-scène* closest to baroque both in its use of light ... and in its creation of a dramatic and oppressive atmosphere' (1996: 158). This is not just indebted to seventeenth- and eighteenth-century baroque but also to the elaborate style of Douglas Sirk's melodramas, a style labelled 'Hollywood baroque' by Thomas Schatz for its extravagance (1981: 245). The film juxtaposes spartan (the cell where Merche and the Mother Superior sleep) and over-elaborated décors (Sister Rat's, Sister Damned's, and Virginia's rooms) and flags up the fact that we are watching a film through, among other things, artificial lighting (the grey light at Yolanda's boyfriend's flat, the blue light when Yolanda arrives in the convent and when she sings at the Mother Superior's party) and frame-within-a-frame shots. The décors are baroque in different ways, for whilst the cells of the two nuns show a spartan lifestyle, their animals and plants offer an elaborate layering of symbolic objects. Virginia's room, on the contrary, is decorated in a manner much more stereotypical of melodrama and, being the exact replica of her room in the house of her despotic father, is the perfect locus for melodramatic action in the film. The room is thus the space where the characters' melodramatic and romantic fantasies can be played out. Significantly, the room/office of the Mother Superior is clearly divided into two very differently decorated sections, the austere sleeping area and the office that resembles a teenage bedroom with artists' posters, teddy bears, and records. This personal space reflects the split personality of the Mother Superior, who is torn by conflicting impulses of asceticism and excess, a conflict she tries to resolve by trying to externalise it through her objects of desire, 'sinful' women.

The use of baroque elements is also highlighted by the multiple occasions in which characters are framed by windows and other architectural features, which again emphasise the film's awareness of its pictorial influences and also the influence of Sirk. The alignment of Yolanda and of the other 'redeemed' girls with the figure of Christ can be seen, for example, in the dinner scene with *mise-en-scène* reminiscent of paintings of the Last Supper (Allinson, 2001: 165) or in Merche's arrest, where the Mother Superior stoops to put her shoes on in a gesture similar to that of Mary Magdalene washing Jesus's feet whilst Merche's contorted body framed by the policemen is reminiscent of Christ in countless Renaissance and baroque paintings depicting the arrest and the flagellation or those of other martyrs such as Saint Sebastian. The most obvious reference to Yolanda as Jesus is the moment when the Mother Superior cleans Yolanda's make-up with a cloth and takes down an imprint of her face saying, 'God forgive me if I feel like another St Veronica.' Yolanda's reaction of astonishment ('What are you doing?' ... 'You're out of it') replicates the feeling of estrangement felt by the viewer.

This constitutes the religious equivalent to what John Mercer and Martin Shingler call 'the hysterical moment' in melodrama where events in the film unravel its 'reality':

> The 'Return of the Repressed' has, in fact, been noted to emerge within the film-text itself, in the form of a discontinuity in the narrative. At certain moments, a breaking-down of 'reality' appears, which can be understood as the hysterical moment of the text. At this point, the *mise-en-scène* has a tendency to become explicitly symbolic or coded, with the added accompaniment of heavily repetitive and intrusive music. (2004: 13)

The Mother Superior is here acting out her specular fantasies by appropriating Yolanda's image. The fact that she wants to keep Yolanda as an image, much in the way of a religious relic or painting, shows how her repression of lesbian feelings and sublimation of those through religion have reached breaking point.

The oppressive atmosphere characteristic of melodrama is also created through the film's use of music. As Mark Allinson states, 'In *Dark Habits* it is the music which from the outset sets the much darker mood than in previous films as much as the visibly darkening skies over the Spanish capital' (2001: 195). This is Miklós Rosza's 'Valse Crepusculaire' for *Providence* (Resnais, 1977), heard during the credits and first scene and towards the end of the film. The 'darkening skies' are used as an excellent preamble for the film to come since viewers are made to wait for the story to begin and Yolanda to arrive at her leisure. Almodóvar chooses to begin the film at dusk in a clear reference to the darkness that is to come. The slow, mournful pace of the waltz contrasts with the fast-paced movements of the city seen at high speed. Yolanda is the first character to be identified with the music that stops as she arrives at her boyfriend's flat only to start again when she is alone in the toilet. The waltz could here be seen as the internal strength of Yolanda's character, who does not seem affected by the fast pace of city life or her bad-tempered boyfriend. It also points to the end of her way of life, as well as that of the nuns. The only other moment in the film when the song is played occurs as the religious community is finally disintegrating. This is a high melo-dramatic point where music supports the emotions of the characters but also points to their slightly exaggerated nature.

'Valse Crepusculaire' also links to the theme of Easter and the Passion of Christ anticipated by the title, since dusk, signalling the night that precedes a new day, is closely related to Easter in Christian iconography. The hazy purple skies of the Madrid evening are the prelude to the death and rebirth of Yolanda from drug addict to confident woman, the end of the film's religious community, and the destruction of the romantic fantasies of the Mother Superior. The whole of *Entre tinieblas* could therefore be seen as an extended crepuscular waltz. It is the music that symbolises the metaphorical blowing out of the candles of hope that both the religious commu-nity and the Mother Superior put so much store by. The final candle to be snuffed out is Yolanda, who has been associated with Jesus, the Virgin Mary, and Virginia, the Mother Superior's former love object. The bell toll of the *tenebrae* ritual is substituted by the heartbreaking scream of the Mother Superior. Almodóvar draws attention to this, at least to English-speaking audiences, by giving Yolanda the artistic surname Bel.

Yolanda is not a Christ-like figure in an anti-clerical or sacrilegious way. It is the infatuation of the Mother Superior that places her in an elevated position. Erotic and religious love have frequently gone hand in hand in Catholicism, particularly in relation to the writings of mystics such as San Juan de la Cruz and Santa Teresa de Avila. Alejandro Yarza describes Almodóvar's aesthetic as camp and argues that his films appropriate and parody traditional Spanish iconography that was associated with Franco's regime (1999: 17; my translation).

While *Entre tinieblas* contains parodic elements in its allusions to religious films of the dictatorship, it is not a parody per se but a melodramatic pastiche that exposes the contradictions in much of Spanish society at the time. As Edwards explains, 'in *Dark Habits* [the comic elements] tend to surround rather than be part of the central story of the relationship between Yolanda and the Mother Superior' (1995: 48). Yolanda and the Mother Superior seem to be living alternately in a melodrama and a tragedy and the elements of comic relief are supplied by a myriad of secondary characters. The sisters' obsessions and quirks, such as Sister Damned's compulsive cleaning and Sister Rat's constant hunger for food and sensational material to write her novels, provide most of the humorous scenes in a film that would otherwise be depressing. However, comedy in *Entre tinieblas* is something that viewers must supply, since any potential comic element is balanced by the serious tone demanded by Almodóvar of his actors: 'In *Dark Habits* there are very amusing things, but they must be said and done very seriously so that they do not become a parody. In parody we do not believe in the feelings represented but here we must believe in them, even if you also find it funny' (quoted in Vidal, 1989: 92; my translation). In a similar way to that of Sirk's films, comic instances in *Entre tinieblas* reveal already existent incongruities within socially accepted practices, including those mainly conveyed through the genre of the folkloric religious film. Nevertheless, Almodóvar's use of the aesthetics of Sirkian melodrama, like his use of the religious film, lulls the viewer into feeling safe within the well-known melodramatic genre markers, only to realise that the plot has become much more subversive than anticipated.

The use of the moving camera to show an intimate, subjective point of view is one of the main devices that align *Entre tinieblas* with melodrama. The camera seems to have a life of its own, following actors at key moments as in the first tracking shot of Yolanda walking through the streets of Madrid. It also anticipates their movements. For example, the tracking gives way to a shot of a building's façade with the camera prying into neighbours' windows much as in the famous opening scene of Hitchcock's *Rear Window* (1954), also quoted in other Almodóvar films. We fleetingly see a lonely figure (whom we later realise is Yolanda's boyfriend) looking out of a window, some people dancing on the floor below, and then the camera focuses on the main entrance. In another reference to *Rear Window*, where Grace Kelly is first introduced through her shadow, Yolanda's shadow and then Yolanda herself enter the frame on the right-hand side and she goes into the house, with the camera following closely behind like a stalker. This sequence suggests an intimacy with Yolanda that, just like the Mother Superior's expectations of intimacy, will not be fulfilled. It places viewers in the role of a voyeur spying on Yolanda's life as happens in melodrama. These unrealistic camera movements alert viewers to the fact that what they are seeing is make-believe but also binds them to the character's story.

Yolanda is not the easiest of characters to like. Her first close-up, as she goes up the stairs, shows her wearing dark glasses even at night. The film, in a trait that is also reminiscent of Sirk, is full of shots of Yolanda through mirrors or mirror-like objects. This is more striking in contrast to the lack of mirrors in the convent except for the lift-up mirror in Virginia's dressing table. Yolanda looks at herself frequently; the nuns look at one another or at her. Mercer and Shingler state that 'Sirk suggested that mirrors were of interest because they produce an image that seems to represent the person looking into the mirror when in fact what they see is the exact opposite. ... Mirrors, then, represent illusion and delusion in his films' (2004: 54). In *Entre tinieblas* the mirror is an object that helps Yolanda shore up and construct her identity. For example, after her boyfriend is rude to her she goes into the toilet, she looks at herself in the three-pane mirror and says 'Forget about him!' After his death she begins to claim her identity back by taking his notebook, reading it, writing in it in his voice, and, finally, destroying it. She is reflected on the bed's chrome base as she steps over her boyfriend's dead body to reach the notebook. This marks the moment when she takes control of her own life, a control that will be threatened by the Mother Superior's narrative of romance and melodrama symbolised by the mirror in Virginia's room.

It is difficult to see Yolanda in any of the mirrors she is presented with. In fact, her face is quite elusive. Even when her face is revealed, it is difficult to fathom her. This may not necessarily have been part of Almodóvar's plan but a consequence of the dynamics introduced by the actor playing Yolanda, Cristina Sánchez Pascual, the producer's wife. Despite its low budget, *Entre tinieblas* was the first of Almodóvar's films to have a producer and be screened and sold abroad. Sánchez Pascual's coldness prompted Almodóvar to change the script significantly, giving more prominence to the group of nuns and therefore turning it into a much more ensemble work than he had initially envisaged.[4] He also changed the ending from one in which Yolanda's adventures continue to the heartbreaking scream when the Mother Superior realises Yolanda has abandoned her. All these readjustments work very well in the final version of the film since, contrary to what the camerawork might suggest, the viewer is seldom allowed into Yolanda's mind and sympathies shift from Yolanda to the Mother Superior and vice versa.

There are several moments in *Entre tinieblas* where camera movements jolt viewers into remembering that they are watching a film. Just before the Mother Superior shows Yolanda into Virginia's former room, the camera is placed outdoors in the cloister framing Yolanda and the Mother Superior at the top of the stairs but, within the same shot, it leaves them and pans to the left, going through another window into Virginia's former bedroom and continuing its movement until the Mother Superior opens the door and lets Yolanda in. This shot is so disconcerting that some critics have imagined the camera going through the wall (Allinson, 2001: 166). This outside–inside movement signifies Yolanda's imprisonment within the convent and her peculiar relationship with the Mother Superior. It is telling that Lucho Gatica's *bolero* 'Encadenados' (chained together) starts as soon as the camera reaches the window frame,[5] the liminal space between freedom and subjection. In Almodóvar's films, *boleros* are frequently musical clues to melodrama, which itself is a genre tied to music as the expression of feeling. The Mother Superior at one point admits that she likes sentimental music and Gatica's 'Encadenados' could be seen as her theme song. The lyrics of 'Encadenados' express ambivalence about love and the love object and are the perfect soundtrack to the Mother Superior's fantasies, fantasies that Yolanda has unwittingly stepped into.

'Encadenados' plays twice more during the film, always in connection with the Mother Superior. Shortly after Yolanda's arrival in the convent, she is seen going to the Mother Superior's room, presumably in search of drugs. There they both sing along to Gatica's song in turns. Yolanda is the mirror image of the Mother Superior, her opposite, her object of specular desire, and what the Mother Superior would like to be but cannot. The Mother Superior seems to have the upper hand on this occasion. Her singing, which happens in her cell, bookends the song. The lines she sings, including 'My fate needs your fate/and you need me much more', could be seen as a romanticised version of her obsession with Yolanda in particular and other 'sinners' in general, but more importantly it is a way of stating her dominance over Yolanda as the provider of drugs and refuge from the police.

However, Yolanda never seems to be as dependent on the Mother Superior as the latter wants to believe. She mimes in a perfunctory way as if only doing it to obtain what she actually wants from the Mother Superior. One of the lines that Yolanda sings along to, 'That's why we will never say goodbye', marks this ambiguity in her feelings and behaviour. Although Yolanda will literally not 'say goodbye' to the Mother Superior, she leaves the convent nevertheless.

The intensity of the Mother Superior's feelings for Yolanda has unfortunately not been seriously explored, probably because of their Sapphic nature. Barry Jordan and Rikki Morgan-Tamosunas talk about the lesbian gaze and point out that:

> Its most effective and striking instance in Spanish cinema probably remains the characterization and structuring of the looks in a much commented sequence from Almodóvar's *Entre Tinieblas*. The impact of the sequence is magnified by the cultural connotations of the two women's identities – cabaret singer and nun – as the Mother Superior mimes a sensual serenade to her female idol, thus reappropriating and recasting erotic specularisation of the female icon in lesbian terms. (1998: 139)

Whilst Jordan and Morgan-Tamosunas are right in identifying the complex 'characterization and structuring of the looks' in the scene, its most unusual aspect is the fact that the Mother Superior is trying to seduce Yolanda but we are not sure of Yolanda's agenda. The play-back singing of 'Encadenados' is thus a slow mating dance where one of the partners is dead serious and the other probably acts in bad faith pushed by circumstance. The two end up literally 'face to face', just like the protagonists of the song. Gatica's *bolero* sums up the Mother Superior's desire to control the women she falls for and her dependence on romantic and melodramatic narratives to survive. What is missing, though, is the context for the Mother Superior's sublimation of her lesbian desire, which she has channelled into religious work. Same-sex desire was unacceptable during the dictatorship and Transition to democracy. Homophobia was widespread. This theme is further explored in *La ley del deseo* (The Law of Desire, 1987), *La mala educación* (Bad Education, 2004), and *Dolor y gloria*.

It also foresees how her one-way relationship with Yolanda will end. The film's use of the *bolero* also sets a more sombre tone, places *Entre tinieblas* within the tradition of melodrama, and, together with non-static camera movements (either tracking or crane shots or a combination of both), shifts the viewer's sympathies from Yolanda at the beginning to the Mother Superior at the end.

If 'Encadenados' shows the Mother Superior and Yolanda as inseparable, Catalino Curet Alonso's 'Salí porque salí' (I Left Just Because I Left), mimed by Yolanda at the Mother Superior's party, signals Yolanda's control over the Mother Superior and her breaking away from her sphere of influence. 'Salí porque salí', first heard briefly when Yolanda is working in the club and signifying her independence, is *salsa*, which has the same 4/4 time as the *bolero* but with a faster tempo. Thus, whilst seemingly paying homage to the Mother Superior and her love of sentimental music, Yolanda turns that same music against her:

> For you I won't even have one miserable look.
> It was better to bury in the past
> your forbidden love.
>   Again I walk the same old path.
> Again, with a smile upon my face.
> If I came to your love it was just because I did.
> And if I left your love it was just because I left.
> ...
> Nothing you say, Mother, can make me change.
> Now everything is different.
> Things aren't what they were.
> I'm alone. I'm very happy and my life is all my own.

In a series of close-ups, we see the Mother Superior surprised, apprehensive, aroused, and embarrassed. Yolanda's desertion is even more ironic because she is dressed as the Lady of the Forsaken during her performance and because the stage (bathed in blue light and framed by two red curtains) replicates Yolanda's arrival in the convent, only this time she is leaving it. The *salsa* even refers to a 'path', echoing the Eucharistic hymn of the arrival scene. If Yolanda was the Mother Superior's path then, now she sings about her imminent return to her own life, disentangling herself from the path traced for her by the Mother Superior's fantasies. Thus, Yolanda's and God's desertion from the Mother Superior's life are equated once more, a proleptic reference to when the Mother Superior goes cold turkey. Once again, the religious and the profane or sexual are conflated by song and *mise-en-scène*.

The fact that Yolanda is given Virginia's room replicates the Mother Superior's former infatuation with Virginia, thus reinforcing the specular nature of the nun's desire. This is not clearly seen in the film, but several things point to it, including the nuns' reactions to the fact that Yolanda is given Virginia's room and how she is seen as a stand-in for Virginia, finishing Virginia's painting or leaving with the Marquise at the end (Yarza, 1999: 64–5). Virginia's room is the main locus of melodramatic action, the other one being the Mother Superior's office. This can be seen in the room's *mise-en-scène* that, save for the religious images on the walls and the double *prie-dieu*, could have been taken from a 1950s American melodrama. Whilst this type of décor would have been seen as quite modern during the 1950s, it looks dated in the film. The Mother Superior realises this when she suggests swapping a painting of the Virgin for a poster of Mick Jagger. The end of the scene shows Yolanda sitting on the bed sighing, possibly realising how far this old-fashioned domestic space is from her image of herself as an 'adventurer'.

If Yolanda seems deflated on entering the convent, the Mother Superior is inconsolable when she discovers that Yolanda has left it. This is the final high melodramatic point in the film and the moment when the camera leaves the convent and the film ends. The Mother Superior enters Virginia's (now Yolanda's) room, realises that Yolanda has left, and screams in despair. She angrily throws the now useless key to the floor. There is a cut to Sister Manure lying in bed as she hears the scream and rushes to the Mother Superior, then another cut as she gets to the door and the camera begins moving out of the open window into the darkness as the opening bars of Lucho Gatica's 'Encadenados' are heard. The film ends with a freeze-frame shot of the Mother Superior being consoled by Sister Manure.

This shot establishes a parallel between the conclusion of the film and the end of the scene where Yolanda tells the Mother Superior that she is going to stop taking heroin. Both happen in the same room and both scenes are shot from the cloister and framed by windows. As Allinson suggests, 'framing can also serve to separate or even incarcerate characters. In *Entre tinieblas*, when Yolanda tells the Mother Superior they should both give up heroin, they are filmed in a long shot from outside two windows, separately, as if in a confessional. The windows reveal them in the same space but firmly kept apart' (2001: 188). Both characters are trapped by their addiction to heroin and Yolanda in particular is trapped by her dependence on the Mother Superior at that stage. The second shot shows only Yolanda's window, now wide open after Yolanda's flight and occupied by the Mother Superior. The open window signifies Yolanda's freedom but also the Mother Superior's unrestrained pain, her heart as open as the window and as vulnerable as the Sacred Heart of Christ, which is the order's symbol.

Almodóvar changed the ending from comic (Yolanda living with the Marquise and going out with her grandson) to tragic. This radical shift in tone turns *Entre tinieblas* from a comedy starring Yolanda to the story of the Mother Superior's tragedy. Like Yolanda, the botanist turned singer, Almodóvar specialises in hybrids, in his case film hybrids. Although the comic elements are there, the overall effect is not comic even taking into account the nervous laughter produced by the surreal. Just as in tragicomedy there are tragic elements that finally lead to a comic (if incongruous at times) conclusion, here we find potentially comic events leading to a tragic ending. *Entre tinieblas* is thus more related to modern drama, particularly its comic tragedies, than to sexploitation films. In contrast to Almodóvar's previous two films – *Pepi, Luci, Bom y otras chicas del montón* (Pepi, Luci, Bom and Other Girls on the Heap, 1980) and *Laberinto de pasiones* (Labyrinth of Passion, 1982) – *Entre tinieblas* ends in loss and despair. Even his relentlessly bleak next film, *¿Qué he hecho yo para merecer esto?* (What Have I Done to Deserve This?, 1984), offers its main character some hope at the end. *Entre tinieblas* is apparently lighter in tone than the latter film, but on closer inspection it reveals a darker story, that of the end of lesbian romantic dreams.

It is also a film that wants to argue for the freedom of modern Spain by re-using old tropes from the film genres of the dictatorship, religious iconography, and traditional songs, but ends up sympathising with those who could have been portrayed as agents of repression, the obsessed nuns who are more in the dark than they would like to admit. After all, Almodóvar is more interested in the forsaken, the obsessed, and the heartbroken than in those who find their way in life. In an interview with Jon Halliday, Sirk commented on how he dealt with sentimental material: 'You have to do your utmost to hate it – and to love it' (quoted in Mercer and Shingler, 2004: 44). Just like Sirk, Almodóvar seems to do his 'utmost to hate ... – and to love' his material, including the damaged women in the convent, trying to make the most of a society that for too long had frowned upon their desires. Almodóvar's magnificent obsession with the religious films of the dictatorship combines a fascination with them, a desire to show their shortcomings, and also to move on. Significantly, Almodóvar wrote the notebook that appears in the film. Yolanda's boyfriend explains his infatuation with Yolanda, his muse, thus: 'Yolanda, don't think you're so important. You're just one of my tools. At times you seem to realise that and I hate you for it.' Loving and hating his source material, Almodóvar seeks to transcend the folkloric religious film but nevertheless comes back to it, as in Gatica's *bolero*, as a source of torture and delight. For it is not just in his latest films that Almodóvar revisits his past or that his past catches up with him.

Notes

1 The third genre Higginbotham identifies is the 'cinema of the crusade', a genre with historical and religious undertones, the purpose of which was to engage in patriotic nation-building.

2 During the dictatorship, both foreign cinema and films made in Spain were heavily censored and the Church was the main enforcer of this censorship. Before any foreign film was shown, the local priest would have a private screening where he would indicate what should be cut. The Church also established a system of rating from 1 to 4, which indicated whether the films were suitable to be seen or should be avoided by 'good' Catholics. Film scripts had to be submitted to the government for scrutiny before filming began and many religious films credit their religious advisers.

3 'Jesus spoke to the Pharisees again. "I am the light of the world," he said. "Whoever follows me will have the light of life and never walk in darkness"' (John 8: 12).

4 This difficult professional relationship is a precursor of the fictional disagreement between Salvador and Alberto in *Dolor y gloria*.

5 *Boleros*, not to be confused with Spanish traditional boleros (clothing), are better known in English as slow rumba. They originate in Cuba and are slow danceable songs with melancholy lyrics.

3

High windows and ugly aesthetics: *¿Qué he hecho yo para merecer esto?*

In *¿Qué he hecho yo para merecer esto?* (What Have I Done to Deserve This?, 1984) we are far from *la movida* whilst still in 1980s Madrid. *¿Qué he hecho?* is set in a poor working-class high-rise neighbourhood, the Barrio de la Concepción, adjoining the M-30 motorway. It was developed in the 1960s to house many of the people who had moved from rural areas of Spain to find work in the capital; here drugs are not taken as re-creation but out of need. Modernity and 'progress' are not signified by sequins and sunglasses as in previous films but by a sprawling city and a dispossessed population who barely make ends meet but crave mod cons. The film takes its cue from 1960s family films such as *La gran familia* (The Big Family, Palacios, 1962), where a large family copes with financial difficulties. Almodóvar's film, however, subverts these feel-good films. Here, the family pet (a lizard) is the most colourful object in a flat where the mother is a sex-starved drug addict, the father is obsessed with an old relationship, the eldest son is a drug dealer, and the youngest son prostitutes himself with the consent of his mother.

The main protagonist is Gloria (Carmen Maura), a housewife who is forced to do cleaning jobs on the side to help the family finances and takes amphetamines to cope with her awful life. Her husband, Antonio (Ángel de Andrés López), is a taxi driver who spends all day working and dreaming of the time he spent as a guest worker in Germany. He is the typical man of the time: demanding, incommunicative, and brought up in a patriarchal system that once allowed him absolute power over his wife. The couple have two sons, Toni (Juan Martínez), who pushes drugs and forges signatures, and Miguel (Miguel Ángel Herranz), who sleeps with his friend's father and is prostituted to a dentist (Javier Gurruchaga) later in the film.

The grandmother (Chus Lampreave) also lives with the family, creating further tension. Gloria accidentally kills her husband with a *jamón* bone during a marital dispute. This brings about the final disintegration of the family. Other storylines include a prostitute neighbour, a single mother who abuses her child, and the rather thin story of a couple of alcoholic writers who inadvertently provoke the argument that leads to Antonio's death. The film's central event (in which Gloria kills Antonio with a *jamón* and then makes a broth with it that she tries to feed to the policemen investigating the murder) quotes one of Hitchcock's television murder mysteries and is itself quoted several years later by Bigas Luna in *Jamón, Jamón* (1992).[1]

Like *Volver* (2006), *¿Qué he hecho?* partakes of neo-realism's emphasis on ordinary people, its episodic structure, and its refusal to pass judgement on the characters' actions. However, it departs from neo-realism in style. Almodóvar explains to Nuria Vidal that there is a link between the film and neo-realism, 'but not in its planning or *mise-en-scène*. More in relation to the intentions of the film' (1989: 116; my translation). The film revisits the life of the housewife glimpsed in *Pepi, Luci, Bom y otras chicas del montón* (Pepi, Luci, Bom and Other Girls on the Heap, 1980) but without Luci's escape route of becoming a groupie or being a masochist.

Most viewers would not at first identify *¿Qué he hecho?* with Almodóvar's aesthetic. It is not pop, like the early films, or as stylised as the later films. It is kitsch, particularly in the family flat, but not kitsch filtered through the camp sensibility that is normally associated with Almodóvar's cinema. The *mise-en-scène* is full of objects familiar to Spaniards who lived through the 1970s and 1980s. Almodóvar designed the sets with what I call a working-class-kitsch-baroque aesthetic in mind, the perfect background for a melodrama whose protagonists are neither affluent (as in most Hollywood melodramas) nor – to Spaniards – exotic because of the familiarity of what we see on screen. This working-class-kitsch-baroque aesthetic is not normally the product of careful planning but of years of accumulation of objects. The working class cannot afford to have good taste. The objects in the house are not terrible in themselves, but they clash. Working-class-kitsch-baroque could thus be defined as being eclectic without being postmodern. Gloria and Antonio's flat contrasts with those of her middle-class employers and the sexologist, which are less cluttered and follow 'bohemian' middle-class decorative style. Almodóvar mentions to Frederic Strauss how 'the dull colours reflect the ugliness which surrounds the life of the character portrayed by Carmen Maura. Re-creating that ugliness was as hard as creating the brilliantly colourful sets of *High Heels*. *What Have I Done to Deserve This?* is, in fact, my only film where everything one sees stems from a realist intention' (Strauss, 2006: 50). The 'ugliness' that Almodóvar speaks of relates to the situation Gloria finds herself in. There are few bright or colourful objects (the red vases and pink throw stand out in a frankly soulless home). It is, in fact, a re-creation of the *feísmo* (ugly aesthetics) of the real apartment blocks in the Concepción.

Almodóvar's attention to the detail of social reality makes this one of his most difficult films to place. It is not realist, or overtly postmodern, or pop like his early films. Nevertheless, there is still humour and splashes of surrealism, including the presence of a pet lizard and the abrupt shifts to television programmes. The film's black comedy also makes it difficult to classify. As Almodóvar comments:

> *What Have I Done to Deserve This?* is a film where again one finds several cinematic genres. Most of all, it alludes to a form of narrative that I'm particularly fond of: Italian neo-realism. For me, Italian neo-realism is a sub-genre of melodrama which specifically deals not just with emotions but with social conscience. It's a genre which takes the artificiality out of melodrama, while retaining its essential elements. In *What Have I Done to Deserve This?* I replace most of the codes of melodrama with black humour. Therefore it isn't surprising that the audience first takes the film to be a comedy, although it's a very tragic, pathetic story. (quoted in Strauss, 2006: 44)

Almodóvar's descriptions of neo-realism as melodrama 'with a social conscience' and of *¿Qué he hecho?* as melodrama with black humour that resembles neo-realism are useful. The film does not blame society directly for its characters' plight but contains neo-realism's values. Hence it is difficult to make clear distinctions between what is and is not artificial and realistic in the dialogue, *mise-en-scène*, and photography. Editing also plays a major part in this confusion, providing opportunities to establish parallelisms between the actions on- and off-screen, for example, during the credits scene and Gloria and Antonio's lovemaking.

Spanish reviewers at the time of release disliked the fact that Almodóvar combined what they considered a realist style with a surrealist plot. Juan Arribas, for example, compared *¿Qué he hecho?* unfavourably to Almodóvar's early films, arguing that in films like *Pepi, Luci, Bom* 'the informal character of the filmic narrative composed a homogeneous whole with the plot and extravagant characters' whereas by *¿Qué he hecho?* Almodóvar 'has learnt how to use the camera and follow his characters so it is not enough to film any old story. The director needs to revise his initial ideas and know how to match what he wants to say with how it will be told' (1985: 269–70; my translation). Arribas wants content and form to follow established generic and stylistic patterns. In his opinion, Almodóvar's improved filming technique and the serious content of the film should not allow for departures from a (neo-)realist style.

Núria Triana Toribio cautions against reading the film 'sociologically, as a semi-documentary', pointing out that 'the way Almodóvar processes the material (often associated with postmodern production in general) resists such a reductive approach.' (2003a: 227). *¿Qué he hecho?* is another accomplished hybrid that is neither a 'semi-documentary' nor a purely playful postmodernist product. Whereas Triana Toribio is right to warn against seeing too much reality in the film, Almodóvar's use of 'postmodern production' techniques is not necessarily used with a postmodernist intention. One of Almodóvar's most prevalent postmodern traits is pastiche, but the appropriation of advertising and other genres by Almodóvar is not devoid of political undertones. The shots from appliances show how characters – Gloria in particular – are alone and only 'seen' by the things they use. As Varderi points out, 'only the objects know of Gloria's existence' (1996: 200; my translation). These shots also offer a stark contrast between the reality of family life and the ideal lives portrayed in advertising. As Almodóvar tells Vidal, 'I shoot from inside things because white goods are the only witnesses of the life of this woman. She mops, cleans continuously and nobody sees her, except for these things. In this way I turn all the propaganda about wonderful home objects on its head, since these are terribly shabby' (1989: 119–20; my translation). Miguel's discovery of an empty fridge is particularly shocking as viewers are used to food and drink adverts showing well-stocked modern fridges.

Paul Julian Smith establishes an important distinction between specific generic traits such as 'immobile' camerawork, which can be associated with neo-realism, and the overall aesthetic of the film:

Almodóvar follows some neo-realist precepts in this film in his use of working-class protagonists, vernacular dialogue, and implied social criticism. With his frequently immobile camera he also coincides with a favourite neo-realist tendency: the primacy of *mise-en-scène* over editing ... But where theorists such as Bazin argued that neo-realists 'respected the ontological wholeness of the reality they filmed' through such techniques, Almodóvar deprives them of any such transcendent quality. (2014: 58–9)

Reality is not treated reverentially, but there is transcendence even in the funniest scenes. This is one of the main reasons why the film enraged Spanish film critics such as Diego Galán, who complains that the film 'mocks the everyday life of an amphetaminic housewife' (1984). *¿Qué he hecho?* does not mock housewives. On the contrary, it seems to me to be fully on their side, even if Almodóvar chooses to demonstrate it by exaggerating their plight and suggesting outrageous solutions to it. The film offers indirect satire, particularly Menippean satire, with a loose narrative structure and representatives from various strata of society whose actions are laid bare by the camera.

The camera is often static, but this is not necessarily out of a neo-realist desire to be unobtrusive. It is due to a desire to convey the claustrophobic atmosphere of the flat and of the characters' social circumstances. The sets were minuscule and there was thus little space in which to move. As a consequence, there is very little camera movement and what there is, as Juan David Correa Ulloa has noted, is usually vertical. Correa Ulloa interprets camera angles above or below eye level as occurring after 'moments of tension, tranquillity, violence and relaxation: for example, the most peaceful moment at home is filmed from above, whereas the most violent, the murder, is filmed from the floor' (2005: 70). However, this is not necessarily so. Whereas it is true that 'the most peaceful moment' – Gloria sitting on the sofa at night sniffing glue – is a high-angle shot, the murder scene is not 'filmed from the floor'. In fact, the low-angle shot happens just before Gloria turns on her husband as he hits her because she will not iron his shirt.

This angle seems justified by the point of view of the lizard who happens to be between the couple as they argue. This violent event is bookended by high-angle shots of the lizard on the floor in quick succession. This distraction softens the violent argument, which can hardly be seen as a result of the blinding kitchen light. The scene also points to the importance of the lizard in relation to the overall symbolism of the film. The first sign that Gloria is bleeding comes from two drops of blood that fall on the lizard's back. Only then is Gloria's bleeding nose shown. The lizard thus becomes green and red, precisely the same colours that Gloria is wearing. But whereas the lizard's cold-bloodedness is skin deep in that its greenness is only masked by the red drops of someone else's blood, Gloria's coldness is all on the surface. Her red jumper is barely covered by the green cardigan just as her anger and jealousy were barely disguised by her half-hearted attempt to make dinner. This is the clearest indication that the lizard and Gloria are inextricably linked in the film, however surreal it may seem. Gloria struggles not to show emotion but to show love. In this sense, although she is redder than the lizard and more prone to violent reactions, she shares its apparent detachment from family life.

One might condemn Gloria's mothering if it were not for the fact that Antonio's fathering is even worse. In fact, perhaps Gloria's tough love is a reaction to having been emotionally starved herself, particularly by Antonio. Whereas Antonio has his mother to fall back on, Gloria has nobody. She is one of the most solitary characters in all of Almodóvar's films, a filmmaker who is justifiably famous for his female communities. Rebeca in *High Heels* and Raimunda in *Volver* are similarly solitary, although Gloria's plight has no solution. Rebeca and Raimunda both have mothers with whom they can be reconciled; Gloria can only aspire to be a good mother herself.

Just as low angles do not automatically imply violence, so do high angles not necessarily show tranquillity. Gloria's moment of peace is shot from a high angle but, looking back at Almodóvar's previous film *Entre tinieblas* (Dark Habits, 1983), one could interpret this as a way of showing how Gloria is trapped by her circumstances and her addiction. In *Entre tinieblas*, high camera angles have been described as showing the point of view of God, but Almodóvar explained to Vidal that he used them 'because it is a way of trapping the character against the floor. You sink them and that is good for the narrative. In these shots what I am most interested in is the geography that comes out of the décor: the floor, the walls, the contours of the furniture' (1989: 67; my translation). As Gloria sniffs glue, she allows herself a moment of forgetfulness just before she returns to homemaking. However, this is simply a parenthesis snatched out of a reality that she cannot escape. She quickly goes back to work, gluing together a broken figurine and checking on her children in bed.

Gloria can only relax when her family are asleep. She is not seen sitting on the sofa or by the heater at any other point. She is always working, either for other people or for her family. Her relaxation is drug-induced, as artificial as the thought that the flat is a family home. Gloria is gluing together a figurine of what looks like a lamb: pastoral, nostalgic, and certainly idealised. This figurine is like her family life, fractured and imperfect. This truth is revealed by the crack in the figurine that, unlike the famous broken bowl in Henry James's *The Golden Bowl* (1904), cannot even be said to incarnate beauty. Gloria and Antonio's broken dreams are not artistic or sublime, but commonplace. Yet the shattering of those dreams is seen to be just as (if not more) painful than those of characters aiming for higher things such as the caricatured middle class. Like the figurine, Gloria is broken and can only survive through taking amphetamines and sniffing cleaning products and glue. Gloria is surrounded by the colour pink in the throw, the plastic flowers, and the glow of the heater. Yet she is not touched by the artificial warmth of the living room. Her clothes are green most of the time, suggestive of the colour of money that she lacks and her emotionally cold life.

Synthetic green is a poor substitute for the rural life that the family have left behind to live in the city. There is a clear dichotomy between city and country in the film. As Kathleen Vernon points out, 'contrary to the director's declarations about making films as if Franco never existed, *What Have I Done?* depicts a world created by the urban non-planning of the Franco years, growing out of a policy that actively sought by passive neglect of urban social services to discourage immigration to the "corrupt" cities' (1993: 33). This world was depicted critically by Spanish black comedies such as *El Pisito* (The Little Apartment, Ferreri, 1958), *El Verdugo* (The Executioner, Berlanga, 1963), and *El Inquilino* (The Tenant, Nieves Conde, 1957), as well as sympathetically in more conservative films such as *La ciudad no es para mí* (City Life Is Not for Me, Lazaga, 1966) and *La gran familia*. In such films, the city is seen as the locus of corruption and moral degeneration, a situation that can only be overcome by a return to the country or by the intervention of a representative of rural Spain. In the case of *La ciudad no es para mí* this figure is an elderly relative, a grandfather who embodies the reactionary values of the dictatorship. Almodóvar seems to support this idea of the rural as beneficial in later films as evidenced in the recovery of Leo in *La flor de mi secreto* (The Flower of My Secret, 1995) and the suspiciously utopian endings of *¡Átame!* (Tie Me Up! Tie Me Down!, 1989) and *Kika* (1993). At this point in his career, however, the ideology of the dictatorship was too close to be endorsed.

¿Qué he hecho? parodies this thinking through the character of the grandmother who stereotypically wishes to return to the country. With her fetish for wood gathering, addiction to sparkling water and fairy cakes, and amusingly realistic turn of phrase, the grandmother can be interpreted as benign but she can also be mean and manipulative. She is a displaced character for whom there is no place in modern society. Her desire to return to the village, which neither Antonio nor Gloria share, is finally realised when she convinces her eldest grandson, Toni, to take her home and find work as a labourer. This is a return to the place his parents had to leave because of the lack of prospects. This return is seen by Gloria as undoing all the hard work she and Antonio have done to give their children more opportunities. Like Bud Stamper (Warren Beatty) in *Splendor in the Grass* (Kazan, 1961) – a film that Toni and the grandmother see at the cinema in Madrid – Toni has given up on his parents' dreams of improvement.

Almodóvar places a visual aporia at the heart of the grandmother's nostalgia that enables viewers to deconstruct it. The grandmother's nostalgia is symbolised by the lone tree she likes to visit to collect wood and where she finds the lizard. The composition and photography of this scene cite the most famous scene in arguably the most famous Hollywood melodrama (a film that also idealises rural society), the Tara scene in *Gone with the Wind* (Fleming, 1939), where Scarlett O'Hara swears, in a barren field next to what looks like a dead tree, that she will never be hungry again. In this scene, Scarlett's and the tree's black silhouettes are seen against the deep orange of the sky at dusk. In *¿Qué he hecho?*, the silhouettes of the grandmother and Toni are seen against a similarly vast sky in a similarly barren landscape. The sky is blue and the tree is almost a mirror image of the tree in *Gone with the Wind*. This quotation immediately brings to mind the poverty and suffering that can exist in the countryside, an aspect of rural life that Toni has not experienced and the grandmother probably does not want to remember. The Spain of the 1980s is not the USA during the American Civil War or the 1930s. However, it is safe to assume that Gloria and Antonio must have moved to Madrid before their children were born, probably during the 1960s. At that time there was a great wave of internal migration from the countryside to industrialised cities such as Barcelona and Madrid and emigration to other

European countries such as France and Germany. Whereas the situation in rural Spain was not as desperate as in the 1940s (commonly known as the years of hunger in Spain), it was still difficult to make a living and many young men and women left to work in factories or to provide services in the big cities. *Gone with the Wind* is not as obvious an intertext as *Splendor in the Grass*, but it is used to undermine the conservative narrative of the latter film. The return to the village is also, as Vernon comments, an ironic rewriting of the neo-realist film *Surcos* (Furrows, Nieves Conde, 1951), in which a family leaves the country for the city to find poverty and unemployment and finally return to the countryside (1993: 34).

Gloria's discomfort with even the thought of rural existence can be seen during her two brief encounters with an old lady from the village, played by Almodóvar's mother (Francisca Caballero). In the first scene, Gloria does not recognise the woman who seems to know everything about her and becomes visibly agitated as a result. During the second encounter, the old lady tells Gloria that she 'looks awful'. The harshness of rural life is not disguised by Almodóvar, although it is treated comically. Nevertheless, the old lady is not atypical in Spain. Thus, some of the most realistic aspects of the film can be interpreted by certain audiences as surreal or fictive, whereas the fictional scenes in the family home can be interpreted as realistic. This should be a warning against trying to see the film as either straight realism or surreal.

The use of sets rather than shooting on location goes against neo-realist precepts. Almodóvar questions the realist credentials of neo-realism in comments to Vidal:

> Neo-realism took the cameras out into the street because it wanted to capture real life. And this is a lie, because cinema is never reality. Cinema is a story that some man has invented. Unlike with neo-realism, 80% of *¿Qué he hecho yo* ... is filmed in a studio, using sets. All the interiors are sets, the corridors, the lifts, the stairs. Everything is in a studio, but you can't tell. Only the exteriors were filmed in the neighbourhood of the Concepción. What happens is that although they were sets, they were minuscule and they produced an impression of total claustrophobia. (1989: 118; my translation)

Viewers are alerted to the film as constructed from the very first scene. As Gloria goes to work in a martial arts school, she is seen walking through a square among a film crew, whose presence she observes curiously. The presence of the crew (the very same crew who are preparing to shoot the scene) punctures the illusion of reality. Music adds to our metacinematic awareness. The film employs an Italianate fast waltz with strings typical of Spanish black comedies and Italian neo-realist films. Hence, from the very first scene the viewer receives contradictory clues.

This metacinematic effect is later reinforced by insertions of adverts and television programmes that the family watch, including a scene where we are shown the filming of a Spanish *zarzuela* for television,[2] with Almodóvar himself miming a popular *tonadilla*,[3] 'La bien pagá' (Well-paid woman), alongside his then musical collaborator Fanny MacNamara (Fabio de Miguel) disguised in period clothing. The song seems to begin extradiegetically as Gloria and Antonio are having sex but soon cuts to the filming of the television programme that we later discover Toni and the grandmother are watching. In two clever cuts the viewers have jumped from the film's illusory reality (the lives of Gloria and her family) to the make-believe of film and television (the set where the song is performed) and finally to the living room where Toni and the grandmother are watching television (Almodóvar's and MacNamara's performance framed by the TV screen). The clever game of reality and fiction comments on the events in the house. Toni and the grandmother are watching what seems to be an intimate scene, a couple breaking up, just as viewers are watching a similar simulation: Gloria and Antonio's lovemaking.

The blatant artificiality of the filming of 'La bien pagá' makes it impossible to view the performance as anything other than spectacle. As Triana Toribio explains:

> this is a past whose representation provides no clues for its definite location, since the clothes are too artificial (signalling fancy dress rather than period authenticity), and the décor, a pastiche of those of TVE *zarzuelas*, flaunts its constructedness by including posters of Almodóvar's own films. In this way, the sudden irruption of neorealism is disrupted by the combined effects of a background which evokes the director's origins as a punk-underground film-maker, and also low-budget escapist television productions. (2003a: 235)

The cross-cutting of shots also invites connections between the song and the couple's relationship. 'La bien pagá' could ironically refer to

Gloria, who is not rewarded for her efforts within and outside the home. As Marvin D'Lugo states, the performance of 'La bien pagá' 'is a camp moment, but one that reinforces the multiple scenarios of coupling and of the status of women, conspicuously those of wife and prostitute' (2006: 43). Whilst Antonio is laying Gloria down on the bed, she asks him for money to take their youngest son to the dentist and other household bills. The money never materialises and she remains 'unpaid' for her services.

The link between marriage and prostitution is made even clearer by having a prostitute – Cristal (Verónica Forqué) – live next door. Besides financial difficulties, the issue that causes most friction between Gloria and Antonio is Antonio's disapproval of Cristal and demand that she be banished from their house and from Gloria's life. Antonio is afraid that Gloria will be tainted by association, a common fear in societies that consider women to be masculine property. Gloria is not keen on the connection with prostitution either but sees Cristal as a person rather than as a prostitute. Yet in a patriarchal system the distinction between 'honest' women and prostitutes is a fallacy. In effect, both Gloria and Cristal have to resort to sex to obtain money, but whereas Cristal achieves this, Gloria gets neither sexual satisfaction nor economic compensation for her sexual availability and other 'work' within the marital home. Yet the home is where Antonio wants Gloria. He follows well-rehearsed patriarchal arguments reinforced by forty years of dictatorship and Catholic and fascist rhetoric about femininity in Spain.

One could think of Antonio as a one-dimensional character, the patriarchal *pater familias*. However, he is as limited and oppressed as Gloria. His labour is also badly paid, his rude behaviour due to his immense dissatisfaction with life. As he says to his mother: 'I work my arse off all day long. When I get back home I have to eat half-burnt chicken and there's no fucking wine!' Part of this diatribe is aimed at Gloria, who has burnt the chicken, but the underlying problem is the family's difficulties to live on what they make in the city. Antonio, however, is unaware of (or unwilling to see) the sacrifices that Gloria makes so that he can have anything to eat. She has a burnt leg and no one else has dinner. Gloria even gives him the last bits of *jamón* that she had been saving for the youngest son. Antonio wants to live in a patriarchal heaven, expects dinner on the table, a clean house, and ironing or sex on demand. In return, he believes he simply has to work as hard as he can.

Antonio's backstory is relevant, having been a guest worker in Germany who has come back to live and work in Spain. His insistence on remembering his migratory past with nostalgia, particularly his relationship with his former boss Ingrid Müller (Katia Loritz), causes tension with Gloria. If Gloria escapes through amphetamines and glue, Antonio does so through remembering his stay in Germany and his relationship with Müller, obsessively playing the German song 'Nur nicht aus Liebe weinen' by Zarah Leander. This is peculiar, since migrants usually idealise their home countries, not the receiving countries. It transpires that Müller merely used him to forge Hitler's letters and make money.[4] Antonio is thus also the subject of the ironic song 'La bien pagá' since he, like Gloria, has not been paid for his love and labour.

Antonio and Gloria's initial argument about Cristal develops out of Antonio's need to reaffirm his own honesty rather than hers. He has just turned down a proposal to forge Hitler's memoirs and takes his anger out on Gloria, who is unaware of this. During the argument they discuss what is important in life:

ANTONIO   There are more important things than money.
GLORIA   Really?
ANTONIO   Yeah, decency for one. If I weren't honest, I could make a
          bundle, but I happen to be a decent man.
GLORIA   Does decency cut your appetite?
ANTONIO   You heard me. I forbid you to see Cristal! And you're not
          going back to that writer's!

Viewers have the benefit of having seen Antonio reject the writer's proposal to commit fraud but Gloria has not. When Antonio talks about 'decency' he is referring to himself as much as her. He has displaced his feelings of guilt about his past forgery onto Gloria, whom he blames for talking to Cristal and breaking the rules on femininity promoted during the dictatorship that discouraged women from taking on any public activity (Domingo, 2007: 91; my translation) and gave husbands the right to decide whether their wives could go to work.

The world of the housewife in the early 1980s in Spain was changing slowly, but the insidious effects of the recent past are at play in Antonio and Gloria's relationship and values. Gloria is hypercritical of herself as a mother, telling a neighbour that 'I'm not such a

good mother either'. She does not complain about having responsibility for housework and parenting. As Almodóvar commented in a
1982 interview with Maruja Torres, 'the world of the housewife both
amuses and fascinates me because it is monstrous in its alienation. I
would like to make a serious film about this; one could build a good
argument in favour of housewives' (quoted in Vidal, 1989: 115; my
translation). *¿Qué he hecho?* is not strictly 'serious' but the underlying
message behind it is.

This critique of patriarchy is reinforced in the television short that
Almodóvar made for Spanish national television (TVE) to promote
the film. The short film, *Tráiler para amantes de lo prohibido* (Trailer
for Lovers of the Forbidden), was broadcast as part of a now mythical
cultural programme, *La edad de oro* (The Golden Age), on 29 January
1985. It is a musical version of *¿Qué he hecho?* where a woman (Josele
Román) with two children is abandoned by her husband (Poch,
the leader of a rock band called *Derribos*), who leaves her for a rich
foreign woman (Bibiana Fernández, also known as Bibí Andersen).
Unable to make ends meet, the wife resorts to stealing shopping bags
and prostitution. She meets a painter who is making the poster for
¿Qué he hecho? and invites her to the film premiere. Meanwhile, the
husband is ditched by the fickle beauty and, in a typical male chauvinist show of jealousy, tries to have a fight with the painter. She
shoots her husband and starts singing what can only be described as
a song celebrating her freedom. By Almodóvar's own admission in
the interview preceding the film, it is 'a pretty atypical trailer' in that
it advertises the film but does not show any footage from it.

The short film is a masterpiece of surreal parody. The main action is
told through miming hit songs. Each of the main characters has their
own style of music. The wife sings *boleros* and the husband *flamenco*.
There are many parallels with *¿Qué he hecho?*, from the wife turning
prostitute to make ends meet to the main event of the killing of the
husband. The murder scenes are quite different, however. Whereas
in the short film the wife shoots her husband as he is opening his
pen-knife and is first indifferent, then elated, in *¿Qué he hecho?* the
murder is less intentional since Antonio only dies because his nape
hits the sink. Nevertheless, the sense that the female protagonist has
got rid of a waste of space who neither cared for nor deserved her
is the same in both films. If anything, the short film goes further
than the feature film in exposing the relief felt by the wife. It also
rewards the murderer more, since the wife continues her happy stroll

with her new boyfriend, whereas in *¿Qué he hecho?* Gloria is on the verge of committing suicide by the end.

Tráiler para amantes is an accomplished short film in its own right and also a wonderful companion piece to *¿Qué he hecho?*, less nuanced than the feature film but more playful. In *Tráiler para amantes*, for example, the wife sings a Spanish version of Édith Piaf's 'Non, je ne regrette rien'. The last line of the song, 'today I begin to live', coincides with the ending of the film. *¿Qué he hecho?* lacks this sense of optimism. Gloria purges the house by re-decorating it but does not seem any happier. She returns home to an empty, pristine flat and has nothing to do since nobody has been there to create a mess while she was away. She walks along the corridor looking into the empty bedrooms, noting that everything is clean. Finally she opens the balcony and steps out.

Vidal appropriately calls this Gloria's '*travelling* of loneliness' (1989: 294; my translation, emphasis in original). The music that accompanies this 'travelling of loneliness' is first heard as Gloria says goodbye to Toni and the grandmother and they leave Madrid. Composed for the film by Bernardo Bonezzi, it is later used extensively in *La ley del deseo* (The Law of Desire, 1987). Paul Julian Smith rightly criticises Miguel Albaladejo for constructing an analogy between the two films: 'Albaladejo sketches out an Oedipal scenario which is repeated in the later film: after the loss of the hated father, the gay son returns to the mother figure and the plot circle is closed. The analogy does not quite hold' (Smith, 2014: 62). It is more productive to look at emotion rather than plot in order to establish links between both uses of the same melody. Loneliness and atomisation seem to be the most likely link between the two films. Before she is alone, Gloria has no theme tune. She is presented at the beginning through a theme that recalls neo-realist detachment and is shortly after identified by her husband's theme song, Leander's 'Nur nicht aus Liebe weinen'. The only other moment in the film where she could be identified with music is the night-time tune, which starts as a drum machine marking time as she is sniffing glue and checking her children are asleep. However, this tune is more a transition from night to daylight than a theme song. The same rhythm is heard as she climbs up the stairs laden with shopping bags. If anything, these repetitive sounds could represent Gloria's humdrum personality, her ticking along, the metallic tones highlighting the fact that Gloria has become an automaton. Almodóvar explains to Vidal that Gloria has become a machine. That is why the most pathetic moment is when she says goodbye to her son and the grandmother. If this film supposedly tells the story of this woman's liberation, it is at this point when she is fully liberated. She does not have the burden of children. ... She has killed her husband and nothing has happened; she is alone and tranquil at home and has nothing to do because everything is clean. This is the moment when she is most lonely. The worst thing about the life she has had is not the life itself, but that she has had no time to realise that she did not have her own life. At this moment she is a free woman but she has no desires. Her life has no meaning. She goes out to the balcony and the temptation of throwing herself out into the void is huge. But this would have been too terrible. I could not end like this; I could not leave her there alone. That is why the younger son arrives. (1989: 146; my translation)

The arrival of the younger son is not, as Albaladejo muses, the closure of an Oedipal scenario where father and son compete for the mother but a reason for Gloria to continue living. Just as Leo is snatched from death as she tries to commit suicide by the voice of her mother in *La flor*, so is Gloria metaphorically woken up by the sight of her younger son, someone who may still need her and whom she desperately needs. She may not miss her role of wife but she clings to that of mother. Her pained stare is thus a precursor to that of Manuela in *Todo sobre mi madre* (All about My Mother, 1999) and Julieta in the eponymous film. The final theme song is more orchestrated, elaborated, and, crucially, louder than the previous repetitive tunes that replicate the patriarchal doctrine that women should work tirelessly and, importantly, quietly. Hence the 'travelling of solitude' is Gloria's first and only true theme tune.

The film's ending returns to a pseudo-neo-realist framework with four static shots of the housing estate receding from the window that signal an invitation to the viewer to make generalisations from what they have seen. Gloria's window is just one of many windows in one of hundreds of flats in that particular neighbourhood. This ending alludes to a classic of Spanish literature, Camilo José Cela's *La Colmena* (The Beehive, 1951). *¿Qué he hecho?* is a comedy like Almodóvar's other early films, but an extremely bleak one. Reviewers have missed Almodóvar's indirect satire of the 1980s, of the hopes of the left that life would be better after Franco's death and of the right that there was an ideal past to go back to. It also punctures illusions

that Madrid and Spain by extension were becoming richer, more cos-
mopolitan, and culturally sophisticated in the 1980s by depicting the
exact opposite of *la movida*. The protagonists are not moving on. They
live static lives where movement is only possible by going backwards,
not forwards. Whereas in his early comedies Almodóvar retreats
somewhat from the outside world into the world of *la movida*, with
¿Qué he hecho? he goes into several of the homes he had previously
ignored and satirises the wonderful life that had supposedly opened
up for Spaniards with democracy and industrialisation. The death of
Antonio, the small dictator in the family, solves little for Gloria, who
cannot see beyond her socially pre-determined roles. Similarly, the
death of Franco, although making possible huge advances legally and
economically, left many Spaniards unsure of their own place in life.

Notes

1 Almodóvar has commented that he was not aware of this intertext and
   explained that he got to the murder weapon through the martial arts
   theme of the film.
2 A Spanish musical drama or comedy that combines declamation and
   singing, operatic performances and popular songs.
3 A brief, popular Spanish song.
4 This forgery was probably inspired by the publication of extracts from
   Hitler's diaries by the German magazine *Stern* in 1983, which were
   revealed to be fakes within two weeks. Despite Antonio's fake letters and
   Toni's business forging signatures, forgery is strongly associated with
   middle-class hypocrisy in Almodóvar's films. Here, Müller convinces
   Antonio to forge Hitler's letters and writers propose he forge Hitler's
   memoirs. In *Todo sobre*, Sister Rosa's mother is engaged in forging
   Chagall paintings whilst snobbishly refusing help from Manuela, whom
   she thinks is a prostitute.

4

Faking Spain: *Matador*

Matador (1986) is the most symbolic of Almodóvar's films. After the ugly aesthetics of *¿Qué he hecho yo?* Almodóvar surprised his audience again with a highly stylised film. The visual excesses of the film point to what at first seems a return to the colourful zaniness of the early films with a murder mystery plot and tale of sexual perversion closely linked to Spanish cultural symbols, particularly bullfighting. *Matador*, however, continues Almodóvar's attacks on complacent attitudes towards democratic Spain and his ambivalent use of cinematic and other traditions. Despite *Matador's* incisiveness, its use of typically Spanish symbols and traditions that can easily be interpreted as local colour may obscure its deconstruction of these.

The film explores desire and repression in relation to death and the urge to kill (and die) using the trope of the *corrida* (a bullfight but also related to the Spanish slang for ejaculation [*correrse*] since both words derive from the verb *correr* 'to run'). There are a series of murders for which would-be bullfighter Ángel (Antonio Banderas) claims responsibility but which have actually been committed by two different people, a lawyer called María Cardenal (Assumpta Serna) and a retired bullfighter called Diego Montes (Nacho Martínez), who is also Ángel's teacher. Diego and María realise that they are both murderers sharing a similar passion for sex and violence and decide to kill themselves whilst having sex during a solar eclipse. Although Ángel has previously confessed to the crimes, which he has witnessed due to paranormal powers, he is exonerated when it is discovered that he faints at the sight of blood.

The actions of the characters are not overtly judged. Indeed, there is some empathy for Diego and María, whose reasons for killing are explored through their dialogue. They believe themselves

different from other people, *matadores*, as opposed to simply killers.
The distinction between a *matador* and a murderer is subtle. Whereas
matador is a term derived from the verb *matar* (to kill), it is normally
used as a pejorative adjective to describe something extremely ugly.
This meaning of *matador* is particularly relevant since fashion is an
important aspect of the film. The title, *Matador*, signals Almodóvar's
consciousness of film as something purposely ugly or tasteless.
This self-consciousness is in line with Almodóvar's use of kitsch
objects and clothes more as a statement of his aesthetics and politics
than simple props. It is also quite a joke in that viewers are invited to
enjoy a film that is *matador*, that is to say, a film that parades its own
tastelessness and use of kitsch, particularly symbols of Spanishness
such as the bullfight.

   The word *matador* is also used as a noun, in card games, and for a
bullfighter who kills with a sword. The use of *matador* as the film's
title distances characters and viewers from the actual murders and
attempts to transform killing into something acceptable and even
desirable. It removes the actual implications of killing by associ-
ating it with games and cultural traditions. In the process, it also
plays up to Spanish stereotypes of *matadors* and of Spain as a nation
obsessed with bullfighting and *fiestas*, an image promoted during
the dictatorship and still prevalent in many quarters. These stereotypes colour interpretations by non-Spanish critics. For example,
Colombian critic Juan David Correa Ulloa comments that 'the film
was seen with suspicion by a public that did not like the demystifica-
tion [Ulloa uses the word *desacralización*, or removal of the sacred
from] of one of its national symbols. The director was conscious of
the risk he was running in placing the religion of Spaniards at the
centre of his film' (2005: 79; my translation). Considering bullfighting a 'national symbol' and using religious language to talk about it
is very much in line with Francoist representations of Spain as the
land of bulls and *flamenco*. As Marsha Kinder points out, 'during
Spain's neo-Catholic revival in the 1940s ... the baroque fetishization
of sacrificial death in the popular arts helps to empower both the
religious orthodoxy of the church and the absolute power of Franco'
(1993: 142). Correa Ulloa talks about bullfighting as 'the religion
of Spaniards' and refers to the film as 'demystifying one of Spain's
national symbols', perpetuating the myth of all Spaniards as obsessed
with this tradition when this is not the case. Leora Lev explains how
during Franco's rule 'the *corrida* enacted an illusionistic drama of

national identity that compensated, in the popular imagination, for the Spanish disenfranchisement from international politics wrought by Francoist isolationism, as well as for domestic socioeconomic disempowerment resulting from a virtually immutable class hierarchy' (1995: 75). For many Spaniards bullfighting is precisely 'an illusionistic drama' that replicated the Roman maxim of 'bread and circus' for the masses. Although there remains significant support for bullfighting in some parts of Spain and among a certain generation of Spaniards, it cannot be seen as a fundamental part of Spain's 'national identity', mainly because there is no such thing as a Spanish national identity. For every person who identifies with this tradition there are others who feel that it annuls their experience as citizens of Spain.

In fact, Almodóvar's use of 'typically' Spanish symbols such as the paraphernalia of bullfighting, the gypsy palm reader, and the strict Opus Dei mother follows established patterns of parody within his films. He is also indebted to a prominent surrealist Spanish film-maker working in exile, Fernando Arrabal, whose *L'Arbre de Guernica* (1975) uses bullfighting as a source of grotesque parody to question the aftermath of the Spanish Civil War. A surrealist film, *L'Arbre de Guernica* is much more biting and critical of Spanish national symbols than *Matador*. One of its most memorable scenes is a bull-fight in a village occupied by Franco's forces where the bullfighter is a military chaplain and the sacrificed bulls are not animals but dwarves. *Matador*'s parody of Spanish symbols can be traced back to more politically charged films such as those by Arrabal and interpreted as politically inflected despite the lack of explicit politics. Ernesto Acevedo-Muñoz, for example, relates the film to the 'cultural baggage for Almodóvar's generation':

> Almodóvar's experiment with *Matador* thus ends in an overly dramatic, clichéd romantic setting that is clearly a parody of itself. Ultimately what the film's entire scenario and *mis[e] en scène* suggest is a very reflexive look at the meaning of cultural baggage for Almodóvar's generation. The movie's ornate combination of the literal and metaphoric cultural symbolism of Catholicism, repression, bullfighting, Spain's Fascist past, sexual inadequacy and sexual abuse, and its exploration of the physical and psychological wounds of the past represent up to its release in 1986, a summary and deeper elaboration of Almodóvar's topics so far. (2007: 78)

In *Matador*, traditional symbols of Spanishness are exaggerated in a way that makes their artificiality apparent. For example, both the setting of María and Diego's final sex scene and their behaviour create an accumulation of symbols and stereotypes that prevent us from taking them too seriously. When Diego and María stop to buy roses the stall is manned by a gypsy, as signified by her dress, hairstyle, and Andalusian accent. This is confirmed by her offer to read Diego's palm. On arrival at María's house in the country Diego and María bathe together in a bathroom decorated with Moorish tiles, which reinforce the idea of the couple's decadence. The extradiegetic music – a popular *bolero* titled 'Espérame en el cielo, corazón' (Wait for me in heaven, sweetheart) – begins at this stage and provides continuity as Almodóvar cuts to the couple in the lounge already dressed up and ready to have sex/kill one another. In addition to this, the *bolero*'s association with romance and seduction provides a romantic atmosphere for what could otherwise be seen as a fetishised, sado-masochistic sexual encounter.

The scene contains very little dialogue and so music and *mise-en-scène* take centre stage. The *mise-en-scène* is saturated with symbolic objects such as the red roses (in vases as in melodrama and scattered on the floor), a bull skin rug by the fireplace, and the bullfighter's silk and gold outfit with frilly shirt and a *capote* that Diego spreads on the rug.[1] María's outfit is contemporary but also symbolic: tights and a corset under a cape designed by Francis Montesinos (the Spanish designer who Almodóvar himself plays in the film and whose outfits feature in the film's fashion show). This cape, a modern version of the traditional cape or *capote*, is black, red, and yellow, echoing the colours of the bullfight and the Spanish flag. María is styled both after a bull (in black) and after a *matador* (with a *capote* in red and yellow). Significantly, her *capote* is red whereas Diego's is pink. Pink is the colour of the type of *capote* used to tease the bull, red is the colour of the *muleta*, a much lighter cape with which the bullfighter leads the bull to his sword. María is therefore dressed 'to kill' whereas Diego's outfit is more playful and less dangerous. As Alicia Hernández Vicente (2003) has noted, it is María who kills in the end, not Diego.

The ending of the film with the detective saying that he has 'never seen anyone so happy' also seems to justify Diego and María's actions. However, as Hernández Vicente states,

> I do not think that this statement is totally correct since there was a pact that one of the parts did not fulfil.

There were two pins, two matadors and an obsession with the only
end of reaching complete happiness ... both Diego and María wanted
to reach a climax with their only and true lover, a dead but satisfied
lover. Because of this, one of them had to be sacrificed so that the other,
Diego, could have what he wanted. This is why María asks him to look
at her with pathetic frustration, so that he can see her dead. But it is too
late; he has not finished his job. (2003: 31; my translation)

Hernández Vicente explores the contradictions of an ending that may
appear to be 'happy' but is not, particularly for the 'frustrated' María
who has to reach orgasm and die on her own. Visually, the couple do
not look 'happy' either.

The final shot is a tableau of Diego and María's dead bodies lying on
a pink *capote* and red and yellow silk. These are roughly the colours of
the tricolour Spanish Republican flag, which is red, yellow, and purple.
The light makes their bodies look sculptural. This effect will later be
repeated in *La ley del deseo* (The Law of Desire, 1987), a film on which
cinematographer Ángel Luis Fernández also worked. The emphasis
is on María's naked torso and nipples at the centre of the composition with secondary light points including Diego's hip and the faces of
both characters.[2] This is also a return to the *chiaroscuro* employed by
Almodóvar and Fernández in *Dark Habits*. In *Matador*, however, the
style is late baroque, with close attention to the details of the body and
textures of cloth. The emphasis on Diego's thigh further brings to mind
Gian Lorenzo Bernini's similar emphasis in *Ratto di Proserpina* (The
Rape of Proserpina). Uncharacteristically for the baroque, however,
neither of the figures has any expression. They are relaxed, statuesque,
but there is none of the extreme emotion conveyed by baroque painting
and sculpture in their faces. This aspect of the final composition recalls
a pre-Raphaelite style with its emphasis on spirituality and necrophilia.
María's face with her half-open mouth and unnaturally folded arm are
reminiscent of John Everett Millais' *Ophelia* (1852), although María's
face lacks the ecstatic expression of Ophelia (Figure 4.1).

Necrophilia features prominently in *Matador*, evident in the use of
snuff films as well as the characters' own actions, including not only
Diego and María's murders but also Diego and Eva's foreplay as she
plays dead, Eva's use of a red wedding dress and pale make-up to try
to win Diego back, the fashion show's blend of sex, death, and violence as represented by the killer bride, and the use of a spiked chain
by Ángel's mother.

4.1   A tableau of Diego's and María's dead bodies (*Matador*, 1986)

María's characterisation is closer to the Gothic. Her introduction associates her closely with death as an agent, not a passive victim. She is the possessor of a sophisticated version of the bullfighter's sword with a curbed end. Bullfighters call the curbed end of their sword 'death'. Thus, María is both the bull and the bullfighter, death by sword and death by goring. She is the embodiment of Diego's death drive and particularly of his wish to have died in the bullring. This interpretation is reinforced by the symbolic use of the eclipse that, however ridiculous a trigger for the couple's final rendezvous, replicates in astrological terms what is happening with Diego and María. During a solar eclipse the moon comes between the sun and the earth so that its shadow falls on earth and obscures the sun. Both María and Diego are associated with the bull and, by extension, with the moon. As Nuria Vidal explains, 'the bull and the moon have a special relationship as symbols ... The bull is seen as a lunar animal and is associated with the night. ... From all these connections between bull and moon a deeper understanding of *Matador* comes about' (1989: 299; my translation). María is also associated with the moon because of her gender. Just as the moon eclipses the sun, so María eclipses Diego in the last scene. This is not the first time that Almodóvar has used astronomy in his films. In *Laberinto de pasiones*, Sexilia's phobia of the sun is traced back to an early childhood trauma and associated with her father. In 1988, Almodóvar told Vidal that the use of trauma and the Oedipal complex was 'no more than a joke about the cheap psychology used by cinema' (1989: 60). *Matador* does not attempt to explain the characters' actions with psychology but resorts to astronomy in much the same way.

Neither the sex nor the violence in *Matador* are particularly extreme in themselves. By the mid-1980s, Spaniards had been freed from censorship for a decade. This phase in Spanish film cinema, known as *destape* (uncovering), refers to erotic and pseudo-erotic films and other cultural products that relied on eroticism or soft-porn during the years after censorship was abolished in 1976. The production of violent films was also a consequence of the abolition of censorship, with films of the late 1970s such as *Pascual Duarte* (Franco, 1975), *Camada Negra* (Gutiérrez Aragón, 1977), and *El crimen de Cuenca* (Miró, 1979) already employing some of the techniques used in *Matador*. As Kinder explains,

> We can already note certain patterns emerging ...: the eroticization of violence, by targeting the genitals and by using fetishizing close-ups, ellipses, and long takes; the specularization of violence for spectators both within the film and in the movie theater; the displacement of violence onto surrogate victims, especially animals, children, and women; and the displacement of violence from one sphere of power to another, between sex and politics, between private and public space, and between the body, the family, and the state. (1993: 137–8)

Despite these disturbing traits, Spanish cinema is no more violent than other national cinemas (Kinder, 1993: 137). The suppression of violence in cinema during the regime led to it being used by anti-Franco filmmakers as an oppositional cinematic language. Just as in *La ley*, it is the first few minutes of *Matador* that are the most trying for spectators. After the initial montage of snuff films and Ángel's vision of María killing a man there is very little in the film by way of sustained violence. In the rest of the film we are shown Ángel's memories of his visions, particularly Diego's two murders. The first murder is softened by cross-cutting and the use of a long shot; the other murder is shot in medium and extreme close-ups, but the woman's make-up and grotesque facial expressions prevent us from seeing her as a 'real' woman. The woman also looks similar to another woman seen being murdered in the snuff film at the beginning, producing a sense of familiarity with events.

Matador is neither a film that outraged Spain due to its use of bullfighting nor as violent and sexually explicit as it first seems. One only has to compare it with one of its main intertexts, *Ai no korîda* (The Realm of the Senses, Ôshima, 1976), to see this. Almodóvar has talked about *Matador*'s relationship with *Ai no korîda* (Vidal, 1989: 173) and in the Pressbook of *Matador* he acknowledges the role of screenwriter Jesús Ferrero in 'turning this Latin drama into something more Japanese or more universal' (quoted in Vidal, 1989: 159; my translation). Both films explore sexual pleasure and violence as tied intrinsically to the death drive. Ôshima's original title, Bullfight of Love, makes an oblique allusion to the bullfight as a sexual battle with a number of rounds that ends with one of the 'partners' dying and the other taking his genitals as a trophy. The use of Spanish culture ends there, with Ôshima using Japanese cultural symbols and traditions such as geishas and kimonos to unravel Japanese pre-war nationalist rhetoric. It is thus not surprising that Almodóvar and Ferrero thought of using the trope of the *corrida* when thinking of developing a plot where two characters goad each other on and end up dead, a film that also unravels stereotypes of Spain and Spanishness.

Nevertheless, the influence of *Ai no korîda* goes beyond the trope of the *corrida* and extends to, for example, the colour palette (gold, pink, red, black, and white) and the composition of certain shots, particularly the final tableau with the dead bodies of Diego and María. Mark Allinson has perceptively associated these colours in *Matador* with bullfighting: 'The visual style of the film as a whole gives primacy to pinks, yellows and reds – the colours of the capote and the muleta, respectively' (2001: 30). This is a purposeful choice of colours as there are explicit references to the nation as 'divided'. Diego and María play the bull and the bullfighter in turns and the film's use of the bullfight is never straightforward. As Almodóvar states: 'María Cardenal and Diego Montes compose a great bullfight in which roles are interchangeable. There are times when she is the bullfighter and vice versa, as in life, sometimes one behaves in a masculine and feminine way, depending on the situation, although the essence of each of us is clear' (quoted in Vidal, 1989: 166; my translation).

Whereas the blend of feminine and masculine 'behaviours' by María and Diego is signalled through their dialogue, the film does not manage to deconstruct gender roles as thoroughly as Almodóvar seems to think. The dialogue between María and Diego when she shows him her fetish collection is one example of how the dialogue tries and fails to deconstruct gender roles:

MARIA   Diego. I have looked for you in all my lovers. I imitated you when I killed them.

DIEGO   Why haven't you contacted me before?

MARIA   I didn't know you were still a matador.

DIEGO   I tried to avoid it, but I couldn't. Giving up killing was like giving up living.

MARIA   Men think that killing is a crime. Women don't see it that way. Every male criminal has a feminine side.

DIEGO   And every female killer, a masculine one.

During this exchange, María and Diego put forward the theory that killing and androgyny go hand in hand. Social taboos are directly related to the Law of the Father as María makes a distinction between men who 'think killing is a crime' and women placed outside social norms who 'don't see it that way'. And yet the whole scene revolves around tired stereotypes of masculinity and femininity that the scriptwriters – Almodóvar (original story) and Jesús Ferrero (screenplay) – never dismantle. Both men and women are treated as homogeneous groups reflecting essential values. Femininity is seen as outside social rules and morality, as implied by María's comment that women do not think that killing is a crime. This goes back to the traditional placing of women alongside nature and natural impulses (the private sphere) and men alongside culture and society (the public sphere). The assumption that killers have masculine and feminine sides is undermined by María's early admission that she has 'imitated' Diego when killing her lovers. Thus, María – as a woman – is both the root of the killings and a mere copycat of Diego the *maestro*.[3]

Given this ideology, it is unsurprising to find María styled as a *femme fatale*, a career woman (a lawyer to boot) in a Spain where women were slowly accessing professional jobs. Women lawyers are always portrayed unsympathetically by Almodóvar. María is also a dominatrix alternating power suits and fetishist clothes to seduce and murder unsuspecting men. The association of working women with unnatural, masculine tendencies was endlessly made by the Catholic Church and *Sección Femenina* (the feminine section of the Fascist movement in Spain) during the dictatorship. It is disappointing that María is portrayed both as a career woman and as a vampiric domi-natrix complete with high heels, lacy tights, corset, dark hair, and red lipstick and nail varnish. Her weapon of choice, the pin, and her entrapment of men through dress align her predatory femininity with the spider, an association repeated in *La piel que habito* (The Skin I Live In, 2011). This, together with her black outfit, places her in a tra-dition that sees female sexuality and reproductive power as threaten-ing. During María's first killing, her clothes, make-up, and hairstyle are reminiscent of those of Elsa Lanchester in *Bride of Frankenstein* (Whale, 1935), echoing Frankenstein's own fears in Mary Shelley's original novel that a female creature who could procreate would be much worse and more frightening than a male one. Like other Gothic texts, *Matador* shares a distrust of female sexuality and active women, together with a taste for necrophilia and scopophilia (particularly in relation to dead women's bodies).

While the dialogue in *Matador* attempts to show that María and Diego are equally androgynous, narrative and *mise-en-scène* do not support this. María, not Diego, is the *matador*. She dies by her own hand, using her own weapon. The camera focuses on María when-ever she is within the frame whilst Diego fades into the background. The only moment when he becomes the object of the gaze is when he is dressed in his *traje de luces* (bullfighting suit), either in the home video of his goring or during the final sexual rendezvous with María. Unlike the women in the film whose bodies are fetishised both whilst dressed and naked, Diego loses his appeal as soon as he takes the suit off. As Ann Davies points out,

> *Matador* detaches to some extent the equation between female identity and masquerade by implying that men such as Diego can also enact the latter – though to do so they take on some female characteristics, in par-ticular that of being the object of spectacle. A link nonetheless persists between woman – and particularly the *femme fatale* – as masquerade and Spain as masquerade. (2004: 15)

Matador emphasises femininity as performance that is not depend-ent on sex assigned at birth. Femininity, as in many other films by Almodóvar, is seen as masquerade. Masculinity, on the other hand, is not always expressed as spectacle but as something that male characters have to prove and is closely linked to feelings of homophobia and sexism. For example, Ángel's attempted rape of Eva (Eva Cobo) is a way of proving to Diego and himself that he is not gay. Nevertheless, women's performance of masculinity is still beset by sexist stereotypes and represented as an existential threat to men, an unseen, internal characteristic as when María goes into the men's toilets at the cinema and warns Diego not to 'trust appearances'.

Diego and Maria are not the only characters to switch roles. Ángel and Eva also exchange roles of attacker and victim. Ángel is also both voyeur and object of the gaze. These shifts have been attributed to diverse factors. Ernesto Acevedo-Muñoz, for example, relates Ángel's changing role from attacker to a failed and pitiable man to Almodóvar's turning 'attempted rape into its own weapon of revenge and humiliation against perpetrators' (2007: 21). Whereas it is true that some of Almodóvar's least likeable characters are often actual or would-be rapists (the policeman in *Pepi, Luci, Bom* or Paco in *Volver*), Almodóvar's sympathies are not always firmly on the victim's side. Ricki in *¡Átame!* and Benigno in *Hable con ella* (Talk to Her, 2002) are portrayed sympathetically, as is Ángel in *Matador*. Ángel is also the object of the gaze of the detective (Eusebio Poncela) and the psychologist (Carmen Maura), both of whom are attracted to him.

The detective's gaze is particularly revealing as it provides a clear link between bullfighting and homoeroticism. This is clearly seen during his visit to the school, where his gaze focuses on the male students' crotches and buttocks while they practise their killing skills. The students are wearing worn tracksuit bottoms and so the direction of the gaze is not related to bullfighting as a feminine masquerade in this instance but to homosexual desire. These shots are similar to those in the initial scene of *Laberinto de pasiones* and *Los abrazos rotos* (Broken Embraces, 2009), where both female and male desires for men are linked by a shared focus on male genitalia. Music is used in *Matador* to link the detective's and Diego's gazes; Almodóvar has used the same theme for the detective's voyeurism and Diego's own spying on María, a voyeurism shared by viewers. From spying on women, first Eva (through Ángel's Norman Bate-ish gaze in a shower scene) and then María, the film moves seamlessly on to spying on men: Ángel during his arrest and the bullfighting students as they practise.

Whereas the gaze by male characters is most frequently related to sexual gratification, women who observe or spy on men are presented as dangerous and slightly deranged.[4] This is the case of María herself and of Ángel's mother, Berta, an Opus Dei member who always thinks the worst of her son. Gwynne Edwards notes that Berta 'is introduced, revealingly, by her harsh imperious voice, reminiscent of Bernarda Alba, the most famous oppressor in Spanish literature, demanding to know what he is doing behind the locked door of his bedroom' (1995: 169). Berta is related to the Mother Superior in *Entre tinieblas*, played by the same actor, in her distaste for closed doors and need to control the people she loves. She is also a precursor of other castrating mothers in Almodóvar's films such as Antonio's in *La ley*.

Berta is characterised by her urgent, domineering knocks on Ángel's bedroom door. An oversized portrait of her sits by Ángel's bedside table where we might expect the portrait of a girlfriend or idol. Ángel himself seems to think that this is the place for girlfriends' pictures as he had previously asked Diego whether the portrait of Ava Gardner on his bedside table was that of his girlfriend. Ángel's mother is therefore standing in for (and blocking the presence of) a love object in Ángel's life. Berta and Ángel's relationship can be analysed in Oedipal terms, with Ángel standing in for his father (Berta frequently says to Ángel that he is like his father) and Berta refusing to allow Ángel any autonomy or personal development. Her insistence that he go to church and confess to his Spiritual Director is particularly sinister. This is not the plea of a mother worried about her son, but that of a fanatic using him.

Berta, Ángel, and the priest are inextricably bound together in a relationship that cannot be fully understood. Their connection is highlighted by the fact that they all wear red clothes in the church scene. The priest wears red vestments for mass, which are traditionally worn when celebrating the Passion or martyrs of the Church. Both Ángel and Berta sport red V-neck jumpers. After mass Ángel is forced to go to the sacristy and tell the priest that he wants to confess. This short scene of a reluctant Ángel and a delighted priest is slightly disturbing since the priest, who is taking his vestments off, looks Ángel up and down. Although there is no clear intimation that there is any sexual frisson other than the priest's look and the fact that Ángel has avoided the church for some time, Ángel's experiences within the church could be part of the explanation for his guilt complex and wish to prove that he is not homosexual. It may well be that Ángel has been sexually abused and is not believed at home. This would be in tune with the portrayal of priests in other films by Almodóvar such as *La ley* and *La mala educación* (Bad Education, 2004). In any case, he is the victim of psychological abuse at home.

In fact, Ángel's confession to the rape of Eva and to the murders at the police station are a direct consequence of his going to church and of his mother's request that he confess. Instead of waiting for the priest he goes to the police station. Almodóvar talks about how

> Church and police station are a continuation, and not the opposite, of each other. When he decides to confess he leaves religious feeling behind. This character is related to Hitchcock and Patricia Highsmith, but in Hitchcock we have deceptive criminals and here we have someone intent on falsely accusing himself. He wants to be guilty. Guilt is a feeling his mother has fostered in him since childhood. (quoted in Vidal, 1989: 175; my translation)

Ángel is particularly similar to Hitchcock's most memorable criminal-victim Marnie in his association with red, the fact that he is let down by his own mother, and has possibly been abused. Not only does Ángel want to be seen as guilty and capable of the crimes he accuses himself of, he also wants to save his teacher, Diego, from himself and the police. Part of this may be due to his wish to fulfil his mother's low opinion of him. Just before leaving the church, he is associated with a statue of Christ's Passion (again in red). Ángel's self-sacrifice follows what is normally seen as feminine behaviour. Despite his confession and the fact that he knows where the bodies are, Ángel's claims are never treated seriously by the police. For example, the policewoman at the reception exclaims 'Some women are lucky' when he says that he has raped a woman. The detective also seems to think it more likely that he has been the victim of a rape rather than the perpetrator.

Eva's relationship with her mother is similarly unhealthy. Eva looks weak and powerless (a cultivated look to please Diego) but she must have a strong personality even to begin to disagree with her mother with whom she cannot even feel angry. Eva's mother is the eternally supportive, 'modern' mother who lives her life vicariously through her daughter. There are many (mostly comic) instances of the mother's interference with Eva's life, but the most revealing signs of their relationship and the mother's vampiric preying on the daughter are the fact that she talks about Eva using the plural 'we' on many occasions and that she wears Eva's clothes. This is particularly obvious during the fashion show, where the mother wears the clothes that Eva was wearing during her attempted rape. These clothes, reminiscent of the bullfighter's outfit in the use of pink for the jacket and tights, are in the twisted logic of the film almost an invitation to be raped, a way of teasing the would-be rapist in the guise of the ultimate tease, the bullfighter.

Almodóvar himself is teasing us by dressing up his film with some of the best known symbols of Spanishness. In 1988, two years after the release of *Matador*, Spanish painter Daniel Quintero painted Almodóvar in a bullfighter costume remarkably like that of Diego. In the portrait Almodóvar also wears an ornamental comb and smokes a cigar. The painting points to both gender performativity and deconstruction of Spanishness in Almodóvar's work. Looking at both *Matador* and Quintero's painting, we are not sure whether to take the symbols they employ as ironic or in earnest. *Matador* is obsessed with Spanish national and religious symbols. It is also conscious of its own aesthetics, particularly obvious in its use of colour and composition. As Correa Ulloa explains, 'the film was conceived and edited with deliberate symmetrical takes; at first, the most evident comparison is that of bullfighting and power-relations in all couples' (2005: 76; my translation). All the characters are shown to be doubles or *doppelgangers* of one another, changing roles and moving into subject–object positions recently vacated by other characters. The film is an intricate combination of couplings and threesomes, including those of mother–child, victim–killer, voyeur–object, criminal–detective. The detective, Ángel, and Diego share many characteristics and form a triangle that is most obvious at the end of the scene when the girls' bodies are dug up. Ángel talks to Diego as the inspector looks on, then Ángel leaves and the inspector occupies his place as he talks to Diego with María filling his previous position as an observer. There are many other triangles: Eva–Diego–María, Diego–Eva–Ángel, and Berta–Ángel–the priest, for example.

Two versions of Spanishness are placed in dialogue: the traditional, Catholic, right-wing Spain fostered by the dictatorship (the Spain of bullfights and tambourines) and the 'modern' Spain of the 1980s Transition symbolised by the fashion world that was also promoted by the socialist government. Both are equally constructed and fictitious. The film is aware of this well-known concept and teases viewers who may want to interpret it in relation to Spanish politics.

The fashion show is called 'Spain Divided' in a clear allusion, as Smith notes, to 'the topos of "the two Spains", of the painful divisions notorious in Spanish history, but in a playful register which deprives such clichés of their continuing resonance' (2014: 75). The designer (played by Almodóvar though originally it was supposed to be the actual designer Francis Montesinos) comments on the two Spains being 'the envious and the intolerant', and that he belongs to both. The two Spains coexist in the film. The film contains a myriad of details inspired by traditional Spanish symbols, but these are frequently shown out of context or exaggerated to create humour. An example of the former is the mini-Spanish flag used by the two models shooting drugs. The latter can be seen, for example, in María's outfit during the show with long fake black tresses and make-up that emphasises the stereotype of the olive-skinned, dark-haired Spanish woman as portrayed by popular painters such as Julio Romero de Torres.

Stereotypes such as the passionate Spaniard who kills for love can be traced back to nineteenth-century French Romanticism and even further back to the Early Modern Period. At this time, Spain was treated as a non-European part of Europe, its inhabitants described in orientalist terms and stories written about this mythic rather than real place. It is therefore understandable that the film was perceived differently in Spain and abroad. Smith comments that Spanish reviewers saw the film as 'fantasy' whereas foreign critics were prone to seeing it as a product of Spanishness:

> The more perspicacious [Spanish] reviewers (such as Vicente Molina Foix and José Luis Guarner) suggested that Almodóvar had transformed 'racial tradition' into fantasy, elegantly denaturalizing the *españolada* and creating an 'admirable piece of nonsense [*disparate*] for Hispanists'. Hence, while foreign critics tended to see the film as re-presenting (and thus reconfirming) national traits assumed to transcend both cinema and history, Spanish critics (whether favourable or not) saw the film as representation, as the reworking of a cultural tradition that carried within it, necessarily, a certain social history. (2014: 75)

Critical reaction outside Spain is steeped in the orientalist tradition described above and perpetuates stereotypical ways of looking at Spanishness. It is tempting to see the film as a heightening or reworking of authentic Spanishness. Similarly, dismissing it as 'nonsense' lets viewers off the hook and discourages them to think about what Spanish symbols are doing in the film. Both the stereotypes and the counter-stereotypes are artificial. In the same review that Smith cites, Guarner refers to Almodóvar's 'postmodern taste' (1986: 30) but there is more to *Matador* than postmodern playfulness. Smith's own use of the term 'denaturalizing' with reference to the *españolada* is telling. An *españolada* is a film, show, or literary work that exaggerates stereotyped Spanish traits. If we accept Smith's argument that *Matador* denaturalises the *españolada* by pointing out the artificiality and lack of authenticity of the genre, it is twice removed from the stereotypes it uses. The tug of war is therefore not between a 'confirmation of national traits' and a 'reworking of a cultural tradition'. *Matador* reworks a cultural tradition that is fake.

The film thrusts cultural symbols in our face, challenging their naturalness. Almodóvar does filmically what *movida* pop painters such as Las Costus did by painting stereotypical images of women in *flamenco* dresses with trains, flowers in their hair, and so on all done in acrylic paint. As Davies says, it is 'woman … as masquerade and Spain as masquerade' (2004: 15). Bullfighting and the bull are some of the most iconic symbols of this imaginary – even Romantic – Spain. Spain is also known as *la piel de toro* (the bull's skin), allegedly because of the similarity of the Iberian peninsula to a bull's skin but more probably as a way of reinforcing the mythology surrounding bullfighting, passion, and Spanishness. *Matador* is clearly alluding to this, most obviously in Diego and María's final rendezvous on a bull's skin but also in the use of costume, hair (dyeing Assumpta Serna's blonde hair jet black and alluding to traditional hairstyles), colours, and plot. There is a clever allusion to the myth of Spain as the land of passionate romance and bullfight in Diego's photograph of Ava Gardner, whom Ángel takes to be his girlfriend. García de León notes that Ava Gardner is frequently mentioned by Almodóvar in relation to childhood memories of the cinema, but Gardner, she says,

is much more than a star's name. Ava Gardner is a kind of fetish of a particular era, 1950s Spain, not only for Almodóvar but also for many other Spaniards. We are talking … of Spain's sentimental chronicle. Underdeveloped, backward, internationally isolated …, the perfect environment for the Americans … and, in this case, the American star who comes to make a film and falls for bullfighter, actor and poet Mario Cabré. This becomes a national love story, as if through this Spanish man, full of national stereotypes, the whole country had touched Hollywood's splendour and, at the same time, America's splendour embodied by its film stars. (1989: 52–3; my translation)

Gardner occupies almost exactly the same space in Diego's bedroom that Pope John Paul II occupies in Ángel's. The two photographs – religious leader and American actor seduced by a Spanish bullfighter representing Spanishness – signify the mythology that fuelled Spanishness during the dictatorship and that is still present to a lesser extent in ideas about contemporary Spain.

Not all Spanish critics see through Almodóvar's 'masquerade' of Spain. Teresa Maldonado, for example, states that '*Matador* was a change in the abandonment of *feísmo* style and kitsch to delight itself in a very Spanish mannerism' (1989: 184; my translation). Maldonado notes the artificiality and decadence, but she qualifies it as 'very Spanish'. Vernon and Morris talk about this conundrum:

films like *What Have I Done* and Almodóvar's next picture, *Matador*, reveal a much more complex relation to Spain's historical and cultural past than the director's much-cited disavowals or historical memory would suggest. ... The commercial viability of such explorations of Spanish 'authenticity' both at home and abroad was not lost on the decision makers at the Ministry of Culture, who awarded *Matador*, the first Almodóvar film to qualify for government financial support, the maximum subvention of 50 percent of production costs. (1995: 9–10)

Almodóvar explores Spanishness constantly in his films, never more explicitly than in *Matador*. As well as highlighting the artificiality of myths surrounding Spanishness, *Matador* also perpetuates them. Those already convinced by the Spanish myth will see the orientalist, Romantic Spain of Mérimée. Like any good satire, *Matador* is convincing in its representation of that which it also critiques. Marvin D'Lugo says of the detective in *Matador*: 'Out of such a character, who outwardly embodies the forms of continuity with the past but inwardly disavows its stern judgmental posturings, *Matador* seeks to rewrite the mythologies of Spanish cultural identity.' (1995: 137). The same could be said for the whole film.

Notes

1 A *capote* is the heavy cape (pink at the front and normally yellow at the back) that bullfighters use to tease the bull. It takes its name from traditional Spanish capes, which it resembles.

2 Following the bullfighting theme, a slang term for large or prominent nipples in Spain is *pitones*, bull's horns.

3 *Maestro* means teacher. It is also used to refer to skilled bullfighters as a compliment.

4 For example, in *Labyrinth of Passion* Sexilia is treated for being a nymphomaniac. In the short film *The Cannibalistic Councillor* (dir. Almodóvar as Mateo Blanco, 2009), a female councillor who seems to advocate eating men admits to being fixated with men's crotches, even as a child.

5

Other voices, other stories:
La ley del deseo

La ley del deseo (The Law of Desire, 1987) was the first film made by
El Deseo S.A., the production company started by Pedro and Agustín
Almodóvar in 1985 to give Almodóvar more control over his films
and take advantage of the new state funding introduced in 1983 with
the Miró Law. Unfortunately, the Spanish government was reluctant
to fund *La ley*. According to Almodóvar, El Deseo S.A. 'received no
help at all from the ministry. The television stations also refused to
buy the rights' (quoted in Strauss, 2006: 64). One can only speculate
as to the reasons why the film was not deemed suitable for funding;
Almodóvar thinks that the identities and sexualities of the main characters influenced the decision:

> There is no longer any official censorship in Spain, but moral and eco-
> nomic censorship still exist and I felt them keenly while making *La ley*.
> It's the key film of my career. I've received many prizes for my films
> in Spain, but none for this one. I don't mean one should measure the
> worth of a film by the number of prizes it wins, but the silence was sig-
> nificant. The subject of the film discomfited the members of the com-
> mission for the advance. I was already well known at the time, both in
> Spain and abroad, and I was forcing the system to face its own contra-
> dictions. (quoted in Strauss, 2006: 64)

La ley is a male melodrama-cum-thriller whose main characters
are gay (Pablo, Antonio) and trans (Tina). The film explores trans
issues well before queer trans studies and trans theory emerged
fully. It depicts gay sex and portrays the many ways in which gay
and trans people are perceived as different from an imaginary cis and
heteronormative mainstream, empathising with the gay and trans

characters just as the Aids moral panic was at its height. In placing gay and trans characters at the centre of the film and expecting the Spanish government to fund it, Almodóvar also highlighted how LGBTQ+ issues were still taboo. The decision not to fund the film reflected public opinion: two years after the film's release, statistics from the Spanish Centre for Sociological Investigations (CIS) showed that '50% of Spaniards believe that homosexuality is "a crime"' and 'Spaniards continue to show serious misgivings about homosexual behaviours. They show themselves tolerant in private, but intolerant in public' (quoted in García de León, 1989: 63; my translation).

Homosexuality had been formally criminalised in 1954 with the revision of the old vagrant laws. This was replaced in 1970 by the *ley de peligrosidad y rehabilitación social* (Law on Dangerousness and Social Rehabilitation). This law was partly repealed in 1979 but not abolished until 1995. Homosexuals were considered social threats and could be arrested and imprisoned, as well as sent to work camps and mental institutions. Even after Franco's death, they were not included in the amnesty for political prisoners that took place during the Transition and it was not until 2010 that they were recognised as victims of the dictatorship. Brígida Pastor analyses the legacy of the criminalisation of homosexuality in *La ley*, highlighting the role of the police (2005: 448). The image of Spain as a tolerant country fostered internationally by subsequent governments during and after the Transition is not entirely correct. Even today, when Spain boasts some of the world's most progressive laws regarding gay marriage and adoption rights, these remain under threat by a number of conservative parties and Catholic groups. The situation of LGBTQ+ communities was shared in other countries at the time, with gays in particular being the focus of intense homophobia and misreporting due to the Aids epidemic around the world (cf. Watney, 1997).

La ley highlights the social scrutiny of gays and trans individuals. Journalists ask the main characters intrusive personal questions about their sexual lives. Men such as Pablo's lawyer (Agustín Almodóvar) stare at trans woman Tina's breasts before remarking 'She's like a real girl!', to which Pablo's doctor (Nacho Martínez) retorts 'Of course she is!' The police suspect Pablo (Eusebio Poncela) and Tina (Carmen Maura) of murder instead of the seemingly straight man Antonio (Antonio Banderas). The most insidious and damaging stereotypes about gay men, stereotypes that were prevalent in the media (in Spain and elsewhere) at the time of the film, are uttered by Antonio, a closeted homophobic gay man. Antonio raises the spectre of the Aids epidemic in the middle of a sex scene:

ANTONIO   You don't have any venereal diseases, do you?
PABLO   Why do you ask me that now?
ANTONIO   Because you're so promiscuous.
PABLO   No, it's OK. I've never had anything. Not even crabs.
ANTONIO   Those diseases terrify me.

Tellingly, Antonio's preoccupation with venereal diseases is prompted by his desire to be penetrated by Pablo, thus showing the persistent link of Aids to (particularly gay) penetrative sex and promiscuity. As Simon Watney explains, the Aids panic that swept the world in the mid-to-late 1980s was portrayed as

'a gay plague' ..., as if the syndrome were a direct function of a particular sexual act – sodomy – and, by extension, of homosexual desire in all its forms. ... The entire discourse of Aids turns round the rhetorical figure of 'promiscuity', as if all non-gays were either monogamous or celibate and, more culpably still, as if Aids were related to sex in a quantitative rather than qualitative way. (1997: 12)

Additionally, Antonio vents his anger at discovering Pablo has another lover by drawing on the traditional representation of gays as predatory immoral monsters: 'You're a pig. If I were 16 instead of 20, I'd report you for being a child molester.'

Despite the difficulties experienced by El Deseo in raising the funds needed to make La ley, it was the fourth biggest film in Spain in 1987 and Carmen Maura was awarded the Goya for best actress. Internationally, the film was much more successful. Marsha Kinder remarks that '[w]hen The Law of Desire [sic] proved critically successful at the 1987 Berlin Film Festival and did well commercially in foreign markets, the Socialist government touted its universality and used it to promote Spain's culture industry—a strategy that was similar to Franco's use of oppositional figures like Saura, Querejeta, and Buñuel to promote a more liberal image of Spain abroad' (1993: 432). The Spanish press was not as impressed: the film was dismissed as having no narrative control (Cerdán and Fernández Labayen, 2009: 135).

More than thirty years after its release, it is clear that La ley is an important film in Almodóvar's career that anticipates themes and characters that recur in later films: the writer/artist as protagonist, the exploration of sibling relationships, celebrity and mass media, sexual abuse including child abuse, and the censorship and recovery of memory. Its main achievement is the emotional force of the story that combines elements of melodrama and thriller in a series of triangular relationships at the centre of which is Pablo, a filmmaker and theatre director who is keen to control his love life in the same way he controls his film scripts. Pablo says that he wants passion and entire devotion in love but his love object, Juan (Miguel Molina), cannot meet these requirements. Pablo gets more than he bargained for when casual lover Antonio is revealed to be an obsessive psychopath who kills Juan and kidnaps Pablo's sister Tina before trading her for Pablo in a thrilling denouement.

Antonio succeeds in becoming Pablo's mourned lover instead of Juan. This is unexpected since, visually, the connection between Juan and Pablo is stronger than that between Pablo and Antonio, as seen, for example, in the telephone conversations Pablo holds with both before the crime. In the first one, Juan calls Pablo and, in true 1940s style, the screen splits to show both Pablo and Juan holding telephones and facing one another. Immediately after, Pablo puts the phone down Antonio calls and the screen is similarly split, but Antonio and Pablo face away from one another, signalling their emotional distance. Pablo prioritises the melodramatic missive to Antonio over the much less exciting letter to Juan. The way Pablo ends Juan's phone call gives viewers a clue to his dissatisfaction with Juan as a romantic partner. When he senses that Juan is about to declare his love, Pablo removes the receiver from his ear with a pained expression.

Pablo only cares for Antonio once he is dead. It is as if he is unable to feel love unless it is narrativised as a fiction or elaborate memory. As Isolina Ballesteros says, 'After his suicide, and while Pablo embraces him in a Pietà-like composition in front of Tina's kitschy altar, the music of ... "Déjame recordar," conveys a grief for a love that springs forth only when it is too late and can thus only be remembered' (2009: 77). Antonio is elevated to an object of veneration once he is dead, as signified by the *mise-en-scène* in the final tableau. His white underwear links him both to Christ and the man masturbating in the opening scene, his sacrifice being on the altar of desire. When 'Déjame recordar' (Let me remember) starts, the audience are prompted to reconceptualise the story as a romantic tale of doomed passion. Behind Pablo and Antonio, candles set fire to the

5.1   Pablo embraces Antonio in a gay Pietà (*La ley del deseo*, 1987)

altar, indicating the extent to which Pablo's love for Antonio is liter-ally ignited by his suicide (Figure 5.1).

The quiet yet all-consuming fire in the flat contrasts with the explo-sion and fire caused by the typewriter that Pablo has thrown out of the window in his despair at Antonio's suicide. The fires point to two ways of experiencing passion. The more melodramatic explosion caused by the typewriter (white like Antonio's underwear) reflects a passion fuelled by fictional heteropatriarchal relationship models leading to murder, kidnap, and, ultimately, suicide. Pablo's feel-ings are less explosive – as signified by his blue underwear – but no less indebted to fictional models of romantic relationships.

The blue and white lights of the police car blend, symbolising Pablo and Antonio's sexual intercourse. Almodóvar frequently uses inani-mate objects instead of sexual intercourse metonymically, in a form of 'cinematic excess' as theorised by Kristin Thompson, 'a device that has *no* function beyond offering itself for perceptual play' (1977: 57). As well as the lights, two key rings inside the police car – a miniature bunch of bananas and an orange golf ball suspended from the same chain and clanging together – metonymically stand for intercourse. Acevedo-Muñoz interprets this use of editing as 'a show of restraint' and states that 'the effect is both comical and paradoxical' (2007: 94); however, the jump cuts encourage viewer association, which can be interpreted differently, as a poetic device too. To me, the image is both kitsch and meaningful. It suggests a more spiritual union of opposites signified by the blue–white lights because pulsating light is caused by the combination of light and darkness that Pablo and Antonio represent.

The other prominent pulsating light is the lighthouse associated with Juan, golden like the moon in this scene (a moon also alluded to in the music and later on in the shape of Antonio's bitemarks near Juan's mouth) and the top of Juan's vest. The lighthouse has been seen as a strong phallic symbol (Arroyo, 1992), but its light is also a symbol of a love that accommodates and of flexible identities. It could also hint at Juan's bisexuality. Juan has been interpreted as straight by some critics (Arroyo, 1992: 42), who blame heterosexuality for the failure of his relationship with Pablo. However, this is not clear in the film and in fact Pablo is reassured of Juan's love many times. If anything, Juan is more likely to be bisexual or asexual. On the other hand, the white lighthouse building is connected to Antonio's inflexibility through his white underwear and the blinding white light of his motorbike. Despite Antonio's efforts to show Juan that Pablo favours him by claiming that he is wearing Pablo's shirt, it is Juan who is closest to Pablo through his gold and blue vest. Antonio, on the other hand, is wearing a black leather jacket over the shirt and grey jeans, a look that emphasises his taste for a monochromatic palette, points to him as the villain, and reveals his need to hide his homosexuality under a heteronormal façade. Sadly, Juan is dressed in a black suit by his family for his wake in an obvious attempt to normalise him.

Light thus separates and brings Pablo's two lovers together. Indeed, Antonio and Juan might be each other's doppelgänger, Antonio as the evil twin trying to replace Juan in Pablo's affection. It is not coincidental that Antonio's arrival coincides with Juan's departure. Antonio could also be seen as Pablo's doppelgänger as he dresses like Pablo during the murder scene, perhaps externalising his desire that Pablo discard Juan by himself. Antonio could be seen as a displacement of Pablo's own passionate feelings for Juan and his pent-up anger at Juan's departure. The fact that he personifies all that Pablo wants in a lover should alert viewers to Pablo's possible hand in his arrival. A possible psychoanalytic reading of the film is to interpret Juan and Antonio as figments of Pablo's imagination that he has lost control over.

The eye-like light and metacinematic elements of the opening credits bring to mind the essentially voyeuristic nature of cinema. This is reinforced by the voyeurism in the first scene, which is in fact the last scene of Pablo's fictional film *El paradigma del mejillón* (The Mussel's Paradigm). In this scene, a young man is asked to undress, rub his crotch on a mirror in an obvious reference to same-sex pleasure and identification, and masturbate in bed by an unseen man who afterwards pays him. Almodóvar refers to the unseen man as a director:

> the role of the director as manipulator is explained. The director pays someone else to do and say what he wants. An actor is paid to embody a fantasy, to be the voice and body of a fictional character. ... It is a sort of prostitution, in a non-pejorative way. This is in the first sequence and this is why it is so uncomfortable, even for me. (Vidal, 1989: 210; my translation)

The scene is uncomfortable because of the power dynamics of the director in charge, but it can still be arousing even though (and perhaps also because) the viewer is made fully aware that the young man is acting on orders. Acevedo-Muñoz bemoans the fact that the scene with 'the gorgeous young actor' is interrupted: 'Almodóvar cruelly breaks the illusion revealing the two middle-aged, overweight, balding men who are actually providing the sensuous voices' (2007: 80). Mark Allinson similarly states that this scene 'represents a new take on the male gaze: in a challenge to the great male directors who directed female stars for the pleasure of male viewers, here a male directs another male for voyeuristic pleasure' (2001: 106). Almodóvar has said that 'the first sequence is the hardest to view because of a cultural concept. Even if one is not homophobic, there is something that is culturally unacceptable: a man, who knows that he can be penetrated, never verbalises it. Saying it aloud is something that is impossible to bear ... In fact, I invented the dubbers simply to make the sequence less hard' (Vidal, 1989: 208; my translation). Almodóvar is also playing with viewers, teasing them with sexually explicit images that are quickly revealed to be contrived. He is not only turning the tables on the male body as the object of the cinematic gaze but also creating confusion in viewers by asking them to collude in it.

For this reason, this objectification of the male body is not similar to that of the female body in the commonly described male gaze of cinema. Even as the scene invites spectators to assume the projector's point of view and to indulge in narcissistic pleasure (the shot of the actor's crotch rubbing against the mirror from his point of view forces spectators to assume his gaze), it makes the control of the male body on display so obvious as to become impossible to ignore. What Laura Mulvey described in 1975 as '*to-be-looked-at-ness*' (1997: 442; italics in original), the quality a woman's body is given in a cinematic context that objectifies her and guides the spectators' gaze, is reinforced here by the passive position the young man is forced to adopt but to such an extent that he cannot simply be observed unproblematically. Unquestioned *to-be-looked-at-ness* is present not so much in this first scene as in the subsequent scene depicting Antonio re-imagining/ enacting the moment of objectification that reveals his narcissistic identification with the young man. The fragmented male body is offered as a means to scopophilic pleasure via close-ups of Antonio's fly, face, and open mouth. This objectification of Banderas' body reoccurs in subsequent shots of Antonio, particularly the sex scenes.

The gaze in the initial scene may be said to be male since the director is male, but the subject position can be occupied by anyone who imagines themselves in this powerful position, and power and pleasure go hand in hand in desire. As Watney explains,

> the movement of desire involving difference *within* the same sex is able to find ready-made instances of analogy within mainstream culture, and to make identifications with them, putting scenarios from heterosexual culture to new, unauthorised usage. At the same time it is important to remember that sexual identification on the part of gay men is always mobile, able to assume different roles and positions, which are always also power relations. (1997: 73)

What Almodóvar refers to as being 'impossible to bear' is only so if the viewer identifies with the young man and finds it difficult to accept another person's control. This is made clear during Antonio and Pablo's first sexual encounter, when Antonio's question, 'You want to screw me, don't you' (in Spanish 'You want to penetrate me, don't you?'), turns Pablo on and prompts the consummation of the act. The initial scene is arousing if spectators buy into the power game. Almodóvar has said that sex scenes are not interesting unless they are used to say something else (Vidal, 1989: 205). Here, as in the other sexually charged scenes in this film, sex is used to represent the desire to be desired.

Power relations in the film are not as clear as they first seem. The characters who seem most in control (Pablo and the director) may in fact not be so. Pablo is a prisoner of his desire to be desired and, as Kinder explains in a 1987 interview with Almodóvar, the product of his past:

> Isn't Pablo like his father—a seducer who prefers young boys and who's never totally committed? Doesn't he reenact his father's seduction of his brother and also inspire his lovers to make a sacrifice? Pablo may want to be in control, but isn't he shaped by his father as Tina was? Aren't his scripts and movies vehicles for patriarchal ideology? (1987: 41)

Kinder's psychological explanation is convincing. In addition to this, Pablo's illusion of control is manufactured by Antonio, who acts as bottom in his first encounter with Pablo, assuming 'the "feminine" role in the sexual act itself (from a patriarchal perspective)' (Acevedo-Muñoz, 2007: 85). Antonio, however, quickly takes the lead in the relationship. In patriarchal ideology, penetration is commonly seen as an assertion of power; Antonio reflects this way of thinking when he tries to rape Juan. However, it can also be used to gain power over somebody else. Antonio is trying to control Pablo even when he is the one being penetrated, something that women such as María in *Matador* (1986) also do. This is particularly obvious here because both characters are men. As Watney states, 'homosexuality problematises the parallel identification of powerlessness and passivity with the figure of the biological female as submissive and penetrated' (1997: 28). Antonio's self-assurance may derive from his subscription to the mainstream conservative, male chauvinist ideology. Pablo calls him 'reactionary' at one point and he says, 'I am what I should be', in Spanish '*Soy como hay que ser*', a common expression to indicate that one follows conservative social precepts. The idea behind this expression is that anyone who does not agree with your views is wrong and unnatural. Antonio's conservatism leads to violence and brings him closer to other male chauvinist characters in Almodóvar films. As Allinson notes, Almodóvar does not simply provide positive images of gays and lesbians (2001: 101).

There are at least four layers of cinematic consciousness that make viewers aware of the fact that they are watching a film and that film-making is itself artificial. These layers are best described as a series of Chinese boxes that fit into each other, from largest to smallest: the spectators' reality; Almodóvar's thriller, *La ley*, including the premiere of Pablo's film, *El paradigma*; the ending of Pablo's film,

El paradigma: the dubbing and post-dubbing of a film containing the first scene where a young man is told to masturbate; and the film being dubbed in *El paradigma*, where the young man is told to masturbate by a fictional director. It is not entirely clear whether the dubbers and the final approval of the film's edited version are part of Pablo's *El paradigma*; they could just as well be Pablo's flashbacks to his editing choices as he agonises about the audience's reaction in the lobby of the cinema. It is likely that the dubbers are part of Pablo's film because we only see the main characters once we are aware that what we have seen before is a film-within-a-film. The two realities are separated by two jump cuts: one to a hand marking the end of *El paradigma* on a film reel, the other to a red curtain that opens to reveal the ending of *El paradigma* during its premiere and Tina congratulating Pablo. This first scene is thus a film-within-a-film-within-a-film, but viewers are not aware of this until the word *FIN* (The End) appears and the cinema curtain opens. It is the first time that the red curtain, a recurrent prop with its connotations of theatricality and performance, is used by Almodóvar. Opening rather than closing, the curtain marks a symbolic opening of the actual Almodóvar film with another set of credits. Although the first scene is important to the rest of the film, this clear distinction tells spectators that everything we have seen until then is fictional and, crucially, everything we will see from then on will continue to be so.

The actual title of the film, *La ley del deseo*, does not appear until the three main characters are in the frame. It is at this point that the image freezes and changes to black and white as they are captured by a photographer in attendance (one can hear the click of the old-fashioned camera). Tina and Pablo are in the background embracing while Antonio steals the limelight as a passer-by in the foreground. The caption, 'Un film de Almodóvar', appears in the same frozen image. This is extraordinary as Almodóvar had already claimed ownership (as director and scriptwriter) in the opening credits. Lauren Films and El Deseo are also credited twice. This doubling of production company, distributor, and director points to the impossibility of extricating the initial scene from the film as a whole and shows why it cannot be called, as Marvin D'Lugo does, a 'precredit sequence' (1995: 138).

The beginning of *La ley* therefore includes a complex net of meta-cinematic references to the filmmaking process that recur in later films. This exuberant *mise-en-abyme* warns viewers that *La ley* is not as straightforward as it may seem. It is also telling that Pablo's film contains the word 'paradigm', meaning example or model. Could *El paradigma* be a model for *La ley*? There are certainly many parallels one could draw, starting with the title. 'Mejillón' (Mussel) is Spanish slang for homosexual. Mussels open when heat is applied, like Antonio, whose homosexuality is revealed when his desire for Pablo forces him to own up to it. Spectators are also forced to own up to their own voyeuristic acts.

Antonio functions as a link between the action in *El paradigma* and *La ley*. On exiting the cinema, he goes directly to the public toilets to masturbate, repeating the actor's words in *El paradigma*: 'Fuck me. Fuck me'. On entering the cubicle, the toilet seat is seen from above in a shot that echoes the credits as the toilet seat is red and the electric light is reflected in the water at the bottom to create a blindingly white circle. It is as if the lights were coming on in a studio and we are revealed to be voyeurs. Antonio's trousers are red so the inference is that white (underwear, semen) will be next. This idea of Antonio as shooting a white target is also seen later on as he plays in an arcade with a rifle. Significantly, Pablo walks past, placing himself in between rifle and target. Pablo is ultimately Antonio's target and Antonio is the seducer. Marsha Kinder analyses the dramatisation of the Oedipal father–son relationship in *La ley* and states that 'Antonio spends the rest of his life, and the movie, gaining control over the dictatorial director, even though it makes him become equally manipulative' (2009: 284). Kinder's essay concentrates on brotherly rivalry in several Almodóvar films, but she ultimately tracks the source of rivalries to the father. Kinder's thesis can be expanded to include non-biological brothers as Antonio places Pablo in a parental role and Juan becomes a rival sibling as well as rival lover.

Antonio has made Pablo his object of desire, but Pablo is probably a substitute for the lack of parental love in his life. Antonio's behaviour combines his mother's obsessive controlling characteristics (she seems to embody the superego with its normalising function) with a patriarchal urge to possess the love object and eradicate any competitors. Antonio wants to be his mother and love his absent father. Both figures are displaced onto Pablo, who acts as a blank page for Antonio to fill with his desire. When Antonio trades Tina for Pablo, he tells him: 'I needed to have you like this at any price.' The English subtitles – 'I needed to see you at any price' – lose some of the strength of Antonio's statement that in Spanish implies that Antonio wants to have Pablo at his mercy. Behind Antonio's rhetoric of victimhood lies an urge to command and control Pablo. When Antonio feels that he is losing his grip on Pablo, he becomes unstable. Antonio's entrapment in patriarchal power structures can be seen in his family home. As Brígida Pastor states, the house's 'rigid iron bars illustrate the cultural imprisonment of Antonio and his mother' (2006: 17), also seen in the panopticon-like stairway with a cleverly placed gilded mirror used by Antonio's mother to spy on him. Both Antonio's and his parents' beds feature elaborate crochet coverlets that give the impression of enclosing the characters as they are in bed. The pattern is reminiscent of lattices (celosías in Spanish, a word derived from celos/jealousy), which are the product of patriarchal thinking, used to hide the women in the house to protect family 'honour'. The house, with its baroque furniture and grandeur, functions as a place where the characters' pent-up emotions are displaced, something reminiscent to what Schatz called 'Hollywood baroque' (1981: 245) where the oppressive atmosphere makes objects metaphors for the characters' psychic states. Almodóvar's Sirkian use of mirrors and other framing devices isolates characters and distances viewers from them.

Antonio's theme song, the bolero 'Lo dudo' (I doubt it), expresses his certainty that nobody can love Pablo as much as he does and his fear of abandonment in the form of extreme bravado. The song is after all a daring scream from a lover about to or just having been jilted who says 'I doubt/that you will get to love me/like I love you./I doubt/that you will find a purer love/than mine'. Antonio plays 'Lo dudo' during his final rendezvous with Pablo. Nevertheless, 'Lo dudo' originates with Pablo; it is first heard as Pablo types to it and reflects Pablo's feelings after Juan's departure. Alejandro Varderi notes that, by using this Latin American song, Almodóvar 'deconstructs existing male chauvinism in both continents, redirecting it towards men' (1996: 161; my translation). 'Lo dudo' is a declaration of confidence that in fact hides Pablo's and Antonio's vulnerability, a vulnerability that is openly acknowledged in the other main theme song in the film, the French chanson 'Ne me quitte pas' (Do not abandon me).

'Ne me quitte pas' is associated with Juan (Vidal, 1989: 241) but also originates with Pablo; it is first heard intradiegetically, Pablo playing it just as Juan arrives, and is also part of his staging of Jean Cocteau's La voix humaine (The Human Voice, 1930). Pablo sublimates his break-up with Juan through song and play. Both 'Lo dudo' and 'Ne me quitte pas' reinscribe Pablo's abandonment as a child by his father and express the character's feelings as befits melodrama. The songs are part of the film's melodramatic excess, 'orchestrating the dramatic ups and downs of the intrigue' (Elsaesser, 1987: 50) as well as gesturing towards unexplored traumas in Pablo's past, traumas that he represses and projects on to his sister Tina, to whom he advises that the show will be hard because it 'will bring back painful memories'. Both Tina and the child Ada (Manuela Velasco) act out abandonment on and off stage; Tina and Ada have just been left by Ada's mother. This breakdown follows the pattern of Tina's previous two significant relationships, with her father, who seduces and abandons her, and Father Constantino, her 'spiritual father'. Father Constantino is a precursor of Father Manolo (Daniel Giménez Cacho) in *La mala educación* (Bad Education, 2004) and both share a narrative intertext in Almodóvar's short story, 'La Visita'. Ada's role in Pablo's adaptation of *La voix* seems to be that of an alter ego to the main character. It also links the loss of adult love to that of a child abandoned by a parental figure. In this respect, she is also externalising Pablo's repressed childhood trauma.

Pablo's new film script is another text that he associates with Tina's experiences but in fact also speaks to his: Laura P is bent on revenge after her lover abandons her, but revenge backfires on her. Pablo has co-opted the lighthouse as one of the settings for the story, which indirectly relates the script to his relationship with Juan. Both Pablo and Laura P end up with a limp. Laura P is a version of Pablo several times removed, hence the initial P in her name and his adoption of Laura P as an alias to write to Antonio. Pablo has, after all, been abandoned by his father (and brother, soon to be sister), too. Kinder rightly states that Pablo must forgive Tina for taking the father away from him (2009: 284). These feelings could have resurfaced following Juan's departure. Despite these connections, Pablo associates Laura P with his sister Tina and tells her that there is 'a certain affinity' between the character and her life, 'regarding your problems with men'. Pablo could be referring merely to the melodramatic aspects of Tina's life, but the fact that Laura P cuts off her leg takes on a different dimension when viewed against Tina's life because Tina has had Sex Reassignment Surgery (SRS). The story of Laura P could thus be a fantasy based on speculation about Tina's trans identity, the details of which Pablo ignores. Laura P is thus a composite of Pablo and Tina.

The behaviour of both siblings with regard to loss is similar in their use of creativity, Tina's directed towards the creation of herself and Pablo's as an artist. The siblings fail to confront the past for most of the film. Their rejection of history responds to Nietzsche's 'antidotes to history', as discussed by Paul Ricoeur: '*the ahistorical and the suprahistorical*' (2006: 292).

> 'Ahistorical' is associated with 'the art and power to be able to *forget*' and the ability 'to enclose oneself in a limited *horizon*'. ... We now know that this forgetting is not historical but unhistorical. As for the 'suprahistorical,' it directs the gaze away from the future and carries it toward the eternity-dispensing powers of art and religion. (2006: 292)

Tina's antidote is ahistoricity, removing any memory object that can remind her of her past as a cis boy, hence her request for Pablo and her mother to give her all of her childhood photographs. Whereas Tina seems to express her grief and happiness openly, she has not really spoken of her most important relationships and losses, those of her father and Father Constantino. Pablo's focus on the arts places him firmly in the suprahistorical camp. Both are well-known strategies employed by artists of the Madrid *movida* as explained in Chapter 1. More broadly, they speak to Almodóvar's preoccupation with traumatic memory and historical past, something that will become more apparent in his later films. It is only when the siblings discuss the past openly that their relationship, as signified by the childhood photographs that Pablo had kept but rips after an argument with Tina, can be rebuilt. Tina repairs the photographs in a reparative act and takes them to the hospital on the day she tells Pablo everything about her past with their father, which, as he had previously reminded her, is part of his. Tina's view of the past changes from conceiving it as her individual property, 'Don't you dare touch anything in my life, no matter how ridiculous. ... No one's going to play with my failures. ... They're mine, understand? Mine!', to recognising that collective memory is essential: 'Your amnesia leaves me without a past. I'll go crazy if you don't remember.'

Spectators hear the story of her sexual relationship with her father when she tells Pablo, who has lost his memory but did not know the details anyway. Tina's tone is unexpectedly restrained. As we have seen in previous chapters, asking actors to underplay scenes is a key trait of Almodóvar's style and allows us to read as plausible the most contrived stories. Tina's revelations could be material for melodrama, but unlike Pablo's life that is dramatised, Tina's traumatic backstory is played down.

Despite the differences in tone, Pablo's and Tina's experiences run parallel and are the product of the same event. The happy traditional family is shown to be a myth, for the father abuses at least one of the children and neglects both. The siblings are presented as modern and urban, a contrast to Antonio's family background. However, all the characters are struggling with the reality that Spain may have changed on the surface but, as Tina says to Father Constantino about herself, is 'still the same deep down'. Tina has not been able to overcome the effects of her traumatic childhood. Even her chosen name – Tina, a feminised shortening of Constantino – points to the fact that she is not over her relationship with the priest. A precursor of other trans characters in Almodóvar's filmography, Tina encompasses the contradictions that are split into doubles in the latter films.

Spanish society, as we saw at the beginning of the chapter, was still deeply transphobic and homophobic when *La ley* was made. This is apparent, for example, in the way the alternative family made up of Tina, Pablo, and Ada is described in one of the first monographs on Almodóvar's work published in Spain: 'Ada lives without mother or father, in ... an environment that is remote from a family (a transvestite and a filmmaker)' (García de León, 1989: 77; my translation). García de León does not accept Tina and Pablo as parental figures and refuses to accept Tina is a woman as seen by her use of 'transvestite'. The film, however, portrays this family unit as strong, with loving individuals supporting one another. Arroyo describes the family in the film as affirming patriarchy and an obstacle to the formation of the homosexual couple that transgresses patriarchy (1992: 42). In fact, the representation of a successful alternative family structure does not affirm patriarchy. On the contrary, it undermines it by presenting an alternative to the traditional family still defended by many in contemporary Spain.

Tina's observation to Father Constantino – 'I'm still the same deep down' – is a profound comment on the irrelevance of biological sex when it comes to feelings and a person's identity. The play that Pablo directs and Tina performs says it all. *La voix*, a female monologue by Cocteau, dissects the end of a relationship in a long telephone conversation between a woman who has been jilted and her ex-lover. At the beginning of the film, Pablo's model pick-up, who is hoping for a part, asks if a man could not do the monologue. Pablo assuredly answers 'No'. Tina's presence is both affirming her womanhood (she is a trans woman actor delivering a female monologue) and exposing the patriarchal fault lines of society by drawing on a binary conception of gender roles in order to undermine it. Even though the destruction of the set was improvised (Vidal, 1989: 237–8), it is a powerful visual execution of the constraints placed on all the characters by society, particularly in terms of gender and sexuality. The characters in *La ley* cannot resolve the contradictions they embody, but they do succeed in exposing them.

6

Pure theatre: *Mujeres al borde de un ataque de nervios*

Mujeres al borde de un ataque de nervios (Women on the Verge of a Nervous Breakdown, 1988) was the film that propelled Almodóvar to international stardom and made him a household name in Spain. The Oscar nomination for best foreign picture created a great deal of excitement. Foreign recognition seemed essential for the director's acceptance in Spain. Almodóvar was still a pariah among a majority of Spanish film critics but scholars were beginning to treat his work seriously. The film broke records in Spain (it was seen by three million people) and abroad. As Paul Julian Smith notes:

> There seems little doubt that *Mujeres* is Almodóvar's most popular work. It remains at the time of writing the only Spanish film to have grossed more than one thousand million pesetas in the domestic market; and it was sold to Spanish television (with *La ley del deseo*) for the unprecedented sum of two hundred million pesetas. The commercial success of *Mujeres* abroad was also exceptional, making Almodóvar the biggest-grossing foreign-language director in the US for 1989. (2014: 101–2)

Mujeres is also a film that Almodóvar keeps coming back to with a partial remake as a film-within-a-film in *Los abrazos rotos* (Broken Embraces, 2009), *Chicas y maletas* (Girls and Suitcases), and further intertextual references to it in *Los amantes pasajeros* (I'm So Excited!, 2013). *Mujeres* brought Almodóvar to an older generation of Spanish viewers, those brought up during the dictatorship, because it is a comedy without obvious sex and drugs. It overcame, to use Almodóvar's own mother's words, the director's reputation for being 'very filthy' and having 'too many sex scenes' (Francisca

Caballero, quoted in *All about Desire*, 2001; my translation). This, in turn, provoked accusations among fans that he had sold out. Some critics shared those feelings: 'With *Women on the Verge of a Nervous Breakdown* (1988), *Tie Me Up, Tie Me Down!* (1989), *High Heels* (1992) and *Kika* (1993), Almodóvar's aesthetic has lost its transgressive character' (Varderi, 1996: 76; my translation). Thus, *Mujeres* marks Almodóvar's breakthrough abroad and in Spain, his success running alongside increasing suspicions about his credentials as an experimental filmmaker.

It is perhaps fitting that TV rights for both *La ley* and *Mujeres* were sold together since – as Linda M. Willem (1998) explains – they are both intertexts of Cocteau's *La voix humaine* (The Human Voice, 1928). *La ley*, as seen in the previous chapter, features a production *of La voix* directed by the main character – Pablo (Eusebio Poncela) – with his sister Tina (Carmen Maura) as the female lead. Originally, Almodóvar had intended to work on another film after *La ley*, a project titled *Tacones Lejanos* (High Heels) that bears some resemblance to the film with this title he did complete in 1991 and to *Volver* (2006). But he wanted to film quickly and this project required more preparation (Vidal, 1989: 257). *Mujeres* was born as an experimental gap-filler and, as such, is an off-shoot of his previous film, *La ley*. As Almodóvar says:

> The origin was *The Human Voice* by Cocteau just as Carmen did it in *The Law of Desire*, which I like a lot. Adapting the text I had almost thirty minutes so I had to do something to expand it. A work of introspection. This led me to imagine that woman forty-eight hours before this crisis point and see what leads her to this final telephone conversation. (Vidal, 1989: 258; my translation)

What had originally been conceived as a female monologue filmed in one set and with ten or so commercials in between grew to a film with a cast of thirty-five and incessant comings-and-goings all over Madrid.

Mujeres is, according to Almodóvar, 'really a version of *The Human Voice*, even though it is not similar or owes anything to it, because it does not contain a single line from the play' (Vidal, 1989: 258; my translation). This accords with the more flexible definition of adaptation described by Linda Hutcheon: 'what is involved in adapting can be a process of appropriation, of taking possession of another's story, and filtering it, in a sense, through one's own sensibility, interests, and talents. Therefore, adapters are first inter-preters and then creators' (2006: 18). Hutcheon pursues an analogy between adaptation and Darwin's theory of evolution: 'To think of narrative adaptation in terms of a story's fit and its process of mutation or adjustment, through adaptation, to a particular cultural environment is something I find suggestive. Stories also evolve by adaptation and are not immutable over time' (2006: 31); *Mujeres* is thus not just an adaptation of *La voix*, it is also a version of the adaptation partly seen in *La ley*. In addition to this, *Mujeres* is in intertextual relation with every other adaptation of the play. It is very possible that Almodóvar had seen a filmed version of the play starring Ingrid Bergman (Kotcheff, 1966), for example. Whether or not he has does not impede viewers from relating Pepa's fuchsia pyjamas to Bergman's bright pink nightdress or noticing the focus on similar objects such as the full ashtray, the drink by the bedside, the black-and-white photographs of the lover, and alarm clocks, the tick-tocking of which dominates Kotcheff's opening and is also prominent in the opening scene of *Mujeres*. The alarm clock does not stop when the woman wakes up in Kotcheff's version and contrib-utes to the mounting pressure as the woman waits for the telephone to ring. In effect, the clock is an aural expression of the woman's tension. In *Mujeres*, the tick-tock starts after the alarm goes off to signal that Pepa continues sleeping and pauses during her dream and Iván's dubbing scene. The clock stops as soon as Iván starts leaving a message on Pepa's answering machine, waking Pepa up (as it metaphorically wakes Lucía from her state of forgetfulness in the mental hospital). This, however, is only a temporary relief since Pepa does not manage to speak to Iván, who has left a message and put the phone down. The answering machine is a clever addition that allows Pepa and the viewers to hear Iván without actual com-munication taking place between the couple.

Kotcheff's adaptation of *La voix* is also prominent in the other main intertext of *Mujeres*, *La ley*. During Tina's performance of *La voix*, she destroys the traditional (like Kotcheff's) set with an axe. The bedroom space in this set is extremely similar to Tina's own bedroom, with green walls, a semi-circular recess into which the bed is fitted, and even a wall-mounted bedside light with an angel playing an electric guitar wearing sunglasses. In short, Tina plays the woman in Pablo's production of *La voix*, but she is also seen as that same abandoned woman in the rest of *La ley*. This offers yet another intertextual link to *Mujeres*. If both Tina and Pepa are versions of the woman in *La voix*, it follows that Pepa is also a version of Tina, the abandoned woman, albeit one with a better wardrobe. Pepa is also more active than Tina, to whom things seem to happen instead of her making them happen herself.

Discussing the play, Tina and Pablo have the following exchange:

TINA   So you don't like me as an actress?
PABLO   Don't be a pain. I like you and the public likes you, don't they?
TINA   Yes, but ...
PABLO   But what? You should be delighted with yourself.
TINA   I am. But some days the show depresses me.
PABLO   I told you it would happen.
TINA   I love doing drama ... and crying, and talking on the phone.
        What I don't like is always being slovenly.

There are multiple intertextual references in this passage. Maura's previous role for Almodóvar was Gloria, the housewife in *¿Qué he hecho yo para merecer esto?* (What Have I Done to Deserve This?, 1984), a 'slovenly' character. Even though Tina herself is not 'slovenly' (on the contrary, she is dressed in modern sexy outfits), viewers familiar with Almodóvar's films may think of this slightly older film. It is also possible to look forward. Pepa is also an abandoned woman like Tina and the woman in *La voix*; each of them is waiting for her ex-lover to contact her throughout the film. But, crucially, Pepa does not allow herself to become 'slovenly'. She is Almodóvar's response to Tina's fictional complaint about her characterisation in Pablo's play. In Pepa, Almodóvar has created a woman who may be desperate to get her lover back but does not allow herself to become the wreck that the woman in *La voix* becomes. Pepa changes outfit seven times in two days (eight if we count the purple cardigan she puts over some clothes when she goes out at night to look for Iván). Except for pyjamas and the cardigan, all of them are suits, most of them including tight miniskirts and matching jacket and blouse. Pepa may be looking for Iván frantically, but she does not forget to match her outfits, jewellery, and shoes.

In the Pressbook for *Mujeres*, Almodóvar justifies the choice of wardrobe for Pepa in a clear defence of the character against comments by Susan Sontag:

Pepa wears heels and tight miniskirts too much. The truth is that they suit her, but they also force her to walk in a way that Susan Sontag (as she said to *Elle* magazine after visiting the shoot) does not think appropriate for an autonomous contemporary woman. I understand and agree with Sontag when she opposes gender polarisation, but this has nothing to do with Pepa. A woman must be free even to choose her clothes. I respect those who imitate Barbie as much as those who dress like Charlot [Charlie Chaplin's character, The Tramp]. (quoted in Vidal, 1989: 383; my translation)

Almodóvar's defence sounds a little dated and not particularly progressive. In declaring his respect for women who dress in both hypermasculine and hyperfeminine fashion, Almodóvar plays down the fact that Pepa's choice of clothes reveals a patriarchal culture at work, even in a woman who on the surface appears to be independent.

Pepa's clothes signal her status. She is a professional middle-class woman who earns enough to own several distinctive suits, matching shoes, and accessories. Even though she is late for work and a doctor's appointment, she still takes time to dress impeccably and apply make-up. As Peter Evans explains,

From one point of view, Carmen Maura's highly colourful visual appearance in *Women on the Verge* contributes to the overall use of colour to commemorate release from past austerities; from another, as in Warhol's over-cosmeticisation of Elizabeth Taylor and Marilyn Monroe, tube skirts, high heels and colour augment the ambience of mask and counterfeit perhaps even more strikingly projected by Julieta Serrano's Jackie Kennedy-as-Wicked-Witch-of-the-West-crossed-with-Norman-Bates'-Mother's look as Lucía. (1996: 70)

Pepa is the main focus of spectator's gazes and her attire reflects the fact that she is on show. Spectators identify with her and her appearance gives them narcissistic pleasure. In addition to this, Pepa is a woman in a society that values women's appearances and puts a great deal of pressure on women who are in the limelight as she is due to her media job. Her characterisation as a woman who may be financially independent but still depends emotionally on Iván would not be believable without her desperate desire to look good.

What Mulvey calls 'to-be-looked-at-ness' is part of Pepa's character: 'In their traditional exhibitionist role women are simultaneously looked at and displayed, with their appearance coded for strong visual and erotic impact so that they can be said to connote *to-be-looked-at-ness*' (1997: 442; italics in the original). Pepa takes on both the traditional male and female functions for characters in narrative film. She is both the driver of the action, actively chasing Iván and helping her friend Candela, and the main source of spectacle as she is present in nearly all the scenes. Pepa's image is important to her job as an actor, as seen in how the customers at the chemist gossip about her appearance: 'She's nothing special' and 'She's thinner than on TV'. Pepa enters the chemist to ask for sleeping pills for which she has no prescription. She is treated courteously by the chemist and given the tablets. In a similar situation, Gloria in ¿*Qué he hecho?* is refused No-Doze without a prescription by a chemist who insults her, calling her 'an addict' and treating her with contempt. I cannot help but think that clothes contribute both to their profiling and to different social reactions to them; Gloria is clearly working class and poor whereas Pepa's outfit displays her comfortable circumstances.

However, Pepa has not been born into the middle class as indicated by her language and behaviour. The fact that she keeps chickens and ducks in the penthouse terrace points towards rural roots. In addition to this, her role in a television advert for washing powder as the 'mother of the assassin' adds to her image as an Everywoman. For Spanish audiences at the time, the actor who plays Pepa, Maura, also reinforces the idea that success has not come easy to Pepa. Maura is herself middle class but was perceived in Spain to have had a long career without major breakthroughs and not to be as attractive as stars of her generation.

In terms of class, Pepa is right in the middle of the women in the film, with Candela's origins being the humblest as denoted by her common Andalusian accent and rural origins and Marisa and Paulina Morales as the most obviously upper middle class. From the moment Carlos and Marisa arrive in the penthouse with a view to renting it, Marisa uses every opportunity to put the penthouse and Candela down. She uses formal language to address Candela as a way to keep her distance and point to her social superiority. This comes to a head as Candela pointedly says, 'educated people know not to snoop around'. Marisa puts Candela in her place by keeping the formal way of address but rudely asking her to 'shut up'. The next exchange cements Spanish-speaking viewers' impressions that Marisa is of a higher social class than Candela; when Marisa asks Carlos if he knows who is with his father in a photograph, Candela blurts out, 'That's Pepa! Who's it going to be?' (in Spanish, '¡Es la Pepa, quien va a ser, la Pepa!'). Using the feminine article 'la' in front of 'Pepa' is vulgar. Marisa immediately asks Carlos about Pepa without using the article.

Paulina Morales and Iván's wife – Lucía – also use formal language to create distance when they speak and Pepa adopts the formal register to reply to them, even when being rude in response to their own rudeness. This says a great deal about the film's underlying theme of appearances versus reality and ties in with Pepa's need to dress well. It also relates to Lucía's obsession with her looks.

The need to gain approval from men is at the bottom of Pepa's and Lucía's need to look good. Lucía asks her father how she looks and bases her fashion sense on a period twenty years earlier when Iván left her and she became mentally ill. Pepa puts up a front in the face of adversity. As Carmen Maura explains:

> Of course that [wearing high heels and a tight miniskirt] will be uncomfortable, but I will pretend otherwise. For a character like Pepa high heels are the best way to deal with her anxiety. If she forgets her looks, her spirits will be irreparably lost. Exercising coquetry is a discipline and it represents her main strength. It means that her problems have not dragged her down. (quoted in Vidal, 1989: 384; my translation)

Pepa needs to look good because being good-looking makes her feel worth loving and desirable, which is precisely what is being undermined by Iván's behaviour. Thus, Maura's comments tie in with Sontag's views about what the clothes represent culturally, an over-reliance on appearance to build up women's self-esteem, a self-esteem that is all too frequently related to their relationships with men.

My siding with Sontag in her analysis of what the clothes represent culturally does not mean that I believe that Pepa ought to be dressed differently. Pepa's miniskirts and matching accessories are important elements of her characterisation. In a study of hysteria in Almodóvar's films, Brad Epps points out that *Mujeres* 'opens with a house, and a woman, in need of a man. This need and its overcoming structure the body of the filmic narrative. Centred in Pepa, it is played out in a number of other women' (1995: 116), including Candela, Marisa, Lucía, Paulina, and even Vienna in the clip from Nicholas Ray's *Johnny Guitar* (1954). Even a very minor character such as Ana is seen to depend on her relationship with her biker boyfriend although by the end of the film she is thinking of buying his bike and ending the relationship. It is telling that the only time that Pepa leaves the house looking dreadful happens precisely after she 'overcomes' her need for Iván. On the way to the airport to stop Lucía from killing Iván, Pepa is covered in *gazpacho* and barefoot. She rushes to the airport not because she wants to talk to Iván but because she wants to stop Lucía from killing him.

This heroic act could belong in the realm of fantasy as the rejected woman saves her ex-lover who then regrets how badly he has behaved towards her. Pepa gets to be the one who says no to Iván in a wishfulfilling ending. Edwards explains it as follows:

> In the end, it is not he who abandons her but she who literally turns her back on him, walking away into a different future. The woman who, throughout the film, has been beset by panic and anxiety, desperate to find her absent lover, finally finds him only to become aware of the folly of her previous desperation, for this man who, about to embark for Stockholm with someone else, is quite unworthy of her. In addition, having previously decided to let her apartment, Pepa now changes her mind and resolves to keep it because she likes the view – in other words, her final decisions are made to please herself. (2001: 101)

Edwards is right that Pepa keeps the penthouse because she likes it but there may be another reason for this. She originally says to the estate agent that she needs a smaller apartment now. This is clearly in response to being single. However, Pepa knows at this stage that she is pregnant and if she plans to keep the child she will need the large apartment. Pepa's change of heart about the penthouse may be linked to her decision to have the baby even without Iván.

Mujeres was filmed only three years after abortion had been legalised in Spain, although it was only possible to abort legally if the mother had been raped, the foetus had serious anomalies or a serious illness was detected, or if the mother's mental or physical health was at risk by continuing with the pregnancy. In practice, it was still hard to access abortion until 2010, when the mother's right to choose up to the first fourteen weeks of pregnancy was enshrined in law.[1] During the 1980s, doctors and clinics carrying out legal abortions in Spain were under pressure not to do so and abortion still carried a social stigma. It was only later on that some doctors started interpreting the risk to the mother's mental or physical health more widely, thus allowing many more women the option to abort. Many women, especially the better off such as Pepa, would have had to resort to going abroad but others would have had to abort illegally. Pepa's doctor does not seem likely to help her opt for a termination as he advises her to 'look after yourself and don't smoke. Look after yourself and you'll be fine.' Moreover, Pepa's peculiar remark to Iván at the end, 'but it's too late now. Two hours too late', points towards a time constraint that may have been dictated by the possibility of having a termination or, less dramatically, to the moment when she decided to have the baby and forget Iván.

For this reason, I am in two minds about Pepa's journey during the film and certainly about the ending, which Epps describes as 'a sort of bedraggled feminist triumph (women do not need men)' (1995: 116). The ending is positive in as much as Pepa has come to terms with the break-up of her relationship and Marisa's reaction to discovering Carlos and Candela together offers an alternative model of feminine behaviour. Marisa is disbelieving but quickly moves on to have a quiet conversation with Pepa. Her self-sufficiency has already been high-lighted in that she has been able to have an orgasm on her own whilst sleeping. Pepa is matter-of-fact. Epps points to this moment as 'the calmest communication in the film' (1995: 117) and it is indeed calm, but not the only one. Pepa is also calm on her way out from Paulina's office, just after slapping her and, crucially, during the police's visit. It seems as if under pressure Pepa is more than capable of being both violent and remarkably serene. The ending is not necessarily 'a bedraggled feminist triumph' but the outcome of what Florence Redding Jessup has called 'a reasonable decision' (1994: 306) by a woman to face up to the fact that her ex-lover does not want her and that she will have to raise their child on her own.

However good the ending is for Pepa's well-being, it is not really a happy ending, let alone a 'feminist triumph'. Pepa cannot rationally do anything else. She has resigned herself to what she cannot change and she now faces a difficult journey bringing up a child by herself in 1980s Spain, a society that frowned upon single mothers. She does not want or need Iván less, but she has come to accept that Iván will not meet these needs. She could have talked to Iván at the airport but, given his track record as partner and father I doubt (and Pepa obviously does too) that he would have improved his behaviour second-time around. Significantly, Pepa decided long before meeting Iván that she was not going to share the news of her pregnancy with him. She had initially placed her results letter in his suitcase, only to take it out, rip it, and bin it on her way down to throw the suitcase away. In between, Carlos had told her that he had not been allowed to meet Iván and that his mother hates him because he 'represents those years without Iván'. Pepa replies that she loves him because he's 'the one good thing Iván ever did'. This conversation is the turning point in Pepa's journey. She moves away from romantic love to motherhood, focusing more on herself and her friends than on her obviously doomed chase of Iván. One could say that this focus on maternity also prompts Manuela's move to Madrid in *Todo sobre mi madre* (All about My Mother, 1999).

Looking at Pepa's predicament and behaviour from this angle changes our perception of her. The film title points towards women's hysteria as they are 'on the verge of a nervous breakdown' for different reasons, but they all have to do with men. It is therefore understandable that the critical focus so far has been on the women's mental health and behaviour. Epps's essay on hysteria in Almodóvar's films is a good example of this, but other studies such as those by Acevedo-Muñoz (2004) and D'Lugo (2006) emphasise the women's instability. Almodóvar is also aware of the importance of self-control in the film: 'Julieta's character [Lucía] is essential. It represents what all the other women in the film could become if they don't control themselves'. (Strauss, 2006: 88). This doubling reoccurs in *Los amantes*. While it is true that Lucía acts as Pepa's alter ego, the idea of control is misleading here. Lack of control seems to relate to mental illness, when in fact it is the opposite. Pepa is behaving in a perfectly understandable way when she is anxious and angry with Iván. Her encounter with Paulina also warrants her response, as Paulina is completely unreasonable in Pepa's mind and the audience's sympathies remain firmly with Pepa. The most unstable characters in the film – Iván, Carlos, Lucía, and the terrorists – are also, paradoxically, the ones who exercise the most control over their emotions. Lucía is able to pretend that she is well in order to be discharged from hospital. Carlos seems weak and conformist but in fact he simply ignores Marisa and seeks thrills with Candela. He is, as his own mother realises, a young version of Iván ('He takes after his father').

Iván prefers avoidance tactics to uncomfortable conversations. Pepa complains about this to Carlos: 'He never says anything or admits to anything. He never ever criticises.' Iván displays a pattern of behaviour that is passive-aggressive. He does not address negative feelings. Instead, he expresses them indirectly through actions rather than words (for example, by not arranging to talk to Pepa and avoiding her at all cost) and blames other people for his shortcomings as, for example, when he leaves a message on Pepa's machine suggesting that she is the one avoiding him and saying 'I really want to talk to you. I miss you.' Pepa recognises Iván's lies and voices her thoughts as she hears the message, engaging in a conversation with a man who does not want to hear her. For example, to Iván's 'I really want to talk to you. I miss you', she retorts 'I can see'. As Evans says, the film portrays 'Iván as someone falsely accusing Pepa of avoiding contact with him, refusing to acknowledge the expiry of his own feelings for her as he strives to transfer his own guilt on to her (a strategy which in its repudiation by Pepa further stresses the film's radical sexual politics)' (1996: 37).

Even during the final rendezvous at the airport, Iván's apology and offer to discuss matters is surprising given his previous behaviour: 'Pepa I'm ashamed. I've treated you so badly. I feel terrible.' Someone with passive-aggressive traits would find it very hard to come up with an apology and accept that he has done anything wrong. This apology fits into the wish-fulfilling element in the ending. It is also a hollow apology since neither Pepa nor the viewer feel that they can trust Iván's words after the number of lies he has been seen to utter. The song in the final credits – La Lupe's '*Teatro*' (Theatre) – sums it up well:

> You are pure theatre
> well rehearsed falsehood
> studied simulation.
> Your best performance
> was to destroy my heart
> and now that you cry to me truly
> I remember your act.
> Excuse me if I don't believe you ...
> it seems like theatre to me.
> (my translation)

It has been clear for a while that Iván is merely a well-mannered womaniser. Iván is, after all, a Slavic variant of John (Juan in Spanish), and his name conveys his indebtedness to the legendary Don Juan.[2] As Edwards points out, 'Pepa and Lucía, both abandoned by Iván, are merely part of his collection, to be thrown aside when he tires of them' (2001: 92). The same can be said of Paulina, already exasperated by his constant acquiescence.

Edwards cleverly relates Iván's treatment of women to the credits sequence:

> the cut-outs – the scissors are surely significant – suggest pictures from magazines which might be pinned on bedroom or office walls. These are, in other words, beautiful women as objects to be looked at, not as individuals to be understood. Secondly, the cut-outs emphasize, for the most part, bits of women – eyes, face, lips, arms, legs: in short, the physical features of women that the majority of men focus on and find most attractive, both fragmenting and dehumanizing the whole woman in the process. Again, they suggest a collection – the shot which includes the butterflies surely makes that notion quite clear. (2001: 92)

The opening credits were designed by Juan Gatti, a photographer who also works in fashion and is a major collaborator of Almodóvar in the development of promotional materials such as posters and pressbooks. The fragmentation and dehumanisation of women is part of the sequence's 1950s American women's fashion magazine look, a look that is indebted to the opening credits of *Funny Face* (Donen, 1957). The credits introduce the viewer to what Almodóvar has called 'a kind of elegant pop aesthetic' he associates with 'the feminine world the film goes on later to explore more deeply' (Strauss, 2006: 85). In doing this, they also highlight how fashion as a visual form itself objectifies and dehumanises women. The same goes for cinema. Mulvey's *to-be-looked-at-ness* is prevalent in the credits, both through the mimicking of fashion shots and the filmic nature of the credits. As she says, 'conventional close-ups of legs ... or a face ... integrate into the narrative a different mode of eroticism. One part of a fragmented body destroys the Renaissance space, the illusion of depth demanded by the narrative; it gives flatness, the quality of a cut-out or icon, rather than verisimilitude, to the screen' (1997: 443). The drawings, which in Spanish are aptly called *figurines*, are idealised representations of women. Sometimes they are made from real models (tellingly called mannequins though they are women).

Mujeres' cinematography makes substantial use of close-ups, the filmic equivalent of the fragmented body in the opening titles. This is more common in melodramas and tragedies rather than comedies, as Almodóvar noted to Fredric Strauss:

> I don't respect all the laws of comedy in *Women on the Verge* ... The format, the sets, the dramatic structure are all comedic. The performances of the actors too; they speak very fast, as if they aren't thinking about what they're saying. But in comedy you'd shoot two shots and medium angles as opposed to close ups. You'd never shoot an extreme close-up as I do with the microphone in the dubbing sequence. And the rhythm of the film isn't entirely comedic either. ... But there were also subjects I wanted to deal with in the film which weren't comic. (2006: 82)

Conventional close-ups of legs, hands, faces, and other body parts occur repeatedly. Pepa's legs are shown frequently in close-up, as is her face. One of the most emblematic shots in the film is an extreme close-up of Pepa's hands as she chops tomatoes to make *gazpacho* and cuts herself. This close-up is echoed later on in *Volver* in two scenes in which Raimunda washes a knife and remade in Mateo Blanco's *Chicas y maletas*, the film-within-the-film in *Los abrazos*. Another is the shot of Pepa's shoes (and legs) as she paces her apartment waiting for Iván's call. Candela's body is also cut up in some sequences, most obviously during her attempted suicide and rescue where a close-up of her bottom with Carlos's hand on it as she is lifted up is prominent. The close-ups of women's bodies are used in the conventional way but also to aid characterisation (Candela's earrings, Pepa's impatient shoes) and provide insight into the characters' emotional state.

The close-up that Almodóvar mentions is, however, not of a woman but of Iván's mouth as he dubs Sterling Hayden's part in *Johnny Guitar*. This is not the first extreme close-up of Iván's mouth. The first one happens just a minute before at the beginning of Pepa's dream, with Iván (spraying his mouth) before speaking platitudes to typecast women into a microphone. Clearly the focus of the extreme close-ups is Iván's voice and its power, which may be in itself erotic. Iván's voice stands for him throughout the film and will bring to mind to many Spanish viewers other roles played by Fernando Guillén, including his dubbing career. Although Iván's groomed voice is sensualised and presented as a major factor in his ability to seduce women, his body is not treated as spectacle. This is reserved for the female characters.

The idea of women as specimens to be collected is also present throughout the film in the attitudes of the main two male characters – Iván and Carlos – and, most significantly, in Pepa's dream. The famous black-and-white scene shows Pepa's anxiety about Iván's unfaithfulness, fickleness, and dishonesty. A tracking shot follows Iván's walk as he utters flirtatious remarks to a series of female stereotypes that are mostly silent. The women reply on just two occasions to his comments, mostly dismissively. The dream sequence thus builds Iván up as a Don Juan, generating sympathy for Pepa. Paradoxically, publicity stills marketed the film as containing a collection of women (particularly the poster with all four female protagonists sitting on a sofa in a similar position) and with the director as owner/creator, as in the publicity shot of Almodóvar sitting down and all the main actors, all women except for Banderas, lining up next to him.[3] These highly staged publicity shots are also in line with those of gendered American comedies that influenced the film such as *How to Marry a Millionaire* (Negulesco, 1953) but also comedies such as those starring Doris Day and Rock Hudson or Katharine Hepburn and Spencer Tracy, particularly films like *Pillow Talk* (Gordon, 1959), where the telephone is crucial to the plot. The film harks back to the 1950s partly as a wink to Hollywood's Golden Age and partly to point to the lack of evolution in a Spain where the social revolution of the 1960s did not really happen. For many Spanish women, the ideals and roles of the 1950s, which emphasised femininity, motherhood, and domesticity, were still dominant.

Almodóvar has called *Mujeres* 'a realist comedy in the American way, that is to say, very false' (Boquerini, 1989: 98; my translation). This insistence on artificiality is seen in the clearly made up sets, including a composite skyline of Madrid, Pepa's flat as an idealised living space with décor similar to that of American melodrama, and the prevalence of primary colours. It is also introduced thematically through scenes that invite reflection on film as an artificial, constructed medium, most notably the beginning of Pepa's dubbing scenes, which begin in the projection room and, in the second instance, show the projector at work and follow the beam of light overhead to reach Pepa.

The flat is seen as a simulation of reality from the beginning, with the first shot being that of a model of the block of flats with an ideal rising or setting sun and palm trees. There is a cut to the 'real' flat and then further cuts to the interior and bedroom. In the bedroom, the camera shows different items from the bedside table. This opening is reminiscent of the beginning of *Rear Window* (Hitchcock, 1954), a film that is quoted several times in *Mujeres* and at the heart of which there is also a man unable to commit to a relationship with a woman, both 'insist[ing] that the film is merely reflecting another film, not reality ... at the same time as questions about commitment and personal relationships are raised' (Evans, 1996: 18). The flat also denotes the artificiality of romantic discourse by contrasting very real elements, such as the chicken coop, with the showroom artificiality of the rest. The chicken coop doubles as a sign of the yearning for a lost rural world, a theme that recurs in Almodóvar's films, and as a way of signalling that the flat used to be Pepa's and Iván's love nest. This patently artificial set is also the result of Almodóvar wanting to shoot something cheaply without many exterior scenes. This emphasis on artificiality draws attention to the problematic nature of gender constraints and construction in the film. If proof was needed as to the seriousness behind this comedy, Almodóvar's placing of Lucía's apartment next to the Madrid Women's Institute should help (Jessup, 1994: 309). Only a year after the film's premiere, Almodóvar asked, 'What is frivolous and what is transcendent?' (quoted in Maldonado, 1989: 168). *Mujeres* manages to be both.

Notes

1 Abortion rights were under threat in Spain as late as 2014, when the conservative government of the time had to withdraw a proposed bill to revert to the 1985 law.
2 See Jessup (1994) on the links between José Zorrilla's play, *Don Juan Tenorio* (1844), and *Mujeres* and a defence of Almodóvar as a feminist.
3 Banderas's case is interesting here as his character seems emasculated during most of the film. Carlos does not display hypermasculine features although he is predatory. This, in a way, makes his inclusion in the 'all-girl' group possible.

7

On the verge of a genre breakdown: ¡Átame!, Tacones lejanos, and Kika

Almodóvar endured a critical, if not necessarily commercial, slump in the early 1990s with the releases of ¡Átame! (Tie Me Up! Tie Me Down!, 1989), Tacones lejanos (High Heels, 1991), and Kika (1993). Responses to these films were very different in Spain and abroad. In Spain, ¡Átame! was the biggest-grossing domestic film of the year and critically it was well received (cf. Flores, 1990; Guarner, 1990), whereas Tacones received lukewarm responses and Kika was savaged critically. The battle to avoid an X rating in the USA for ¡Átame! (lost by distributor Miramax, who released the film unrated, with consequent loss of audiences and revenue) is well known, including Almodóvar's rant in the Spanish daily El País against US hypocrisy and censorship (Almodóvar, 1990). In the UK and Spain it was released with an 18 certificate, as were Tacones and Kika. This helped secure Almodóvar's reputation as an enfant terrible after the mainstream success of Mujeres, but it obviously affected revenues. For the first time, criticism outside Spain was mostly negative, accusing Almodóvar of being a covert or, at best, unconscious male chauvinist. Reactions to Kika were particularly harsh. Of the three films, the most palatable to mainstream audiences, Tacones, has received the most critical attention, with the other two being relatively overlooked. The underlying reason for the critical and commercial blip in Almodóvar's trajectory at this point may well be due to his increased experimental playfulness with genre and tone.

¡Átame! is a case in point. Critically well received in Spain, the film raised numerous eyebrows abroad because of its depiction of violence against women. Margaret Walters summarises objections to the film thus: 'Is the vauntedly non-macho Almodovar [sic] instead just a self-flattering fantasist, an unreconstructed chauvinist at heart?'

(1990: 40). This debate continued in discussions of *Kika*, particularly in relation to the prolonged rape scene. Both *¡Átame!* and *Kika* are indirect satires of contemporary society, as well as sending up the genres they cannibalise, namely the slasher movie, porn films, and the thriller in the former and the thriller and reality television in the latter. As Mark Allinson notes, '[i]n Almodóvar, the assumption of an all-encompassing male gaze is problematic for a number of reasons. Where male characters assume voyeuristic or sadistic roles, this is critically questioned, and identification lies with the female characters' (2001: 81). Allinson goes on to explain that '[a]s well as a critique of patriarchy's instinctive violence, [*¡Átame!*] represents a satirical twist on politically incorrect sub-genres based on voyeuristic and sadistic titillation for men' (2001: 79). This is also the case in *Kika* where the footage of the rape calls into question Ramón's (Àlex Casanovas) use of Kika (Verónica Forqué) merely for his own pleasure and where characters who knowingly exploit other people – Andrea (Victoria Abril), Nicholas (Peter Coyote), and Ramón – are portrayed unsympathetically. In contrast to Allinson, Walters suggests in an early review of *¡Átame!* that in previous films Almodóvar's 'mocking, flamboyantly provocative style served to defuse their excesses. And his high-camp instincts, at once parodic and envious, enabled him to say something witty about at least one aspect of femininity—the sense in which it is always learned, made up, performed' (1990: 40). Whereas Walters is right about Almodóvar's recurrent deconstruction of gender, she fails to see that it is precisely the lack of obvious mockery, flamboyancy, and excess that signals *¡Átame!*'s satirical presentation of the ideological ties that love, family, and – by extension – nation bind around individuals. Because *¡Átame!* can easily be taken as straightforward (note the outrage and the accusations, but also the praise mainly in Spanish and French reviews), it is paradoxically a superbly achieved satire.

Satire is achieved through blending genres. Both *¡Átame!* and *Tacones* ultimately explore the links between love and violence, the former as a romantic relationship in search of a replacement for maternal love via horror, the latter as violence against a romantic object as a response to maternal neglect through melodrama and the murder mystery. *Kika* combines the murder mystery with screwball comedy to parody reality television and satirise contemporary Spanish society. The films pick at uncomfortable wounds where the discourses of romantic or filial/maternal love open up to reveal the capacity of those acting in their name for horror, exploitation, and violence. All could belong to the genre of black comedy that from the 1960s 'broke taboos of taste by mocking serious subjects' (Blandford, Grant, and Hillier, 2001: 54). They certainly are inverted satiric comedies that attack the social order rather than its deviations. Thus, the films paradoxically reinscribe and resist the discourses they tackle, allowing for shocked distancing as well as implicit acquiescence by the viewer.

Critiques of Almodóvar's films based on distaste of his breaking of contemporary taboos around gender violence miss the point completely. As Smith shrewdly asks in relation to ¡Átame!: 'What, then, if this cult of the surface is read as critique, as a means of investigating the questions of pornography, heterosexuality, and femininity?' (1992: 207). The 'trouble' with the films seems to be that they do not wear their politics on their sleeve; ambiguity causes discomfort and anger. Linda Hutcheon discusses parody as crucial to postmodern aesthetics, highlighting how it is paradoxically used to 'subvert' (1988: XII). She recognises that 'unresolved paradoxes may be unsatisfying to those in need of absolute and final answers' (1988: 21). Following Hutcheon, I think it is more productive to consider the open nature of the films' aesthetics as an attempt to breach established order through playfulness or what Mikhail Bakhtin has called the carnivalesque, a complex system of meaning that emphasises the 'multiaccentuality of the sign' (Dentith, 1995: 23). His analyses of how carnivalised writing takes 'the carnival spirit into itself and reproduces the inversions, parodies and discrownings of carnival proper' (Dentith, 1995: 65) apply to film just as well. Bakhtin already noted the ambivalence of carnival itself, as both reinforcing and resisting official culture and power. Pam Morris defines carnival as 'another term for a social centrifugal force which opposes the centralizing imposition of the monologic world' (1994: 20) and 'carnivalized literature' as taking 'from medieval carnival the inversion of power structures, the parodic debunking of all that a particular society takes seriously (including and in particular all that which it fears)' (1994: 250). As Simon Dentith notes, the carnivalesque 'provides a malleable space, in which activities and symbols can be inflected in different directions' (1995: 75). Blending disparate genres, using irony, and including multiple divergent voices, the films enable different discourses to interact without giving prevalence to one particular voice. Moreover, although the plots of the films have specific and defined endings – Marina (Victoria Abril) and Ricki (Antonio Banderas) get together, Becky (Marisa Paredes) dies

after reconciling with Rebeca (Victoria Abril), Kika leaves Ramón –
the existence of these other discourses makes accepting the endings
as closed (particularly in ¡Átame! and Kika) near impossible.
Numerous distancing techniques are employed across the three
films, including mise-en-abyme, defamiliarisation of 'normality',
incongruity, and exaggeration. The most obvious of these is mise-en-
abyme, which in Tacones is best seen in Rebeca's photographs of the
home she shared with her husband, which she shows to TV viewers.
It is also present in Becky's showbiz background, Femme Letal's
(Miguel Bosé) tribute act, television news footage, and a musical
number in prison. In Kika and ¡Átame!, mise-en-scène already points
to artificiality, and mise-en-abyme is reinforced by the characters'
backgrounds (writer, photographer, make-up artist, journalist, actor)
and embedded television programmes. Andrea Scarface is a case in
point, where her whole characterisation (in particular the costumes
designed by Jean Paul Gaultier but also her make-up and hairstyle
during television appearances) could be considered mise-en-abyme.
Andrea's signature costumes draw attention to the artificiality of
the programme she fronts, the footage she edits, and, by extension,
Kika itself. Her mannerisms and traditionally inspired hair (centre
parting, bun, and curls stuck to her face) mimic flamenco movements and are reminiscent of the tile mosaics in the background
during Femme Letal's act in Tacones and indeed also Femme Letal's
styling, which is itself a tribute to Becky's. Juana's (Rossy de Palma)
hairdo in Kika is a (childish) version of this, with only the upper part
of the hair tied back with a big artificial red flower. These multiplying images of the 'traditional' Spanish woman pepper Almodóvar's
filmography – from Pepi's (Carmen Maura) dressing up as a chulapa
to Zahara's (Gael García Bernal) styling as a cuplé singer in La mala
educación (Bad Education, 2004) – and a clear reference to Romantic
representations of Spanish women imbued in (particularly Castilian
and southern Spanish) customs and manners. The paintings of
Francisco de Goya are emblematic of Spanish art's use of these
images of Spanish folkloric femininity, which in turn can be traced
to European Romanticism and its orientalisation of Spain as exotic
due to its Jewish–Muslim culture (cf. Hutcheon, 1988: 153–67). As
Silvia García Alcázar has noted in relation to the Romantic for Spain:

> The origin of everything would be found in those faraway paradises, dif-
> ferent worlds where one could live outside norms and in contact with

wild nature. ... The big problem for [writers] was the distance they had to travel to reach those exotic marvels. This is where Spain started to play a leading role and became the ideal place to know the oriental legacy without leaving Europe. Granada, Sevilla and Cordoba became must-see places for the lovers of Islamic style and thus the Romantic image of our country [Spain] was complete. (2011: 203)

The influence of European Romantic orientalism in images of Spain and Spaniards is crucial to understanding *Tacones* and *Kika* stylistically. Their high-camp, postmodern aesthetic not only deconstructs gender and sexuality but also targets Spanishness itself, like *Matador* (1986). In particular, the films satirise the belief that Spain is different from the rest of Western Europe. Spain's othering via orientalism was reinforced by centuries of indigenisation, culminating in mass tourism in the twentieth century and the use of these stereotypes by Spain itself. Almodóvar is not the only member of the *movida* to use Spanish kitsch with a camp aesthetic. Artist duo Las Costus, whose flat was used in *Pepi, Luci, Bom* and whose paintings can be seen there and in *Carne trémula* (Live Flesh, 1997), are notable examples of this.

Satire of Spain as oriental other is not constrained to high-camp moments in the films, however. In fact, it is most potent when most invisible, so much so that it can be taken as straight, realist, or 'documentary' as, for example, in the ethnographic footage in *Kika* about the Easter tradition of *Los Picaos* that is reported in a section of Andrea's television programme – *The Worst of the Day* – titled 'Bloody Ceremonies'. This is real footage from a Spanish town that routinely appears on Spanish national television at Easter. In 1998 it was declared an event of regional tourist interest, and in 2005 the central government declared it of national tourist interest. The real footage is framed by Andrea's elaborate bandages and blood costume as a way of highlighting Spanish television's sensationalism and Spain's Gothic self-exotisation. Andrea is sitting on the television, which is in turn dangling from a trapeze, emphasising the circus-like element of the show and its carnivalesque elements (Figure 7.1). The seemingly implausible plot device of having criminal Paul Bazzo escape during the ceremony is not as ludicrous as it seems in a country where some prisoners are still reprieved on Maundy Thursday.

The distorted mirror of Spain that the film offers via high-camp and realist footage is not simply reinstating Spain as the other of

7.1   Andrea Scarface introduces 'Bloody Ceremonies' (*Kika*, 1993)

Europe, but as the other of itself, mystified by nearly extinguished medieval traditions that are still supported in the name of tourism or religion. Established religion, also crucial in the iconography of *¡Átame!*, plays a major role in the image of Spain as other but is here used to resist this discourse. Spain as a stranger to itself is obvious in the reverse shots of Kika, Ramón, and Juana watching the programme in a mixture of fascination, disbelief, and horror. Although the TV footage is more realistically shot than the film in which they appear, the brightly dressed characters in the obviously designer-created set could be seen as more 'real' or closer to most audiences in Spain and abroad, due in particular to their reaction of astonishment to the show. And yet they are not so distant. Juana admits to letting her brother abuse her to prevent him from raping other women, for example. Kika and Ramon's lovemaking scene happens straight after the television show and starts with a panning shot of the knick-knacks in their bedroom, which includes multiple religious artefacts. This kitsch collection highlights the emphasis on the ritual rather than the spiritual. The recycling of kitsch religious artefacts is one of the constants in Almodóvar's sets. It reflects contemporary Spain's apparent detachment from its mythical identity through postmodernity but ultimate identification through it.

Significantly, the footage of both *Los Picaos* and Kika's rape as shown on TV have the same background music, thus aurally flattening both events and signalling their importance as spectacle.

The presence of fast-paced percussion (almost like riffs in mambo) make the footage ludicrous, thus pointing to how reality television treats everything similarly, depriving its subjects of humanity in the search for larger audiences, as Andrea explains later on being upbraided about showing the rape. The music works to distance TV viewers from the rape; the experience of watching the initial rape scene (however artificial and edited it is) is very different from that of watching the recording shown on television, which sensationalises it. *Kika* is full of such metacinematic moments that unravel the way the mass media works within the film and satirise its role in the narrative of the nation.

In an interview, Almodóvar talks about the rape scene in *Kika* as a 'culminating scene': 'you realise that the worst thing that has happened to this girl is not that she has been raped, but what happens next. The rape scene is key to understand Kika, a brave and positive woman, who in this situation tries to convince her rapist and negotiate a way out. What she cannot stand is her rape being on television' (quoted in Llopart, 1993: 2). Almodóvar was thinking about this long rape scene early on in the project, viewing it initially as a means of humiliating the rapist since he could not have an orgasm. In the final version, Paul Bazzo (a pun on the Spanish term, '*polvazo*', a big fuck) comes several times. The scene is devoid of the sexual frisson or victim identification of many conventionally filmed rape scenes. Paul Bazzo's comic-strip staying power is matched by Kika, who, Almodóvar explains, 'starts by resisting Paul, but the second he puts the knife to her throat she becomes practical' (quoted in Strauss, 2006: 130). Neither of Kika's responses looks authentic; both are incongruous. Overall, the scene could do with more editing, but the exaggeration of the rapist's and victim's behaviour asks questions about what film viewers expect from these scenes.

With its long takes, the scene acts a none-too-subtle aporia at the heart of the film that ensures viewers are uncomfortable in the role of voyeur they have thus far adopted. The role of the spectator is highlighted by the positioning of observers, either outside the frame (the voyeur filming from a different building) or inside (Juana and the policemen). The voyeur and Juana are particularly ineffectual and morally compromised as one does nothing and the other is complicit in the crime. The policemen take long to prise Paul away from Kika and he still manages to have a third orgasm before escaping. Christopher Mildren discusses how long takes confront viewers' compromised positions in relation to Roy Andersson's films:

> More discomfiting and confrontational is Andersson's exploitation of the role the spectator has in creating meaning from the image during the long take, by including a passively observant audience in the screen frame. This device satirically mirrors the actual viewers' incapacity to affect the action on-screen, while implying that this is also a moral choice. Passive viewing of the cinematic image without ethical engagement is provocatively equated with passively witnessing unjust events in the real world. (2013: 152)

Mildren's insightful analysis is equally relevant to the rape scene in *Kika*, even more so since the main object of critique in the film is reality television and the consumption of sensationalist news stories by contemporary audiences: 'the long take aesthetic satirically plays on the heightened awareness that extended duration generates for the spectator in order to implicate the viewer in dilemmas of ethical responsibility encountered by the protagonists. ... These are the "time-images" described by Deleuze, which essentially have time itself as their object' (Mildren, 2013: 148). Heightened viewer awareness and implication play a part in the negative reactions to this crucial scene.

Almodóvar envisaged this scene as comic in its portrayal of Kika's 'optimism' and 'the strength women can call on in difficult, not to say critical, situations. ... I wanted to show this because it's a feminine trait I admire a great deal' (quoted in Strauss, 2006: 130). The long scene was also conceived to develop into a comic moment:

> It's also what makes the scene funny. If I'd written half the scene it would have stayed merely violent. You have to imagine that it doesn't last twenty minutes; Paul Bazzo is on top of Kika for three hours, the situation has time to develop. The horror of rape becomes irrelevant; a thirteen-stone man is on top of you and after a while you want to scratch your nose, have a pee, you think of the shopping, the phone calls you have to make, all kinds of domestic worries spring to mind.(Almodóvar, quoted in Strauss, 2006: 130–1)

The scene backfired badly as this sketch-like concept that uses postmodern defamiliarisation techniques is undermined by the way the long shots interpellate viewers. The conflation of the initial rape scene with the voyeur's footage shown on television also contributes to the negative reaction.

As Acevedo-Muñoz notes, 'in Almodóvar's films sexual violence is often treated as an allegory of Franco's repressive regime and state apparatus' and 'suggests the possibility that Spain's Transition into democracy and away from the Fascists' violent, authoritative ways is not complete, that the country might still be in danger of a return to a reactionary state' (2007: 10; 24–5). This is clearer in films with more authoritarian characters but not so much in *Kika* where the rapist is portrayed as animalistic and mindless. In *Kika*, structural violence against women is shown in the way the rape is reported. Explicit violence distracts viewers from the serial murders that Nicholas is carrying out (one of the bodies is transported in a trunk in the foreground but viewers' attention is focused on the rape taking place in the background). It also diverts Ramón from dealing with the traumas of his past. Almodóvar implies that the Spanish nation behaves similarly, gorging on sensationalism and moralising stories that only happen in the present tense. The past is forgotten, buried, not spoken about, at least until Ramón decides to read his mother's diary and realises that Nicholas's claim to be the victim is untrue.

Whereas in *Kika* the nation and characters live in the present despite an unresolved past that will come back to haunt them, *¡Átame!* and *Tacones* make more explicit links to the characters dealing with their past. *Tacones*, for example, contains two lengthy flashbacks where Rebeca remembers her supposed murder of her authoritarian stepfather to free her mother (and herself) from him and her mother's subsequent betrayal in leaving her. *Tacones* is highly intertextual with a key Spanish film of the Transition, *Cría Cuervos* (Raise Ravens, Saura, 1976), a film that critiques the final stages of Francoism through the memories of a young woman who thinks she killed her authoritarian father as a child. In *Tacones* and *¡Átame!*, distance is also achieved through defamiliarisation techniques, be it through Rebeca's heart-to-heart in front of the television cameras as if she is addressing a confidante rather than millions of anonymous viewers or Ricki's unnerving search for and performance of 'normality'. Naturalistic performances, even in implausible situations, are an Almodóvar trademark; using this technique erodes the boundaries between acceptable and unacceptable conduct, madness, and sanity.

When Ricki is discharged from the sanatorium in *¡Átame!*, the director asks him what he will do next and he states he wants to lead a 'normal' life and have a family, to which the director replies that he is not normal. Throughout the film, Ricki strives to act and sound 'normal' and a romantic relationship with Marina is the most normal thing he can think of. The situation denaturalises what he does, such as his use of greetings like 'Honey, I'm home' or his handiwork in Marina's house. This is incongruous in a kidnap situation, but perfectly in keeping with Ricki's impersonation of a would-be husband. It also links Ricki to another character played by Antonio Banderas in an Almodóvar film, Antonio in *La ley*. Just like Antonio, Ricki demonstrates his suitability as a partner by taking on traditionally male roles in the home. Unlike Pablo in *La ley*, Marina is taken in by Ricki's performance. Ricki's desire to form a family is not simply about the future. He is trying to re-create a lost past as his search for his family home in Granadilla – now in ruins – demonstrates. He has just one photograph with his parents in front of the house before they died and he was taken into care. Tellingly, he sits in the same spot he was sitting in as a child in the photograph. In effect he is still tied to his childhood. As Almodóvar remarks, 'Antonio [Banderas] plays the part as if Ricki were ten' (quoted in Strauss, 2006: 97).

All three of the films discussed in this chapter depict characters attempting to reconstruct an idealised past. Ricki in *¡Átame!*, Rebeca in *Tacones*, and Ramón in *Kika* all seek to go back to a childhood space where they can be reunited with an idealised mother. To do so, they also re-produce families that attempt to re-create these childhood spaces and relationships. Marsha Kinder writes about maternal identification in *Tacones*, disentangling the Oedipal structures of the film. Kinder identifies Rebeca's photographs as 'fetishistic substitutes for her dead husband (a strategy of the masochistic aesthetic, at least according to Deleuze), but he turns out to be merely a secondary fetish for motherlove' (1992: 42). Ricki's family photograph is also a primary fetish for the mother, and Marina (whom Ricki wants to save and be loved by) could be seen as a secondary fetish. Ramón's voyeurism is closely linked to the mother and his relationship with Kika is a way of substituting the father-figure and re-enacting the Oedipal narrative that has been truncated by his mother's death.

By far the most obvious *mise-en-abyme* in *¡Átame!* is the use of the metacinematic film-within-the-film. Marina is an actor filming a b-movie where she is the final girl (the last character left alive to confront the killer). In the final scene of this film, Marina's character confronts the Midnight Phantom, who has been terrorising her and wants to take her 'somewhere quiet where we can be happy'. Marina's character says that the Midnight Phantom offers death, not happiness, lassoes him with a red telephone cord, and jumps out of the window to safety where she is left hanging. The ending is ambiguous despite the final girl's apparent victory. The Midnight Phantom is vanquished in the home but Marina's character is still tied to him through the cord, her life still dependent on him. Red ties Marina's character and the Phantom like an umbilical cord. The Phantom doubles as Marina's boyfriend, who was on the line shortly before the appearance of the Phantom. This prompts a deconstruction of Marina's relationship with her boyfriend, one that anticipates the preoccupations of the film as a whole. For Marina has just ended a brief telephone conversation with her boyfriend, to whom she has just said: 'Darling, I'm afraid the whole future is ours.' She has also been asked by him twice whether she 'idolises' him and she has agreed impatiently. The insecure boyfriend does not seem to offer a credible and desirable alternative to the Midnight Phantom. On the contrary, he seems another version of him.

This ending is also related to Marina's biography. Earlier in the film, she admits to a journalist that she worked in a circus lassoing and taming horses as a child, a story overheard by the director Máximo Espejo (Maximum Mirror, Paco Rabal) and used by him to change the ending of his film. Thus one could argue that all of the male characters in the film are lassoed and perhaps ultimately tamed by Marina. This is an interpretation I would like to extend to the film as a whole, where Marina asks to be tied but ultimately has also tied down her aggressor. This may at first sound like the stereotypical argument that women are responsible for men settling down. However, whilst apparently acting of their own free will once Marina escapes, both Marina and Ricki are subject to the discourses about romantic love, the traditional family, and heteronormative 'normal' life. Both are tied by the red telephone cord, and both acquiesce to these binds because they are subjected to these discourses. Whereas ¡Átame! has been read as the subjection of a woman by a man until she agrees to be his romantic partner with the ending thus seen as problematic, it may be more productive to analyse it using Foucault, as the subjection of two people to existing discourses of power regarding ideas of romantic love. Whereas the characters are subjected to these discourses, the film itself resists these very discourses.

One defence of the film has been the distinction between sanity and madness, in effect arguing that the film's actions are those of a mentally handicapped person and a recovering drug addict. However, the film goes beyond such binaries to question the boundaries between normal and abnormal behaviour, thus tugging at comfortable assumptions within a heteronormal society. Ricki aims to lead a normal life, which he idealises as romantic love, heterosexuality, having children, and having a home and a job. But Ricki's methods do not at first seem 'normal'. Before shooting ¡Átame!, Almodóvar said about the film that it 'is in reality the story of someone who tries to create a love story as he would study for a university degree: through effort, strength of will, persistence. Can passion be designed in advance, can it be planned and motivated in another person?' (quoted in Edwards, 2001: 107). Ricki is one of a number of characters in Almodóvar's films who must start their lives afresh after life-changing events. He resembles Víctor Plaza, the main character in *Carne trémula*, who is wrongfully convicted of attempted rape and murder and has to rebuild his life after prison. Unlike Víctor, however, Ricki does not have many memories of a family or a house to fall back on. Both Víctor and Ricki set up to rebuild their lives with a plan, and their plans include romantic relationships with women. But whereas Víctor uses the prison-service's rehabilitation programmes to become a more compliant citizen, validated through learning, effort, and a desire to prove himself different from the criminal he was mistaken for, Ricki's only aim is to leave his institutionalised existence, primarily by learning how to play 'sane' (just as Lucía in *Mujeres*). Víctor is fully subjected to social discourses about behaviour, whereas Ricki pretends to comply but is ultimately resistant.

Ricki's obsession with having a normal life is therefore suspect and understandable since this is what, in his opinion, will prevent him from being institutionalised again. His methods are also fully consistent with his upbringing. Ricki is treating Marina as he has likely been treated himself, replicating discipline tactics such as restraint and 'reasonable' talk possibly learnt in children's homes, reformatories, and the asylum. He is, in effect, re-educating Marina into his 'normality'. In turn, his normality has been shaped by his exposure to discourses about heterosexual love, comic strips, and experiences of institutionalised violence. Ricki, however, strips the love story to basics, performing love and companionship (romantic gifts, helpfulness, sharing a home) in such a way as to undermine them from within. His obsession with these discourses makes the film as a whole encourage viewers to question practices that are otherwise widely accepted. This is further emphasised by a conversation about *Midnight Phantom* between director Máximo Espejo and the editor in the cutting room:

EDITOR   It's more of a love story than a horror story.
MÁXIMO   It's hard to tell them apart.

The confusion of genres chimes in with the blurring of reality and representation, most notably in the initial still of Ricki's painting of the sanatorium (also seen in the director's office) that fades to a still of the very same building. The painting heightens the building's traits in a similar way that the film as a whole highlights the characters' actions. The painting's colour palette – red, green, and blue – dominates the film, with red and green dominant in Marina and Ricki's characterisation and natural green in the shape of overgrown vegetation and plants throughout.

In satirising romantic love and family life, Almodóvar follows a characteristic of Spanish cinema analysed by Dominic Keown:

> The free-living couple, however, regress into orthodoxy as Rikki [sic] falls for Marina and, following convention, insists that she become the mother of his children. The bonds with which he binds her to the bed, reminiscent of the same motif in *Viridiana*, are merely the exterior representation of those ideological apparatuses. ... Marina, instead of analysing her situation, submits to the paradigm offered, inviting Rikki [sic] to subject her further. Although the ties that bind her at the end are invisible–her need to act as a dutiful spouse–she drives off to find her partner in what will, significantly, constitute another happy ending, we are reminded of the extravagant dissimulation of the protagonist at the climax of *Belle de Jour*. (1996: 70)

Keown sees a movement from 'free-living' to 'orthodoxy' in the couple, but both Marina and Ricki are subject(ed) to social constraint from the beginning and remain curiously unreadable at the end. The ending of *¡Átame!* is inconclusive since, after escaping, Marina 'chooses' to remain tied to her kidnapper and invest in his dreams of 'normality' and happiness. As she drives off into the sunset with her sister Lola to one side and Ricki in the back seat singing a Spanish version of 'I Will Survive', Marina is tense and cries. Lola seeks to reassure her that she and Ricki get on well, but one wonders whether Marina cries for happiness or something else. The lyrics of 'I Will Survive' point to Marina's and Lola's resilience due to their flexibility, 'I will resist to keep on living ... I'm like the reed that bends but does not break'. Paradoxically, Marina has done the most bending. Ricki has not wavered in his objective to achieve a family and Marina's love. This is consistent with their names, as Marina originates in Latin and means 'of the sea' whereas Ricki is a diminutive of Enrique, from the German for man of the house. As usual in Almodóvar the characters' names reveal a great deal about them.

The endings of ¡Átame! and Kika are remarkably similar. Characters escape towards an idealised provincial family life and a simple family celebration respectively. Kika's ending is more optimistic. Kika decides to start again, wiping Nicholas's blood from her left breast (where the heart is). She does not follow Ramón in the ambulance, nor does she mourn Nicholas. Wiping the blood away symbolises her rejection of the maternal role imposed on her by these two men, a role that is particularly obvious when Nicholas asks her to hold him in a way that is reminiscent of a Pietà as he is dying. As well as wiping the blood away, Kika wakes up Ramón from his cataleptic fit by placing a bedside lamp on his big toes. Her seemingly remarkable recovery from shock – much like her contained behaviour during and after the rape – looks contrived and is certainly another way of creating distance from the material.

All of the main characters in these three films are orphans, yet only Kika seems able to move on. She seems to suffer from the adult equivalent of disinhibited attachment disorder. Kika's most outlandish characteristics, such as her willingness to go off and lack of reticence with strangers, may be traceable to her need for attention and love that perhaps was triggered by being orphaned at an early age. Ramón, on the other hand, is overtly reticent and closed, perhaps an inhibited attachment disorder causing fear of rejection. Motherhood is thus a prominent theme in Almodóvar's films well before Todo sobre, and the subject of returning to the (imaginary) mother or an (imaginary) place recur in his films. It is not only places that characters remake; people are increasingly manipulated into becoming other than they may otherwise be. Thus Marina in ¡Átame! is an early example of a constructed subject under duress, a construction that generates violence in *Los abrazos* and ends with gender reassignment and facial transplant in *La piel*. Ricki is an early, poorer, institutionalised version of the surgeon Robert Ledgard in *La piel*. Both of them are played by Antonio Banderas, who also plays Antonio in *La ley*. Banderas incarnates a number of obsessive men who attempt to reshape the world according to their patriarchal ideas.

The figure of the Immaculate Heart of Mary as the ultimate model of devotional motherhood links the films' iconography. The same painting of the Virgin appears in Ramón's headboard in *Kika* and multiplied by three above the bed in *¡Átame!* Significantly, in *¡Átame!* the triptych is accompanied by a remarkably similar (and similarly multiplied) triptych of the Sacred Heart of Christ. Both are concerned with love, but in the heart of Mary it is the love she has for God and her son, whereas the Sacred Heart of Christ represents the love of God for humanity, a love that is mostly rejected or ignored. The choice of paintings in *¡Átame!* emphasises the similarities of both figures, as is traditional. Jesus and Mary are clothed in the same tones (red and blue) and have similar expressions and nearly the same body posture. Their similarity is emphasised by the long (1.33 min) backwards tracking shot used, from an extreme close-up of the caption 'S. COEUR DE MARIE – SAGR. CORAZÓN DE MARIA' at the centre of the collage to the full view of all six images. The pictures are clearly a postmodern collage, as seen by the shadows between posters, framed to appear as one. The relationships within the three films discussed here are also collages of expected roles and mimicry in a search for love in general and, ultimately, maternal love.

The search for that impossible love results in fixation with fetishes and – to use Baudrillard's terminology – the attempted reproduction of a non-existent original, a simulation. Thus, Marina and Ricki's relationship is a simulation of a heterosexual couple but also an attempt to return to the mother by both. The choice of Granadilla for Ricki's backstory and the location of the final scenes of the film prompt an interpretation of the film in relation to the recovery of historical memory and the difficulties encountered by a post-Transition Spain in creating new social relations without falling into old patterns. Granadilla was a thriving town until the mid-1950s, when a reservoir was planned and all lands and homes were expropriated by the state. Residents held on until 1964, when they had to abandon their homes, now the property of the Spanish government. The state took

7.2   Ricki and Marina bond in the bathroom (¡*Átame!*, 1990)

away Ricki's parents' home and, after their deaths, Ricki himself was institutionalised. Like contemporary Spain, Ricki attempts to build a new life but can only think of re-creating his family photograph. Significantly, the breakthrough in his relationship with Marina comes in the bathroom (which contains a shower curtain with a map of Spain) as he mentions that their reflection reminds him of his only memory of his parents (Figure 7.2).

In *Tacones*, Rebeca copies her mother Becky, marries Becky's former lover, befriends an impersonator of her mother, and, finally, bears his (her mother's) child. Kika becomes a stand-in mother for Ramón, who relives his early voyeuristic experiences spying on his mother and her partner by photographing his sexual acts with Kika. Ramón's fetishism and voyeurism go hand in hand with his profession as a lingerie photographer and link him to Andrea Scarface, the psychologist turned journalist who films crimes and has turned herself into a footage-making machine.

Hearts feature prominently in ¡*Átame!*, *Tacones*, and *Kika*, as well as in *Todo sobre mi madre* (All about My Mother, 1999) and *Julieta*. Paul Julian Smith has traced the heart in ¡*Átame!* from the heartbeat of the opening credits to the heart-shaped chocolate box Ricki buys for Marina:

> the conceptual and emotional work in this film is carried out by the image itself and not by the plot, which is flagrantly derivative. The

slippage from heartbeat to Sacred Heart to chocolate box suggests, in purely graphic form that physiology is inseparable from symbolization, that the body is already bound up in the image repertoire of a culture that precedes and envelops it. (1992: 205)

This use of iconography also works across films. The sacred heart is present in *Entre tinieblas*, for example. Hearts also feature prominently in *Todo sobre* (Esteban's heart, Blanche's heart-shaped jewellery case) and *Tacones* (Becky dies of angina).

An ailing heart leads Becky to nostalgia and regret as she tries to make amends with Rebeca and returns to her childhood flat. The melodramatic ending with the mother taking the blame for the daughter's crime is effective and in keeping with the genre. However, it is not clear whether Becky's motives are altruistic or theatrical as the crime would heighten her status as a legend. Tellingly, Becky does not know where the heart is, as she asks Femme Letal for her right-hand artificial breast: 'Right. The one from the heart.' She nevertheless receives the correct breast, perhaps showing that Letal as Becky has the heart that she never had towards her own daughter. Becky's retreat to the porter's lodge of her childhood and her memories of seeing high heels through its window contrast with their significance in Rebeca's memories. For Becky, high heels were a sign of success and freedom, for Rebeca, the loud reminder of her mother's abandonment and her anxiety over her return.

¡Átame!, *Tacones*, and *Kika* are films about the past as much as the present, where memories intrude into everyday life and characters seek out to replace or enact that which has been lost. The films pull at conventional behaviour through stretching genre boundaries and ignoring contemporary moral codes connected to gender politics and violence. Ultimately, all three films hold a distorted mirror to society to highlight how what is considered 'normal' is perhaps not so. Similarly, they satirise Spanishness as the recovery of an idealised past that was probably never there in the first place. Ricki, Rebeca, and Ramón all yearn for the maternal, imagining a relationship where maternal love is boundless. Becky also dreams of love, her daughter's and – most importantly – that of her country after a long stay in Mexico. Whereas in a film like *Tacones* melodramatic aspects obscure the parody despite the *mise-en-abyme* warning viewers not to treat it too seriously, ¡Átame! and *Kika* satirise so well that they have been taken to be the object of their satire. Postmodern experimentation with an ethical undercurrent has taken Almodóvar and his viewers to the verge of a genre breakdown, a welcome one as well.

8

The end of romance:
La flor de mi secreto

La flor de mi secreto (The Flower of My Secret, 1995) was heralded as the first in a new, 'mature' phase by both the director and the press. In an interview before the UK release, Julia Llewellyn Smith outlines what was to become a familiar narrative: 'Just as the masses were beginning to lose patience with melodrama that seemed no longer subversive but merely smutty, along comes *The Flower of My Secret* – a tender, understated drama about a middle-aged woman who has teetered over the verge into full-scale breakdown' (1996: 31). The story of Almodóvar's transition from *enfant terrible* to mature filmmaker has been recycled with both negative and positive spins. Varderi, for example, identifies Almodóvar's financial success as prompting the end of his experimental and transgressive cinema as early as *Mujeres al borde de un ataque de nervios* (Women on the Verge of a Nervous Breakdown, 1988):

> In Almodóvar's case experimentation was due to budgetary concerns, more than to his desire to hold a critical standpoint against the *establishment*: as soon as he had enough financial backing, Almodóvar devoted himself to ... making commercial 'art' cinema, where abstract and surrealist elements of the first vanguard, intertextualised in parody, pastiche, and irreverence towards what was established in the 1960s vanguard, have been lost ... the Almodóvar aesthetic has lost its transgressive character. (1996: 76; my translation)

José Luís Sánchez Noriega is even more explicit about this aesthetic change, still writing off *La flor* as a flawed film due to its lack of empathy with the main character: 'The major error that was *Kika* has been somewhat overcome by *The Flower of My Secret*, a film where the

Manchego director seems to mostly abandon the style he was known for to make more stripped back and classic cinema' (1996: 274; my translation). Carolyn Ueda and Margaret Smith attribute the change to an exhaustion of taboo-breaking: 'What happens to a filmmaker who has pushed all the boundaries? In Almodóvar's case, he's turned back the clock' (1996: 39). More recently, Sally Faulkner has labelled *La flor* as 'Almodóvar's "middlebrow turn"' (2013: 210) because of its 'fusion of serious subject matters, accessible treatment, high production values and high cultural references' (2013: 212). Although the 'film did not do particularly well in the global market' (Kinder, 2004: 11), in Spain it was critically well received and seen by nearly a million people (Sotinel, 2010: 61).

La flor is neither an aesthetic break nor the end of Almodóvar's exploration of taboos and social boundaries. The film's aesthetic departs from the postmodern comedy of *Kika*, but it is satirical and delves deeply into personal relationships and (romantic and filial) love as much as his previous films. Like these films, *La flor* is concerned with overcoming trauma and loss, in this case mostly Leo's loss of her husband Paco (Imanol Arias) and the betrayal of her best friend Betty (Carme Elias) but also the potential loss of her livelihood due to her breach of contract. The main difference between films from *Women on the Verge* to *Kika* and *La flor* is in tone. Where previous films contained a higher rate of comic or unconventional takes, *La flor* is much more sober and conventional in tone.

Almodóvar has commented on how he often shoots a scene using different tones, a 'serious and conventional way' and a 'crazy idea' and chooses which to go with during editing: 'Now, I can shoot the scene in a serious, conventional way and then go on to try the crazy idea I may have had. I did this on *High Heels*. When we were editing I almost systematically chose the conventional takes, the most serious ones. But with *Kika* it was the opposite; we opted for the takes that were all the most wild and exaggerated' (quoted in Strauss, 2006: 110). If Almodóvar followed this editing method with *La flor*, he must have always chosen the 'serious, conventional' takes for this film, which tonally and visually is closely related to *Tacones lejanos* (High Heels, 1991). The blues that dominate Becky's (Marisa Paredes) flat are present throughout *La flor*, for example, particularly in the presentation of Leo and her home. Almodóvar's films deal with loss and recovery but do so within different genres and using different tones. Thus, although there is a noticeable shift in style it is not a break with what had come before and certainly not an indication of maturity, which is perhaps more to do with genre perception than the films themselves since drama and tragedy are generally perceived as more mature and serious than comedy and satire. However, as we have seen throughout this book, Almodóvar is usually at his most comic when most cutting about social issues.

Almodóvar calls *La flor* a 'drama', but he also states that 'it's a much more optimistic film than *Kika*' (quoted in Strauss, 2006: 152). If it were a play I would suggest it is a tragicomedy in the classic sense, a tragedy that ends with a comic (meaning happy, not funny) ending, as Leo and Ángel get together to toast the new year, the *zapateado* show is a success, and Leo seems to have begun recovering from the break-up with Paco. The ending in Ángel's apartment, which is reminiscent of the postmodern sets in *Kika* and the apartment in *¡Átame!*, revisits the earlier style as 'comedy' is established. But for most of the film the colour palette, set design, characterisation, and music fits the genre of drama. As Almodóvar says:

> The look of the film is stripped down, austere. I had originally imagined the film as being more extravagant, but I gradually discovered that the more sober and austere it was, the more expressive it would be. It's the austerity that gives meaning to this film: I've made films before about abandoned women, but I've never made such an economical film, one which speaks such a simple cinematic language. (quoted in Smith, 2014: 174)

This more 'austere' look tampers the film's comic or hyperbolic moments, such as when Leo offers to pay a junkie to help her remove her boots or her encounter with Ángel during the student protest. The set is, however, closer to melodrama's grand houses as Paco leaves Leo for good and tells her that there is nothing she can do to improve things. It is this style that fits preconceptions of drama that encouraged reviewers to hail *La flor* as a mature film.

Almodóvar himself has fostered the idea of the film's maturity in interviews. For example, in discussion with Strauss about the depth and emotion in the main character, Leo, he says: 'What all this means is that *The Flower of My Secret* is a mature film, more mature than all those I've made so far. And it's true I'm now over thirty and I don't like thinking about it. I hate saying it's a mature film, but it's obvious and what can I do?' (quoted in Strauss, 2006: 155). Whereas it is true

that many early Almodóvar movies were ensemble films and characters were not as developed, there are plenty of psychologically complex
characters throughout his filmography. The pop aesthetic of the
early films did not allow such depth, but who could say that Gloria
(Carmen Maura) in *¿Qué he hecho yo para merecer esto?* (What Have
I Done to Deserve This?, 1984) is not on a par with Leo? In fact, the
two films have been linked: 'More than a story, *The Flower* offers a
number of situations about a woman's loneliness; the housewife of a
working-class neighbourhood from *What Have I Done* is now a more
educated woman with more options, but with the same family background' (Sánchez Noriega, 1996: 274; my translation). The plot – 'the
story of a woman abandoned in the city' (Smith, 2014: 172) – is also
reminiscent of *La ley del deseo* (The Law of Desire, 1987) and *Mujeres*:
Pepa's (Carmen Maura) plight is also Leo's. They have both been dis-
carded without closure. Both wait for a never-made phone call. Both
contemplate suicide or murder (Leo carries it through but fails à la
Shirley MacLaine in Billy Wilder's *The Apartment* (1960), a film she
mentions; Pepa takes sleeping pills and thinks of killing the reluctant
Iván. Both women prepare the men's favourite dishes to retain them.
Both are resilient enough to overcome their unsatisfactory situations.
Finally, both women may seem completely down, but their attention to
their wardrobe says otherwise: 'Leo is one of those women Almodóvar
always dresses stylishly, even when she's caught in the rain, in bed, or
driving nervously around the streets of Madrid. ... [W]e're aware that,
despite all her suffering and tears, she's a woman who could never give
up' (Ueda and Smith, 1996: 40). This description applies as much to
Pepa, who has by the end of the film become 'the mistress of her own
solitude' (Almodóvar, quoted in Smith, 2014: 172).

An interesting difference between the characters' plights is Pepa's
pregnancy. Leo and Paco are childless, whether by choice or design
we are not told. The film focuses on this in an understated way. As Leo
waits for her friend Betty to open her door, a young girl goes past and
Leo turns to look at her. *La flor* lingers on children playing on a school
playground below Leo's window on several occasions. We see them
just before we are introduced to her. Their voices wake her up at the
beginning of the film, just as Iván's voice wakes up Pepa in *Mujeres*.
In fact, these two scenes are very similar, from the initial focus on
the sleeping body of the woman to the meandering camera showing
the personal items on the bedside table and the ticking clock in the
background. A further similarity is the abundance of photographs of

the absent men, men who are perhaps self-centred and with whom the women in these films are obsessed.

The children are seen and heard more clearly as Leo tries to call Paco in Brussels the morning after he tells her off for ringing late. Their playful voices are the background to Leo's failed second attempt at communicating with Paco. Children are juxtaposed to books. For example, the wind blows Leo's window open and turns the pages of her books to the noise of play. Writing romance novels has firmly been established as Leo's occupation, with literature as a substitute for the children she and Paco do not have.

Leo's new novel – which her publisher rejects – features a strong mother–daughter relationship in a plot that will form the basis for *Volver* (2006). The publisher reminds Leo that the series is called 'True Love', adding: 'Why give us the story of a mother who discovers that her daughter killed her father after he tried to rape her? And to keep it secret she puts him into the freezer of the restaurant next door.' To which Leo replies, 'The mother has to save her daughter. You'd do anything to help your child.' At this point the publisher reminds Leo of the escapist aim of her writing, talking about how 'children take our lives away' and 'novels give us the illusion of living'. Just as Leo sublimates her love for Paco through writing romance, once the relationship is over the fictional figure of the husband is turned into a would-be incestuous rapist and killed. The other husband in the novel plots to kill his mother-in-law to see his estranged wife again. These are two opposing narratives, one of wish-fulfilment where the husband still loves her, the other of revenge. The fictional child is here the driver of the plot, and the strong mother–daughter bond replicates that of Leo and her mother (Chus Lampreave) and feeds off the strong family ties between them and her sister Rosa (Rossy de Palma). The 'true love' in Leo's latest novel is that of a mother for a daughter.

As Almodóvar explains, it is the mother's voice that 'brings Leo back from the dead. Her voice is like the aroma of a delicious meal simmering in the kitchen that drifts down the corridor to Leo's room and wrests her from her final sleep. Leo hears her mother on the answering machine saying she feels ill, that her blood pressure is high, and she thinks, if I die, my mother will die too' (quoted in Strauss, 2006: 155). In both films, it is the wider community of women and children who secure the main characters' recovery from romantic disappointment. Leo mutters, 'Mamá, mama'. Next to the telephone is a photograph of Rosa and her children. Again there is a parallel with *Mujeres*. The sleeping Pepa and Leo become conscious of the voice on the telephone and respond by getting up frantically. The main difference is that in *Mujeres* spectators are allowed to see Pepa's sleeping body, whereas in *La flor* we are unsure if Leo has died and only see her once she has woken up. The lack of camera movements make these scenes moments of both suspense and reflection.

Leo's return to the village in La Mancha has been interpreted as Almodóvar's desire 'to go back to his roots' (Correa Ulloa, 2005: 106). The status of the countryside, and particularly that of Almodóvar's region, La Mancha, is regularly used to justify a number of critical positions. Spanish critics have used it to distinguish him from the middle-class filmmakers of the 1970s and 1980s (D'Lugo, 2006: 12). D'Lugo refers to one of the earliest studies of Almodóvar's work by Garcia de León and Maldonado, who describe the connotations of these rural aspects in perceptions of Almodóvar. Although their study partakes of the clichés it describes, it is useful to see the rural–urban distinction being made in distinctive middle-class terms. D'Lugo relates what he calls the 'simple correlation between Almodóvar's roots in rural Spain during the second decade of the dictatorship and his later cinematic sensibilities' to a theory usually espoused by film critics outside Spain: 'The clichéd equation between Almodóvar and Spain or Almodóvar and Spanish cinema, made by foreign commentators, is valid, since his biography dramatizes on the individual level the metaphorical migration of Spanish culture toward integration into modern European culture, social practices, and even politics' (2006: 12; 4).

However, the films treat the rural in a more complex way that these narratives of Spain divided into rural-poor-uneducated and urban-sophisticated-European would have us assume. They show cities as composed of a variety of people, many of whom have rural origins regardless of their present social class, but they do not overtly advocate for the movement from the country to the city as an improvement in social conditions. Many of the characters who have migrated to the city – such as the *flamenco-pop* singer in *Pepi*, the family in *¿Qué he hecho?*, Marina and Ricki in *¡Átame!*, Leo's family and Blanca in *La flor*, Víctor's mother in *Carne trémula* (Live Flesh, 1997), and the main characters and their neighbours in *Volver* – struggle to get by. In fact, in *La flor*, Leo's writing supports her mother's home in the country and her sister's family in Parla, a satellite city near Madrid that underwent a huge increase in population in the late 1960s and 1970s due to internal migration from Spanish provinces.

Food is crucial to understand the relationships between these characters, many of whom visit their villages periodically to see relatives and load up on local produce. It also extends to the recurrent nurturing of characters in Almodóvar's films, who feed those they love with traditional dishes (Pepi's cod dish, Pepa's gazpacho, Rosa's squid and cod, Leo's mother's roast peppers). Most of these migrants take many of their rural customs with them to the city whilst others attempt to distance themselves as much as possible from their rural origins.

Leo's and Rosa's homes are paradoxical in this respect. Rosa, arguably the sister who has stayed closer in terms of class to her origins, favours a kitsch baroque aesthetic with furniture that is ostentatious and too large for the space she inhabits. Leo's flat partakes of a Hollywood Baroque aesthetic in its grandiose setting (note the doors, communal stairs, and use of raised flower vases) (Assumpta Serna) but is a much sparser space, mostly crowded with books and plants, with photographs of her husband and a political map of Spain the most obvious decoration. The plants, however, give Leo's origins away, as she uses the mezzanine to re-create a rural *patio* with hanging pots that are carefully tended. The veneer of sophistication present in Leo's wardrobe extends to her home, but details such as these highlight her origins as much as Pepa's chicken coop in *Mujeres* or María Cardenal's Chinchón retreat in *Matador*. This leads me to believe, contrary to D'Lugo's theory discussed above, that without being overt about it until *Los amantes*, Almodóvar's films resist the narrative imposed on them. They are not, and have never been, straightforward representations of a new, modern Spain after Franco's death. Spanish culture may be changing, but these changes are neither as quick as it would seem nor as widespread as it has been implied. The reinscription of a Romantic orientalist geography where rural or traditional Spain is placed firmly outside Europe also seems misguided, as it posits 'modern European culture' as a model to be imitated and tags the 'integration' of 'Spanish culture' as desirable progress. As we shall see further in the discussion of *Los amantes*, Spain's transformation into a 'European' country did not proceed as expected during the Transition.

Almodóvar insists on placing the rural inside urban homes. The fascination of urbanites with Spain's others (see the screaming competition on television that Leo cannot countenance) is an empty distancing gesture that may work somewhat, but the same Leo who thrives in the city also sleeps under an elaborate lace coverlet. This coverlet, on which Leo lies down to die, is as significant as Becky's death in her childhood flat in *Tacones*. Lace is directly linked to Leo's mother through cinematography. When Leo is in bed after fainting on arriving in the village, her mother is shot through lace as she closes the curtains to the sound of church bells, turning to look at Leo and sighing. It is only when she approaches Leo in bed that we see her without the lace 'filter'. Leo's village bed also has a lace coverlet and her bedside lampshades have a lace pattern. Leo's life is in tatters; returning to the village is a chance to recover one's way, and lace (with its repetitive actions, like prayer, and community building use) is the symbol for this. The sound of bobbins moving starts at this scene's close. We only realise what it is as it cuts to lace being made. In fact, the bobbins echo the sound of Leo's typewriter, thus linking both pursuits as the opening credits do in emphasising printed letters as a net.

Lace is also the object that links Leo and the mother to the wider community of women in the village. As Edwards points out, 'rural Spain is presented as a source of emotional recuperation, lacemaking as an image of female solidarity' (2001: 156). But, as the lacemakers' scene shows, the recovery is not achieved by fully immersing in the rural but by using it as a springboard to return to the city and rebuild the self in a safe environment (which in this case is rural, but in other films is not). During the lacemaking scene a recovering Leo sits among the women and asks them for a traditional song about Almagro, a large town in the area renowned for silk lace. Lacemaking in this area was passed on by mothers to daughters, making these tight-knitted communities. This scene could be simply about local customs were it not for Leo's presence among the women in red leggings, white and red pinny, straw hat and Walkman. Leo does not look like someone who can make lace. The chit-chat and song provide entertainment, highlight the aural as important to Leo's relationship with her past and mother, and mark Leo as both outsider and insider. Leo's *faux pas* in asking what is a needle and her scant knowledge of the song's lyrics point to this position. Leo is clearly recovering but a return to the village for good is not an option. Her recovery will be marked by a return to Madrid to start again on her own and a burgeoning relationship with Ángel, a man whose very name highlights his blended masculinity and femininity, as opposed to soldier ex-husband's Paco, a nickname for Francisco, evoking the most notorious military man of all, General Francisco Franco.

Almodóvar may be idealising La Mancha in general in this film, and female solidarity in particular, but instead of returning to a specific place he is 'improving on reality' (Almodóvar, quoted in Strauss, 2006: 158). As he says: 'There is a certain nostalgia in the film, it's true. But I never go back to my childhood village, I've never even shot there. It's a neighbouring village in the film. But there's a kind of idealization of place' (quoted in Strauss, 2006: 162). This 'idealization of place' is certainly not the product of a wish to return, a subject he develops in *Volver*, but of a wish to change reality due to the ambivalent feelings about the region he has left:

> The minute the film arrives in La Mancha, it acquires a charge which is very moving for me and which I didn't expect. I was born in La Mancha, and I lived there for eight years. These years taught me that I didn't like the place, that I didn't want to live there, and that everything I would do in life would be contrary to what I saw in La Mancha: the way of living, thinking, of actually being these people. But, having made the film, I also discovered that I belonged to La Mancha, even though I no longer go there, even though my life represents the opposite of that of an orthodox Manchego. The white streets of the village, the whitewashed walls move me a lot. They were the first streets I saw. (Almodóvar, quoted in Strauss, 2006: 162)

This narrativisation of La Mancha as the place he fled but is still receptive to is typical of Almodóvar. I would not want to assert a correlation between Almodóvar and his character, Leo, however. Leo may feel like Almodóvar, yet we are not told this. What we can see is the difference between her life in the city and life as experienced in the village, and that lack of social connections in the city other than her (soon to be ex-) husband, housekeeper, and one friend have amplified her feelings of loss during the break-up of her marriage. The village with its readymade friendship group of neighbours is presented as a social restorative for Leo, and the 'idealization of place' may be more Leo's than Almodóvar's. After all, Leo is the driver of the narrative and the subjective point of view is normally hers.

This subjective representation of place may also be due to an emphasis on predictable narrative clues. *La flor* is (as is customary in Almodóvar) metacinematic and calls attention to itself as a film. It is also metanarrative, commenting on the film itself as a derivate product of romance and tragedy from the opening credits, which appear on a background of drafts from the film script. This is not only commenting on the film as film, but also on Leo's life as fiction, as emphasised by the use of pathetic fallacy; it rains when Leo misses Paco and the sun shines after she learns that Paco will have some time off work and her review has been accepted by the newspaper.

For critics such as Correa Ulloa, it is tempting to see Leo as Almodóvar's 'alter ego, this time a female one, of a director decided to return to his roots' (2005: 106; my translation). Varderi suggests that Almodóvar's career mirrors that of Leo and talks about a 'clear auto-biographical return to La Mancha through Leo, a writer who needs to go back to her origins to develop a new style and move from the *low* of romance to the *high* of literary fiction' (1996: 212; my translation). However, Leo has already moved away from romance into fiction and completed a novel before her final breakdown and retreat to the country. If one were to look for a biographical link to her new style, it seems that her crumbling relationship with Paco is the likely source. As for Almodóvar, his choice of 'conventional takes' may be due to previous resistance to his experiments with tone but also to a different type of engagement with satire that is less reliant on the 'wild' and the 'exaggerated' and, for this reason, more likely not to be noticed. Leo's is the journey of the artist, not literally in her return to her roots but because she uses writing in a transformative way.

The film dissects Leo's feelings about the end of this relationship from sadness tinged with optimism to despair and, finally, acceptance. Leo's change of genre is not due to her movement from low-brow to high-brow but to a depression fed by the lack of closure in her failed marriage. As the opening credits graphically illustrate, Marisa Paredes' character is stepping out of a personal and artistic crisis that has made her see everything in black. This mock death chimes in with Leo's attempted suicide, her change of genre and breaking of her contract, and the fragility of the rose that symbolises her writing persona, Amanda Gris. The rose that appears in the anthology's cover is realist, but the opening credits show it as a collage that signals the constructedness of Leo's writing persona, romance itself, and the discourse of love. It also points to how easy it is for all these discourses to come apart.

As Almodóvar has noted, Leo's trajectory in dealing with the break-up follows closely that of a person dealing with bereavement:

> *The Flower of My Secret* is a film about pain, about a pain of almost epic proportions. But it isn't an epic film about pain. This pain is the pain

of abandonment, a pain which I believe one feels as physically as death. No matter that for the rest of the world the person who has gone continues to live. For us, the relationship is the same as if they had died. Perhaps the serenity you spoke of arises from the fact of filming pain. (quoted in Strauss, 2006: 160)

Not only does the film explore pain, it also focuses on the repression of that pain through an unconscious refusal to accept reality. A reviewer in *The Washington Post* put it succinctly: Leo 'refuses to face the possibility that her husband ... does not love her' (Anon., 1991: 51). Like the mother in the role-playing scene at the beginning of the film, Leo holds on to the hope that her marriage is not over. It is this journey from refusal to acceptance and partial recovery from loss that the film outlines.

For this reason, the initial training scenes for transplant staff and the 'trope of the brain-dead youth' are neither a 'minor episode', as Marsha Kinder suggests in an otherwise incisive article (2004: 11) nor simply relevant as a precursor of *Todo sobre mi madre* as is commonly believed, but an integral part of the story and its analogy of pain through physical and spiritual loss. Kinder analyses how this opening 'trains us how to read the main plot' (2004: 12) and notes how it tricks the audience into thinking that the role play aimed at reflection and training is the 'main plot'. Whilst this is certainly true and reinforces the film's metacinematic aspects, I would argue that the opening is indeed the beginning of the main plot in a coded way, much like Pina Bausch's performance at the beginning of *Hable con ella* (Talk to Her, 2002) is a prelude and commentary on the film as a whole. The overtly fictional opening points both to our emotional investment in fiction (hence its relevance to Amanda Gris's work and the film as a whole) and to how fiction is and can be used as training for the 'real' world and as a blueprint for how we interpret it. Leo might not be wilfully blind; the romance narratives she writes could be preventing her from seeing into her failed marriage to Paco. Likewise, the mother played by nurse Manuela (Kiti Mánver) during role play cannot understand what the doctors tell her because her son's death does not feature as a possibility in her mind.

Whereas Kinder says that Leo 'is the one who is figuratively comatose' (Kinder, 2004: 13), I would suggest that the marriage is 'comatose' and Leo is in the position of the mother, in denial rather than brain-dead. The film's working title – 'Is there any chance, however small, of saving what we have?' – points to this. Leo also has to accept the transplant of her husband to her friend Betty later on. Although it may seem far-fetched, the mother's pain of losing a child is firmly linked to that of losing a partner through break-up. This perspective is represented by Leo when she talks to Paco about herself as a war victim. Paco, voicing conventional understanding of bereavement as more traumatic than break-up, sees this as exaggerated and selfish. But is Leo in a position to be as detached from the experience as Paco and Betty desire her to be for their own conscience?

Betty does not follow her own professional advice in her dealings with Leo and Paco. First she is caught in an uncomfortable psychologist-friend-lover role with Paco, then she forgets her own advice to fellow professionals: 'it's vital that you don't judge the relative. Pain and fear justify any reaction, even the most offensive.' Instead, she lectures Leo on several occasions on how she should act. She does not apply what she knows about grief to her friend's relationship:

> BETTY   Brain death is hard to explain and to understand. The relative is in the depths of grief. They're ready to grasp at any hope, however small or absurd it may seem. Donation can't be discussed until they have fully understood and accepted the death. It must be explained clearly and tactfully.

Paco and Betty, instead of being clear with Leo, hide behind half-truths. Betty sets up Paco when he calls her at home so that Leo can figure out the situation between them, but Leo is too ready to believe Paco and save her marriage. Betty will only be straight with her friend (I am not sure she is being tactful) after Leo has understood that her marriage is over. Moreover, she makes the same mistake the doctors commit during role play in diminishing the importance of Leo's suffering:

> BETTY   You're not the only woman who has problems with her husband.
> LEO   That's no consolation.

The professional outside grief sees the case as one of many. The bereaved, on the other hand, is experiencing 'the pain of abandonment' rather than thinking about it. What for some is a common occurrence, for the grieving relative is a singular experience:

DOCTOR 1   These things happen every day.
MOTHER   Every day? It's not every day I see my son die.

Brain death and transplants are therefore not as secondary as it could seem.
Likewise, the story of a 'woman who has problems with her husband' appeals to more general issues surrounding grief, as well as puncturing Spain's over-confident self-image in the 1990s. *La flor* achieves this through its veiled satire of the couple and their friends, of the military's new image as protecting human rights in Yugoslavia, and of the ruling socialist government that was eroding worker's rights at the time. *La flor* is a subtle poisoned dart satirising Spain's euphoria at supposedly leaving behind the dictatorship and Transition. It is no coincidence that Paco is in charge of a peace-keeping mission abroad whilst advocating repression and censorship at home. Neither is it surprising that the disintegrating middle-class couple is sometimes so stylised as to suggest self-parody. Fouz-Hernández and Martínez-Expósito suggest as much when they state that Leo and Paco partake of transvestism:

> But the more encompassing and 'unlimited' sort of transvestism that J. Smith illustrates, amongst other scenes, with the moment ... (1996 [sic]) when husband and wife dress up (fetishized masculinity in his military uniform, iconic femininity in her formal dress) for a re-encounter that has been ritualistically turned into a performance, is, in fact, present everywhere in Almodóvar's films as a matter of style. (2007: 154)

Just as in previous films, the slightly over-emphasised roles open up the film to an analysis using Foucauldian notions of subjection to discourses of power in relation to romantic love, masculinity, and femininity. The use of colour in the flat, for example, matches Leo's and Paco's characters. The space where they are most affectionate, the corridor and lobby, are warm, whereas the bedroom, bathroom, Leo's study, and most significantly the external door and stairs are all painted in blue or grey. Blue-grey is also the colour of the glass-bead picture frame that Leo shatters as she throws a photograph of herself and Paco kissing. This frame is associated with masculinity in its alignment with Paco's green-grey uniform and opposition to Leo's red dress. It also signals the precarious nature of the couple's

relationship, held together by a cold, fragmented frame. This fragmentation is replicated in the couple's disjointed reflection in the
lobby mirror. The tiff about the paella is also revealing; Paco complains that it
is cold to Leo's aside, 'I'm not'. The kitchen is the most ambiguous
space, full of Blanca's warmth and painted in a tone similar to that of
the lobby. Leo's efforts are dampened by Paco's intransigence despite
a fleeting smile on his face when he sees the food. The literal meaning
of cold paella is obvious, but in Spanish *pásarsele el arroz a alguien*
(someone's rice has become overdone) also connotes a missed opportunity, being too old (or too late) to do something. It is a clear reference
to the couple's missed opportunities in repairing their relationship
but also perhaps an allusion to their childlessness (the expression is
commonly and crudely used to refer to women beyond fertility age).

Almodóvar started shooting the film with this key scene (Almodóvar,
quoted in Smith, 2014: 175) not just for the main plot but also for the
style of the film overall, including the use of hyperrealism to 'recover
the Technicolor of the 1950s present in the films of my childhood'
(Almodóvar, quoted in Varderi, 1996: 211; my translation). Paco and
Leo are playing at husband and wife, man and woman, soldier and
writer, as part of a display of performative middle-classness, a performance that in Leo's case slips repeatedly because of her pain and in
Paco's does not but is used in a passive-aggressive way. If Leo resembles Pepa (*Mujeres*), Paco is another Iván. Whilst Iván hid under the
pretence that he did not want to hurt Pepa's feelings, Paco flees to
Brussels and constructs a narrative of national solidarity to avoid confronting Leo. Whilst the film can be interpreted as a straight drama,
these aspects lead to a more ironic treatment of the material. As
Edwards states in relation to *Tacones*: 'Detractors of the film have sarcastically alluded to Almodóvar as an interior decorator, but they fail
to understand that the beautiful surfaces of *High Heels* are intended
to create a contrast to the passions that rage in the hearts of the characters, as well as to suggest, much as Buñuel does in many films,
that bourgeois life is a façade' (2001: 135–6). This adds rather than
detracts from *La flor*'s impact, although it is true that it can also make
it easier to ignore the film's critique of contemporary Spain. Varderi
views the style negatively:

> The alleged seriousness of the flamenco dance by Joaquín Cortés dis-
> places Andalusian folklore to ridiculousness given its lack of context.

This is the opposite effect to the one Cortés produces in *Flamenco* (1995) by Carlos Saura.

Similarly, the potentially transgressive and censoring power towards the socialist government [of the time] that lies behind the student protest as the first overt expression of a political conscience in Pedro Almodóvar's cinema disappears in favour of a purely aesthetic effect. (1996: 212; my translation)

Varderi is right to note the decontextualisation of contemporary *flamenco*-inspired dance in the film that turns 'seriousness' into 'ridiculousness'. When considered alongside gender exaggeration, use of stereotyped occupations such as the military and genres such as romance and drama, it is obvious that the film is mocking contemporary Spain's recycling of old (frequently orientalist) stereotypes in an attempt to position itself as a modern European state. The dance scene performed by Blanca and her son (played by internationally famous dancer Joaquín Cortés) is a postmodern ending to a show called *Una soleá apoteósica*, a spectacular *soleá*. An apotheosis is also the ending of a light show, and the *soleá*, in this case Miles Davis's music, is at the same time the ending and the self-referential comment about the show. The title is hyperbolic and the dancing physical, beautiful yet slightly overdone. The characterisation contrasts with that of the dancers at either side of the stage in more traditional *flamenco* costumes and the final virtuoso *zapateado* (dance associated with *flamenco*, similar to tap) by Cortés is both a reference to his trademark steps and a comment on how Andalusian folklore has been updated for modern consumption in Spain and abroad. As in other occasions, the show is both a reinforcement and critique of traditional orientalist stereotypes about Spain.

The film's aesthetic adds to rather than detracts from its 'transgressive and censoring power', going beyond single political points (the student protest reminiscent of the 1990s protests by student doctors) to encompass not just the political establishment but also how Spain is mining European Romantic orientalist folklore to position itself both within and outside Europe. The seemingly joyful protesters' ditties against the president of the time, Felipe González, and their jibes about how Spanish youth is being 'shafted' every which way are not only effective as a summary of the political context at the time (particularly if one remembers the real student protests) but sadly they remain relevant even today. Spanish youth and workers as a whole are the forgotten victims of successive governments' squandering of resources and vanity projects. The students chant that Felipe will have to heal the flu, a sarcastic remark made even more so by the film's use of Spain's success at organ transplant. The doctors we see at the beginning were once students. Leo and the protesters have been forgotten by Paco and the government respectively. The white gowns do create a beautiful background, but it is also a medical background where Leo is supported by Ángel, a background where leaflets resemble snow in a cold winter sun against blue skies and bare trees, a whiteness also pointing to the sanitary ware prominent in Leo and Paco's love language. This final link is emphasised by Leo's collapse on seeing the advert 'Te quiero a ti. Roca' (I love you. Roca) in a shop window. The dot on the i has been replaced by a red heart as Leo's red hat is barely seen among the white gowns. White rocks are also a clear reference to Leo's name. Although 'leo' literally means 'I read', it is a shortening of Leocadia, a name whose etymology is Greek, meaning the one who looks after her people (as Leo does) or the one who comes from Laucade, Laucade being an island with white rocks. As Faulkner suggests, the 'tilting crane shot ... lifts the image, and our attention, up and away from the workers in order – problematically perhaps – to continue the narrative focus on Leo's emotional slide' (2013: 213).

Although *La flor* looks at first like a departure from Almodóvar's distinctive aesthetic and exploration of sensitive political and social topics, it is not. The film is markedly different in tone from his comedies but satire and irony continue to support its metamodern attack on social discourses around love, gender, and social inequality. Ryan Prout analyses how in *La flor* and *Todo sobre mi madre* (All about My Mother, 1999) 'the fictional transplant dramas ... can be read as depictions of Spanish identity' (2004: 45), seeing transplants as framing national identity as a success story. This is also true of international contemporary *flamenco*-inspired dance such as Cortés's and the participation of Spain in peace-keeping missions such as the one in Yugoslavia. *La flor* attacks all three success stories. The large political map of Spain showing its autonomous regions that presides over Leo and Paco's bedstead witnesses the couple's final break-up as Leo accuses Paco of 'volunteer[ing] for the Peace Mission to escape the reality [in the original, the war] you had to face here'.[1] The end of the discourse of romance with the dissolution of the couple and dispersion of the glass balls that form the picture frame are a not-too-guarded allusion to the civil tensions within the Spanish state. It reminds me of another, small and less-defined, map on the shower curtain in the background when Ricki and Marina get together in *¡Átame!* (cf. Acevedo-Muñoz, 2007: 129). If, as Acevedo-Muñoz says, 'the essence of Almodóvar's aesthetics has always been ... the desire to make logic out of chaos, and to rebuild the family and the nation out of its own fragmentation and the trauma of the past' (2007: 7), *La flor* shows us how the post-Transition system that kept the main discourses of the nation in place is not working.

There is a guarded warning about this in the film, as Leo visits Ángel at the daily newspaper *El País*, founded in 1976 (only a year after Franco's death) and closely associated with socialist ideology. *El País* (the title means, the country) is a symbol of Spanish Transition. In the film, an establishing shot makes explicit it is *El País* Leo visits. Ángel and an incidental character (Agustín Almodóvar) admire the printing press, saying:

ÁNGEL   This is the place I love most.
CHAR.   It's like the heart and the arteries.
ÁNGEL   If this doesn't work *El País* doesn't work.
CHAR.   And even if it worked, it doesn't ...

The double meaning of 'El País' as a newspaper and the country is put to good use in this dialogue, where the editor could be referring to both and the other character seems to talk about the country not working well. This ambiguity has been lost in translation, as the English subtitles have Ángel refer to the newspaper explicitly. As Prout explains, 'the exchange is important because it establishes somatization of the nation state within which the media (especially the print media) are established as being the lifeblood of Spain's national identity and where, in turn, seemingly chance remarks about the relationship between parts of the body and nationality assume a greater significance' (2004: 50). Prout sees this exchange in a positive light, but the final remark disrupts the link between the press and the idea of a democratic country. The incidental character doubts that the country works well despite the newspaper doing so. For this reason, I would go beyond Prout's analysis to suggest that this scene directly identifies Spain with the brain-dead patient, whose (democratic) body seems to be working smoothly thanks to machinery (oxygenation in the case of the teenager, alleged free press and democracy in

Spain) but is actually dead. Thus, although the *Organización Nacional de Transplantes* 'seems to be a living testament to the new Spain of democratized power' (Prout, 2004: 54), it is also one of a number of discourses of democratisation and success that Spain was telling itself at the time, even as it is clear that such Europeanisation and modernisation are mostly aesthetic. In *Los amantes*, Almodóvar goes further to show idle conveyor belts and an empty airport, a clear sign that oxygenation machines have been switched off on the country.

Note

1 Autonomous regions were mentioned in the 1978 constitution but not formalised until 1981 and 1992 with the agreement of the two main political parties in Spain, Partido Popular (PP) and Partido Socialista Obrero Español (PSOE). These include four historical nations (Andalusia, the Basque country, Catalonia, and Galicia), as well as a number of other regions.

9

Circle lines and memory work:
Carne trémula

Carne trémula (Live Flesh, 1997) was seen as a change in direction
for Almodóvar in three ways. First, it is an adaptation from a novel,
the eponymous thriller by Ruth Rendell. Second, it was, as José
Arroyo pointed out, 'his "straightest" yet – camp figures less than in
his other films and, interestingly, not to *Carne trémula*'s disadvan-
tage' (1998: 51). Finally, the film is often interpreted as an explicitly
political work and as a clear break with Almodóvar's previous non-
engagement with Spain's past and the dictatorship in particular
(Allinson, 2001; Arroyo, 1998; Correa Ulloa, 2005; Smith, 2014).
Carne trémula includes a muted opening with a black-and-white scene
where a woman is rushed to hospital to give birth during a State
of Emergency, allegedly in 1970 (I will discuss dating inaccuracies
below), and ends with another similar situation in late 1990s Spain as
the main character's voice-over comments on Spain's improved socio-
political circumstances. Vibrant colours only appear gradually, as the
film moves to the present and Spain moves from dictatorship to the
period after the Transition in the mid-1990s. This may be a filmic reference to dark Spain during the dictatorship and to the muted palette
of left-wing Spanish filmmakers. It also corresponds to the film's *noir*
style that privileges volume and shadows unlike pop's flat, colourful
surfaces. The appearance of colour in *Carne trémula* corresponds to
the supposed improvement of the characters' lives, but it is checked
by its obvious artificiality and the depth created by lighting.

The film's obvious reference to and engagement with historical past is, however, not straightforward. Although *Carne trémula*
seems to open with historical fact – the decree declaring the *Estado
de Excepción* (State of Emergency) by Manuel Fraga, the Francoist
Minister of Information and Tourism (who was still active in politics

in the 1990s and founded the conservative Partido Popular (PP)) – things are not quite what they seem. As Steven Marsh points out:

> historical reference in this film, in spite of its assertions of accurate realism, is far from precise. Such claims are founded upon the documentation (the on-screen reproduction of the original decree declaring the State of Emergency) and in the genuine radio broadcast blaring out in Doña Centro's living room. ... The opening sequence is fraught with exacting verisimilitude and yet the year is wrong. Almodóvar is mistaken. The State of Emergency to which the radio announcement refers ran from January to March of the previous year, 1969, before it was discontinued. ... One can only speculate as to the reasons why Almodóvar chose 1970, but it is intriguing that his one contribution to analysis of national teleology should be factually flawed. (2004: 57)

The decree cited in the film is from 24 January 1969. The wrong date could simply be a typo since it is unthinkable that the researchers who must have had to look up the original document to quote it and find the radio broadcast would not know when it was issued. It is likely, however, that the date has been altered on purpose, just as the text of the decree has been modified slightly to emphasise the government's actions and strip it of Francoist rhetoric. For example, the original decree claims that 'the defence of peace and progress and Spaniards' right to exercise their rights, unanimously desired by all sectors of society, has forced the government to ...' (Spain, 1969; my translation), but the film elides the reference to how the government is merely 'defen[ding] peace and progress' as 'desired by all sectors of society'. Much of the institutional language of decrees, present in the radio broadcast, is excised and the next section of text – ostensibly still between inverted commas to denote a faithful quotation – keeps to the spirit of the decree but not the letter, explaining what articles of the law were suspended, which are only cited numerically in the original decree. The main ideas are further emphasised by highlighting words and phrases successively. This way of setting out the historical context is effective but not as accurate as it leads viewers to believe. As we will see, this is not the only historical inaccuracy in the film. I point these out not to lay charges of inauthenticity at Almodóvar but to move the debate beyond 'accurate realism' to how the film appropriates and reconfigures the past, as much as it re-creates Rendell's novel, for its own purposes.

The opening of *Carne trémula* reconstructs the past, replacing memories that simulate first-hand experience. This has been called 'prosthetic memory'. As Pam Cook explains, exercises in 'prosthetic memory'

> lay themselves open to charges of lack of authenticity, of substituting a popular version for the 'real' event, and to accusations that presenting history as dramatic spectacle they obscure our understanding of social, political and cultural forces. ... Yet, in the very act of addressing audiences as nostalgic spectators and encouraging them to become involved in re-presenting the past, the media invites exploration and interrogation of the limits of its engagement with history. (2005: 2)

The pre-credits sequence in *Carne trémula* appeals to nostalgia in its use of period props such as the post box and bus, but it also undermines it through camp, humour, and parody. Madame Centro's (Pilar Bardem) humorous asides and dramatic actions are one of the main features of the sequence. For example, when the bus driver tells her 'Are you crazy, or what? I could have killed you!' she retorts matter-of-factly 'These high heels will kill me.' The situation is made worse by the deserted streets of Madrid during the State of Emergency, but Centro (meaning centre and also focused and keeping calm) relies on her wit to deliver her friend Isabel (Penélope Cruz) safely and the comic tone ensures that the audience does not fear for the characters.

The use of Christmas lights as constructed counterpoint to the dire social situation highlights the façade of normality under the State of Emergency. Note, for example, the workers removing the bulbs from the star at the beginning and the clearly artificial setting of Víctor's birth. The incongruous lights, as well as the beautifully lit monuments of Madrid with a Happy Christmas sign, heighten the sense of overexposure to fake happiness. The Christmas lights also cite one of the most memorable scenes of a popular film of the dictatorship, Fernando Palacios's *La gran familia* (The Big Family, 1962), a comic drama about a large lower-middle-class family's struggle to make ends meet. This film has been seen as political propaganda from the regime as it depicts an idealised, happy family. The Christmas market scene shows the younger boy getting lost and his family's search for him and it starts with a low-angle shot of a Christmas star in the night sky over the now closing market.

In *Carne trémula*, the link to Francoist investment in the family is reinforced by the jolly voice-over from a fake *NoDo* (the dictatorship's newsreel) announcing Víctor's birth just as the title of the film appears. This is the type of feel-good story that would have been used in the highly censored news, but the closing prediction that the young child would have 'a life on wheels' proves not to be true in a Spain that is no longer a dictatorship but where miscarriages of justice for those who are poor can still happen. The parody of the *NoDo* shows Isabel being visited by city dignitaries to appear in the news and showered with presents for the child, but also two stern nuns (nuns ran many Spanish hospitals at the time) and two gossipy middle-class wives looking on disapprovingly. All these features point to a conscious undermining of nostalgia in something similar to what Annette Kuhn calls 'memory work', only using a simulated past rather than a photograph: 'memory work is a conscious and purposeful performance of memory' (2002: 157). Kuhn's ideas on 'memory work' provide a different way of thinking about the historical sequence as it can be seen as a way of thinking about the present:

> Besides in its nature referring to events which cannot be retrieved or fully relived, then, remembering appears to demand no necessary witness, makes no insistence on the presence of the rememberer at the original scene of the recollected event. Remembering is clearly an activity that takes place for, as much as in, the present. Is memory then not understood better as a position or a point of view in the current moment than as an archive or a repository of bygones? Perhaps memory offers a constantly changing perspective on the places and times through which we – individually and collectively – have been journeying? Perhaps it is only when we look back that we make a certain kind of sense of what we see? (2002: 128)

It is significant that Isabel sends Víctor a photograph of herself holding him as a young child and a newspaper cutting of the news about his birth when she learns that she has cancer, saying that Víctor had asked to have them repeatedly. Víctor carries those around in his Bible, just as Ricki carries a photograph of himself as a child with his parents in *¡Átame!* (Tie Me Up, Tie Me Down, 1989). Víctor is full of questions for his mother when he visits her grave and is keen to figure out the extent of her maternal sacrifice in being a prostitute for his sake. Curiously, in Almodóvar's next film *Todo sobre mi madre* (All about My Mother, 1999), Esteban (Eloy Azorín) asks his mother, Manuela (Cecilia Roth), 'Would you prostitute yourself for me?' But Isabel Plaza Caballero's grave offers no answers. Ricki is also drawn to his parents' old house. Víctor and Ricki are trying to form their own families, but by doing so they are also trying to understand their own family history. Memory influences our present and vice versa, and this works for personal and collective identities. Both Ricki and Víctor are rebuilding their lives after traumatic events, just as Spanish people were finding their way and Spain was creating a narrative of new Spanishness during the Transition. Víctor and Ricki are optimistic about their future and, like *¡Átame!*, *Carne trémula* ends (perhaps too) positively.

Overall, *Carne trémula* seems to buy into the narrative of Spain moving beyond the dictatorship and becoming a modern country, albeit with hiccups such as Víctor's wrongful conviction. Ultimately, its form contradicts this superficial optimism. The late 1990s saw the beginning of the large housing bubble that made the current financial crisis worse in Spain, but the optimism of those years is reflected in the evening Christmas shopping scene at the end of the film. Colourful Christmas lights are reflected on the windscreen. In contrast to this opulence, the star is also present, but as part of a makeshift nativity at the orphanage. Víctor's optimism and his comparison between his birth and that of his son twenty-six years later form part of the narrative of progress dominant in Spain until the 2008 financial crisis.

Víctor's comments about everyone being at home watching the Spain versus Malta football match should warn us against Víctor's complacency. Most Spaniards born in the mid-1970s or earlier would remember the famous Spain–Malta match, not in 1996 but in December 1983, when Spain won 12–1 to qualify for the 1984 European Championships. The obvious socio-political improvements noted by Víctor seem dampened by the mention of football, the nation's most popular sport (which Almodóvar dislikes). Thus, the link between direct violence exercised by the totalitarian state and cultural violence employed to prevent the population from questioning the system is present despite Víctor's optimism and the fact that the traffic jam suddenly disappears. The film's scrutiny of post-Transition Spain (during which Víctor is unfairly convicted in 1984) and contemporary Spain points to a more problematic take on historical memory and the widely accepted narrative about Spain's exemplary Transition from dictatorship to democracy. Smith sees Víctor as 'the embodiment of a national narrative whose grand theme is reminiscent of a nineteenth-century novel: the definitive shift from dictatorship to democracy' (Smith, 2014: 185). This optimism seemed justified in the late 1990s, but Almodóvar – whether intentionally or not – inserts enough warnings for audiences not to get carried away.

As Morgan-Tamosunas states, 'the surface optimism of the narrative closure is disturbed by an almost obsessive structural and stylistic emphasis on circularity' (2002: 186). Circularity recurs in latter Almodóvar films and can nearly always be traced back to personal and social trauma. Marsh explains that 'Almodóvar does not break with the past – indeed, in this film he disavows discontinuity – instead he seeks to produce a kind of simultaneity that emerges in the seemingly immobile forms of monuments and masculinities; in doing so he destabilizes (or displaces) both of them.' (2004: 59). Whereas Víctor espouses linear progression in his final address to his unborn child (a reflection on his past and the past of Spain, which begins diegetically but becomes a more traditional voice-over typical of *film noir*), the circular structure of the plot encourages 'simultaneity'. Thus, the voice-over seems at best misguided. Víctor's statement about Spain is deeply ironic.

The historical reference, *noir* elements, and practical disappearance of camp in *Carne trémula* offer a clue to the changing social and political situation in Spain, but not necessarily straightforwardly. It is true that Almodóvar has been increasingly outspoken since the mid-1990s, particularly when the conservative PP has held power, a party originally called Alianza Popular, which was founded in 1976 by top Francoists including Fraga Iribarne – the Francoist minister quoted at the beginning of the film – and closely linked to the ideology and establishment of the dictatorship. Those encountering Almodóvar in the twenty-first century may be surprised to hear that for decades he insisted on his apoliticism and rejected the idea of engaging with the dictatorship. For example, in a 1988 interview in *Paris Match* he said: 'I don't even want to allow the memory of Francoism to exist in my films' (quoted in Martínez-Vasseur, 2005: 109; my translation). Smith relates the overt politics of *Carne trémula* to the rise to power of the PP for the first time in Spain's new democracy: 'The Almodóvar who has protested for almost twenty years that Spaniards can hardly remember a Dictatorship that has no resonance for his youthful audience, here bravely assumes his country's history and dares to speak on behalf of a nation that is now ruled by a rightist government' (2014: 185). The 1996 PP victory is key in terms of national narrative as it marks the perception of Spain as having successfully completed the Transition to democracy with the election of a conservative government for the first time since the dictatorship. Spain was finally seen as a country with full democratic credentials. This image was at play with the 1992 Barcelona Olympics and features in *Carne trémula* as a signifier of the country moving on whilst Víctor is in jail. The film, however, undermines these narratives, using *noir* to create suspicion of authority and social structures during the Transition, structures that are seen to still work for untrustworthy policemen and include a failing justice system (Víctor's imprisonment for a crime he did not commit, Sancho's impunity, and Clara's defencelessness against domestic abuse) and the social exclusion of Víctor and his mother as opposed to the privileges of Helena. Writing on the historical period of *noir* in the USA, Paul Schrader explains that the end of the war and Depression meant that the film industry was released from the need to keep 'people's spirits up' and 'promote patriotism' (1972: 9). Although the USA and Spanish contexts and periods are different, Spain's optimistic national narrative of the late 1990s has similarly freed Almodóvar to explore the country's past and uncertain future in a more sombre way, despite the use of camp in the pre-credits sequence. The use of *noir* therefore makes sense, as generically *Carne trémula* is doing for Spanish society what *noir* generally did in 1940s USA, as well as partaking in *noir*'s exploration of masculinity.

The film centres on a miscarriage of justice and highlights the structural violence that still pervades Spanish society during the Transition period. It emphasises distrust of authority, suspicion, and deceit, as well as casting doubt on the ethics of the actions of its main characters, making much of it in line with the dominant aesthetics of *film noir*. As Tatjana Pavlović states, '[t]he sense of fatalism is reinforced through *film noir* elements: shootings, births, deaths, violence, revenge. In addition, *Carne Trémula* enacts a cycle of ironic and tragic commerce: lovers, wives and entire lives are exchanged' (2006: 164). One of the most obvious features of *noir*, high contrast, is present in key scenes, particularly the pre-credits scene and the run-up to the first shootout in Helena's flat but also during key moments such as the sex scenes and the second shootout. Pam Cook and Mieke Bernink summarise Place and Peterson's (1974) elements of *noir* thus:

> *noir*'s chiaroscuro 'low-key lighting' which eschews softening filters and gauzes and 'opposes light and darkness, hiding faces, rooms, urban landscapes – and by extension, motivations and true characters – in shadow and darkness'. ... [N]oir's *mise-en-scène* 'designed to unsettle, jar, and disorient the viewer in correlation with the disorientation felt by the noir heroes'. Typically, they argue, noir is distinguished by the use of 'claustrophobic framing devices' which separate characters from each other, unbalanced compositions with shutters or banisters casting oblique shadows or placing grids over faces and furniture, 'obtrusive and disturbing' close-ups juxtaposed with extreme high-angle shots which make the protagonist look like 'a rat in a trap'. Overall, the visual style of *noir* described by Place and Peterson amounts to a disorientating anti-realism which exists in opposition to the harmonious *blanc* world of the realist film. (2004: 185)

Carne trémula combines scenes with *noir* elements, realist scenes (such as the basketball celebrations, day scenes in Madrid, and some of the care home scenes), and scenes where 'the harmonious *blanc* world of the realist film' is challenged through other means including (as in *Kika*, 1993) colourful, artificial sets such as David and Helena's flat. The beginning and end also partake of a fabulist tradition that includes the story of Jesus' birth at Christmas and is obvious in Víctor's storytelling to his unborn child. As well as *chiaroscuro*, the film contains unsettling *mise-en-scène*, most notably in Helena's parental home with confusing layout, dark entrance hall where dark paintings dominate the background, stairs with wrought-iron banister, and entrance doors where the policemen's doubling shadows foretell Sancho's animosity towards David (the gun in Sancho's shadow points to the nape of David's shadow on the wall). The *mise-en-scène* at Víctor's shanty in La Ventilla neighbourhood is also initially disorienting.

'Claustrophobic framing devices' are also present throughout, including shot-reverse shots of David and Helena with the 'ban-nister casting oblique shadows [and] placing grids over faces' (the semi-circular shadow over David's face foreshadows his dependence on a wheelchair); a shot of Clara through a red flower wreath at the grave of Helena's father, also foreshadowing her death; framing that shows Sancho and David at loggerheads visually in the police car and Helena's flat; and the notable shot between Víctor's legs in the final shootout as Sancho holds Clara's hand to lift the handgun seemingly towards Víctor, only to turn it against himself. The circle (the revolver's muzzle) and triangle (legs) in the composition are recurring shapes in a film that emphasises circularity in both temporal and spatial terms, including the repetition of events and situations (shootouts, love triangles, parental deaths, and the choice to commit a crime or not), the wheels of buses, motorbike, and wheelchairs, the idea that Víctor is stuck in a life written for him due to his humble origins signified by his aimless travel on the circular bus line, and the recurrence of Madrid landmarks such as the roundabout with the Puerta de Alcalá monument (Víctor's birth and his first appearance as a young man) or the KIO towers by his home.

The circle is associated with inescapable fate and to the wheel of fortune in Greek and Roman mythology (the Greek goddess Tyche and its Roman equivalent Fortuna are frequently represented with a wheel, and Tyche wears a mural crown to represent cities). The protagonist is shown as an easy target by the target-shaped rug at Helena's father's flat. Concentric circles mark the spot where the young Víctor, unaware of his fate, stops on hearing Helena's voice. Víctor has been hit by Cupid's arrow and in wooing upper-class Helena seals his fate. Red concentric circles are also associated with Clara (earrings, wreath), the other character who consistently loses out due to social structures, in this case patriarchal ones that lock her in an abusive marriage and lead to her murder by Sancho. The final shootout highlights the rings that bind her, the wedding bands that both she and Sancho wear are emphasised through their glinting in the close-up of their interlocked hands around the revolver. It seems like a deliberate choice as Sancho's ring is on his left hand as it should be, but Clara's has been placed on her right hand instead so that both rings appear in the shot.

Smith identifies circularity as key to the film:

> The structural device here is the circle: the son becomes a father, the daughter a mother. Born, as we have seen, on a bus, the baby Víctor is presented in a mischievous black and white parody of the *NoDo* or Francoist newsreel with a lifelong bus pass which we will use to travel Madrid's own circle line. The revolving wheels of the bus and wheelchair match the illuminated star decorations to which Almodóvar's

camera tilts up in the opening sequence and from which it tilts down at the close. Circularity is even built into the casting. (2014: 185–6)

Smith's is a perceptive exposition of the multi-layered use of circularity to structure the film. In his keenness to tie the thematic to style, however, he would have the camera tilting down at the end of the film when in fact it stays up looking down at the busy street. Even during the final credits, the camera tilts up again to show the Christmas star from the pre-credits sequence. The circle is complete, but the camera stays up, not down. This is significant as the upward movement complements Víctor's nostalgic optimism as it echoes the endings of religious films such as *Marcelino pan y vino* (The Miracle of Marcelino, Vajda, 1954) and contributes to the gentle ending of the film, which Almodóvar has called 'a Christmas tale', adding: 'I hate Christmas, but I like Christmas tales, especially if they are very sad' (quoted in Correa Ulloa, 2005: 115; my translation).

The triangle (and the cross, which shapes four triangles as in the wire netting in Helena and David's apartment) is also ubiquitous, not least in the numerous unbalanced compositions but also geographically as Víctor moves along important avenues in Madrid (cf. Marsh, 2004) in triangular routes with the Puerta de Alcalá and the Puerta de Europa as vertexes. The latter building is also known as the KIO towers and 'nicknamed by Madrid wags – as a phallic symbol – "*las entrepiernas*" (the crotch)' (Marsh, 2004: 59) and is the building with a cross on its façade that dominates Víctor's neighbourhood. As Marsh explains, 'Víctor is a victim of the initial rivalry between Sancho and David. He not only lives provisionally in-between the two towers of La Puerta de Europa, he also operates in-between the times of the two rival policemen and, significantly, he cuckolds both of them; Víctor infiltrates their masculine space' (2004: 59). Whilst Víctor may be seen as a victim initially, by the end he has succeeded in (re)creating a family with Helena and his life is materially and emotionally secure. Sancho and Clara have become victims of rivalry, this time between Víctor and David, for Helena. Víctor's legs are not those of a victim but of a man who resists what must be a strong desire to shoot the person responsible for his imprisonment, someone who says that women do not belong to men, no longer seeing them as objects to be possessed by men as he did at the beginning of the film. Víctor's victory comes with self-control in the face of social structures stacked against him. He wins by not giving in to direct violence. Víctor is almost too good to be true, just as the democratic Spain he depicts at the end of the film and his marriage to Helena. Smith points to the contradictory nature of the film:

> Surprisingly, then, this stylistic circularity gives way to a faith in linearity, even progress: both Spain and Víctor are decidedly different and better at the end of the film than they were at the beginning. And so, Almodóvar, proclaimed for so long as the quintessential postmodernist, seems to have rediscovered not only masculinity, in his newly tough and tender male characters, but also modernity. (Smith, 2014: 186)

The surprise that Smith alludes to can only come to those who frame Almodóvar's work firmly within postmodernism and pop aesthetics. However, Almodóvar favours content over form from the beginning of his career, even as the content is expressed with a style that fits a postmodern aesthetic. The combination of typically postmodern and modern traits is analysed in relation to Almodóvar's use of pastiche, and Buñuel in particular, by Sidney Donnell, who argues that Almodóvar 'embrac[es] postmodernism and some aspects of post-structuralist thought without abandoning story-telling and its ability to help him communicate historical truths' (2001: 64). The balance between modernist and postmodernist frames is not always tipped consistently, and the ambiguous ending of *Carne trémula* is a wonderful example of this. Even as the 'faith in linearity, even progress' is undermined by the structural irony, the social critique is not lost. In recent years, this use of postmodern aesthetics with a different, ethical intent has been defined as 'metamodernism' (Vermeulen and van den Akker, 2010).

Víctor's positioning between the historical Puerta de Alcalá and the postmodern Puerta de Europa tells a similar story. Besides being a symbol for masculinity, the actual name of the KIO towers – the door to Europe – points to aspirational Spain, celebrating its new-found place in the European Economic Community. They are a symbol of (post)modernity and capitalism as they were financed by the Kuwait Investment Office (KIO) and are the headquarters of a bank. However, they are also associated by most Spaniards who remember the 1990s with fraud on a large scale; they are now seen as a symbol of what is wrong with Spain's financial sector as they are owned by Bankia, a banking conglomerate formed in 2010 and the source of several political corruption and fraud scandals that have even seen

9.1 Establishing shot of Víctor's neighbourhood, dominated by one of the KIO towers (*Carne trémula*, 1997)

a former PP minister convicted of embezzlement. The KIO towers are thus a powerful visual symbol of a divided Spain where a corrupt establishment takes everything from those less privileged. It is fitting that Víctor lives in the neighbourhood of La Ventilla, which, as the film shows, was expropriated by the state to build a main avenue and better housing around the towers.

The composition of the establishing shot of Víctor's neighbourhood is dominated by triangular shapes. The low-angle shot already encourages a triangular set up, while the grey, oblique railing guides the gaze towards one of the KIO towers with the huge cross in the right-centre of the frame. To the far right, only a limbo-like grey sky is seen (Figure 9.1).

The camera tracks right to show the derelict neighbourhood of La Ventilla and Víctor picking his way to his mother's shantie. Unbalanced compositions are also typical of *noir*, but this time a low-angle shot replaces the more common high angle of *noir*. The entrapment effect, however, is similar, with the low-angle shot having the advantage that it also makes unbalanced social structures and thus 'structural violence' apparent. Whereas it would seem that class is primarily at stake here, gender inequality is also at play. Clara makes the relationship clear when she first compares the neighbourhood with war-torn Sarajevo, later stating that she knew she would 'end up like this neighbourhood, expropriated and destroyed'. Clara is the body bearing the brunt of masculine confrontation, a live geographical space.

Carne trémula has its fair share of high- and low-angle shots. Beginning with the pre-credits scene featuring low- and high-angle shots and the high-angle shots of Víctor on Helena's circular rug, of Helena looking back as she escapes during the first shootout, and Víctor exercising in prison, *Carne trémula* also uses a high angle during some sex scenes, particularly Víctor and Helena's and at the very end.

Norberto Alcover considers the use of Rendell's novel 'an excuse' and the historical framing of the film to record change in Spanish society a gimmick that has nothing to do with the main thriller (1998: 189; my translation). Whilst it is true that Almodóvar's adaptations reimagine source materials substantially and *Carne trémula* is far removed from the novel, it is a masterly adaptation as reinterpretation. Novel and film share characters and the main plot driver in the shootout where Victor, an intruder who is holding a woman hostage, shoots policeman David, who, as a result, is paralysed (cf. Willem, 2002). Both deal with the aftermath of the shootout.

Paul Julian Smith claims that *Carne Trémula* meets some fidelity parameters:

> this opening scene is very similar in the book and the film, with the proviso that Almodóvar's version greatly increases its density and intensity. For Almodóvar, unlike Rendell, integrates the plot by making the girl at the stakeout (Elena) (sic) fall in love with the wounded policeman (David); and, thinking visually as ever, Almodóvar does not limit himself like Rendell to the single viewpoint of the young, psychotic Victor, but rather cross-cuts between the perspectives of the five characters, assembling an intimate and intricate collage. (2014: 182)

Smith refers to the opening scene of the book and what was the opening of the film for a while but was postponed to the third scene. The first shootout is the key to both film and novel. Its result is the same (David is paralysed by a bullet shot by Víctor), but the film's different take on Víctor's guilt and its determination to keep his innocence hidden from spectators and characters alike results in different choices regarding point of view and storyline. Mark Allinson notes the similarities and, crucially, differences between film and novel:

> Some elements are almost perfectly transposed: the garage which contains the furniture that represents Victor's past becomes the dilapidated

house in La Ventilla; both in the novel and the film, David clasps at the
banister as he is shot down by Victor's bullet. Beyond these parallels,
the way in which Almodóvar adapts Rendell's novel says much about
Almodóvar's attitude to genre and to his characters. Where the crime
novelist subjugates her characters to the needs of the plot, Almodóvar
gives full integrity to his characters at the expense of generic integrity.
Even the title is given a markedly different interpretation. Rendell's live
flesh – Chorea, a medical twitch, and a metaphor for Victor Jenner's
psychosis – becomes a metaphor for weak and easily tempted flesh in
Almodóvar. Rendell makes Victor virtually a psychopath; he deludes
himself that he was provoked by David's insistence that the gun was
fake. Almodóvar makes Víctor truly a victim of circumstance. (2001:
152–3)

Almodóvar's *Carne trémula* is a perfect example of what Linda
Hutcheon calls 'adaptation as process' (2006: 18). Both *Carne trémula*
and Almodóvar's other adaptations – *La piel que habito* (The Skin
I Live In, 2011) and *Julieta* (2016) – are creative appropriations of
the source material, acts of 'appropriating or salvaging' rather than
'slavish copying' (Hutcheon, 2006: 20). These films are highly successful adaptations of the narratives they cannibalise.

In Rendell's novel, Victor stalks and befriends David and his
new girlfriend Claire in a bid for revenge. In the film, Víctor stalks
Helena, the woman he was trying to convince to go out with him
when the shootout happened and who is now David's wife. But
David seeks revenge by stalking Víctor, and the revenge is not perceived as such because responsibility, unlike in the novel, does
not lie with Víctor but with David and a new character, David's
senior officer and wife-batterer, Sancho. Where Rendell's Victor
is psychotic and violent, Almodóvar's Víctor is measured and
good natured, almost child-like in his innocent plans for revenge.
Likewise, David is more complex in his possessiveness of Helena
and desire to get back at Víctor. The film's introduction of another
couple, Sancho and Clara, multiplies the relationship triangles and
provides a clear guilty party: Sancho, the character with the most
obviously Spanish name after one of the most famous characters
of Spanish literature who decorates his house with a map of Spain
like the husband in *La flor de mi secreto* (The Flower of My Secret,
1995). Sancho frames Víctor for David's shooting, literally forcing
Víctor to pull the trigger to kill David. The film also provides a final

victim: Clara, who is abused and killed by Sancho, abandoned by David, and left by Víctor.

Almodóvar conflates two of Rendell's characters – the hostage held by Victor and David's girlfriend Claire – in Helena, the aptly named woman whose love David and Víctor covet. Like Helen of Troy, the foreign Helena (spelt by herself as 'Helena' in a beer mat despite what subtitles, etc. tell us) smites those she meets and triggers violence. But, unlike her mythological counterpart, Helena is given a voice and a will, making decisions about her life as she learns of the real reasons for David's paraplegia. Helena switches allegiance from David to Víctor on hearing that the latter was not responsible for shooting the former and that David may have brought Sancho's revenge upon himself by sleeping with his wife. Of course, this reasoning can only be applied if one buys into the masculinist logic of Sancho and David, who see women as their property and other men as breaching their property rights if their wives decide to sleep with them. This is also young Víctor's logic at the beginning of the film and the reason he returns to Helena's flat to demand 'an explanation' as to why she is meeting with someone else when she had agreed to date him that evening.

The 'cross-cutting' of perspectives during the shootout scene allows Helena, David, and the viewers to be misled. The moment Sancho jumps at Víctor is recorded in a circular movement of the camera as it occupies Víctor's point of view. He is only seen once Sancho has hold of his hand. All are unaware of Sancho's reasons for wanting to kill David so the likelihood is that audiences will make an assumption about Víctor's criminality and Sancho's response to imminent danger.

Almodóvar discusses how he uses ellipses to advance the story 'in which the slightest development affects all five of them simultaneously. As I clearly couldn't repeat the same piece of information five times over, I had to resort to a narrative structure that was full of ellipses, almost within individual scenes. That was complicated' (quoted in Strauss, 2006: 168). These ellipses are not just a product of editing or focalisation. *Carne trémula* makes excellent use of characterisation, *mise-en scène*, generic expectations, and music to suggest interpretations that later on are proven unfounded. Pavlović analyses how music misleads the viewer:

> The song heard on the police-car, 'Ay mi perro' (performed by La Niña de Antequera), which narrates the loss of a guard dog, defenseless sheep

and violent wolves, will be a telling metaphor for the relations between the characters. ... Sancho's duplicitous comment to David – 'Look at the lambs we have to protect (...) stealing, scheming, betraying and corrupting each other (...) we're the guardians of a sick flock' – points to *Carne Trémula*'s tragic ironies and the impossibility of distinguishing wolves from sheep or police from criminals. (Pavlović, 2006: 159)

Pavlović is right in highlighting viewer conditioning to consider Víctor guilty, but his kind behaviour towards the unconscious Helena should generate some sympathy towards him. Pavlović analyses the use of the song playing in the police car, 'Ay mi perro', by La Niña de Antequera, which refers to the lambs and shepherd dog, a dog that Sancho directly relates to the police. However, the song tells the story of how the good dog is killed for chasing a female deer in a national park and the owner's sadness. In line with the medieval tradition of courtly love, Víctor could be seen as the dog chasing forbidden love (Helena) and being taken down for transgressing. Likewise, Sancho's music is a warning to David, who has trespassed by having an affair with Clara and who Sancho will attempt to kill using Víctor. The use of 'Ay mi perro' is therefore just as equivocal as the rest of the film. Moreover, an appearance of guilt does not usually translate into actual guilt in either crime thrillers or *film noir*, the main intertextual genres of *Carne trémula*. Additionally, it should be noted how the film reflects generalised distrust and fear of authority in general – and the police in particular – in Spaniards, a legacy of the repressive role of the police during the dictatorship. For a Spanish audience, the police is not necessarily a reliable law enforcer and Sancho's comments about having to protect a 'sick flock' will ring alarm bells to those attuned to the rhetoric of those who saw the Transition to democracy as a disaster and yearned for a return to the dictatorship. The credits scene with its emphasis on the declaration of the State of Emergency as Víctor is born and giving the police the power to arrest anyone indiscriminately should still be fresh in the audience's minds. The State of Emergency may not have been in force as Víctor is confronted by Sancho and David, but suspicion and fear of the police was still at play. The film also seems to encourage audiences to make the connection between the historical frame and Víctor's situation, pointing to how miscarriages of justice continued well into Spain's democratic phase.

Carne trémula exploits the genre of the thriller and *noir* to engage in memory work. The film moves ostensibly forward, but the recurrence of ellipses in form and content induces a backward movement, towards the past. Kuhn establishes a formal link between detective work and memory work:

> the past is gone forever. We cannot return to it, nor can we reclaim it now as it was. But that does not mean that it is lost to us. The past is like the scene of a crime: if the deed itself is irrecoverable, its traces may still remain. From these traces, markers that point towards a past presence, to something that has happened in this place, a (re)construction, if not a simulacrum, of the event can be pieced together. Memory has a great deal in common with forms of inquiry which – like detective work and archaeology, say – involve working backwards – searching for clues, deciphering signs and traces, making deductions, patching together reconstructions out of fragments of evidence. (2002: 4)

In a nation 'characterized by historical amnesia' (Vernon, 1993: 28), it is the emphasis on detective work that stands out. It highlights how accepted national narratives such as that of the successful Transition period may not have been as smooth as commonly thought, scrutinising Spain's recent past perhaps just as much as (or even more than?) the pre-credits sequence set during the dictatorship.

Camp is toned down, appearing nevertheless at crucial moments. As elsewhere in Almodóvar's work, camp has a political dimension of critique. In fact, it appears most prominently in the historical pre-credits opening of the film that addresses the lack of freedom and limited options for Spaniards during the dictatorship. Whilst it is true that Carne trémula is the first of Almodóvar's feature films to make direct reference to Franco's regime and include a long scene set during the last years of the dictatorship, Almodóvar's direct reference to repression during the dictatorship should not be seen as a turn to politics. As seen in previous chapters, Almodóvar's films have always been political and 'consistently offered a critical representation of the rigid patriarchal and paternalistic social structures that underpinned [the dictatorship's] arch-conservative ideology and its relation to a strict and dogmatic notion of Catholicism based on fear and guilt' (Morgan-Tamosunas, 2000: 112). Carne trémula is one more in a series of films engaging with the social and political period of the Transition but the first one to make the connection between contemporary Spain and the dictatorship explicit. However, from his early films Almodóvar is showing post-dictatorship Spain as a (sometimes reluctant) heir to that same dictatorship. The importance of the initial historical scene should not distract us from the fact that it is followed by a longer historical section encompassing the Transition to democracy, and this is a major change in perspective. The Transition and the *movida* had been contemporary to Almodóvar's films thus far; by the time *Carne trémula* was made both had finished and Spain's optimist narrative as a fully fledged, modern European country was firmly established. *Kika*, *La flor*, and *Carne trémula* undermine this optimism, a move that culminates in a return to camp in *Los amantes pasajeros* (I'm So Excited!, 2013). *Carne trémula* is a *noir*-inflected thriller that contains a camp look at the dictatorship, a critical look at how it survived during the Transition, and a suspiciously neat happy ending that questions the narrative of progress in Spain at the same time as celebrating how the country has changed in over twenty years.

10

Remembering children:
Todo sobre mi madre

If *Mujeres al borde de un ataque de nervios* (Women on the Verge of a Nervous Breakdown, 1988) launched Almodóvar's international career and ensured he was taken seriously by the Spanish film industry, multi-award winning *Todo sobre mi madre* (All about My Mother, 1999) cemented his status as *the* Spanish *auteur* to watch. The film's commercial success went hand in hand with prestigious accolades as Almodóvar's new American distributor – Sony – marketed Almodóvar as a great director, rather than an underground filmmaker as Miramax had done previously (Colmenero Salgado, 2001: 37). This was a triumphant vindication for a director who had been alternatively ignored and vilified at home.

Like many of Almodóvar's films, *Todo sobre* tells the story of a woman, Manuela (Cecilia Roth), in desperate circumstances. Repression and censorship are at the heart of the film, which begins by showing Manuela's life in Madrid with a fulfilling job and a healthy relationship with her son Esteban (Eloy Azorín) just before Esteban's seventeenth birthday. Esteban wants to know who his father is but Manuela is reluctant to explain. On his birthday, just after Manuela agrees to tell him 'everything' when they get home, Esteban is killed by a car whilst chasing the actor Huma Rojo (Marisa Paredes) for an autograph. Manuela agrees to donate his heart. Despairing, she goes back to Barcelona to look for Esteban's father – trans woman Lola (Toni Cantó) – to tell her that she had a son and that he is dead. During her search she meets Sister Rosa (Penélope Cruz), a nun pregnant with Lola's baby. The two women's lives and those of actor Huma Rojo, Manuela's former friend Agrado (Antonia San Juan), and Huma's lover Nina (Candela Peña) become entangled. Sister Rosa dies of pregnancy complications and Manuela goes on to raise her son, also called Esteban, but this time she decides not to hide anything from him or prevent Lola from seeing her baby. The film charts Manuela's journey from censorship to acceptance, as well as revealing her and Lola's backstory, as a consequence of the son's death.

Todo sobre has been seen as part of a turn in Almodóvar's *oeuvre* to the serious. Paul Julian Smith includes it in what he has called Almodóvar's 'mature "blue period" (as opposed to the earlier, more florid "rose" films)' (1999: 28), together with *La flor de mi secreto* (The Flower of My Secret, 1995) and *Carne trémula* (Live Flesh, 1997). There is some truth in this periodisation, at least in terms of *Todo sobre*'s technical accomplishments; some of the film's most memorable images are composed of audacious slow pans and podiums with the camera moving along floors, walls, and even curtains. Nevertheless, the term 'mature' is misleading. Whereas Almodóvar's technical ability has increased over his career, the film's smooth surface does not imply a banishment of frivolity. Comic relief is introduced through the character of Agrado and ensemble scenes of women's solidarity and sisterhood. Excess is still part of these films, the ornamental and unusual subsumed into a normalising narrative or displaced onto specific characters. The former is trademark Almodóvar, beginning with his short films and early comedies, where extraordinary occurrences are not given a second thought by the characters. In fact, the more Almodóvar tackles serious socio-political and historical issues, the more he uses comedy and 'florid' cinematic language on the one hand and postmodern distancing techniques on the other.

The film is intensely preoccupied with memory of a personal and historical nature. As Julián Daniel Gutiérrez-Albilla explains, it 'engages with subjective and shared traumas of patriarchal absence, abandonment and domination; with the traces of national and transnational political repression; with loss, death, bereavement, AIDS, social alienation and marginalisation – to name just a few' (2017: 67). Manuela's insistence on living in the present and ignoring the past is thwarted. The film's ostensible capturing of the present and implausibly optimistic ending is underpinned by memory work about Manuela's recent and historical past. It is significant that *Todo sobre* was made in the late 1990s, when Spain's traumatic twentieth-century history was actively being revised academically and culturally. As Juan Carlos Ibáñez states, 'the film speaks to us about the negation or concealment of the past that results in paralysis and the contrary decision to undertake a hazardous journey through the "tunnel of memory," in the words of Almodóvar ..., a journey that leads to the hope of a future free of contaminants of that past' (2013: 163). The film is preoccupied with ending the censorship of the past, which had been justified as beneficial for the younger generation and necessary for a Transition to a stable democracy. This 'commanded forgetting' belongs to what Paul Ricoeur calls an 'abuse' of memory (2006: 452; 443) and was linked to an amnesty for all those involved in the Civil War and the crimes of the dictatorship. As Ricoeur explains, '[c]onsidered in its stated intention, the aim of amnesty is the reconciliation of enemy citizens, civil peace' but, he continues, 'is it not a defect in this imaginary unity that it erases from the official memory the examples of crimes likely to protect the future from the errors of the past and, by depriving public opinion of the benefits of *dissensus*, of competing memories to an unhealthy underground existence?' (2006: 453; 455). Manuela's wilful suppression of the past may be intended for Esteban's good, but its effect is to consign alternative ways of living, represented by her life with Lola during the Transition and in Argentina, to the dustbin. Esteban is not allowed to discover 'the historical past by means of the memory of ancestors', something that Ricoeur calls 'transgenerational memory', which allows the 'transition from learned history to living memory' (2006: 394). Like many other characters in Almodóvar's films, Manuela is, if not necessarily completely forgetting herself, avoiding her memories. This is 'a devious form of forgetting. ... But this dispossession is not without secret complicity, which makes forgetting semi-passive, semi-active behaviour, as is seen by forgetting by avoidance (*fuite*)' (Ricoeur, 2006: 448), one that Julieta in the eponymous film will take to extremes.

Censorship and self-censorship during the dictatorship are also part of this traumatic legacy since the silence of Republican supporters and opponents of the regime was necessary for their and their families' safety. Although not explicitly addressed in the film, this history is surely present in Almodóvar's use of iconic Spanish film star Fernando Fernán Gómez to play Sister Rosa's father. The character suffers from a form of dementia with severe memory loss. Dementia is an obviously metaphorical affliction for a generation who were first unwilling to speak and ultimately unable to do so. Fernán Gómez – best known to art-house audiences as the actor who plays Fernando, the father of two girls in Víctor Erice's *El espíritu de la colmena* (The Spirit of the Beehive, 1973), set in 1940 Spain – reprises his earlier embodiment of the generation who never spoke about the war.

The film's movement towards recognition and acceptance of past events forms part of the cultural shift in Spain towards openly exploring the Civil War and post-war trauma, mostly driven by the inquisitive gaze of those born after the dictatorship, like Manuela's son Esteban, who is determined to find out about his family's past. As Helen Graham explains, this 'grandchildren's gaze', which no longer respects the *pacto del olvido* (Pact of Oblivion), has been central to opening up the story of the Civil War from the 1990s, asking how 'the retrieval of such events [came to] be of such moment to people for whom they are, essentially, "post-memory" that is, neither directly experienced events nor even immediate consequences' (2005: 143). Almodóvar places a new generation at the forefront of the search for answers, not just about their personal past but, inextricably linked to it, the historical past. The past that Esteban wants to recover is embedded in Spain's Transition to democracy and, previously, the experience of repression and dictatorship, this time not in Spain but in Argentina where his parents are from. Thus, Almodóvar places a grandchild's gaze – Esteban's – at the centre of *Todo sobre*.

Esteban functions as a distancing device and a double for the filmmaker/creator. As Emma Wilson explains, during the first scene '[t]he film is marked as the creation and product of the consciousness of the adolescent who will be its victim. Esteban seems to be the author of the film, explaining the possessive pronoun [my] in the title' (2003: 68). This is signalled, as noted by Wilson, by Esteban's invention and writing 'All about My Mother' in his notebook:

> [Esteban] suddenly takes up his notebook again and writes: *Todo sobre mi madre*. ... We see his hand in a close-up as he writes. The film then cuts to a shot of the pencil lead writing directly on the glass of the lens, as if our point of view and the notebook on which Esteban writes are one. The film cuts back to a shot of Esteban and Manuela, both in the frame, on the sofa. In the space between them we see the same title repeated, superimposed over the image, confirmed as the title of the film. (2003: 68)

Wilson persuasively analyses Esteban's role as 'the imagined creator and witness of the film ... for whom Manuela acts' and 'the narrative and action of the film' as 'the wish-fulfilling construct of Esteban the young author' (2003: 72). Besides the structural and cinematographic clues, which Wilson deftly presents, the film constantly reminds us of Esteban as a pervasive creative presence visually; *Todo sobre* is famous for its pans of walls and floors, many of which contain horizontal lines. Esteban is associated with the horizontal line through his clothes; horizontal lines are also present in ruled notebooks and flatlining EEC scan lines. Could the pans of walls in *Todo sobre* be reminders that we are inside the writer's story?

Not only is Esteban a writer, and possibly the writer of the story, he is also Almodóvar's alter ego. Esteban dies on his birthday, 26 September, a date that is uncannily close to Almodóvar's birthday, which biographers say is on 25 September and Almodóvar has said is on 24 September (Méjean, 2007: 183n). First released in 1999 in Spain, the film is told in the present as is typical of Almodóvar films. Esteban's birthday thus also coincides with the birth of Almodóvar as a filmmaker in the early 1980s. Interpreting Esteban as an alter ego for the filmmaker helps us to see the film as a fictionalisation of the need to unearth the past through fiction. Thus, Esteban's fiction is not just his musings about his personal past and his desire to change his mother's stance on censorship but also an instance of 'prosthetic memory'.

Pam Cook employs the term 'prosthetic memory' to describe 'the process whereby reconstructions of the past produce replacement memories that simulate first-hand experiences' (2005: 2). Whilst Cook is concerned with historical cinema and stories of the past, Jonathan Ellis and I have gone further to suggest that '"prosthetic memory', particularly one that makes viewers aware of its own artificiality, may be the best way to remember the past' that has been censored or repressed, as it 'will ... call into question the very acts of remembering and historicising the past' (Ellis and Sánchez-Arce, 2011: 175). This function of prosthetic memory is taken further in *La mala educación* (Bad Education, 2004), *Los abrazos rotos* (Broken Embraces, 2009), and *Dolor y gloria* (Pain and Glory, 2019), but it is already at work here; the film is Esteban's version of his parents' past and fictionalisation of the prevalent teenage death fantasy as well as acting as proxy for the process of historicising a traumatic recent past, be it that of Spain or Argentina.

Todo sobre is also Almodóvar's first historical look at marginal lives in the Spain of the Transition and beyond, a theme that he will retake in subsequent films. Thanks to intertextual links with Tennessee Williams's *A Streetcar Named Desire* (1947), altered in the film to end with Stella leaving Kowalsky, audiences are led to believe that

Manuela left an abusive husband for self-preservation and the interests of her unborn child in mind. It is only discovered later on in the film that Lola is a trans junkie turned prostitute. The Spain of the 1990s was simultaneously recovering its historical past and busy consigning the cultural and social alternatives of the late 1970s and 1980s to the historical dustbin.

During the film we learn that Manuela conceived Esteban whilst in a relationship with male chauvinist non-binary husband Lola (formerly also called Esteban). Lola seems to play the role of the inconvenient trans, a role further developed in *La mala educación*. Like Ignacio (Francisco Boira) in *La mala educación*, Lola is the embodiment of the major changes that took place in Spain in the 1980s and the sense of freedom that took hold of the country, as well as the social rejection of it as more established conservative and neo-liberal views regained ground in the 1990s. Lola's presence is the aporia that unravels the film. The non-binary figure is both reclaimed (Manuela's censorship ends with optimistic signs of social change) and suppressed (Lola conveniently dies whilst her second son – also called Esteban – is a toddler). Lola goes against binary-friendly ideas of trans, performing femininity and masculinity as and when it suits her. Lola's masculinity, the fact that she does not look like or play a binary trans woman conforming to femininity, makes the character more challenging to binary-oriented audiences in contrast to Agrado, who performs a camp femininity and aligns herself with womanhood, most notably in her key speech about authenticity and her transphobic views on Drag Queens. When *Todo sobre* was premiered in Spain, the casting of Toni Cantó as Lola was criticised – just as Miguel Bosé's as Letal in *Tacones lejanos* (High Heels, 1991) had been – on the grounds that Cantó did not manage to move away from masculinity. This view is still represented as seen in Spanish *Vanity Fair*'s 2016 ranking of Toni Cantó as the worst 'Almodóvar boy', citing as a reason that '[s]eldom is an actor playing the role of a transsexual woman credible' (Vegas, 2016; my translation).

Lola is portrayed by other characters as self-centred and controlling, but this, as Silvia Colmenero Salgado points out, is not how she behaves when she actually appears: 'Before we meet her she is portrayed in absolute patriarchal terms, tyrannised, which does not go well with the image we will be given of her. When she holds her son in her arms or cries looking at the photograph of Esteban, the dead teenager, Lola appears as a tender being, with a sweet maternal attitude'

(2001: 125). The film therefore provides a much more complex portrayal than any one character or action presupposes. Although Rosa's
mother rejects the bodily changes Lola has made, these are not the
real problem for Manuela, who complains about Lola being stuck
in masculine, male-chauvinist narratives, controlling towards her
whilst she herself enjoys sexual freedom, and having a strong need
to become a father despite the risk of passing on HIV. Manuela does
not reject Lola as non-binary but, as she says to Rosa, because 'Lola's
got the worst of a man, and the worst of a woman'. Ibáñez shrewdly
points to the transformation of Lola (whom he calls 'Esteban *padre*' in
a refusal to acknowledge her preferred gender) as a 'defection from
[his] shared cause [with Manuela, which] could be read as a case of
ideological evolution similar to that of many of the former members
of the Goliardos troupe', a left-leaning theatre group that Almodóvar
belonged to in the 1980s, a movement from political commitment to
investment in hedonistic entrepreneurship (2013: 166). The narrative
around Lola is reminiscent of that of *Matador*, where the two main
characters combine hypermasculine and hyperfeminine traits. Lola
admits that she 'has always been excessive'.

Colmenero Salgado thinks that impending maternity prompts
Manuela to break with the father, who she perceives as a threat to
herself and the unborn child (2001: 75). Whilst this may be true,
Lola is not necessarily a threat because of her non-normativity (as
Colmenero Salgado implies) but due to her adherence (in Manuela's
eyes) to a patriarchal view of family relations and relegation of
Manuela to the role of the subservient woman. Opposing those such
as Ángel Fernández-Santos who question the usefulness of Lola's
appearance, Colmenero Salgado argues that her presence is part of
the film's use of paternal absence and maternal presence:

> The film is characterised by the absence of fathers whilst mothers
> possess the story's vital strength. The three mothers of the film,
> Manuela, Rosa and Sister Rosa, live their children's tragedies on their
> own, without sharing them with the fathers because they are either
> absent (Lola) or disabled (Rosa's father). ... This absence prompts the
> action. (2001: 89; my translation)

Lola's desire to be involved in her second son's life and mourning
for the first son she never knew upsets the paternal as absence that
is typical of Almodóvar's films. In a series of interviews with Nuria

Vidal, Almodóvar acknowledges that '[i]t is true that there aren't any fathers. I can't write them. They're always absent. Perhaps this may have something to do with myself, I don't know. I didn't have much of a relationship with my father' (quoted in Vidal, 1989: 58; my translation). Manuela writes Lola out of the first Esteban's life of her own volition and cuts contact with her when she disappears with the second Esteban to avoid his maternal grandparents. Lola herself is not willingly absent. It is as if to be able to make the father present Almodóvar has feminised the role. The film's final dedication – 'To Bette Davis, Gena Rowlands, Romi Schneider ... To all actresses who have played actresses, to all women who act, to men who act and become women, to all the people who want to be mothers. To my mother' – signals the importance of Lola and Agrado as 'men who act and become women', but the film itself also makes clear that Lola wants to be a father, not a mother. This is not a contradiction if one considers parental roles as separate from gender.

The figure of the grieving father is further complicated by Lola's association with the grieving Virgin Mary or *mater dolorosa*. Lola's name is a shortening for Dolores ('pains' in Spanish, and also the name of the grieving Virgin). Lola grieves a son as well as the idea of that son and, later on, the son's unconditional acceptance of her difference. Whereas Wilson (2003) insightfully analyses the motif of the grieving mother in relation to Manuela, it is Lola who takes on the Virgin's mantle, not covering her face as she cries for her son and accepting her dispossession by Manuela with grace and understanding. Lola's paternity and her grief without name is a prerequisite for her rehabilitation in Manuela's eyes. Manuela's and Lola's tears (as well as Huma's fictional ones at the end of the film) participate in the imagery of the tears of the *mater dolorosa* as consolation because they 'belong to a universal language of cleansing and rebirth' (Warner, quoted in Wilson, 2003: 67).

Nevertheless, Manuela is allowed a second chance whilst Lola is ejected from the narrative off-screen, in a melodrama that resolves issues in a positive way for cis women at the expense of LGBTQ+ characters. Whereas most critics such as Colmenero Salgado view Lola's gender identity as trans in a way that protects binary thinking – Lola becomes woman/mother instead of man/father – it is my view that Lola's non-normativity is overtly signalled in the film: she is a woman–man/father–mother. Confusion is reserved for those who cannot see beyond gender binaries. Lola's gender identity evokes gender and sexual taboos; her name slips into the many positive and negative connotations of the figure of *la loca*, which means mad or irrational in Spanish, but also refers to (and is used by) particularly homosexual men who perform femininity non-normatively. In Argentina and Uruguay it is specifically used to refer to sex workers, particularly if they are trans. Lola is all of the above. She is *la loca* Lola. Here the main characters' origins are important. Agrado, Lola, and Manuela are all Argentinean who have settled in Spain. The Lola we meet is dying of an Aids-related illness, but she is still a presence in high heels and full make-up. Like Pepa in *Mujeres*, she does not let herself go.

Mark Allinson voices a cis-centred view in his discussion of the film's indebtedness to Hollywood melodrama, which he rightly interprets as a transcription of 'classic melodrama into a European, contemporary, post-feminist version, where friends replace family, and the world of drug-addicts and transsexuals substitutes home and the housewife' (2005: 229). Allinson's astute point about the underground substituting 'home and the housewife' can be taken further. The film is a 'post-feminist version' of melodrama, moving away from cis women as the locus of social tension, transferring it instead to supporting LGBTQ+ characters. Allinson's focus on a traditional critique of melodrama misses this transformation of the genre:

> The domestic sphere in *All About My Mother* is entirely female, even to the extent that the biologically male father, Esteban, has become a transsexual. Male characters remain tangential to the dramatic action, and they determine neither the suffering of the females nor the resolution of that suffering. Consequently, unlike classic melodramas in which according to Ann Kaplan, 'events are never reconciled at the end in a way which is beneficial to women', *All About My Mother* offers a happy ending, in which single motherhood and female friendship have replaced the conventional patriarchal family unit. (Allinson, 2005: 230–31)

The film's happy ending is restricted to Manuela. Transgressive characters either die (Esteban, Sister Rosa, Lola), slot into cis-friendly roles (Agrado, Nina), or their problems are unresolved. It is significant that the film ends with Huma, not Manuela, staring at camera in full costume saying 'I'll see you later' and leaving for the stage, followed by a dedication superimposed on the stage curtain, which is then raised to reveal blackness as the credits begin. This ending is not unproblematic or straightforwardly 'happy'.

As Núria Triana Toribio explains, Almodóvar's versions of melodrama reject Manichaeism: 'Polarization between good and evil, which constitutes another element of melodrama, is often avoided' (1995: 4). Even Esteban, who is mostly portrayed as the ideal son and could easily slot into melodrama's use of children as 'living representations of innocence and purity' (Brooks, 1995: 34), is shown to have a darker side. As Triana Toribio states, 'Almodóvar parodies the conventional happy endings in which a heterosexual bond is established' (1995: 14). In *Todo sobre*, parody is not at the forefront. At the same time, Manuela's happy ending is somehow too neat and self-contained not to warrant careful scrutiny. Just as Manuela's is a story of healing and coping with bereavement, it is also the story of coming to terms with the presence of Lola. This is ultimately not resolved as Lola's absence forfeits any chance of a replacement of 'the conventional patriarchal family unit' despite Allinson's best hopes. Instead, the film moves towards melodramatic 'excess', a term coined by Geoffrey Nowell-Smith in discussing melodrama (quoted in Allinson, 2005: 231). Excess is mostly associated with Esteban, Lola, Rosa's parents' *art nouveau* flat, and Huma's dressing room with its dominant mirror and photographs. Allinson comments that 'Almodóvar does not abandon the compensatory use of classic melodrama *mise-en-scène*' (2005: 231); it is used to show social repression of alternative lifestyles. According to Stephen Maddison, Esteban's character is 'coded' as gay (2000: 272). Leo Bersani and Ulysse Dutoit list Esteban's coding: 'As if artistic sensibility, his father's absence, and his great love for his mother were not enough, his aesthetic tastes leave no doubt – for a public even minimally trained in such codes – about his gay sensibility: Bette Davis, Truman Capote, and Blanche DuBois' (2009: 243).

Saša Markuš splits the film into 'two completely different parts. Manuela lives in a harmonious and exemplary setting with her son, whose death reactivates her youthful links with the *underground*' (2001: 85; my translation). Markuš identifies Barcelona and Madrid as the geographies of these very different settings (2001: 86), Barcelona representing the past, Madrid the present. This distinction is called into question once Esteban dies. Madrid then becomes a space of nostalgia, and Manuela's home with Esteban the imaginary place she returns to when she thinks about her dead son. After Esteban's death,

Manuela's flat is only seen once. The flat is markedly different from the film's first scene. It is now dark and unwelcoming. At the end of the film Manuela returns to Madrid with the new Esteban, but this is off-screen. Moreover, given Madrid's reputation as the centre of *la movida* in the 1980s, a clean distinction between Barcelona and Madrid can only be made in relation to the character's private attitudes to underground movements, not the cities themselves. As Smith explains, 'just as performance and authenticity are gleefully confused, so location and dislocation go hand in hand. The visually striking scene in which cars slowly cruise prostitutes as if in some lower circle of suburban hell is not shot in Barcelona, but in Madrid, albeit with Catalan trannies (more showy than their Castilian sisters) imported as extras for the occasion' (1999: 29). The inner workings of the film refuse strict categorisation of geographical spaces.

Similarly, the early scene of Manuela at home watching *All about Eve* (Mankiewicz, 1950) on television with Esteban already introduces question marks about Manuela's 'harmonious and exemplary' life and, by extension, the 1990s narratives of a successful Spain. Although Manuela's life is reimagined through the lens of nostalgia throughout the film, all is not well in Manuela's and her son's lives. The scene shows the cracks in this idealised life as well-mannered Esteban unexpectedly shows another side to him by using crude language and asking Manuela if she would prostitute herself for him. Manuela replies curtly, 'I've already done just about everything for you', implying via the proximity of her remark to their talk of prostitution that she has done something illegal or taboo. Whereas the film's plot centres on Esteban's death and Manuela's subsequent search for the father and rebuilding of her life, from the beginning spectators are driven – much like Esteban – to find what it is that Manuela hides. Whilst the film relentlessly moves forward, spectators are piecing together Esteban's family history from snatches of conversations and photographic prompts. The past is constantly implied but also left to the imagination.

Unusually in a film so concerned with personal history, there are only two short flashbacks, both of the recent past rather than historical past. The first, as Manuela is about to see *A Streetcar Named Desire* in Barcelona, is of Esteban in Madrid looking up from inside a bar before he meets her at the theatre door and signals Manuela's painful awareness of her loss as Esteban will not join her this time round. The other flashback is Huma's memory of Esteban knocking on her

10.1 Esteban asks for Huma's autograph (*Todo sobre mi madre*, 1999)

taxi window in the rain, a memory that she produces as Manuela is telling her about Esteban's death (Figure 10.1).

Both flashbacks draw attention to how insignificant events can become relevant and even be generated when embedded in a narrative network, in this case the production of a narrative of grief. As Annette Kuhn explains,

> Remembering is clearly an activity that takes place for, as much as in, the present. Is memory then not understood better as a position or a point of view in the current moment than as an archive or a repository of bygones? Perhaps memory offers a constantly changing perspective on the places and times through which we – individually and collectively – have been journeying? Perhaps it is only when we look back that we make a certain kind of sense of what we see? (Kuhn, 2002: 128)

Photographs feature prominently in the film. Old black-and-white pictures of Manuela's past cut in half signal the censorship of the father and of their Argentinean past. Manuela refers to General Videla's dictatorship, which prosecuted left-leaning groups to which Manuela and Lola may have belonged (Manuela mentions that they performed

Boris Vian, 'Cabaret for intellectuals'). A group photograph of Agrado, Manuela, and Lola functions as visual evidence for Agrado's happy memories. Recurrent photographs of the dead Esteban structure the film into distinct parts. As Kuhn explains, 'memories evoked by a photo do not simply spring out of the image itself, but are generated in a network, an intertext, of discourses that shift between past and present, spectator and image, and between all these and cultural contexts, historical moments' (2002: 14). *Todo sobre*'s story is generated through such discourses to encourage remembering and create memories in spectators. It is a memory text that encourages collective and individual remembering.

Camerawork encourages the production of such memories by pausing over selected objects in (sometimes extreme) close-ups. Esteban's photographs are such objects, as are the intravenous bag and drip chamber before the opening credits and Esteban's notebook. As Kuhn states, 'memory work is a conscious and purposeful performance of memory' (2002: 157). The opening scene is the film's most elaborate instance of camerawork being used for memorialisation purposes, the focus being the medical instruments used to save lives and record cerebral death. Camera movements double in their actions, with side-to-side pans and up-and-down pedestals punctuated by pauses over the intravenous drip bag, drip bag and tube, and drip chamber. A dissolve leads to a pan right of inoperative valves on the wall, pause on the wall to focus on 'Un film de Almodóvar', then cut to the electroencephalogram (EEG) scanner with a tilt up the dials, dolly and pan left to show it flatlining (here the first intradiegetic beeping sound). Finally, a tilt up Manuela's uniformed body to her serious face. This complex sequence establishes Manuela as a health professional and provides a memory of the setting for viewers to remember when Esteban is in intensive care being tested for signs of life off-screen.

Repetition is also used to form what Kuhn calls memory 'network'. For example, the doctor–patient role play is repeated for real after Esteban's death and both of these are versions of a role-play scene in an earlier film, *La flor*; Esteban's car accident is rehearsed in a previous near miss, also first seen through a reaction shot of Manuela; Esteban looks out of the bar window towards his mother both before and after his death; Esteban is seen knocking on Huma's taxi window twice; scenes from *A Streetcar Named Desire* appear on several occasions, with Nina or Manuela playing Stella, and with and without

Esteban in the audience, his absence – like Benigno's in *Hable con ella* (Talk to Her, 2002) – signalled by an empty seat.

Wilson speaks of the film's 'compulsion to repeat' (2003: 69). The film is full of doubles, reflections, and second chances, not least the three Estebans, the pregnancies of Stella, Manuela, and Sister Rosa, Manuela's two escapes to Madrid, and Rosa's mother's forgeries. Rosa's mother forges Chagall paintings; we see her copying *Madonna of the Village* (1938–1942), painted during the years of the Jewish Holocaust and finished in exile. This is another instance of a traumatic past being transferred to memory objects and perhaps, as I explain below, of 'multidirectional memory' (cf. Rothberg, 2009). Significantly, Rosa's mother is the opposite of the Virgin and Manuela; she is an imitator of love.

Much has been said about *Todo sobre* and performance in relation to metatheatricality and gender, but not as much about its exploration of repression and memory as performative. Wilson's work is one of the few exceptions to this trend, as is the recent book by Julián Daniel Gutiérrez-Albilla (2017). The urge to control the body and (historical) memory can be seen in the initial focus on the intravenous bag with drip chamber and the advert for nappies, both of which regulate fluids. The undulating red film credits mimic liquidity, blood in particular. Leo Bersani and Ulysse Dutoit note that the film 'begins with appealingly light reminders of the beauty of liquidity, its life-saving virtues, and the relative ease with which an undisciplined flowing can nonetheless be contained and absorbed' (2009: 254). This reassuring notion is challenged during the film, as Esteban dies on a night with torrential rain (torrential rain being common in late September and October in Spain) and Sister Rosa dies during a planned caesarean due to placenta praevia (one of the major causes of maternal morbidity through haemorrhage) and not, as critical consensus has it, from 'the contemporary afflictions of contemporary unmarried motherhood and AIDS' (Smith, 2014: 193), 'AIDS-related complications' (Ballesteros, 2009: 80), or 'HIV complications' (Gutiérrez-Albilla, 2017: 81). Rosa is HIV positive, but she is not seen to develop the syndrome. This distinction is important because it has given way to speculations that her death 'may be interpreted … as a moralising attitude on the part of Almodóvar towards those infected with HIV (Rosa) and those who transmit the HIV virus to others (Lola)' and 'certainly, if unconsciously, perpetuate the dominant, negative and discriminatory cultural discourses and representations of AIDS and the AIDS epidemic' (Gutiérrez-Albilla, 2017: 81). Although characters in the film voice transphobic views (Agrado, Rosa's mother) these views are by no means endorsed. Manuela herself responds with disbelief inflected through the discriminatory discourses that Gutiérrez-Albilla refers to when Sister Rosa reveals that she is HIV positive, but during the film she journeys from this position outlined by Simon Watney (1994; 1997) to acceptance of Lola.

Maternal grief is associated with failure to repress emotion. Manuela's persona cracks during her few outbursts, showing her vulnerability. Because they are unusual, these pivotal moments remind viewers of the backstory and change other characters' relationships with Manuela. Personal grief is, as explained in Chapter 8 and discussed by Ryan Prout (2004), inextricably linked to nationality and national historical memory. Here, it draws on other histories of suffering such as those of the trans community and Aids sufferers. The film alludes to Argentina's dictatorship and repression, one that is inextricably linked to the figure of the mother as hero, as evidenced by Mothers of the Plaza de Mayo's campaign. *Todo sobre* includes the wish-fulfilling news of General Videla's death (in fact, he did not die until May 2013). Videla's pardon in 1990 is another instance of democratic rulers relying on lack of accountability to overcome the past. As Gutiérrez-Albilla notes, Argentina's history 'is evoked' in the film's 'use of tango music in the soundtrack' and the film 'explores how different layers of memories associated with political violence coexist' (2017: 85).

Almodóvar's use of Argentinean history is a productive example of what Michael Rothberg calls 'multidirectional memory', whereby distinctive histories of suffering merge in a dialogical way and can be articulated by inflection through other instances of historical suffering. Thinking of memory as '*multidirectional*' allows Rothberg to explore it as 'a subject of on-going negotiation, cross-referencing, and borrowing' (2009: 3). This history, together with the history of the sidelining of gender non-conforming people, powerfully combine in *Todo sobre* to extend the story of maternal grief into one that recollects and memorialises the unarticulated, repressed memory of the Spanish Civil War and its repressive aftermath. As Rothberg explains, 'multidirectional memory, as its name implies, is not a one-way street' (2009: 6), so by juxtaposing all of these stories of suffering the film not simply narrativises Spain's repressed history but also puts forward a more ambitious narrative about the suppression of LGBTQ+ individuals' suffering both during and after the dictatorship, a suffering that may have decreased in Spain with gradual decriminalisation but has continued to exist due to prejudice against these communities.

In *Todo sobre*, we encounter the old Spanish motif of the glorification of the mother, and particularly what philosopher Miguel de Unamuno called 'the cult of the Mother in agony' (quoted in Kinder, 1993: 246) associated with veneration of the Virgin Mary. Manuela is portrayed as a grieving mother, a kind of secular Virgin Mary. As Smith explains, 'Manuela is Mary in a new Holy Family (hence the appearance of the Sagrada Familia), the grieving mother of a son of doubtful paternity' (2014: 193). Nevertheless, the association with the grieving mother is transferred seamlessly from Manuela to Lola during the cemetery scene as both parents shed tears for their lost son. Tearful expressions of grief become full outbursts, particularly after Manuela communicates to Lola the existence and death of their son. From then on, Manuela's grief pervades her reparative actions as she cares for Sister Rosa and her son. Tears are reserved for Lola, the father who never knew she had a son until it was too late.

Flowing tears and the blood of the dying or dead son are shown as performative by having Huma play the grieving mother in Federico García Lorca's *Bodas de sangre* (Blood Wedding, 1933). *Bodas*, a theatrical intertext that takes viewers back to Manuela's position after Esteban's accident, is another example of Kuhn's intertextuality at work in generating memory. Huma interprets Lorca's text thus:

> There are people who think that children are made in a day. But it takes a long time, a very long time. That's why it's so awful to see your child's blood on the ground. A stream that flows for a minute and yet cost us years. When I found my son, he was lying in the middle of the street. I soaked my hands in his blood and I licked them. Because it was mine. Animals lick their young, don't they? I'm not disgusted by my son. You don't know what it's like. In a monstrance of glass and topaz I would put the earth soaked by his blood.

Jesús González Requena (2015) analyses the scene above in detail, noting that although it is mostly from *Bodas* there are two sentences from another of Lorca's masterpieces, *Yerma* (Barren, 1934), and that there is no laundry scene in *Bodas* but there is one in *Yerma* (2015).

The two sentences are: 'Animals lick their young, don't they? I'm not disgusted by my son.' González Requena's shrewd observation that the scene is played by a woman pretending to be a mother and his identification of the hidden intertext of *Yerma*, a play about a woman who cannot conceive and ends up killing her husband, sheds some light onto the substitution. *Bodas*'s rejection of the father as capable of maternal feelings ('You don't know what it's like' is addressed to the father) is undermined by *Yerma*'s affirmation of strong (even excessive) maternal feelings in a childless woman who imagines motherhood. If maternal feelings are decoupled from biology, men and fathers can also share in maternity and the role of the grieving mother/parent. Nobody questions Manuela's maternal feelings for the second Esteban, who is not her son, and her sisterly/maternal feelings for Sister Rosa. Therefore, Lola's maternal/paternal feelings for her sons and the other maternal relationships in the film need not be questioned, either.

Bodas's 'monstrance of glass and topaz' alludes to *Snow White* and thus to the preservation and exhibition of the dead body, which is picked up in the transplant theme of the film. It also refers to the act of memorialising the dead son. In *Todo sobre* this is achieved through Esteban's photographs and notebook that preserves his voice. We see two different photographs of Esteban. One is a close-up of him smiling that Manuela has in her handbag when she goes to the theatre in Barcelona in what is a re-enactment of her final happy moments with her son. We only find out about the photograph once the performance is over, as she wipes her tears in the toilet just before going to Huma's dressing room. This is a different photograph from the initial one shown in Manuela's Barcelona flat. The other photograph of Esteban is an extreme close-up where his expression is serious. It appears four times and erases the smiling picture to create a unified memory of Esteban as troubled or thoughtful. It is first seen in Manuela's flat as Sister Rosa asks who Esteban is and shortly afterwards appears on Manuela's bedside table. It is the only picture Manuela shows Lola and the one she gives her to keep. It is also present in the last scene in Huma's dressing room, on the looking glass.

It is significant that this picture is chosen by Manuela (and Almodóvar) to represent her son as the smiling Esteban is banished from the film. The extreme close-up and seriousness form an intra-textual network with Esteban's voice-over as Manuela waits anxiously to hear the results of the ECG scan after his accident. This voice-over may be a fragment from his notebook: 'Tomorrow I turn 17, but I look older. Boys who live alone with their mothers have a special face, more serious than normal, like an intellectual or a writer. In my case it's normal, because I'm also a writer.' Esteban's photograph is therefore not simply a memento of the dead son but also a constant reminder to Manuela that due to her choices her son was brought up without a father. Moreover, the link between the serious face and writer – just as that between Esteban and death – is reinforced every time the photograph appears in the film and by Manuela's flashback where Esteban stops writing and looks up at her thoughtfully. Esteban's photograph is not simply a prop for nostalgia; it connects Manuela, Lola, Huma, and Agrado in a continuous remembering, one that also includes Sister Rosa and later on the deceased Lola, and even Lorca's plays. Kuhn shrewdly says of memory texts: 'I have observed the unfolding in memory texts of connections between memory and the past, memory and time, memory and place, memory and experience, memory and images, memory and the Unconscious. Above all I have seen how, in all memory texts, personal and collective remembering emerge again and again as continuous with one another' (2002: 5). Esteban's photograph functions as a memory text in the film, which is itself a memory text.

Esteban's status as an only child without a past is also represented by photographs, this time defaced by Manuela as she attempts to erase her past and, presumably, Lola from her new life with Esteban. Esteban writes about this in his notebook in a moving passage that first appears as voice-over when Manuela looks into her son's empty room and later as Manuela lets Lola read an extended version:

LOLA   *reading from Esteban's notebook* Last night, Mamá showed
              me a photo of when she was young. Half of it was
              missing. I didn't want to tell her, but my life is missing
              that same half.

MANUELA   Keep reading.

LOLA   This morning I looked in her drawers and I found a
              bundle of photos. They were all missing a half. My father,
              I suppose. I want to meet him. I have to make Mamá
              understand that I don't care who he is, or what he's like,
              or how he behaved towards her. She can't deny me that
              right.

Esteban voices the plight of younger generations of Spaniards who have been denied a history and lived lives marked by censorship. The film asks similar questions about personal and historical memory, becoming a text about the re-creation of memory itself through artistic reimagination and the use of multidirectional memory. *Todo sobre* seems an unlikely example of prosthetic memory. It is cathartic only if interpreted as a melodrama focusing on Manuela's plight. However, there is more to this contemporary melodrama. It not only keeps spectators' interest alive in the main plotline but also asks questions about how to deal with traumatic personal and historical pasts, including aspects that are deemed socially and politically taboo, such as non-normative behaviour and the dictatorship in both Argentina and Spain.

11

Still lives: *Hable con ella*

Hable con ella (Talk to Her, 2002) continued the critical and commercial success of *Todo sobre mi madre* (All about My Mother, 1999),
harvesting numerous awards including an Oscar for best original
screenplay, something highly unusual for a foreign film.[1] It is the
third film in what Marsha Kinder calls 'Almodóvar's brain-dead
trilogy' (2004: 9). The use of brain death has changed from motif –
metaphorically alluding to a broken relationship in *La flor de mi secreto*
(The Flower of My Secret, 1995) and to regenerative forces associated
with facing past trauma in *Todo sobre* – to being the central, bodily
expression of the film's main topics: silence, loneliness, and the role
of art in articulating a response to difficult events, including death,
abuse, and national trauma.

The dead or unresponsive bodies that populate these three films
mask other, less obvious links between them, in particular between
Todo sobre and *Hable con ella*. The former is dominated by Esteban's
(Eloy Azorín) recurrent accusation of not having the whole picture of
his past as signified by the mutilated photographs without his father
that his mother, Manuela (Cecilia Roth), keeps; the latter explicitly
mentions the missing father but remains silent on the issue of censored family and national history, which is nevertheless evident in
Benigno's (Javier Cámara) prized possession of half of his parents'
wedding photograph (the father is missing). This half-photograph,
framed and displayed in an attempt to signal a complete family and
national history, accompanies Benigno at home, in prison, and,
finally, to his grave. Like budding writer Esteban, Benigno retreats
into a personal world of the imagination, one that he fails to distinguish from reality. Benigno resembles David Kelsey, the protagonist
of Patricia Highsmith's *This Sweet Sickness* (1960), an intertext of

Hable con ella. Thus, despite the reference to communication in the title, silence and secrets dominate, even as the film boasts one of the most verbose characters in Almodóvar's filmography, Benigno. Speech does not always equate to meaningful communication. As Paul Julian Smith states, in *Hable con ella* 'solitude is the main and uncompromising theme' (2002: 25). Silence (including censorship) and solitude dominate Almodóvar's films from *La flor*.

Hable con ella was hailed for its aesthetic achievements (French, 2002; Smith, 2004b) but also criticised due to the main plotline involving rape. The film tells the parallel stories of two men – nurse Benigno and travel writer and journalist Marco (Darío Grandinetti) – that converge in the atemporal space of a hospital. Benigno first spots Marco during an initial performance of Pina Bausch's 'Café Müller', when he notes that Marco is crying with emotion. The film then shows Benigno's and Marco's lives in juxtaposed scenes: Benigno at work as a nurse taking care of vegetative patient Alicia (Leonor Watling), a dancer who has had a car accident; Marco using his job as a journalist to meet bullfighter Lydia (Rosario Flores) and woo her. We learn that Benigno stalks Alicia before her accident, his obsession leading to her rape and his imprisonment and suicide. We follow Marco's relationship with Lydia from Marco's initial interest to its end as Lydia is gored by a bull and ends in a vegetative state. A friendship develops between Benigno and Marco. Marco leaves Spain when he discovers that Lydia was planning to break off their relationship but returns on hearing the news of Lydia's death and that Benigno is in prison for Alicia's rape. Despite Marco's efforts to help Benigno, he fails to pass on the news that Alicia has miraculously woken up from her coma. Unaware of this, Benigno commits suicide in the hope of entering a coma and joining Alicia in hospital. The optimistic ending shows an incipient relationship between Marco and the unsuspecting Alicia.

Marco's story is given precedence over Benigno's and closes the film, but Benigno's story – continued in Marco's reprisal of Benigno's relationship with Alicia – is the main focus of the film and has generated the most controversy because of Benigno's (repeated) rape of Alicia whilst she is in a coma. Chronology shows that Alicia had already missed a period when the hidden rape scene takes place. Benigno fiddles her medical notes the very same week. When Alicia's pregnancy is discovered she is two months pregnant. Some critics, like Pilar Aguilar, criticise the fact that Almodóvar makes Benigno 'a moving young man in love [with Alicia] who brings her back to life', sarcastically noting that 'after this, it seems that we still have to think that Almodóvar cares about women' (2003; my translation). Whilst acknowledging the complexity of the film, Karen Backstein echoes this view: 'Not only are two vibrant and particularly *physical* female protagonists reduced to stillness and silence during the course of the fable, but Almodóvar represents in sympathetic (though clear-eyed) fashion a man who commits a monstrous act' (2003: 41). Defences of Almodóvar range from a celebration of its aesthetic to an analysis of rape as 'a narrative tool that represents multiple different forms of social, psychological and even cultural damage', or a means for Spain's recovery from its 'national trauma' via a 'promise of national reconstruction' (Acevedo-Muñoz, 2007: 240–1).

The most problematic of these defences are perceptions of Benigno as 'innocent' as voiced by Marco in the film and by Kent Jones: 'This warm, cheerful child-man, half-way between Chayefsky's Marty and Hitchcock's Norman Bates, may be the film's wisest character. He's the most complex innocent in movies since Sheen and Spacek in *Badlands*, but he's more of a real person' (2002: 15). Although Benigno shares an overbearing mother with Marty in the eponymous film (Mann, 1955), the fusion of Marty and *Psycho*'s Norman Bates (Hitchcock, 1960) has a closer precedent in Dennis Potter's Martin Taylor from *Brimstone and Treacle*, a psychopath who befriends a couple caring for their disabled daughter in order to sponge off them and rape her. Potter's TV play was written in 1974 for the BBC and was deemed so controversial that it was shelved for eleven years, eventually being shown in 1987. Before that, a film version directed by Richard Loncraine starring singer Sting as Martin Taylor was released in 1982. The plot of *Hable con ella* borrows heavily from *Brimstone and Treacle*, including a main character whose charm blinds those around him to his criminal actions and a controversial rape that precedes the healing of the disabled woman, as well as Martin's trick of returning Mr Bates's wallet to make the Bates trust him, his disturbing identification with Mrs Bates, and the young woman's accident in the rain. Whereas Martin is clearly characterised as a criminal suffering from mental health problems, the portrayal of Benigno does not offer viewers such a clear moral or psychological picture. Benigno is complex, but not necessarily innocent. His innocence is predicated on his own view of his 'relationship' with Alicia, which he perceives to be a relationship of love and affection, even though Alicia is unable to consent to anything.

Such justification permeates Kinder's analysis, for example, when she states: 'Only the dancer is brought back to life – through acts of love, both verbal and physical, that reawaken her body as a motherland. Though such acts would ordinarily be called "rape," the maternal Benigno performs them as part of his tragic devotion to his beloved, with whom he identifies and to whom he willingly donates his vital organs, even at the risk of his own life' (2004: 18). Kinder's reading of Alicia's body as the motherland is problematically justified:

> Having devoted 15 years to nursing his mother, this mama's boy admires and emulates women's ability to talk about their emotional lives, which is the core of maternal melodrama and, according to Almodóvar, the root of all fiction and narrative. Yet Benigno rejects two patriarchal institutions that frequently play a crucial role in this genre because of their simplistic approach to language: psychoanalysis (with its so-called 'talking cure' and diagnostic labels), and the law (with its binary choices of true/false and innocent/guilty). He resists other binaries (like gay or straight, male or female) and reductive definitions of key words like *brain-dead, psychopath,* and *rape.* (2004: 20)

Benigno's absent father and the unhealthy relationship with his mother are seen as factors in Benigno's behaviour, trauma being a pre-condition of sociopathy. Yet the film only shows Benigno's plight through his own conversation with the psychiatrist. Benigno resists binaries when it suits him, as in his lie to Alicia's father about his sexual orientation. As Ann Davies comments, 'Almodóvar teaches us the danger of resorting to clichés about sexual orientation when assessing people; for in fact other dangers such as Benigno's sexual obsession may thus go unnoticed. And yet, once we realise where Benigno's interests really lie, our possible identification with him and his story might make us relieved that Alicia's father settles for the explanation of homosexuality' (2007: 105).

The film uses an equivocation technique: arousing, assuaging, and finally confirming suspicion. Suspicion is first aroused due to Benigno's closeness to Alicia's body and dismissed due to his supposed homosexuality, which is nevertheless immediately denied by Benigno himself. Benigno employs a similar technique when stalking Alicia, who confronts him. He at firsts confirms her suspicions but immediately offers an acceptable explanation in suggesting he only wanted to return Alicia's lost purse. Alicia is disarmed and cannot refuse him when he asks to walk her home.

Benigno uses a similar trick during his appointment with Alicia's father, giving him enough information about his background to encourage him to pursue therapy, only to refute his claim that his 'adolescence' was 'special' and defend his mother, saying that she 'wasn't disabled, or mad. She was just a bit lazy, you know.' Benigno's use of 'lazy' shows his fixation with Alicia, whose surname is 'Roncero', literally lazy or delayed in Spanish. Although Benigno is aware of ethical limits to behaviour, as demonstrated by his outrage at Dr Roncero's interrogation, he chooses to see himself above such limitations. His piecemeal personal morality picks whatever elements of tradition and modernity suit his obsession. For example, his desire to marry Alicia could well respond to a traditional, Catholic-inflected Spanish moral obligation to marry due to Alicia becoming pregnant. Instead of facing the likely outcome of discovery of his crime, Benigno fantasises about a suitable 'punishment' that validates his romantic narrative and allows continuation of his obsession with Alicia.

Moving beyond psychological interpretations, one could link Benigno's obsession with the mother ('motherland' in Kinder's analysis) to Almodóvar's frequent use of violence in relation to 'national trauma'. As Acevedo-Muñoz notes, Almodóvar 'returns to the recurring motif of the human body as symbolic of the national trauma, and eventually of the possibility of reconstruction' (2007: 240). Both Alicia's and Lydia's bodies could well stand in for Spain, the struggle for self-definition and reimagination in previous Almodóvar films reconfigured as gender conflict. The image of Spain as a nation suspended between life and death has a long history in Spanish culture as exemplified in singer-songwriter Cecilia's song 'Mi querida España' (My dear Spain). Composed and censored in 1975 (the year Franco died), the lyrics refer to Spain as 'dead' *and* 'alive' in a thinly veiled allusion to the last years of the dictatorship. Benigno's imagined relationship with Alicia could stand for the grip maintained on Spain by those who insist on continuing a one-sided relationship, allegedly modernising during the Transition to democracy, but only so that nothing changes.

There is no way of disputing Benigno's point of view. However, besides his lies about Alicia's periods to disguise the pregnancy, Benigno is seen to lie or mislead on at least two other occasions: when Alicia's father questions him about his sexuality and when he says to Marco that he kept his second appointment with the psychiatrist. In his flashback we actually see Benigno ringing the doorbell, but Dr Roncero has previously stated that Benigno never showed and Benigno did not challenge him. Although the actual visit to the psychiatrist may not be relevant, it is important to note that the point of view of the flashback is Benigno's and that we are being shown reality as he recollects or constructs it, rather than as it may have been. The mastery of the film lies in its ability to walk a tight rope between the rule of law on the one hand and Benigno's taboo-breaking justifications on the other, moving viewers to understand and feel pity for a character like Benigno. Almodóvar has attributed this achievement to tone: 'the tone is what really defines the movie. It is very difficult to talk about the movie to people who have not seen it. It sounds almost monstrous' (Arroyo, 2002). Indeed, the plot synopsis could well damn Benigno's actions, but the film is able to generate sympathy for Benigno and his plight whilst making clear that he has committed a crime.

Davies notes that 'Almodóvar has demonstrated an intermittent taste for pathological characters who are presented to us with a certain degree of sympathy. ... Benigno in *Hable con ella* is the most complex and perhaps the most troublesome example of this— precisely because he is such an engaging character' (2007: 104). As Kinder states, 'Almodóvar ... uses his own inventiveness (like Katerina and Bausch) to re-choreograph these transgressive scenarios as fully embodied love stories' (2004: 21). This is precisely what Vladimir Nabokov does in *Lolita*, a narrative precedent of *Hable con ella* in its use of a criminal's first person narrative. Likewise, Highsmith's David Kelsey's point of view permeates most of the third person narrative in *This Sweet Sickness*. In *Hable con ella* Benigno's views of the world are rarely challenged until he tells Marco that he wants to marry Alicia, a completely logical follow-up to his belief that he has a meaningful relationship with her, a belief that until then had seemed a humane attitude to looking after a brain-dead patient.

Benigno's performance of innocence lulls other characters into thinking he is harmless. Even as he is caught by Alicia breaking into her home and spying on her showering, she seems to accept his claim that he is 'harmless'. His name, Benigno – benign in Spanish – is either a conscious give-away or an attempt at reinforcing his harmlessness, depending on whether audiences accept his deeds as criminal or signs of his 'tragic devotion'. In the absence of

Alicia's point of view, the audience is caught in Benigno's narrative embellishments as much as the film's own formal accomplishments. Benigno literally recounts much of the action to other characters. Some of these stories become flashbacks, such as how he met (and stalked) Alicia; others are retellings of events we have already witnessed and are being reported to a third person. As Almodóvar states in the film's Pressbook, men are 'narrators of themselves' (quoted in Smith, 2002: 26).

Male self-expression and self-construction comes at the expense of women in the film, who are silenced by male characters and by the film's own structure until the very end. As Mark Allinson explains:

> for much of the duration of the film, both female protagonists ... are deprived of speech owing to physical trauma. Their silence paradoxically gives voice to their male partners, imposing on the men the need to retell and review their stories. While Benigno ... lives his life merely so he can retell it to his beloved Alicia, Marco ... finds himself obliged to recall (and thus retell) the story of his relationship with Lydia. (Allinson, 2009: 152)

Benigno narrates Alicia as object of desire but also as identificatory model. She stands in for his mother and in fact resembles her, as well as the unconscious Viridiana of the eponymous film by Luis Buñuel (1961). Benigno's monologues are not 'imposed' on him due to Alicia's silence; her silence is his opportunity to prey on her sexually and as a model for his own depleted life. Benigno is not only in thrall of Alicia's body, but of what she represents. Her association with the arts (particularly contemporary dance and art-house cinema) mark her out as upper middle class as opposed to Benigno's more humble origins. Their social backgrounds can be seen in the location and decoration of their homes (Alicia's in an opulent apartment block in a main street, Benigno's much more modest with dated décor). Benigno's job as a nurse in a private clinic would not pay much but he redecorates his whole flat as a sort of shrine to Alicia, in the colour of her bedroom at home and her hospital room. Paul Julian Smith sees Benigno's redecoration of his home on a nurse's salary as a sign that 'hermetic and self-referential, the Almodóvar universe has become immune to social stresses' (2004b: 369). Not so, as late 1990s and early twenty-first century Spain was going through an economic boom period with record levels of personal debt and easy credit. Benigno's 2002 largesse – as opposed to Victor's 1997 make-do approach to improving his home in *Carne trémula* (Live Flesh, 1997) – is a sign of Almodóvar's acute observation of changes in Spain. Moreover, Benigno copies directly from a magazine, a sign of his lack of developed taste. Benigno's interior design is an attempt at class mimicry similar to his copying of Alicia's interests. Hiding behind a bland, impersonal façade, Benigno's bedroom shows the extent to which his fixation with Alicia is a sign of a wider project to remake himself as a modern man and his failure to do so.

Contemporary dance is crucial to this interpretation. As Julián Gutiérrez-Albilla suggests, in Spain 'the search for belated and accelerated modernity, dance, and especially modern dance, was connected with a cultural liberalisation of the country that was in the process of consolidating an empathic system and becoming economically and politically integrated in the modern European Union' (2005: 48). Dance is associated in the film with class and foreignness as denoted by Alicia, Marco, and Alicia's teacher, Katerina. Contemporary dance epitomises Benigno's appropriated utopian aspirational fantasy, but he flounders, as seen in his failure to find a suitable term when Katerina is explaining her new project:

KATERINA   ... when a soldier dies from his body emerges his soul, his ghost, and that's a ballerina. Long tutu, white like the 'Wilis' in 'Giselle', classical, but with blood stains, red.
...
From death emerges life. From the male emerges the female.
BENIGNO   Of course.
KATERINA   From the earthly emerges ... [searching for words]
BENIGNO   The ... beach?
KATERINA   No. From the earthly emerges ...
BENIGNO   The ... water?
KATERINA   (exasperated) No. The ethereal. The ethereal, the impalpable, the ghostly.

Benigno's attempts to talk about ballet show his lack of cultural capital, to use Pierre Bourdieu's terminology, as well as his literal-mindedness. The ballet is the sublimation of traditional ideas about gender, with femininity aligned to life and the ethereal and masculinity to death and the earthly, foreshadowing Benigno's and Alicia's future, where Benigno's crime is the trigger for his death and Alicia's recovery.

Whereas Benigno 'fully playacts being in a relationship without having to deal with the thorny problem of reality or another person's will' (Backstein, 2003: 41), Marco recalls his failure to listen to Lydia and allow her to speak, which shows him to be more aware of the damning silence of his partner whilst in a coma, but also during their short relationship. As Backstein shrewdly points out, 'one irony of the title is that Benigno can only really talk to Alicia when she can neither hear nor respond, while Marco talks to the sentient Lydia in a way that silences her: when he says, after a long car ride together, that "We talked the whole way," she replies, "*You* talked the whole way"' (2003: 41–2). Marco realises his error too late to listen to Lydia and talk to her meaningfully but heeds her wishes retrospectively when he finds out from El Niño that she was about to break up with him. Benigno, on the other hand, never acknowledges that he is not talking to Alicia, but *at* her, imposing his desire on her, first as a stalker and then as a carer.

Marco is not the only one projecting his view of the world onto Lydia's behaviour; Lydia is seen as a woman first and bullfighter second by everyone around her. Her typecasting as a 'desperate woman' (Marco's phrase) is the result of media framing as a woman in love, used and rejected by an unscrupulous man as he seeks out fame at her expense. She is repeatedly questioned about her failed relationship on national television. Lydia may be reeling from the end of her relationship with El Niño de Valencia, but she does not refer to this as her main cause of distress. Instead, she talks about her late father as the major influence on her life. Viewers – like Marco – are primed to believe otherwise and see her as a weak woman despite the obvious physical and mental strength required in bullfighting.

The first time we see her bullfighting is also framed by this narrative of vulnerability through the conversation of El Niño de Valencia and his agent, who think she is trying to impress El Niño:

EL NIÑO   She's gone nuts.
AGENT   She's dedicating it to you. She'd let the bull rip her apart just so that you could see it. We shouldn't have come, especially you.

The use of music in this set piece seems to reinforce this message, as Brazilian singer Elis Regina's 'Por toda a minha vida' (All My Life) plays alongside stylised shots of the bullfighter's balletic movements and beautifully composed body.[2] The song is an oath by a lover to her beloved, promising 'all my life to be only yours and love you like nobody ever loved'. However, Lydia's love object during the bullfight is not El Niño, but bullfighting itself. As Lydia looks up at the crowd, we are given an extreme close-up of the left hand side of her chest that fades to reveal what is inside her heart: an iconic old photograph of a revered bullfighter, Manolete, whilst injured. Glory and artistry occupy Lydia's heart. If bullfighting is associated with any man in Lydia's mind, it is her father, a would-be bullfighter who could only be a *banderillero*.[3] Lydia's aspiration is signalled by the use of red and gold in her costume. Like Benigno, she is trying to move above her station, not only in terms of class but also, more importantly in this case, gender. Here Almodóvar is drawing on contemporary reactions to women bullfighters in Spain, in particular to Cristina Sánchez.[4] The silencing of women on-screen thus functions as an indictment of their socially inferior status off-screen. The scene, like the cele-brated one of Caetano Veloso singing 'Cucurrucucú paloma' later in the film, stops the action. In this respect, it is an example of what Kathleen Vernon has identified as change in Almodóvar's use of music from *Todo sobre*. For Vernon 'song serves the cause of cultural mobility while freezing the advance of the narrative and inviting us to contemplate the translations between geographic, artistic, sexual, and affective registers and identities' (2009: 54). Both 'Por toda a minha vida' and 'Cucurrucucú paloma' introduce reflective scenes on art and devotion, making the link between passion for art and devotion to a lover.

The importance of art is further highlighted in the party scene with Caetano Veloso through a short sequence of an anonymous man swimming. As noted by Despina Kakoudaki, this sequence, which has no narrative function, is reminiscent of David Hockney's 'swim-ming paintings, such as *Portrait of an Artist (Pool with Two Figures)* (1971) [sic], and his numerous lithographs and "camera works" involv-ing pool scenes' (2009: 224) (Figure 11.1).

Immersion in art as pure joy (the swimmer's expression) and pain (Marco's tears) is precisely what Lydia experiences during the bull-fight, and her death is not the result of despair as Acevedo-Muñoz assumes (2007) but attempting a *porta gayola*.[5] These reactions to art are mostly physical, not verbal. As Smith states in his discus-sion of the film's opening scene, 'Almodóvar is suggesting that the meaning of this film cannot be reduced to rational discourse,

11.1   An anonymous swimmer (*Hable con ella*, 2002)

that the "eloquence of the body" (his phrase) must take precedence in aesthetics as in ethics' (2004b: 368). The film's title, *Hable con ella*, is thus more misleading than it seems and should be understood as a question mark as much as an imperative. The last time we see Alicia before her accident she is left speechless by Benigno's violation of her privacy. Benigno's actions place him alongside famous cinematic voyeurs such as Norman Bates (whose name also reinforces normality and, thus, harmlessness) in *Psycho* and, like Norman, he presents himself as a mild-mannered, caring figure devoted to his mother. Benigno's characterisation – his plain jacket and anodyne clothes – is further reminiscent of Norman. Norman's possible necrophilia is also hinted at in Benigno's sexual penchant for Alicia's unresponsive body. Benigno's fetish is shared by two other 'pathological characters' in Almodóvar's oeuvre, Diego and María in *Matador*, who also kill themselves. *Hable con ella* contains other allusions to *Psycho*: a comic one when Marco fetches Benigno's key from the caretaker and she stands behind a glass door on the ground floor, resembling Norman's 'Mother', and a tragic one when Benigno's face is reflected onto Marco's during their final conversation in prison, echoing the famous blurring of Norman's twisted face with his mother's skull. Marco is henceforth not just acting for himself but also acting out Benigno's wishes as Benigno becomes the unseen third person (signalled by his empty theatre chair) in Marco and Alicia's budding relationship. Almodóvar talks of how this reflection in the prison was 'discovered by accident. I asked the DP to light in a way to accentuate this idea of the two men becoming one. ... This is almost a moment of romantic love' (Arroyo, 2002).

Benigno spins a narrative web, much as he embroiders his idealised relationship via monograms of his and Alicia's initials, 'A' and 'B', onto his bed sheets. 'A' can also stand for his mother, Amalia. As Acevedo-Muñoz explains, 'like so many Hitchcock protagonists, from *Notorious* to *Psycho*, Benigno confuses his first, repressive and elusive object of desire, his mother, for Alicia' (2007: 254). He is identified with fabric and texture, as well as textuality. Like Humbert, he is associated with the spider, both in his presentation and due to his association with the silent film-within-a-film, *El Amante menguante* (*Waning Man* rather than *Shrinking Man* as it has been translated in the English version). *El Amante* is in direct intertextual relation with sci-fi classic *The Incredible Shrinking Man* (Arnold, 1957), a film where the shrinking protagonist Scott Carey (Grant Williams) ends up melting away into Nature in a pantheistic ending parodied in Almodóvar's *El Amante* as Alfredo (Fele Martínez) instead disappears into a vagina. A spider associated with Scott's wife (its web rests on Lou's abandoned piece of cake, next to her workspace in the cellar) is seen by Scott as an existential threat and he successfully plots to stab it with a nail: 'One of us had to die.' Scott, who sarcastically refers to himself as 'the child that looks like a man' and who feels that his masculinity is threatened, recovers his masculinity with his victory over the spider only to realise that 'I had thought in terms of Man's own limited dimension. I had presumed upon Nature.' The spider is called 'monster' and 'devil' and its hairy jaws are reminiscent of a vulva, a *vagina dentata*. In *The Incredible*, the spider is a clear symbol of threatening femininity, repository of Scott's displaced anger towards his wife as his power in the relationship wanes with his increasing dependence.

El Amante's Alfredo does not feel threatened or struggle against the feminine. Indeed, he joins it in an exercise of defilement that is regenerative, waning like the moon rather than shrinking/diminishing. As Acevedo-Muñoz observes:

Alfredo returns to the repressive mother from whom he had escaped earlier in his life, presumably as he discovered sexuality. The infantilised Alfredo then, arguably, regresses to the repressed recognition of the mother as the first object of desire when he climbs into Amparo's vagina, trying to return to the womb. ... The name of the hotel where Amparo and Alfredo's consummation occurs (Youkali) is also the name of the much-desired maternal estate in *Kika*. The name, taken from a piece by German composer Kurt Weill (1900–50), is supposedly that

of a utopian island paradise, but in both *Kika* and *Talk to Her*, it signifies the incestuous anxiety of a disturbed young man. (Acevedo-Muñoz,
2007: 254)

Benigno's rape of Alicia is the result of his desire not just to possess
femininity but to blend with it, something already signalled by his
previous theft of Alicia's hairgrip (another thinly disguised *vagina
dentata*) and anguish at being parted from it. Notwithstanding, I
would not go as far as Mark Allinson in suggesting that Benigno's
attitude is 'woman-centered (I dare not quite say "feminist")', or that
'for Benigno, to know women is not to "possess" them, but to tend to
their needs' (2009: 156). In my opinion Benigno is a masochist, on
the one hand educating himself to become the sort of ideal Christian
woman Franco's dictatorship promoted in order to tend his phallic
mother,[6] on the other forever seeking the nurturing oral mother
described by Deleuze: 'in masochism, the mother is cold, severe, and
sentimental like Mother Earth who feeds and kills, and to whom,
in the end, all her children return. She is a cold and severe mother,
but not a sadistic woman' (Geyskens, 2010: 109). Benigno's flashback shows him at home behind white net curtains spying on Alicia,
waiting for his chance to make contact with his prey like a spider.
During the rape scene Alicia is made up like Amparo (Paz Vega), the
female protagonist of the silent film but, whereas Amparo looks like a
grown woman enjoying physical stimulation by her lover (even if she
has not explicitly consented), Alicia is unresponsive and she resembles a girl or doll due to her pigtails and make-up. The beginning of
the scene is shot from the point of view of Alicia's right ear and shows
the end of the right pigtail resting on her shoulder. At first sight it
looks like the pubic area. This is one of the first indications that there
is a more sinister, hidden story. Benigno's careful pulling down of
the hospital gown foreshadows Alfredo's pulling down of Amparo's
bedsheet to discover her body, starting with her breasts.

Benigno identifies with Amparo's boyfriend, Alfredo, who is 'like
me'. We see Amparo's face in ecstasy as she orgasms, then in quiet
contentment following Alfredo's penetration. This is quickly followed by Alicia's expressionless face at rest and Benigno's rubbing
of her thigh towards her pubic area as he says that 'Alfredo stays
inside her forever'. Alicia's face at rest is shown again, followed by
a shot of the lava lamp's mingling of yellow and red substances shot
horizontally. Using the colours of the Spanish flag may be a way of

signalling the attempted merger of old and new Spain, an experiment that fails as the child is stillborn, but succeeds in the rebirth of the modern woman, Alicia, whose body has rejected the maternal burden promoted during the dictatorship in order to live.

With this 'process of cinematic "masking"', D'Lugo speculates, 'Almodóvar problematizes Benigno's identity by a sleight of hand that brings the spectator to occupy the point of view of the rapist, who is also the storyteller' (2006: 113). Kevin Ohi, on the other hand, asks why we should deduce that intercourse has taken place as we only hear Benigno's monologue and Almodóvar is not shy to show sex on-screen. Ohi puts forward the theory that Alicia's is an 'immaculate conception' and *El amante* 'ought to be read ... less for its themes or for what it reveals psychologically [about Benigno] than as one of many scenes depicting scenes of spectatorship', with Almodóvar contrasting the voyeurism of the 'sexualized gaze at exposed bodies and an absorbed gaze at aesthetic spectacles' (2009: 523; 526). Whilst Ohi's analysis of spectatorship in *Hable con ella* is shrewd, there is little to warrant a miracle as explanation for Alicia's pregnancy. By denying physical contact Ohi seems to be occupying 'the point of view of the rapist, who is also the storyteller'. As I have previously noted, Almodóvar frequently uses objects as metonymies for sexual intercourse—for example, in *Pepi, Luci, Bom y otras chicas del montón* (Pepi, Luci, Bom, and Other Girls on the Heap, 1980) and *La ley* – not because he shies away from sexual content or because these acts are not happening. He used this technique in *Hable con ella*; he says:

> to hide what was going on in the clinic. I wanted to cover it up in the best cinematic way and in an entertaining manner. ... I didn't want to show Benigno doing what he did in the clinic. I also did not want to show the audience that image. So I put the silent movie in there to hide what was happening.
>
> But it is, of course, full of meaning. I anticipate what is going to happen later in the film. I also wanted to express the strength of cinema to hide reality. (Almodóvar, quoted in Arroyo, 2002)

El amante is a metonymy that hides an ellipsis, something Almodóvar is incredibly fond of. Just as Nabokov demonstrated the persuasive power of language, Almodóvar shows the ability of cinematic language to build alternative worlds and conceal as well as show. His films are full of secrets and teasing prompts to viewers to go beyond their surface content. These correspond to what has been described in literature as poetic diction, comprising of, for example, circumlocution, elision, personification, and the use of images and intertextuality. The poetic is the main mode of *Hable con ella*, what Almodóvar refers to as 'tone'.

Poetic techniques are used skilfully to equivocate, as Benigno does, and constantly undermine spectators' assumptions. Almodóvar writes in his notes on *Hable con ella*:

> Disrupted time and the mixing of diverse narrative units function best when the action is mental or internal, or occurs in another dimension, as in the films of David Lynch. In this kind of 'fantastic neorealism' or 'naturalism of the absurd' in which I move, plot ruptures suppose a kind of punch in the eyes of the spectator since he's already bonded with the characters and the story, and I pull him away, grab him, and oblige him to follow another character, another story. (Almodóvar, quoted in D'Lugo, 2006: 10)

Paradoxically – and unlike Almodóvar's next film, *La mala educación* – the fragmented narrative is seamlessly absorbed and hidden in the film, which is not as disruptive as Almodóvar suggests. D'Lugo states that 'Rather than diminishing the desire for story, these "punches in the eye" intensify viewers' delight with the storytelling process' (2006: 10). The film is composed not so much of 'punches in the eye' as riffs that appear regularly. Marco and Lydia's story, the contemporary dance pieces that bookend the film, Lydia's mesmerising bullfighting, and the magic performance of 'Cucurrucucú paloma' are variations that 'intensify viewers' delight with the storytelling process', not because they 'rupture' the film's narrative but because they enhance its symbolic plane as the different images in a poem accumulate to become more than the sum of its parts. *Hable con ella* can be seen as foregrounding a mythopoetic function (myth-making using cultural activities such as storytelling, music, or poetry, for self-understanding) in Almodóvar's cinema, hence its 'disrupted time and the mixing of diverse narrative units'. As Richard Lane and Philip Tew state, in contemporary mythopoetic texts 'adjacency of past and present becomes an aesthetic dynamic. ... History is both interrogated and becomes interrogative' (2003: 12). Adriana Novoa's analysis of *Hable con ella*'s use of fairy-tale motifs, the most apparent of which is the 'Sleeping Beauty' myth (cf. Naughten, 2006), observes this juxtaposition, concluding that 'the film employs fairy-tale strategies in critiquing a contemporary society beset by dehumanization and alienation. But ... in making his case, the director imposes a misogynist conception of gender that must be analysed with extreme care. In the very act of subverting relationships between men by reinventing the fairy tale, he recreates utterly traditional female characters' (2005: 225). Whilst I share some of Novoa's and Backstein's reservations about the use of patriarchal tropes of femininity, I am not as forceful in condemning their use since, in this film and even more obviously in *La mala educación*, they are employed to comment on the (sometimes misused) persuasive power of cinema and storytelling, and the complex, sometimes unpalatable, nature of contemporary Spain.

Notes

1 Before *Hable con ella*, the last foreign film to win an Oscar for Best Screenplay was Claude Lelouch's *Un homme et une femme* (A Man and A Woman, 1964).
2 Lydia's body is only focused on during the bullfight and dressing for it, unlike Alicia's which is mined for voyeuristic shots recalling famous nude paintings such as Francisco Goya's 'The Nude Maja'.
3 A *banderillero* is an assistant to the bullfighter who sticks *banderillas* (barbed darts with banderoles) into the bull's back to weaken it at different stages of the bullfight.
4 Cristina Sánchez became a bullfighter in 1996 but 'retired' three years later. Her attorney blamed male bullfighters who refused to appear with her, with some such as Francisco Rivera Ordóñez stating that 'one must have two balls to face a bull and triumph in the main bullrings' (quoted in Amiguet, 2016). Like the fictional Lydia, she was the daughter of a *banderillero*.
5 *Porta gayola* is a spectacular but dangerous trick. The bullfighter waits for the bull to come out on their knees with the *capote* in front of them. As the bull charges, the bullfighter tricks it by swinging the *capote* right to left in a circular way with one hand.
6 After the Spanish Civil War, repressive measures were widely adopted to keep women silent, poorly educated and mostly in the home. A blend of Catholic and fascist ideology was used to 'educate' women into an ideal womanhood, one focused on family and home and subservient to men. Stereotypically feminine activities such as sewing were encouraged (cf. Domingo, 2007).

12

Faking memory: *La mala educación*

Whereas the secrets that structure *Hable con ella* (Talk to Her, 2002) remain on the whole confined to the personal, in *La mala educación* (Bad Education, 2004) narrative ellipses are more obviously historicised. Fredric Strauss talks about the use of ellipses in *Todo sobre mi madre* (All about My Mother, 1999), *Hable con ella*, and *La mala educación*, noting that in the last two films 'the moving back and forth between past and present adds a sense of depth' (2006: 214). Almodóvar concurs, stating that, in *La mala educación*, ellipses 'correspond to the fade to blacks, and are what I think give that sense of depth. They're like black holes which, literally, add a depth to the film, a sombre depth. For the first time, I detailed these fade to blacks in the script since they occur at such precise moments' (quoted in Strauss, 2006: 214). The main fade to blacks in *La mala educación* coincide with elided sex scenes, including the first time that 'Father Manolo' (Daniel Giménez Cacho) abuses Ignacio as a child (Nacho Pérez) and repeated sexual encounters between Enrique (Fele Martínez) and Juan (Gael García Bernal). As well as fade to blacks, the film contains many hard cuts that cause viewer disorientation and the melting of temporal frames. These, and the use of framing and digital manipulation, convey visual meaning in a covert way. For example, as Paul Julian Smith explains,

> Almodóvar uses framing to full effect, as when the black shoulder of the priest swells to fill the screen in a first (unshown) scene of child abuse, or a high-angle shot of a hundred anonymous boys doing gymnastics gives way to a close-up of the child Ignacio, frozen by desire and loss as his beloved Enrique is taken away. Sometimes past and present are linked by dissolves, as when Ignacio-Zahara and his best friend Paca

in 1977 are superimposed over the page of the typescript that tells their tale in 1980. (2004a: 17)

The black shoulder of the priest is an intradiegetic fade to black, which is then followed by an iris wipe (the shot of the shoulder is replaced by the shot of the exercising boys in the shape of a growing ellipsis). This centres attention on the backsides of the supine boys (supine desirable boys and young men in shorts recur in the film) and also literalises an eye-opening scene, as Ignacio is initiated into sexual abuse and adult duplicity ('Fr Manolo' does not keep his side of the bargain and expels Enrique). Obvious digital manipulation also plays a part in (sometimes misleading) meaning-making: Ignacio's trauma during 'Fr Manolo's' first sexual advance shown as a trickle of blood running down his forehead and splitting his head in two; the faces of the crying child Ignacio and child Enrique (Raúl García Forneiro) as they see each other for the last time are transformed into the faces of the adult Juan (who we believe to be Ignacio) and Enrique in what Enrique believes to be an emotive re-encounter.

The film is structured around ellipses, drawing attention to itself as an act of communication focused on the message itself. This is part of a poetic or aesthetic function that foregrounds textual features and emphasises form and medium. Texts where this function is dominant tend to be more opaque, self-referential, metaphorical, and connotative. The poetic or aesthetic is the dominant function of *La mala educación* and metonymy (synecdoche, using a part to mean the whole, in particular) is its elliptical heart. Whereas in *Hable con ella* the secret is how Alicia becomes pregnant, in *La mala educación* the secret is how Ignacio dies and, by extension, how alternative lifestyles and those seeking justice for crimes committed during the dictatorship were silenced during and after the Transition to democracy in Spain.

For the first time in Almodóvar's career, a whole film is set in the past, combining fragments from three historical periods, 1964, 1977, and 1980. In addition to temporal complexity, some of the events are retellings, representations or fictional reinventions, which make the plot fiendishly complex. Almodóvar has spoken about the difficulties he had with the script, which went through twenty drafts (Almodóvar, quoted in Strauss, 2006: 214). This complexity is not gratuitous, however; it partakes of an aesthetic common to Spanish films and literature about the repression of historical memory and the Spanish

Transition. *La mala educación* is a film about the Transition that takes this aesthetic to breaking point. It harnesses it to place LGBTQ+ issues, which were silenced in Spanish culture during and after the Transition, centre stage. Alberto Mira talks about a spiral structure from Ignacio's childhood memory to the short story, the 1980 narrative present, and the film adaptation (2008: 551). The childhood memory is the absent centre of the spiral, the other episodes forming as the focus moves away from or towards that memory. I would suggest thinking of the film as a double helix since the spiral is doubled by metafictionality. This structure pulls viewers in opposite directions both at plot level (characters are shown to have different fates in alternative versions of the story, for example) and in relation to issues such as the film's supposed autobiographical nature, use of history and public memory, and representation of visible yet censored LGBTQ+ identities.

In 1980, filmmaker Enrique Goded is looking for ideas for a new film when an old school friend – Ignacio, whom he has not seen for years – turns up with a short story titled 'La visita' (The Visit),[1] partly based on their time together at a religious boarding school in the mid-1960s. Enrique does not recognise Ignacio but takes the story to read nevertheless. 'La visita' is a wish-fulfilling narrative set in 1977, where 'Ignacio',[2] now grown up and touring with a burlesque company as a trans woman called Zahara, picks up a young man, discovers he is her old school friend 'Enrique', and has sex with him, possibly restarting their relationship. Zahara also blackmails an old priest, 'Fr Manolo', who abused her as a child and plans to help the unemployed 'Enrique' with money. 'La visita' is set in 1977, a crucial year for the Transition, but contains an important analepsis or flashback to 1964 in the form of a short story that the fictional Zahara/'Ignacio' has written about her budding relationship with 'Enrique' at school and 'Fr Manolo's' interference and abuse. Within 'La visita', Zahara/'Ignacio' takes this story to 'Fr Manolo', who reads it. At this point, the 1980 Enrique is reading a story containing a fictionalised version of himself as 'Enrique', where a fictionalised version of Ignacio, 'Ignacio', going by the name of Zahara, makes a fictionalised 'Fr Manolo' read a short story about Zahara/'Ignacio's' version of the events in 1964, which have in all likelihood been embellished but contain enough shared details to convince the 1980s Enrique that the author of 'La visita' is his old school crush.

Enrique decides to adapt 'La visita' but Ignacio – who wants to be known by his artistic name, Ángel Andrade – insists on taking the lead role as Zahara/'Ignacio' and takes the story away when Enrique refuses to cast him. By then Enrique is curious to know more about Ignacio/Ángel and goes to his home town in Galicia, where he discovers that the real Ignacio (Francisco Boira) died in 1977 and that it is his younger brother Juan who has brought him Ignacio's short story. Desire for Juan and curiosity to know why he impersonates his brother prompt Enrique to cast Juan as Zahara/'Ignacio', but changing the ending, possibly as he now knows that Ignacio was trying to blackmail the real Fr Manolo – now a lay man going by the name of Mr Manuel Berenguer (Lluís Homar) – around the time of his death and that after Ignacio's death Mr Berenguer went to his mother's house looking for his stories; in Enrique's adaptation, 'Fr Manolo' and another priest kill Zahara/'Ignacio'. On the last day of filming, Mr Berenguer visits the set and tells Enrique his version of what happened to Ignacio, a story shown through a flashback: that Ignacio was a drug addict who in 1977 discovered Mr Berenguer was the former Fr Manolo; that Ignacio tried to blackmail him, threatening to go public with the historical abuse; that he wanted the money for detox and a sex change; that Mr Berenguer started giving him money because he was smitten with Juan; and that Juan and Mr Berenguer became entangled and decided to kill Ignacio by providing him with unadulterated heroin. After the murder, Juan disappeared from Mr Berenguer's life, but Mr Berenguer has tracked him down. The film ends with Juan/Ángel, now on the way to stardom, turning up at Enrique's house. Enrique, who has been having an affair with him, hoping to figure him out, shuts him out in the cold.

The difficulties encountered in attempting to provide a synopsis are not replicated in the viewing experience. Almodóvar places the audience first and things that may appear convoluted – such as using different actors to play the same part in the story/film and the 'real' 1980 – are great aids to following the action. This casting choice reinforces the idea that characters are the same but different. Following convention, Enrique and Ignacio as children are played by child actors (Raúl García Forneiro and Nacho Pérez). The adult Ignacio is played by Francisco Boira in Mr Berenguer's narrative and in the 'real' frame, as seen in a photograph when Enrique visits Ignacio's mother in Galicia. Ignacio is also played by García Bernal, as Juan/Ángel pretends to be his brother in the 1980s in order to play Zahara/'Ignacio' in the film *La visita*.

García Bernal's 'miraculous four-sided performance' (Gilbey, 2004: 46) enables the audience to distinguish between the character he plays – Juan – and Juan's impersonation of his dead brother Ignacio in 1980, and 'Ignacio', during which time he also takes on the role of Zahara in *La visita*. Juan is a young man who, in 1977, conspires to kill his brother Ignacio, allegedly for being a drug addict but also for being an embarrassment to him due to being a trans woman. Juan seduces Mr Berenguer for money and so he helps him kill Ignacio. The fictional 'Fr Manolo' in 'La visita' (both as Enrique reads the story and, later, in the film version of it) is played by Daniel Giménez Cacho but the 'real' lay man Mr Manuel Berenguer is played by Lluís Homar. Of all the doublings, 'Fr Manolo's' – Mr Berenguer's – is the most unusual and the most revealing about the film's insistence on its own metacinematic qualities. 'Fr Manolo' is not a young Mr Berenguer but an adaptation of Ignacio's fictionalised memory of someone Mr Berenguer used to be. Furthermore, the 'real' Ignacio is only seen through Mr Berenguer's and his mother's narratives, and the film's *mise-en-abyme* leads spectators to think of the 'real' 1980 Enrique, Juan/Ángel, and Mr Berenguer as characters in yet another narrative.

The film's *mise-en-abyme* is substantial, most notably in its inclusion of a thirty-minute film-within-a-film, a portrayal of the creative process from the filmmaker's search for ideas, the use of vintage typewriters and cameras (a Super-8 used by Juan and Mr Berenguer to record sex videos and cameras used to film *La visita*), and dissolves of the short story pages and the adaptation as it is imagined by Enrique whilst reading. As in *Dolor y gloria* (Pain and Glory, 2019), realism is further undermined by showing how the film set of *La visita* is dismantled after the final scene is shot: actors revert back to being themselves, sets are moved away to reveal an industrial warehouse, the golden light that bathes the scene is revealed to be artificial, and so on. Only Juan seems still caught within the film; he is distraught and bursts into tears (Figure 12.1).

Juan's *sang froid* is momentarily abandoned as he embodies his brother's fictional alter ego, Zahara. His tears in this context could simply be crocodile tears (becoming in a character who is associated with crocodiles as predators), but García Bernal's performance of sincere feeling points to two other reasons for this: either Juan is

12.1   The film set of Enrique's film-within-the-film, *La visita* (*La mala educación*, 2004)

deeply committed to acting and is actually upset in reaching the end of his contract or his embodiment of Zahara/'Ignacio' as she dies finally allows him to express his feelings of guilt for conspiring to kill his brother. Both correspond with Peter Bradshaw's analysis of *La mala educación* as being 'about the pleasure of acting, role-playing and fantasy and the way these things can be used as wish-fulfilment, as a way of journeying back in time and conquering the demons of the past, and the present' (2004: 14). Vincent Cervantes argues that 'the performance of Zahara by Ángel works to pardon his own sin, his contribution to her murder' (2014: 431).

La mala educación may be, as Geoff Pingree notes, a film 'in which the director redeems his characters by releasing them to the agony of their own wisdom, ... he frames redemption itself as a process of maturity through suffering' (2004: 5). However, in creating a fictional version of his brother's death at the hands of the person he was blackmailing, this conquest is less atonement than a fictional revision of that past, a revision where the Catholic Church takes all the blame and Juan can mourn his brother's death as part of an obscure past left behind during Spain's Transition to a supposedly democratic, secular country. This use of fictional memory has been called 'prosthetic memory' by film scholars, first in relation to implanted memories in sci-fi (Landsberg, 1995) and later on in the analysis of cinematic representations of the past (Cook, 2005; Ellis and Sánchez-Arce, 2011). Alison Landsberg describes prosthetic memories thus: 'memories which do not come from a person's lived experience in any strict sense. These are implanted memories, and the unsettled boundaries between real and simulated ones are frequently accompanied by another disruption: of the human body' (1995: 175). Juan's feelings and experiences as an actor are his own, yet his embodiment of Zahara/'Ignacio' and reimagining of Ignacio's death through the adaptation are simulated. His body is disrupted as he adapts to what the part requires and this physical disruption ushers in a change in subjectivity as simulated, prosthetic memories alter his identity. Discussing memory and embodiment in *La mala educación*, Julián Gutiérrez-Albilla argues that the film

> asks us to rethink the body of the material force which impacts the fragment of subjective and collective memory. ... Through the film's obsession with embodiment, the subject may activate an engagement with fragments of subjective memory, associated here with the violence and abuse inflicted on the body and subjectivity of the fictional character Ignacio. On a parallel plane, subjective memory is aligned with collective memory and history, associated in the film with the aggression and repression that the Franco regime inflicted on the Spanish national body and psyche. (2013b: 323)

Juan's wish to play Zahara/'Ignacio' stems from ambition and a desire to use the power of film to create a prosthetic memory where Ignacio succeeds and does not die. Even as Enrique changes the ending, Juan still benefits as *La visita* enables him to construct an alternative narrative of his brother's death, and thus a new future for himself. Juan embodies the complex 'relationship between memory and experience' (Landsberg, 1995: 177) and personal and collective memory. As a young Spaniard during the Transition, it is in his interest to keep the crimes of the old regime firmly in the past, suppress his brother's unviable identity, and foster an image of himself as in tune with Spain's changing narrative of itself. This use of cinema by Juan and Enrique is reminiscent of Pablo's in *La ley del deseo* (The Law of Desire, 1987). They turn to what Paul Ricoeur calls the 'suprahistorical', which 'directs the gaze away from the future and carries it toward the eternity-dispensing powers of art and religion' (2006: 292).

Joan Ramon Resina distinguishes between 'history and public memory', explaining that 'the two can obviously merge ... when the historian takes on the role of opinion fabricator, or when history becomes the pretext for narrative effects (rather than the other way around), as in the vogue of historical novels in the decade after the dictatorship' (2000: 13). The danger of historians becoming 'opinion fabricator[s]' is clear, but less so the role of 'narrative effects' in cultural texts tackling traumatic historical issues.

Resina considers this a misuse of history in fostering an appreciation of technical virtuosity as opposed to historical fact, and indeed historical novels and films may be used to foster a public memory that departs from or hides historical data, offering a comforting narrative for those holding power. These narratives encourage 'prosthetic memory':

> the process whereby reconstructions of the past produce replacement memories that simulate first-hand experiences. Such enterprises lay themselves open to charges of lack of authenticity, of substituting a degraded popular version for the 'real' event, and to accusations that by presenting history as dramatic spectacle they obscure our understanding of social, political and cultural forces. (Cook, 2005: 2)

Cook argues that by encouraging spectators to 'become involved in re-presenting the past', these texts 'invite explorations and interrogations of the limits of its engagement with history' (2005: 2). Jonathan Ellis and I have also argued that 'cinematic "false" memories ... may eventually summon real ones or at least prompt a fresh engagement with historical documents', suggesting 'that a "prosthetic memory", particularly one that makes viewers aware of its own artificiality, may be the only way to remember the past' (Ellis and Sánchez-Arce, 2011: 174). *La mala educación*'s two narrative strands offer both problematic 'replacement memories that simulate first-hand experiences' *and* memories 'that make viewers aware of [their] own artificiality', thus prompting a fresh engagement with the past and offering a critique of the creation of a comforting public memory. It also ponders the role of cultural agents, including filmmakers such as Enrique and editors such as Mr Berenguer, in the reinvention of that past and present.

Cis actor Juan's embodiment of a trans woman is also suspect. His is a performance of queer traumatic past, but not an altogether positive one as Cervantes (2014) argues because it is employed to manipulate collective memory. Unlike Almodóvar's *La mala educación*, Enrique's *La visita* does not wear artificiality on its sleeve. On the contrary, it illustrates the creation of a comforting public memory that does not show the 'secret discordance ... between collective memory

and historical memory' (Ricoeur, 2006: 396). As such, and unlike
La mala educación, La visita on its own provides a convenient screen
memory, even as it purports to uncover a traumatic past, in effect
creating a 'structuring of forgetfulness' (Ricoeur, 2006: 450).

Unusually for Almodóvar, the film ends by providing an account
of the fates of the main characters. Despite its closed ending, *La mala
educación*'s structure and mythopoetic aesthetic discourage viewers
from reaching firm conclusions about historical facts whilst at the
same time showing how this very same impulse works in individuals
and societies. This is achieved through Almodóvar's use of a number
of techniques, including self-referential *mise-en-scène* (for example,
the 1980s up-and-coming filmmaker Enrique Goded owns a white
typewriter harking back to Pablo's in *La ley*; Ignacio's typewriter is
either Almodóvar's or very much like it) and 'self-reflexive games'.
For example, as Acevedo-Muñoz notes, when Enrique is imagining
the central short story as he reads, Almodóvar 'cuts from a close-up
of "Enrique's" face ... to the same page in the manuscript where this
action is described' (Acevedo-Muñoz, 2007: 266). In addition, multiple temporal frames of reference aid the proliferation of meaning.

There are three temporal frames of reference – four if we add spectators watching 1980 Enrique interact with Juan/Ignacio and, at the
end, Mr Berenguer – that signal their metanarrative and metacinematic nature by virtue of their multiple allusions to writing and filmmaking: 1964, 1977, and 1980. The first, 1964, marks the year in
which compulsory education in Spain was extended to return (at least
in law) to pre-Civil War circumstances (setting compulsory education
for children from six to thirteen). In January 1977, a law to dismantle the legislative framework of the dictatorship was passed, and in
June the first general elections since the Civil War took place. It is
also the year when the *semana trágica* (tragic week, 23–29 January)
of the Transition took place: killings and kidnappings carried out
by extremists threatened a return to war. The third, 1980, was still
within the complex Transition period (the resignation of the Spanish
president Adolfo Suarez, attempted coup d'état in 1981, and general
elections in 1982 were still to come). It is also the year Almodóvar
released his first feature film.

These temporal frames add to *La mala educación*'s thematic preoccupations, including a critique of the regime's education policies,
especially the unchecked power conferred on the Catholic Church in
education matters,[3] a hold that was exacerbated by the decline of state

education and the proliferation of private schools led by religious orders. The children attending school in the film are coded as relatively affluent. A glimpse of Enrique's mother marks him as lower middle class, whereas Ignacio's background is less clear, as seen by the impoverished family home. Perhaps Ignacio, like Almodóvar, is a scholarship boy with a treble voice. The film's layering of experience is complicated by these echoes of the filmmaker's own life, as well as intertextual links to Almodóvar's previous work, which have led critics to explore its autobiographical nature. As with *Dolor y gloria*, reviews and interviews (Abeel, 2004; Rodríguez, 2004) repeatedly mention these autobiographical connections despite the film's obvious warnings about authenticity and autobiography, leading the filmmaker to deny that the film is autobiographical (in the strict sense of the word) and explain that fiction and reality are slippery and that 'everything that is not autobiographical is plagiarism' (Almodóvar, 2004). In typical Almodovaresque equivocation, there is both affirmation and disavowal of the autobiographical, something he has continued to do.

The second thematic aspect of the film highlighted by the temporal frames is a critique of the Transition for not delivering justice to those who suffered under the dictatorship and for allowing perpetrators to move on unscathed whilst victims were silenced or ignored. The film draws attention to the role played by Spanish culture (and Almodóvar himself as he places multiple references to his own career trajectory) in the elision of discordant memories about the past and the creation of a collective memory whereby the strictures of the dictatorship are something that Spain has left behind. Last, but not least, the film highlights the 'bad education' of Spanish society into homophobia and a lack of viability of alternative identities such as Ignacio's, both during and after the dictatorship. As Marvin D'Lugo points out, the film's title 'has a double meaning of a literal bad education depicted in the plot and also of bad behaviour or conduct. It thereby suggests the continuum from childhood to adult behavior as it has affected Spain's contemporary social life and politics' (2009: 362). Historic homophobia provides Juan with justification for his actions.

The story of Catholic indoctrination and abuse is the screen behind which other issues are obscured in the film and in Spanish reviews. As Alberto Mira shrewdly notes, *La mala educación* echoes social worries stemming from the international scandal concerning sexual abuse by Catholic priests, which was in the news at the time the

film was being made (as well as speculation about possible links to
Almodóvar's own school years), though critical focus on paedophilia
in Spain seems to function as a way of avoiding the confusion generated by a 'homosexual perspective' (2008: 550–1). The paedophilia at
the centre of 'La visita' is used as the tragic element of Ignacio's 1977
tragic–comic revenge story. In 1980 it is turned by Enrique into the
central element of Zahara/'Ignacio's' tragedy in *La visita* featuring
'Fr Manolo' (and by extension, the Catholic hold of Spanish education) as the evil antagonist. Whereas in Enrique's film-within-the-
film the Catholic Church is given the ultimate villain status, this is
not so in *La mala educación* as a whole. The tension between indul-
gence in Enrique's and Ignacio's Manichaean fictions and awareness of the fictionality of Enrique's film and Ignacio's story provides
viewers with both a comforting placement of evil firmly within the
past ('Fr Manolo', the Catholic Church, the dictatorship) and an
unravelling of this story through the 1977 murder plot. Disturbingly,
Enrique chooses to place evil firmly in the past (note the final scene
of the film-within-the-film showing the abusers turned murderers
still in the same positions as in 1964) instead of looking hard at the
present. Enrique chooses not to know more about Ignacio's fate; it
is Mr Berenguer who forces him to hear it: 'the filmmaker is forced
to face the past beyond the fetishized nostalgia that he has reworked
as melodrama, opening up the audience to confront the perplexing
world that is not so easily ordered by genre and Manichean codes'
(D'Lugo, 2009: 376). In 1977, Mr Berenguer is no longer Fr Manolo.
Whereas Ignacio reports trauma and a split identity in a key scene of
his fictional story, Mr Berenguer is not only never brought to justice
but is able to reinvent himself, as many supporters of the dictatorship
did during the Transition, and remain in an influential position, this
time through an editorial role in which he gets to decide what is published and what remains confined to the closet. As D'Lugo explains,
the film is also in a less obvious way about 'the transformation of
the ideologues of the old Francoist order of the 1960s into the new
Conservatives in the 1990s [*sic*] and beyond' (2006: 116).

Sociologist Salvador Cardús i Ros talks about this process thus: 'nat-
urally, no one wished to recall exactly *who* had been *what* during the
previous regime, and even less so to do it while facing the prospect of
having to adapt very quickly to different political coordinates, mainly
through the turncoat activity that came to be known as "changing
[the colour of one's] shirt," a reference to the emblematic uniforms of

various ideological currents' (2000: 20). Mr Berenguer has obviously changed his attire, but Juan's colour-coding and unexplored turncoat activity is more disturbing. Whilst D'Lugo is right in his historical reading, there is another, more troubling aspect of the Transition that the film tackles and that has also been obscured by the focus on the film's obvious villains; the insistence of past 'education' on the collective unconscious of Spanish society, as seen by Juan's transphobia and general conservatism, is hidden in a superb performance but betrayed by visual and aural poetic reverberations in the film.

Juan is a chameleonic character, a cynical murderer who is capable of doing anything to succeed. He poses as a straight young man seduced by an older man, a masculine gay man, a straight actor researching a part that requires effeminacy, and a concerned son frustrated with his elder brother's mistreatment of their mother. Any of these versions of Juan could be prioritised, but the film ultimately foregrounds the view of Juan as calculating and self-centred through the final exposition of the characters' fates as he kills Mr Berenguer. Juan's ruthlessness is confirmed during his last conversation with Enrique, as Juan tells him 'I am capable of much more', to which Enrique replies 'I don't doubt it' before shutting the door on him. Juan asserts his determination to succeed at any cost as well as the sexual possibilities he represents, possibilities that are noted and rejected by Enrique.

Visually, Juan sells youthfulness and an American-inflected muscular version of homosexuality that firmly rejects trans as a viable social identity. Juan's chagrin at Ignacio's unconventional behaviour drives his desire to kill him, and his impersonation reveals the need to control trans representation and gain from appearing as a cis actor playing a trans character. Ignacio's final letter to Enrique, truncated as he collapses on the typewriter, is testimony to the consequences of his murder for trans identity in the collective imagination. Mr Berenguer's and Juan's narratives justify the murder on the grounds that Ignacio was not a 'good' trans, including his drug use and his general disagreeableness. Juan shares more of 'Fr Manolo's' morality than his liberal façade lets on. Both characters are displayed in specular logic reaching out to get something: 'Fr Manolo' in a re-creation of Ramón Masats's famous photograph 'Partit de Fútbol' (1960) and Juan as he dives into Enrique's pool. D'Lugo points to Almodóvar's freezing of the frame in the first instance, 'freez[ing] the representation of the past, transforming it into an object of analysis that will enable the reading subject to scrutinize critically the distortions and contradictions inherent in historical representation' (2009: 376). The second instance – reinforced later on by another shot of Juan in a supine position wearing only white shorts to lure Mr Berenguer – is shot in slow motion and followed by another shot of Juan swimming under water, which quotes David Hockney's 1972 painting, *Portrait of an Artist (Pool with Two Figures)*, a painting linked to Hockney's break-up with Peter Schlesinger. Whether the figures are seen as doubles or not (and whether these correspond to Juan and Enrique as doubles), the homoerotic gaze and figure of the artist as observer of male beauty are replicated in *La mala educación* as Juan (aided by García Bernal's sex symbol status) is repeatedly shown as the object of Enrique's gaze. The pool scene in *La mala educación* has a more positive counterpart in *Hable con ella*. Whereas the swimmer in *Hable con ella* breaks the narrative with a pure expression of joy, *La mala educación*'s bathing scene shows Juan's untrustworthiness as he hides from Enrique's gaze and is seen making time under water. The homoerotic gaze seems to place Enrique as the agent and Juan as the object, but other visual elements mark Juan as the predator and Enrique as the prey. The swimming scene is followed by Enrique's reading of a news story about a woman who hugs a crocodile as it eats her. On being asked what he is thinking about, he replies, 'Hungry crocodiles'. Almodóvar none too subtly cuts to Juan.

Juan is also named after the religious leader of the Trinitarian fathers, the religious order that seems to be the model for the film's 'Turinarios', whose school is called 'San Juan Padres Turinarios'. But even more troubling is the artistic name that Juan choses for himself, Ángel Andrade, which is nearly the same as the pseudonym used by Franco when he wrote the film script for *Raza* (Sáenz de Heredia, 1941), Jaime de Andrade. Spanish writer Manuel Vázquez Montalbán discusses Franco's script thus:

> Franco left behind a clear psychological self-portrait in the script for the film *Raza* [caste or breed, J.L. Sáenz de Heredia, 1942], which he signed with the pseudonym Jaime de Andrade and which recounted in a positive light all his negative childhood traumas as the son of a freethinking, womanising mason who made his poor wife Doña Pilar's life awful. Doña Pilar was idealised by Franco as a natural mother and the mother of Spain, suffering and slandered by Freemasonry and international Marxism. (Vázquez Montalbán, 2000: 223; my translation)

Juan, like Franco, is from the region of La Coruña in Galicia, in north-western Spain and, like him, he seems to revere his mother. In *Raza*, Franco equates the desire to protect mother and country. *La mala educación* displays a similar use of this trope in Juan's justification for murder, which, by extension, criticises the compromises of the Transition in the name of protecting the mother country. Misbehaviour by Franco's father in *Raza* seems to be transposed to Juan's brother in *La mala educación*. The parallels do not end there, as Berenguer and Goded are the surnames of two prominent fascist generals who admired Franco.[4] Moreover, the story of brotherly rivalry and murder for personal gain predicated on saving the motherland is uncannily close to that of those who rebelled against the legitimate Republican government during the Spanish Civil War.

La mala educación does not punish Juan. Neither does it question Enrique's closure of this chapter in his life rather than seeking justice for his childhood crush. On the contrary, there is a marked sympathy with the adult characters ('Fr Manolo'/Mr Berenguer and Enrique), as 'Fr Manolo' is seen battling his infatuation with the child Ignacio and Enrique and Mr Berenguer allow their sexual attraction for Juan to guide their actions. As Almodóvar explains,

> [t]he adult character is aware both of their desire and of the price they will have to pay for that desire; yet they give themselves in all generosity, without heed to eventual manipulations or, worst of all, what eventually happens, the absence of the loved one. Rather paradoxically, the person I make to be the moral hero of the film, in a certain sense, is the priest I want to pronounce as the abuser of a child – when he becomes Monsieur Berenguer, the person who loves with a genuine passion. (Almodóvar, quoted in Strauss, 2006: 225)

Enrique's final action is to close the door on Juan and, symbolically, on the ghosts from his past that Juan ushered in during his first visit. D'Lugo analyses Almodóvar's use of the 'door-opening image ... to suggest the symbolic eruption of the ghosts of the past at the moment in his own professional career when his creativity was built upon the *denial* of recent Spanish history' (2009: 365). However, Enrique is haunted by the past before Juan arrives and after he leaves. Posters of his films adorn his office walls, the one nearest the door being for *La abuela fantasma* (The Ghostly Grandmother). The final frozen frame of Enrique clutching Ignacio's unfinished letter to him shows him posed between wilful elision of the past and surrender to the haunt-ing of untold and untellable stories.

La mala educación thus mirrors the Transition's silencing of alter-native stories, either through murder or 'erasure of the social memory that had been hegemonic up to 1975' (Cardús i Ros, 2000: 19), which ended up protecting those guilty of crimes and perpetuating the regime's moral stance on LGBTQ+ individuals. It is significant that one of the two deleted scenes from the film features the confronta-tion of the fictional 'Enrique' and two policemen with 'Fr Manolo' and Fr José where it seems that the priests will not get away with the murder. In this version of Enrique's adaptation 'Ignacio's' memory of abuse is corroborated by one of the detectives saying 'One of my brothers had the misfortune to go to school here'. The deleted scenes add the discovery of the murderers to the film-within-the-film, but this ending is not as affecting as the ending Enrique (and, ultimately, Almodóvar) finally chooses for La visita. The excision reinforces the view that abuse stays hidden as the voices of victims are suppressed.

Resina suggests approaching 'the literature of the Transition ... in reference to what it leaves out, what it subtracts from what we know from experience or what can be learned from less popular and more inaccessible sources' (2000: 9). This approach reflects 'a sociology of the Transition [which] turns into the analysis of the processes of erasure and reinvention of the collective memory in which ... the media participated with particular enthusiasm' (Cardús i Ros, 2000: 24–5). Memory and the return of this repressed past is a recurrent theme in literature of the Transition such as Jorge Semprún's Autobiografía de Federico Sánchez (The autobiography of Federico Sánchez, 1977) and later narratives dealing with twentieth-century Spanish history such as Manuel Vázquez Montalbán's Autobiografía del general Franco (Autobiography of General Franco,1992). As Ofelia Ferrán explains, 'both novels employ a similar narrative strategy: a supposedly auto-biographical account by an individual is refracted into multiple mem-ories that ultimately create a collective reconstruction of a concealed past or repression' (2000: 217). These texts are characterised by a 'heteroglossia [that] relativizes all claims to a single historical truth and raises the issue of how we know the past' and 'completely under-mines the unitary, monologic, hegemonic representation of the past put forth by an authoritarian force' (Ferrán, 2000: 212). By under-mining ideas of stable authorship, these texts also destabilise the authority of narratives, not only (or not necessarily) their authenticity.

La mala educación, too, highlights the process of construction (rather than completion or closure) of the past by refracting Ignacio's supposedly autobiographical narrative of child abuse into a number of modes, genres, and narratives by different authors. Ignacio's fate is thus explained away in narrative, filmic, and other forms, but viewers are no closer to knowing what happened to him. In fact, the overtly fictional murder of 'Ignacio'/Zahara in the film-within-the-film seems to be more affecting than Ignacio's 'real' death. Prosthetic memories such as this one play a crucial role in the film's critique and reinscription of the Transition's 'processes of erasure and reinvention of the collective memory'. The collaborative nature of film is employed to underline memory-making as a collective process that may or may not be underpinned by historical data.

Filmmaking as archaeological or detective work is also signalled in a trademark Almodóvar shot of the internal mechanism of a Panasonic M146 camera,[5] as Enrique's voice-over explains how he throws himself 'into the shooting of *La visita* as a homage to Ignacio ... and also to discover the enigma of Juan'. The link between filmmaking's exploration of the past as reinvention and Enrique's attempts to penetrate Juan physically and psychologically are neatly expressed visually as the pan showing the inexorable movement of the machine focuses on the timer, a phallic object rapidly hammering away, as Enrique says that Juan 'allowed me to penetrate him frequently, but only physically ... his mystery remained intact'. This image brings to mind the previous sex scene between Enrique and Juan, who engage in anal sex with Enrique as the top, clearly experiencing orgasm, whilst Juan experiences discomfort as the bottom. Juan engages in mechanical sex to obtain the role of Zahara in Enrique's film. At this point it is impossible to tell whether Enrique is (as he says) 'like the woman who threw herself to the crocodiles' or whether it is Juan who is being taken advantage of sexually by Enrique, or both. This scene contrasts with the unshown molestation scenes between 'Fr Manolo' and the young Ignacio and the mutually satisfying masturbation scene between young Ignacio and Enrique whilst they watch a film starring diva Sara Montiel.

This memory of sexual awakening filtered through Ignacio's fiction is significant

> in terms of homosexual experience ...: cinema as private space to share fantasies. The resistance against malign ideas that appropriate your

feelings. The complicity established through an image that, at first, has nothing to do with homosexuality. The diva as intermediary between two sissy children. Sara Montiel as a dazzling figure in the dark of the theatre, but also as symbol of the strength of glamour in the priestly world of Francoism in the provinces. (Mira, 2008: 44; my translation)

The children's gaze uncovers the heteroglossia of Montiel as a sex symbol. The scene as a whole makes meaning a collective enterprise that is dependent on viewers' shared understanding rather than an authoritative narrative. This heteroglossia is also, disturbingly, the linchpin of 'Fr Manolo's' defence of sexual abuse, which he explains away (like Benigno in *Hable con ella*) as love. However problematic, both appropriations of heterosexual eroticism and the discourse of love show that there are conflicting perspectives rather than a single interpretation of the past.

La mala educación's metacinematic features, fragmentation, and multiplicity were not appreciated by everyone. Ernesto Acevedo-Muñoz saw the intricate plot as a distraction: 'Maybe more sensationalist than interesting, it is also Almodóvar's most centripetal structure, to the point of (almost) collapsing unto its own triptych, circular plot' (2007: 263). Ryan Gilbey saw Almodóvar's 'control' of his material as a negative: 'the movie sometimes resembles a clinical experiment in storytelling' (2004: 45). However, the film's 'baroque mannerism' is due to the fact that it 'hides and reveals ... a *horror vacui* that is most fully conveyed to the spectator when the gate to Enrique's house closes in the last scene. In spite of its formal richness, emptiness and lack of true communication ... are the dominant characteristics of the film' (Fuentes, 2009: 435). The architecture of the film as a whole encourages a healthy scepticism of its multiplying narratives. Viewers are offered too much and too little, having experienced a range of genres and styles but ending their viewing experience where they started: with the same character. Enrique, wearing the same pink shirt as in the first scene and having just finished yet another film. Juan Carlos Ibáñez notes that

[t]he epilogue offered in the last frame of *La mala educación* can be read as the closure of a cycle that opens with the prologue in *Carne trémula*. The proleptic summary of the characters' various fates functions to emphasize the return to the present moment from whose vantage point the film's fictional time period of the democratic transition is judged

and found wanting in ideological and moral terms. ... The film thus
traces its own subtle circular structure. (2013: 168)

The Almodóvar of the twenty-first century is able to show the twin tendencies of flight and fight with the past in this and subsequent films,
here by presenting characters who desire revenge and pay for it, like
Ignacio, or who actively run away from and rewrite the past, choosing
straw criminals to avoid questioning the wider social amnesia during
the Transition period, like Juan and (to an extent) Enrique. Enrique
shoots *La Visita* in a realist style. Gilbey highlights this as problematic: 'The slow-motion footage of pubescent boys frolicking in a river
invites us to see the children from Manolo's perspective, when in
fact he is not observing them at any point – the unique reading of
their horseplay belongs uniquely to Almodóvar' (2004: 45). Pingree
(2004) notes the 'homoeroticism' of this and the schoolyard exercise
scene, but fails to realise that there is another filmmaker involved
in these shots: Enrique. It is Enrique who presents the childhood as
nostalgic and shows eroticised boys, perhaps because he is dealing
with the material as a form of memory work similar to that described
by Annette Kuhn in relation to photographs. It is significant that
the river scene is shot in slow motion with heightened use of 'Moon
River' sang diegetically by the child Ignacio. Discussing memory and
nostalgia in cinema, Cook relates 'dream-like slow-motion and step-
motion' to 'a slowing down of cinematic time that seems to resist the
inevitability of history' (2005: 5–6). In contrast, Almodóvar uses slow
motion during the unglamorous death of Ignacio, which is the very
opposite of erotic, and as Juan dives into Enrique's pool.

Ignacio's 'La visita' is based upon Almodóvar's own eponymous
short story,[6] but *La mala educación*, as D'Lugo explains, goes beyond
this, becoming: 'what Fredric Jameson calls "postNostalgia," a formal
visual-narrative strategy that seeks to free its audience from the pull
of pastness by developing a plot that works as a diagnostic apparatus through which to view and question the individual's relation
to the representations of the past' (2006: 116). Whereas Enrique's
film could be seen as nostalgic, *La mala educación* as a whole is not.
Its metacinematic qualities distance viewers from past events and
encourage a distrust of 'representations of the past'. This is crucial
to understanding what makes *La mala educación*, despite the tragic
events it recounts, not a historical drama, or a tragedy, or a realist
tale of childhood abuse, but a metamodern (postmodern in aesthetic

but with underlying ethics) film *noir* that contains a nostalgically shot drama within. Smith discusses *La mala educación* as providing 'a vital lesson of which its main characters remain, for the most part, ignorant: not all stories are to be trusted, however seductive they may seem at first sight' (2014: 182–3). An elliptical film about the reverberations of suppressed personal and historical past, *La mala educación* is best seen 'not as autobiography, but as prosopography—a collective biography for the country in which it is set' (Pingree, 2004: 7). This history of a collectivity is achieved through the film's engagement with prosthetic memory and the dominance of the poetic function in its aesthetics. As Gutiérrez-Albilla states, '[i]f the film's thematic concern with trauma and memory is inherent in the poetics of the cinematic form, it is the linking of the repeated torn surfaces of trauma that I want to emphasize here. In this context, compulsive repetition is linked to the symptomatic, non-narrative performance of trauma' (2013b: 330). Trauma in *La mala educación* is personal and collective.

Despite the film's disavowal and the director's warnings, however, *La mala educación* is frequently remembered as a film about child abuse and a film that 'turns [Almodóvar's] memories into movie masterpieces' (Abeel, 2004: 14). Prosthetic memories are shown to be seductive even when surrounded by signs of their artificiality. In 1980, Enrique is complicit in glossing over the flaws of the Transition, helping to keep the past firmly shut in a discreet historical period (that of the dictatorship). Yet, as Enrique's previous film *La abuela fantasma* (The Ghostly Grandmother) shows, it may seem easy for Enrique to slam the door on the past and shut Juan out of his life, separating private life and work à la Francis Ford Coppola's *The Godfather* (1972), but the past, which is not as neat as he wishes or buried as he imagines, may yet come back to haunt him, as it does in Almodóvar's next film.

Notes

1 I use an unitalicised title within quotation marks for Ignacio's short story, 'La visita', and italics for Enrique's adaptation of it, *La visita*.
2 I use quotation marks to distinguish the short story and film characters 'Ignacio' and 'Enrique' from their 'real' 1977 and 1980 counterparts. Juan posing as Ignacio is thus not differentiated as a way of replicating Juan's deception of Enrique.

3 The 1953 *Concordato* (agreement) with the Vatican, among other things, stipulated that education in Spain had to follow Catholic morality and dogma.

4 Dámaso Berenguer i Fusté (1873–1953) and Manuel Goded Llopis (1882–1936).

5 A similar shot of a projector is present in *What Have I Done to Deserve This?* The Panasonic M146 camera is an analogue period camera widely used in the 1970s and 1980s, later seen in use as Enrique's shooting of his film's end.

6 Almodóvar's manuscript short story 'La visita' is available in Spain's National Library.

13

Motherlands: *Volver*

In *La mala educación* (Bad Education, 2004), one of fictional director Enrique's films is *La abuela fantasma* (The Ghostly Grandmother).
Pedro Almodóvar's *Volver* (2006) makes this ghostly grandmother
a reality in the story of two sisters, Raimunda (Penélope Cruz) and
Sole (Lola Dueñas), whose mother Irene (Carmen Maura) seemingly
returns from the dead to ask forgiveness from her youngest daughter,
Raimunda. Raimunda carries a secret, which is revealed at the end
of the film and which her mother knew nothing about for years: she
was sexually abused by her father, thus her fourteen-year-old daughter Paula (Yohana Cobo) is also her sister. The abuse is only revealed
at the end, although there are hints throughout. The reconciliation
between Raimunda and Irene, which signals personal and family
healing, is the film's framing narrative. The main plot driver, nevertheless, is another instance of sexual abuse; Raimunda's husband,
Paco (Antonio de la Torre), attempts to rape his adoptive daughter,
Paula, who kills him in self-defence. Raimunda, prepared to take the
blame for the murder if need be, spends most of the film hiding and
disposing of Paco's body whilst making everyone believe that he has
left her for another woman.

Cruz plays both the role of a traumatised daughter, a victim of
sexual abuse who becomes estranged from her mother like Sophia
Loren's daughter in *La ciociara* (Two Women, de Sica, 1960), and the
strong mother who supports her own daughter as she in turn becomes
a victim and killer in self-defence, just as Mildred Pierce attempts
to protect her daughter from charges of murder in the eponymous
film (Curtiz, 1945). Raimunda is, in effect, becoming the mother she
wishes her own mother had been and, '[i]n acting on her maternal
instincts, she thus begins the process of her own psychic healing'

(Saenz, 2013: 253). Irene was unaware of the abuse and Raimunda explains that she 'hated [Irene] for not noticing anything'. Raimunda does not know that, when Irene found out, she killed her husband and his lover by setting fire to the country hut they were sleeping in, subsequently disappearing and allowing everyone to think that she was the dead woman next to her husband. In a further twist, the lover was the mother of Agustina (Blanca Portillo), one of the village neighbours. Irene has spent the last three years hiding in the house of her sister Aunt Paula (Chus Lampreave), who she looks after, villagers believing she is a ghost. When Aunt Paula dies Irene tries to talk to Sole, who runs away, scared. But Irene hides in Sole's car and returns with her to Madrid, where she lives with her, hoping to be able to speak to Raimunda one day and ask for forgiveness.

Volver was an immediate hit in Spain and abroad and won numerous international prizes. A comedy sandwiched between two dramas – *La mala educación* and *Los abrazos rotos* (Broken Embraces, 2009) – which blur distinctions between past–present and fact–fiction, it is not surprising that *Volver* (encouraged by Almodóvar's production notes and marketing materials) prompted reviewers to focus on the film's local colour and its autobiographical dimension, aspects that mask the film's engagement with the silencing of the past, the ramifications of unaddressed trauma, and the specularisation of girls and women in cinema and society in general. *Volver* employs mother–daughter relationships (including problematic stereotypes) to critique the persistence of patriarchal structures in contemporary Spain and repeated intergenerational sexual violence as symptomatic of the persistence of Franco's ideological regime well into the democratic era.

In this chapter, I argue that *Volver*'s comic genre and pop aesthetic disguise its serious consideration of difficult issues, much as his earlier and later comedies do. The overt comedy, much of it relating to eschatological bodily fluids and noises such as the mother's smell and farts, performs an act of amelioration and diffusion of painful events by resorting to abjection. *Volver* is the filmic expression of the common Spanish phrase *'reir por no llorar'* (laugh in order to avoid crying).

Volver's seemingly simple narrative structure seems a relief of sorts within Almodóvar's later career, but it contains as complex a take on the haunting of the present by past events as preceding films with seemingly more complex plots. Paul Julian Smith remarks on the film's simplicity in structure and shooting style, noting two narratives that he distinguishes by setting (country and city) and style ('highly coloured' vs 'plainer'):

Rejecting the tricky flashbacks and reversals of *Talk to Her* (2002) and *Bad Education*, *Volver*'s structure seems simplicity itself, with Almodóvar cutting coolly between the highly coloured city narrative (the disposal of a corpse) and the plainer rural strand (the encounter with an all too realistic ghost). The shooting style is similarly transparent: the camera tracks fluidly through the gravestones in the opening cemetery sequence, but more often simply sits alongside the women and asks us to pay attention to what they are saying. The occasional high-angle shots come as a surprise, as when Sole is mobbed by mourners or the camera looks cheekily down on Cruz's cleavage as she slaves over the washing up. (Smith, 2006: 18)

There is indeed a difference between the two narratives although this is not necessarily to do with colour but with lighting and backgrounds. It is true that the exteriors in the country are less colourful due to the sparseness of the Spanish plateau and whitewashed village streets, where the sisters' red car stands out, than the highly populated city centre exteriors, full of graffiti and red buses. As Almodóvar comments, 'Inevitably, I remember my childhood: the whitewashed streets, deserted until 8.30 in the evening. ... I remember the red earth, the yellow fields, the ash green olive trees, and the patios, blooming with life, plants, neighbors, and secrets as deep as wells and loneliness. Female loneliness' (2009: 450). All of these spaces, including the patios (specifically an interior courtyard), are public or semi-public spaces. The patios and ground-floor rooms are halfway between public and private and usually the only accessible part of the house for acquaintances.

The city centre and squares may be colourful, but the peripheral neighbourhoods of the city, with their small illegal housing built by migrants from the country, are not. They resemble the country villages their original inhabitants came from. This can be seen in the courtyard outside Sole's flat and as Raimunda returns to the restaurant laden with shopping. Marvin D'Lugo explains the liminality of these poor migrant neighbourhoods, analysing space in this scene:

The tenuous separation of the past from the present, of the village from the city, is expressed through images and plot elements that at first appear unrelated to the incest narrative. ...

For a moment, the image is jolting as it suggests perhaps [Raimunda's] return to the space of the village. Only as the scene progresses do we recognize that she is in the same Madrid working-class barrio of the preceding scene. As the editing of this scene makes clear, Raimunda is in fact suspended between the rural world she has left and the urban world in which she tries to survive. (2013a: 419–20)

Almodóvar is not conflating the rural and the urban, but showing in mock neo-realist style the architectural history of the peripheral neighbourhoods that proliferated in Spanish cities such as Madrid and Barcelona from the end of the nineteenth century, the growth of which accelerated in the second half of the twentieth century with fresh migrations from country to city. The poor whitewashed streets with one-story houses are as much a sign of the poverty of their inhabitants as of their and the city's hybridity. They are home to an underclass of migrants, originally from rural Spain and in the last few decades from other parts of the world, who sometimes turn to illegal activities out of necessity such as Dominican Regina (María Isabel Díaz Lago) acting as a prostitute or Sole running an illegal hairdressing salon.

There is a subtle hierarchy of housing in the Puente de Vallecas (Raimunda's) neighbourhood and Tetuán (Sole's) neighbourhood, with the more established migrants, mostly Spanish, having moved to flats and the new migratory waves such as Latin Americans occupying the small shanties. Making some of Madrid's poorer neighbourhoods visible – much as he did with the Barrio de la Concepción and La Ventilla in ¿Qué he hecho yo para merecer esto? (What Have I Done to Deserve This?, 1984) and Carne trémula (Live Flesh, 1997) respectively – Almodóvar exposes their absence from narratives of Spain's modernisation. He also revisits the theme of exploitation of these migrants – both of their labour and, in relation to women, their bodies – already present in Almodóvar's first feature film, Pepi, Luci, Bom y otras chicas del montón (Pepi, Luci, Bom and Other Girls on the Heap, 1980).

Migrants maintain some of the 'solidarity' of the village by extending it to their city neighbours, whatever their origins. As Almodóvar points out, 'The solidarity displayed between neighbours is a quality that all characters of Volver bring with them to the city' (2009: 451). This is particularly obvious in the scene discussed by D'Lugo above – as Raimunda makes her way to the restaurant laden with food and stops to talk to her neighbours, who agree to help her by selling her some of their own food.

The film's interiors are not as clearly demarcated by colour as Smith believes. Whereas in the village walls are mostly white and grey in public spaces (the patios and ground-floor rooms), setting off the highly decorated tiles and colourful kitsch furnishings, the private village rooms and city interior walls are painted, tiled, or wallpapered in colours other than white. The colourful furnishings are thus set apart in the village public spaces by the monochrome background but flattened by layers of texture in the private spaces and city interiors. This public–private distinction shows how city living becomes less community-driven and more isolating. Lighting is also different, with village scenes happening mostly during the day and city scenes being predominantly nocturnal. Even during daytime scenes the lighting is different: village scenes are lit using much more pronounced *chiaroscuro* techniques that add depth, possibly using luminosity masks on the darker parts of the picture; city scenes, in contrast, are lit in a much warmer light, only bathed in white in the liminal spaces of the whitewashed peripheral neighbourhood streets, Raimunda's kitchen as she repays her neighbours, and during the montage of Raimunda's many low-paid jobs (this time as a contrast between the minimalist modern look in the world of business and the kitsch home surroundings of the workers servicing these).

Volver's structure is seen as simpler because of its rejection of the 'tricky flashbacks and reversals' of previous films. Whilst it is true that *Volver* does not contain visual flashbacks, it is composed of numerous narrative internal and external analepses (or narrative flashbacks), which are descriptions of previous events. The difference with usual cinematic flashbacks is that past events are not shown but narrated by characters to other characters, thus emphasising the oral aspects of traditional rural Spain and explaining the film's penchant for close-ups, medium shots, and two shots. As Almodóvar says, '*Volver* is told through the eyes of the actors. From the beginning I felt that I needed to see them, and this impulse, somewhat abstract but very powerful, forced me to have the type of shot in which camera location and movements are hardly noticeable. ... Proximity to the actors forces you to use a, let's say, classical method of shooting' (quoted in Fouz-Hernández and Martínez-Expósito, 2007: 461). Thus, a film that appears simple visually is highly complex in narrative terms, inviting us to listen to and watch facial expressions carefully. *Volver* contains thirteen significant analepses, eight of them external, returning to the family history that lies behind Raimunda's trauma and Irene's double murder. The internal analepses explain what has happened in the village in the sisters' absence. All of them are returns to the past and to the village. The film's title, therefore, gives away its main structuring device, which is one of gradual revelation of the backstory by repeatedly revisiting the past.

The film's complex relationship with the past and revision of personal history is conveyed, as in in *Todo sobre mi madre* (All about My Mother, 1999), through objects (including homemade food, traditional furnishings, and photographs). These objects prompt reminiscences in the characters, even if these are not explicit. Sensory stimuli and dialogue containing traditional turns of phrase can be prompts for characters' nostalgia. They may also generate spectators' nostalgia or be seen as kitsch elements of local colour. The antique dolls are a case in point. To the family, they are objects of sentimental and monetary value. However, the younger Paula only likes them because 'they look like they're from a horror movie', which, in a way, they are. Almodóvar is placing horror, like Hitchcock, back into the home, where it often belongs.

The objects that best represent the film's constant return to and turning over traumatic events are not directly referred to, but ever present: the Manchegan windmills, shown in their modern versions as wind turbines. The turbines are the visible sign of the East Wind that blows across La Mancha and a reminder of the most famous episode in Spanish literature, Don Quijote (Don Quixote) tilting at the windmills that he believes to be giants. Madness is, of course, repeatedly mentioned in *Volver*. Many non-Spanish critics mention windmills (French, 2006; Smith, 2006), but only to emphasise the film's authentic local colour or make a link to 'Cervantine myths' (Kinder, 2007: 4).

The turbines are, to use Pierre Nora's terminology, allegorical 'lieux de mémoire' (sites of memory) (Nora, 1989). D'Lugo explains this in relation to the cemetery:

> not only are the music and credit titles suggestive of pastness, but the zarzuela chorus, with its euphoric paean to country life offers an historically specific memory of Francoist culture of the immediate Spanish post-Civil War period which promoted zarzuela music on Spanish radio as a[n] autochthonous form of 'música con *enjundia*' (music with substance) ... The women's ritual cleaning of the graves of family

reflects a society in which mnemonic practices (repeating the ritual in an effort to remember the deceased), attached to oral performances, negate both print and even image culture. (D'Lugo, 2013a: 421–2)

D'Lugo explains the scene's links to post-Civil War Spain and notes how it suggests 'pastness' through music and the women's acts of cleaning graves. This is countered by the less than idealised actions and dialogue, as well as the women's characterisation combining old-fashioned dress with stylish sunglasses. In addition, the credits are formal, which conveys not only pastness but also, due to the superimposition of the title over a granite background resembling a tombstone, death (Gutiérrez-Albilla, 2011). Tombstones are memory objects, standing for lost relationships and providing a space for mourning and also a reassuring sense of closure, which assuages fears about the possible liminal state of those deceased. A tombstone elicits ritualistic remembrance and provides a finite and solid substitute image to that of the decaying corpse of the deceased. A tombstone is, then, both a memory object and a screen memory for trauma.

Drawing on Laura Mulvey, Julián Daniel Gutiérrez-Albilla analyses a related link between the stillness of the title shot and cinematic representation:

According to Mulvey, cinema's relation to mobility is transcended by the camera, by editing and ultimately by narrative, all of which tend to repress the still frame. From this perspective, Mulvey argues that if stillness reinscribes the presence of death, then cinema is inhabited by spectres. If the tombstone and red titles of the film uncannily evoke death, I would suggest that death is brought back here through the stillness of the shot, thereby provoking in us an intellectual uncertainty about the blurring of the boundaries between life and death. (2011: 322)

Indeed, *Volver* is 'inhabited by specters'. Not just the obvious 'ghost' of the mother or the idea of the dead present among the living. Characters are frequently shown to be spectres themselves through reflections (mirrors, bus stops, television screens) and caught up in a spectral narrative where analepsis summons the past without fully fleshing it out visually. This first scene is already setting 'mnemonic practices' against a background of past death, trauma, and Franco's dictatorship.

The wind is explicitly mentioned by Almodóvar as a metaphor for his own memories: 'I feel that my films are getting progressively more autobiographical. At least, I am much more aware of how my memories stroll along the sets, like the breeze along the streets of Almagro [Almodóvar's home town] at night' (2009: 451). As Thomas Sotinel comments, 'Volver is not a light film. Its central theme is death and absence, especially that of Francesca [sic] Caballero [Almodóvar's mother, deceased in 1999]. In the production notes, Almodóvar describes the shoot as a "second, painless mourning"' (2010: 87; my translation). The wind as memory work is also conveyed through the cemetery scene's intertextual relationship with Written on the Wind (Sirk, 1956) and Gone with the Wind (Fleming, 1939). The cemetery scene alludes directly to Sirk's masterpiece, linking the wind to unstoppable emotion and the relentless interference of the past. Volver's relationship with Gone with the Wind is less clear and much more complex; both films comment on traumatic historical pasts employing regional stereotypes and idyllic settings (including rivers and mills), but Volver avoids Gone with the Wind's problematic endorsement of nostalgic feeling, managing instead to convey the personal drama of the main characters and their nostalgic yet self-aware relationship with their rural roots.

Volver is just as ambivalent about contemporary Spain's façade of successful modernisation, which hides traumatic historical memories beneath apparently harmless nostalgia for post-Civil War rural Spain, keeping the horror of the situation in check with its comic tone. Volver conflates the personal and the historical in a bid to rebuild the national home, attempting to 'reimagine, to reinhabit, to recuperate, or to reappropriate a rural space which becomes a kind of utopian, maternal space as a therapeutic cure for the traumas produced by patriarchy, and the latter's association with Francoism' (Gutiérrez-Albilla, 2011: 331). It is not coincidental that Volver was released in 2006, just a year before the Ley de memoria histórica de España (Spanish Historical Memory Law, 2007) was passed to recognise and expand the rights and entitlements of those who were persecuted or suffered violence during the Civil War and the dictatorship. In the wake of debates about the need for such a law, the film asks metaphorically how families and countries recover from such violence and whether memory contributes to the process of healing.

Tonally and visually, Volver is described by Almodóvar as a pop comedy: 'It is a pop comedy (pastel colors wouldn't suit it); a false local film that involves a drama with surrealist elements; it isn't a horror film, but some characters inhabit the darkness within the houses, the dim back rooms' (2009: 457). This description encapsulates the complexity of *Volver*, a film that can be read on many levels, from a naive enjoyment of its relationship to Spain's *Españoladas* tradition and recording of local manners to an inquisitive evaluation of the problematic recycling of nostalgia and closure for family and collective history. As Smith notes, '"Volver" means "going back" or "coming home". And [... it] stages at least six returns: to comedy, to women, to his native La Mancha, to his actress-muses Carmen Maura and Penélope Cruz, to the theme of motherhood in general, and to his own much mourned mother in particular' (2006: 16). As Gutiérrez-Albilla explains, the film 'attempt[s] to "act out" and/or "work though" personal traumas perpetrated by dead paternal figures (Raimunda's father and husband), or, in a more allegorical and oblique manner, the collective traumas perpetrated by the Francoist regime' (2011: 326). This collective trauma is 'the darkness within the houses, the dim back rooms' that *Volver* continually revisits.

Silence around traumatic events drives the present-day action in 2005 (Paco's attempted rape of Paula, her accidental killing of him, and Raimunda's efforts to hide it), the reported action that took place in 2002 (Irene's rage on being told that Raimunda had been sexually abused by her estranged husband, her double murder as revenge, and subsequent life in hiding looking after her elderly sister), and the original traumatic abuse perpetrated around 1991. The sexual abuse of Raimunda by her father is the repressed trauma that, even as mother and daughter clear the air, is left unexplored. It is important to refer to these events as abuse, as opposed to 'incest' as Jean-Max Méjean (2007: 178; my translation) and D'Lugo refer to them. Raimunda did not consent to sexual relations with her father, which makes any sexual activity either sexual abuse or rape. The focus on incest rather than abuse makes Raimunda at least partly responsible for the events as opposed to the victim of a crime. This leads Méjean to see Raimunda's journey in *Volver* as a 'path to salvation. [She] reflects upon her past, accepts it and even seems to abandon all form of sexual desire, transforming into some sort of pure spirit; she, who had even committed incest' (2007: 178; my translation). Considering the events of 1991 as sexual abuse enables me to see Raimunda's journey as one of confrontation of trauma, healing, and reconciliation with the mother, and Raimunda's lack of sexual desire as either a consequence of her trauma or simply not the priority of an over-worked mother (we see Raimunda doing three different physical jobs on the day Paula kills Paco). Doing so also removes moral judge-ment from the victim. I prefer instead Noelia Saenz's argument that *Volver* shows how sexual abuse has 'marked [Raimunda's] sexual-ity' and her focus on 'the sexualising of adolescents as problematic' (2013: 254).

The film denounces the specularisation of women's bodies in eve-ryday life and on screen through references to Irene's misguided coaching of Raimunda to sing in a competition and Agustina's appearance in a reality TV programme. This is aided by the use of Cruz in the lead role and heightened by an intradiegetic comment on Raimunda's large bosom, as well as media focus on the pros-thetic bottom used to characterise Cruz. However, the film's focus on Raimunda's and Sole's behinds can be seen as a critique of this specularisation in the allusion to Marnie's deliberate use of her body in Hitchcock's film to attract and deceive men. As in *Marnie* (1964), lingering shots on women's bodies become uncomfortable cinematic experiences (and memories) once the abuse is revealed. Laura Mulvey analyses how 'feminist curiosity is specifically alerted and aroused by spectacular images of woman. The very excess of these images indicates that they conceal, or distract from, some-thing troubling to the psyche, a mask, as it were, that, once recon-figured as a sign, reveals coded traces of repression and abjection' (2012: 1). These shots seem objective, but may not be so, and they disrupt the narrative by drawing attention to the problematic use of women's bodies as the object of the cinematic gaze. Many of them are high-angle shots, which can be associated with an undeclared spectral presence, in which case they are likely to be aligned to those of Raimunda's father or Paco's. Another high-angle shot, this time of mourners during Aunt Paula's funeral, also seems to be from the deceased's point of view.

The father figure's elision from the film can be seen in the framing of the parents' tombstone, where the beginning of the inscription with the father's name and date of birth have been excised. He is turned into a cypher, a function within the film rather than an indi-vidual; his name is not uttered once, a sign of the trauma associ-ated with him. The other abusive father in the film, Paco, is given Franco's first name (Paco is a shortening of Francisco), but the film's action revolves on how to get rid of his corpse, a comic take on how mother and daughter try to put the attempted rape and resulting manslaughter behind them.

Physical bodies are much easier to dispose of than psychological burdens, and yet the film seems to support talking as a way to heal (Irene and Raimunda) whilst at the same time conveying closure through freezing and burying the past (Raimunda and Paula). In this respect it is important to note that whereas Raimunda and Irene find catharsis in recounting past events, the mother who aims to protect her children through silencing personal history recurs in Almodóvar's work and these mothers are generally found – despite their good intentions – to be misguided in their censorship. Raimunda, much like Manuela in Todo sobre, refuses to tell Paula who her father is. This knowledge may not have prevented Paco's attempted rape, but being aware of a history of sexual violence against women may have prepared Paula for Paco's actions and provided some context to her mothers' difficulties in self-regulation and dissociation. These difficulties are acknowledged by the family as Raimunda is seen as being temperamental and, at times, cold. Irene, for example, says that she is 'not a bad person but has a nasty streak' and 'she's got a lot of temper'. Talking to Irene, Paula says that 'at times, she's really stroppy', then asks Irene how Raimunda got on with her: 'When she was little, the apple of my eye, but as a teenager for some reason I didn't know, she grew away from me until I lost her completely. Your mother didn't love me. It really hurts when a daughter doesn't love her mother.' Raimunda displays classic signs of an anxious-avoidant insecure attachment due to trauma. As Raimunda explains to Irene towards the end of the film, 'I hated you for not noticing anything.' And so Raimunda, carrying the burden of abuse, remains silent and withdrawn. Irene asks Paula what Raimunda has told her: 'Nothing, she doesn't like to talk about that time.' Raimunda's silence is matched by that of her Aunt Paula, who knew about the abuse but only told Irene years later, when trying to defend Raimunda against her mother's anger. Silence is how the village deals with family secrets; a veneer of normality covers up scandals.

As in Todo sobre, Los abrazos (2009), and Julieta (2016), in Volver regenerative forces are associated with facing past trauma and talking about past events whereas silence and repression are seen to generate and perpetuate pain for individuals and across generations. Volver's textbook happy ending might cause us to gloss over the traumatic pasts and uncertain futures of its characters. After all, the silenced abuse only comes to light towards the end of the film as indirect speech by Irene. Raimunda cannot bring herself to talk about her abuse, although she seems keen to discuss her current predicament vis-à-vis Paco's manslaughter and Paula is eager to know the identity of her father. Irene's reported speech and other narrative analepses make up for the gaps in the characters' pasts, but even then she focuses on her reaction to the news rather than the abuse itself, explaining how she had accused Raimunda of being a '*descastada*', subtitled into English as heartless or uncaring. This is a highly despective noun meaning Raimunda is alienated from her family and implying she is ungrateful and rejects her origins and identity.

Irene's description of Raimunda adds a layer of meaning to the film's title. *Volver* takes its title from a tango by French-Argeninean Carlos Gardel. Sang with a *flamenco* arrangement by singer Estrella Morente and mimed by Raimunda in one of the film's key scenes, it is a song about the experience of migrants' return to their home towns and countries, of how returning means facing past sorrows, possibly related to failed love. The loving but tense relationship between the song's narrator and her motherland is appropriated by the film to refer to a similar focus on mothers and daughters. Raimunda's interpretation begins in medias res. This is another instance of Almodóvar pausing the narrative to invite reflection (Vernon, 2009: 54) to show how art sublimates experience. In addition, as Marvin D'Lugo notes, 'the tango has been raised here to a more prominent textual position as it strategically underscores the film's principal narrative and further serves as a catalyst for action and the transposition of the protagonists' identities within the broader and even political scenarios' (2013a: 414). Make-up and framing place Raimunda's tearful eyes centre stage, guiding us from the bright lights of the party to the dark street where Irene hides. The love object sought by the singer could be both the land and an unrequited love. Cross-cutting points to the loving relationship being that of mother–daughter and the shadows as being both the past and the disavowed trauma, where the maternal figure is located.

Irene's cathartic revelation comes during the film's dénouement, in an amazing reconciliation scene between her and Raimunda, comprising of Irene's monologue punctuated by Raimunda's brief questions and additions. It is a four-minute scene depicting a night

walk through the deserted streets of one of Madrid's poorest neighbourhoods. The scene ends with the camera retreating slowly from
the characters as if to allow them time alone. Raimunda smells her
mother as she bends to hug and be hugged by her. Their position
is exactly the opposite of Marnie and her mother during Marnie's
failed attempts to reconnect with her. Their posture is, however, like
the position of Maddelena and Maria's in *Bellissima* (Visconti, 1951),
during Maddelena's realisation that her dream for her daughter to
become a film star is harming her and that she has been exhibiting
her daughter as if she was a circus performer, much like Irene did to
young Raimunda.

Bellissima is directly quoted in *Volver*'s final scene, when Irene is
watching television just after injecting Agustina with painkillers. The
scene quoted is the first bedroom scene between Maria and her father,
where he acts surreptitiously, kissing her on the lips, telling her not
to tell her mother and promising her an ice cream. Spartaco could
merely be spoiling Maria. Inserted within *Volver*, however, *Bellissima*
acquires much darker connotations. If in both films mothers lose
track of reality as they strive to turn their daughters into media stars,
could the father's kindness in *Bellissima* hide a similar act of abuse to
that discovered in *Volver*? Raimunda is characterised like the mothers
in *Bellissima* and *La ciociara*. The link between Maddelena and Irene
is less obvious. Both deliver injections to ease their neighbours' pain
and are seen to be blind to the abuse their daughters are being subjected to in their pursuit of fame until it is too late. Maddelena is first
introduced having 'lost sight' of Maria. Irene herself states that she
'was blind' on two different occasions, about her husband's cheat-
ing to Sole and later to Raimunda about her husband's abuse. Irene
is thus characterised by blindness. This is reinforced by the *mise-en-
scène*: we encounter Irene for the first time in a photograph in Aunt
Paula's house. She is resting in a rocking chair, her eyes closed as if
asleep.

Despite previous claims of despising psychoanalysis, Almodóvar
himself described *Volver* as 'a foolish and crazy attempt to bring my
mother back from the dead, back to life' and an exploration of his
childhood (*Informe Semanal*, 2016). The film is thus not simply concerned with memory objects but is a memory object itself. Almodóvar
admits to making the film at least partly to narrate his mother back to
life. In doing so, he returns to but changes the characterisation of an
earlier story he had been planning to film about a ghostly mother who

haunts her two daughters. In 1988 Almodóvar discussed this project with Nuria Vidal thus:

> it could be defined as a variation of *The House of Bernarda Alba*. It is a story with a ferocious and intolerant mother who makes her daughters' lives impossible, but in a different way. This one has killed her husband and would like to kill her daughters. It is a mother mad with intolerance but also mad due to the easterly winds. ... Supposedly the mother has died in a fire started by her, but she has not really died and starts appearing to one of the daughters as if she was a ghost for fifteen years. (quoted in Vidal, 1989: 251; my translation)

By 2006, the mother has evolved from a typical castrating mother like Bernarda Alba, a familiar figure of hatred in Spanish cinema (Kinder, 1993), to an avenger willing to defend her offspring to the point of standing up to patriarchy in the killing of her abusive husband. This change in plot is first floated in a previous Almodóvar film as if the director was letting the viewer in on his change of heart. In *La flor de mi secreto* (The Flower of My Secret, 1995), Leo submits a thriller to her publishers for their 'True Love' series. Leo's publisher is aghast: 'The story of a mother who discovers that her daughter killed her father after he tried to rape her? And to keep it secret, she puts him into the freezer of the restaurant next door?' Leo retorts: 'The mother has to save her daughter. You'd do anything to help your child.' More than a decade later, prompted by his grief, Almodóvar returns to this fictional story within a fictional film to make a film that is close to home personally and nationally: the desire for a strong caring mother(land) to return and make peace with her children over past violence. In this way, the blind mother of earlier generations is transformed into a mother who asks forgiveness and is willing to talk to her daughter. Almodóvar's optimism in this film reflects the optimism of mid-noughties Spain. In this sense, *Volver* was and is a vital artistic contribution to the country's continuing debate over whether to return to history or place a tombstone-screen firmly over it.

14

Archaeology in the dark:
Los abrazos rotos

Los abrazos rotos (Broken Embraces, 2009) is a companion piece to *Volver* (2006) and *La mala educación* (Bad Education, 2004). All tackle the theme of memory and trauma through private stories of grief, which nevertheless resonate with current Spanish debates on the recovery of national history, particularly the history of the Spanish Civil War and the ensuing thirty-six-year dictatorship under General Franco. Marsha Kinder notes that both *La mala educación* and *Los abrazos* 'have an important character (Lena or Ignacio), who is already dead when the film begins, and who is seen only in flashbacks and in the creative works of others' (2010: 33). *Volver* also contains an important 'dead' character, Irene. *Los abrazos* returns to the issues of parental censoring and mother–child relations present in *Todo sobre mi madre* (All about My Mother, 1999), *Volver*, and *Julieta* (2016).

Los abrazos is indeed self-referential and highly intertextual, layering references to art, cinema, and previous Almodóvar films. Yet the plot is neither as complex as that of *La mala educación* nor as deceptively linear as that of *Volver*. It contains a story-within-a-story-within-a-story, two films-within-a-film, and a number of minor character narratives that complement the main action. These metacinematic traits are, as in previous and later films by Almodóvar, not there to disguise shortcomings or display technical virtuosity in an empty postmodern gesture but, as Marvin D'Lugo explains, as 'a meditation both on the cinematic artifice and the potential of movies to illuminate the meaning of individual and collective experience' (2013b: 213). The film can be seen as partaking in what Robin van den Akker, Alison Gibbons, and Timotheus Vermeulen call a metamodern structure of feeling:

Metamodern artists often employ similar strategies to their postmodern predecessors in the way that they eclectically quote past styles, freely use older techniques and playfully adopt traditional conventions. Indeed, they, too, recycle the scrapheap of history. Yet, in doing so, metamodern artists attempt to move beyond the worn-out sensibilities and emptied practices of the postmodernists – not by radically parting with their attitudes and techniques but by incorporating and redirecting them towards new positions and horizons. (2017: 10)

Almodóvar has always employed postmodernist techniques and past styles with an ethical intent; his use of postmodernist 'attitudes and techniques', similar to the description of metamodernism above, has indeed increased after the millennium. *Los abrazos*, like *La mala educación* and *Kika* (1993), dresses itself in postmodernist clothing to reach towards new ground ethically, historically, and filmically.

The framing narrative involves a blind scriptwriter going by the name of Harry Caine (Lluís Homar), formerly a sighted film director called Mateo Blanco, his agent and production manager Judit García (Blanca Portillo), and her adult son Diego (Tamar Novas), who is friends with Harry and assists him in scriptwriting. Judit, a single mother, is extremely protective of both Harry and Diego but has a number of secrets that she refuses to disclose, including her betrayal of Mateo in helping financier Ernesto Martel (José Luis Gómez) 'destroy' Mateo's last film *Chicas y maletas* (Girls and Suitcases) by using the worst takes for each scene after Mateo runs away with his leading actor (and Martel's partner), Lena (Penélope Cruz). Judit discloses the latter to Diego and Mateo fourteen years after the events, in a three-minute monologue similar to that of Irene in *Volver*.

As in *Volver*, the revelation leads to healing in their relationship. It also leads to a second revelation: Mateo is Diego's father. As D'Lugo points out,

'the confession gives privilege to the female voice, revealing Judit's power to control the destiny of the male's illusion of mastery (Mateo's film)' … The monologue, structurally akin to Carmen Maura's extended confession to her daughter as the end of *Volver* proposes a dramatic telling that supersedes cinema's power to merely 'show'. Judit's story exposes the errors of Mateo's version, ennobles the much maligned Ernesto Jr and facilitates the restoration of Mateo's film. Her revelation facilitates the (re)construction of the new cinematic family (the filmmaker, his son and his spiritual and professional muse, Judit). (2013b: 223)

The power of the female gaze and voice is already apparent in the opening scene, which starts with Harry/Mateo's reflection in a young woman's eye as she observes him and describes herself as a preamble to casual sex. Thanks to Judit's revelations and ultimate control over Mateo's negatives, sound tapes, and other material, the film ends with Mateo, Diego, and Judit re-editing *Chicas y maletas*. The position of the characters – Diego between Judit and Mateo – signals how their relationship has become closer, Judit no longer sitting between the two men as during her revelations.

Despite this happy ending, and as in other films by Almodóvar, the tragic story-within-the-story persists in viewers' memory more than the framing narrative. There is very little action in the 2008 present with most of the significant events shown through flashbacks to 1994. The 2008 narrative could be seen as an excuse to tell a gripping *noir* drama: the story of how in 1994 Lena and Mateo become lovers, their flight from Madrid to the island of Lanzarote (one of the Canary Islands) to escape from Martel's grip, and Lena's subsequent death in a car accident. Nevertheless, the action-lite 2008 provides a way of meditating upon the past and the role of re-membering (both as recall and putting sections of the past together as the broken members of an unamendable body or story) to move forward into the future. Just as *Girls and Suitcases* must be re-edited, so must the character's lives. After Lena's death, all the other characters exist in limbo until they deal with their traumatic pasts. The trigger for this re-membering is the death of Ernesto Martel, the man who terrorised Lena and ruined Mateo's career as a director.

The 1994 events are told in two nearly uninterrupted flashbacks by Harry/Mateo to Diego, prompted by Diego's question, 'Will you tell me why my mother is so afraid of Ernesto Junior?' Ernesto Jr (Rubén Ochandiano) is Martel's son, who now goes by the artistic name Ray X and tries to get Harry/Mateo to co-script a thinly disguised autobiographical film about how his father is responsible for his unhappy life. Ernesto Jr's impulse to obtain revenge and his inability to move on from his unhappy childhood show that he is still controlled by his father. The relationship between the two Ernestos 'as indicated by their names (and Almodóvar's press notes), ... is based on the relationship between Ernest Hemingway and his son Gregory, who, after the death of his famous macho father, had a sex-change operation' (Kinder, 2010: 33). After his father's death, Ernesto Jr comes out as gay and adopts the artistic name Ray X.

Ernesto Jr/Ray X marks a watershed in Almodóvar's filmography by being the first of his characters to define 'himself explicitly as "gay". ... This is also the first film where a politically charged word such as "homophobia" is used in the Almodóvar canon' (Mira, 2013: 99). Ernesto Jr/Ray X's story is a far cry from the script that Mateo wants to develop, based on Arthur Miller and his son, on 'the strength of the son who survives without any grudge against the father who'd ignored him'. Nevertheless, Ernesto Jr/Ray X's story is closer to Mateo's life than it at first seems. Ernesto Jr is intimately connected to Mateo and Lena's story; he is first and foremost Lena's companion, fervent admirer of Mateo's work, and coded closeted teenage homosexual infatuated with Mateo. Much more sinisterly, he spies for Martel during the shooting of *Chicas y maletas*, under the guise of recording a making-of documentary. Scholarship on *Los abrazos* focuses on the relationships between biological fathers and sons, ignoring the important near-parental relationship between Mateo and Ernesto Jr. If Diego (also coded gay, incidentally) is Mateo's biological son, he is also the artistic son of his scriptwriting alter ego Harry, who he learns from. Ernesto Jr/Ray X, on the other hand, is the thwarted artistic son of Mateo the director, who he admires and learns from during the shoot of *Chicas y maletas*. Ernesto Jr/Ray X has thus been 'destroyed' by both his biological and his artistic fathers. Instead of nurturing and guiding Ernesto Jr's obsession with filmmaking, in 1994 Mateo only sees him as his father's proxy. Unbeknownst to Mateo, Ernesto Jr witnesses (and records) the fatal car accident and calls for help, as he is following Mateo and Lena when it happens. This, however, is only revealed at the end of the film, when Harry/Mateo accuses him of Lena's murder and Ernesto Jr hands him his documentary to prove his innocence. Harry/Mateo's baseless accusation shows 'Mateo's self-absorption as scriptwriter and director who otherwise sees the world either as movie dialogue or screen images' (D'Lugo, 2013b: 223). At this point Harry/Mateo is immersed in *noir* and sees the world in Manichean terms, seeing himself and Lena as wronged and both Ernestos as the villains; it is not coincidental that Mateo's surname is Blanco (white). Kinder believes that 'in most Almodóvar melodramas, even murderers, kidnappers, and rapists are sympathetic; it's only in noir that he presents this Manichean division between good and evil' (2010: 33). I am not as sure as Kinder that this is the case. Whilst Harry/Mateo tries to read the situation in terms of 'good and evil', he is undermined by Judit's assertion that Ernesto Jr 'has got nothing to do with it' and proven wrong by the footage of the accident. *Los abrazos* does not present Ernesto Jr or Ernesto Martel as pure evil. Ernesto Jr may be an accessory to his father's psychological abuse of Lena and has become an angry young man, but he is not violent or a murderer. Ernesto Martel is abusive, but there is no indication of his involvement in the accident that caused Lena's death and Mateo's blindness. Promotional materials in the DVD describe the film as 'a story of "amour fou", dominated by love, jealousy, treachery and fatality'.

There is a third temporal frame in *Los abrazos*: the backstory of how Lena came to be Martel's partner in 1992, which provides sympathy for Lena's plight as she is seen to become Martel's partner out of gratitude for helping her dying father. Martel can also be seen as a substitute father for Lena, albeit one who is abusive and exploits her sexually. Noelia Saenz analyses the various forms of domestic violence employed by Martel to control Lena, including physical (beatings, endangering her life, sexual slavery) and psychological (surveillance, psychological blackmail) abuse, stating that *Los abrazos* 'is one of the most overtly serious portrayals of domestic violence in all its manifestations' (2013: 255). Lena is coerced into becoming Martel's sexual partner, most notably in the scene of their weekend in the island of Ibiza, where she vomits after six consecutive coitus. Violence against women recurs in Almodóvar's films, and although it is treated with apparent levity in *Pepi, Luci, Bom y otras chicas del montón* (Pepi, Luci, Bom and Other Girls on the Heap, 1980), *Matador* (1986), and *Kika* (1993), it nevertheless always refers to power relations. Whereas in Almodóvar's previous films sexual violence was 'often treated as an allegory of Franco's repressive regime and state apparatus', it is important to note that, as Ernesto Acevedo-Muñoz states, 'the feature of treating traumatic sexual encounters, abuse and repressive authority figures as partially analogous to Spain's troubled past under Franco evolves visibly throughout [Almodóvar's] career' (2007: 10). Most of the traumatic sexual encounters in Almodóvar's films happen during either the Transition or the contemporary period. For this reason, they may not just comment on Spain's recent past but also its present and the continuation of circumstances that allow gender and social violence to continue into the democratic period.

In *Los abrazos*, Martel is not even Spanish but Chilean. His nationality seems irrelevant in the transnational period but, nevertheless, Chile's transition to democracy after a similar military dictatorship to Spain's offers innumerable points of contact with the situation of Spain. Martel 'functions', as Saenz notes,

> as a critique of the transnational model of global capitalism, which serves female bodies as sites of labor and sources of pleasure. It is not a coincidence that Lena worked as Martel's secretary and needed to resume her sideline as a call girl out of financial necessity. Because of his wealth, Martel could provide the medical care that her ailing father required and thus secure Lena in exchange, a factor that emphasizes the threat of transnational forces to the national gendered body. (2013: 256)

Martel is able to buy Lena's sexual services because of her 'financial necessity'. Despite Lena's nod to Luis Buñuel's *Belle de Jour* (1967) in her choice of Severine as her call girl name, she is not in control of her body or life. Her real name, Madgalena (shortened to Lena), already brands her as a fallen woman. Lena's 'fall' is not only because of her low salary but also due to the dire straits of the Spanish national health service as depicted by Almodóvar (cf. Sanderson, 2013). Public and private hospitals are a constant in his cinema, which represents private clinics as always well appointed. Public hospitals do not fare so well, the exception being *Todo sobre*. *Los abrazos* takes place in the 1990s, a time when there was social alarm at proposals to privatise the newly established (in 1986) national health service by the back door. These plans were outlined as long ago as 1991,[1] but they have only been implemented in stages (mostly after the 2009 financial crisis began) because of social resistance to them. From the vantage point of 2009, just as the financial crisis was affecting public finances, Almodóvar reflects on the role of global capitalism on basic health care.

John D. Sanderson describes how Lena's imprisonment in Martel's gilded cage is shown visually: 'when Lena has begun her affair with tycoon Ernesto Martel, the first shot of her at his home shows her in front of a mirror trying on a striking piece of gilded jewelry that strongly resembles a set of chains, a conjunction that might well be read to symbolize how she has surrendered her freedom for his wealth' (2013: 482). Lena is also indebted to Marnie, of Hitchcock's eponymous film, in her initial characterisation (grey suit, white shirt, excessively correct demeanour) and later entrapment by the man she works for, an entrapment that is signalled by the red of Martel's office wall, the blinds of his house in Ibiza, and the red clothing Lena wears whilst she is with him, as opposed to the blues and natural colours associated with her and Mateo. Their relationship is depicted as suffocating and deadening, as seen in the reference to René Magritte's *The Lovers* (1928) series of paintings noted by Smith (2009). It is also expressed through depictions of food: Lena cuts up fresh tomatoes for Mateo's film but is held by Martel from behind against an engorged still life painting of overripe, wrinkly peaches.

Lena's decision to ask Martel for help happens in 1992, the year 'of the "spectacularisation" of Spain through the Olympic Games, Expo Sevilla and the designation of Madrid as the European Cultural Capital' (D'Lugo, 2013b: 216). Lena thus not only represents 'vulnerability' due to 'her subordinated position as a woman of limited financial means, which trumps any power she has over Martel as a Spanish national' (Saenz, 2013: 256), she could well be a personification of Spain itself, caught up in an unhealthy relationship with global capitalism yet relishing the benefits of it until she realises that she is unable to break free. Lena could have left Martel before she does but, following the Francoist Christian logic of self-sacrifice and her own desire to be an actor, decides to remain with him until Mateo's film is finished. Mateo is, additionally, not an alternative to Martel but a continuation and development of Lena's (and Spain's) 'spectacularisation', since Mateo is also bound financially to his producer.

The situation above is not a far cry from how *Entre tinieblas* (Dark Habits, 1983) came to be made, only in this case the would-be producer approached Almodóvar and two other filmmakers in a bid to save his marriage to Cristina Sánchez Pascual, who became the lead actor (Correa Ulloa, 2005: 64).

Herrera interprets *Los abrazos* as a work of 'synthesis that reflects more than any other [Almodóvar's] cinephilia and his personal world as tailor of images' (2012: 69; my translation). Kinder also considers the 'remix [of] many of his motifs from previous works' as deriving from 'Almodóvar's celebration of cinema' (2010: 34). Smith similarly suggests that the film 'reveals Almodóvar's nostalgia for his own back catalogue' (2009: 19). I interpret this differently. Whereas *Chicas y maletas* – the version of *Mujeres al borde de un ataque de nervios* (Women on the Verge of a Nervous Breakdown, 1988) contained within *Los abrazos* – may elicit nostalgia among fans of Almodóvar if taken in isolation, its placement within *Los abrazos* (which acts as a sort of making-of documentary) leads to a reflection on the film-maker's role in contemporary Spain, especially the entanglement of spectacle with the financially driven spectacularisation of contemporary Spain as 'modern' for consumption at home and abroad. Mateo's plight in 1994 is that of the up-and-coming director dependent on either the government or private backers to make films. The filming of the pop comedy *Chicas y maletas* is clearly affected by events off-camera. Mateo's efforts to hide the real situation by asking Lena to act light-heartedly and rewriting the script to incorporate Lena's broken leg embody Almodóvar's own public attitude towards the dictatorship and Transition in Spain early on in his career and his similar attempts to work despite past and present violence. *Mujeres* as remade in *Girls and Suitcases* is, ironically, more an engagement with the filmmaker's (and the country's) politics and compromises than a nostalgic return to a so-called golden age.

In 2006, Almodóvar talked to Fredric Strauss about his desire to take the same pseudonym he later gives Mateo, Harry Caine:

> To take a pseudonym is an effective way of fighting against time. You start all over again, which is what I'd like to do: to reshoot an earlier film, with all the freedom that implies. ... When you make your first film, there are no pressures: you have no line, no style, no audience yet, you're starting out. So I thought of taking a pseudonym. I found a name: Harry Cane [*sic*]. Because if you say it quickly it sounds like Hurricane, a typhoon. But my brother has forbidden me to use a pseudonym. We now have our company, it took us long enough to get where we are, so we're not starting again. (2006: 165)

Harry Caine is clearly marked as Almodóvar's blind double (note the pun on cane). Not only is Harry/Mateo physically blind, he is also unwilling to see the price he and his film will have to pay for financial backing. Almodóvar allows himself some fun in 'reshoot[ing] an earlier film' without compromising the Almodóvar brand, but at the same time he comments on the material and political circumstances emerging filmmakers endured as he started out. This makes *Los abrazos* not simply a refracted comment on the 1980s narrative of Spanish modernity but also a criticism of the continuing role of the establishment in democratic Spain from the vantage point of 2009.

Harry's opportunity to re-edit *Chicas y maletas* is Almodóvar's dream come true but also a comment on the 'duplication and doubling' (Delgado, 2009: 40) contained more generally within photography and film. In his discussion of photography as 'not only generator of fiction, but also continuation of life in memory, memory shaper, mummification of time' (2012: 69; my translation), Herrera mentions Jean-Claude Seguin's observation on photography's role in *Kika* as doubling images and senses (2012: 70–1; my translation). Whereas Herrera concludes that the film ends up being 'a reflexion about death, about the impossibility of art ... to express the truth of life' (2012: 72; my translation), the intertextual and metacinematic characteristics of *Los abrazos* suggest otherwise. The iconic shot of the Moviola, a device used to edit films until the late 1990s, functions as a 'metaphor for the process of telling and unravelling a story' (Almodóvar, quoted in Delgado, 2009: 43). The end of the negative in the Moviola dissolves into a shot of the stairs reminiscent of Hitchcock's famous tower scene in *Vertigo* (1958) as Mateo runs down to see Lena, who has just been assaulted by Martel, signalling the unravelling of both the editing of *Chicas y maletas* and, more importantly, of Mateo and Lena's plans. Just as in *Vertigo* the stairs become a metaphor for the delayed disclosures that change our perception of the story and for Scottie's and Madeleine's inability to escape their tragic fate, so in *Los abrazos* the Moviola and stairs alert us to the fragility of art and the role of fate in life. The circular shapes of the Moviola and spiral staircase remain a constant in the film, from Lena's earrings to the movement of César Manrique's mobile sculpture at the roundabout where Lena dies. Manrique called these sculptures wind toys: this one in particular is called *Fobos* (Fear), named after the son of Aphrodite, goddess of love, by Ares, god of war. Fear is appropriately begotten by the characters representing love in the film, Lena, and conflict, Martel (Mars is the Roman name for Ares). Thus doubling and duplication are inextricably linked to chance (the wind, the car accident) and fate (the end of the negative replicating the mythical threads of life cut by the fates). They point to what may happen as well as providing alternative destinies for the characters. This is also one of the effects of the ghosts raised by intertextuality, be it Madeleine from *Vertigo* or the couple in *Viaggio in Italia* (Journey to Italy, Rossellini, 1954), another film quoted in *Los abrazos*.

Told as another flashback prompted by Harry/Mateo's listening to Martel's obituary, Lena's backstory can only be a visual flashback of

Lena's own recounting of this story to Mateo in 1994. This flash-back helps Mateo's characterisation as possibly suffering from sec-ondary traumatisation syndrome (as well as personal trauma). He experiences extreme emotional distress in response to Lena's experi-ences of physical and psychological violence at the hands of Martel. Such a reading certainly accounts for Mateo's reluctance to remem-ber the traumatic events experienced by Lena even before she met him. He avoids anything to do with his relationship with Lena and its tragic ending. Mateo goes as far as changing his name to Harry, burying his former self personally and professionally to avoid think-ing about his traumatic past. In hospital he refuses to answer to his given name, telling Judit that 'Mateo is dead'. Judit tells the doctor, 'His work revolves around images. I guess that for him living in the dark is death.' Blindness may make his professional life impossible, but the darkness within caused by Lena's death is just as perma-nent. Significantly, Mateo's memories are prompted by Diego as he himself recovers from a near-death experience.

Almodóvar returns to filmic flashbacks, a typical trait of *noir* that he had abandoned in favour of narrative analepses in *Volver*. This time his focus is not on healing and reconciliation (though healing is implied in the re-telling of past events and the re-editing of Mateo's film and reconstruction of his photographs) but on the act of breaking bodies, lives, and relationships. As D'Lugo explains, the film exposes 'the force of self-consuming cinematic illusion' and counteracts it by exposing

> the psychological traumas it masks. The key to that deconstructive project lies in foregrounding a cluster of tropes of classical Hollywood noir cinema that emphasises the human voice. These include the prominence of voice-over, flashback, the particular privilege given to telephones as auditory props and, finally, the scripting of exposing monologues that recall some of the origins of film noir in radio dramas. (2013b: 213–14)

Whilst D'Lugo is right in noting the warnings about 'self-consuming cinematic illusion', the reparative power of this same illusion is present in the film. Memory is always constructive, and cinema can be a prompt for redintegration (the process of recalling an entire memory using a small part of it or other knowledge), thus aiding memory construction through encouraging perceptual memory in a safe context. The exposure of cinema as an 'illusion' is thus crucial

to its potential healing role. Notwithstanding, as evidenced by its
title, *Los abrazos* focuses less on psychological healing work (which
is gestured towards in the optimistic ending) as on the reconstructed
traumatic past, the importance of constructive memory, and an awareness of its limitations. These limitations are overcome within the
film by resorting – as in *La mala educación* – to 'prosthetic memory',
described by Cook as 'the process whereby reconstructions of the
past produce replacement memories that simulate first-hand experiences' (2005: 2). The deliberately broken narrative tells of broken
relationships and lives, which include the main love story between
Mateo and his leading actor, Lena; a secondary tale of unrequited love
between Mateo and Judit leading to revenge; and a third story based
on Martel's abusive infatuation with Lena. There are also a number of
other stunted or curtailed non-romantic (but no less intense) relationships, such as the friendship between Harry/Mateo and Diego and
the love–hate felt by Ernesto Jr towards his father.

Davina Quinlivan discusses how the 'aesthetics of hope and reparation' present in *Los abrazos* are complicated by an aesthetic of 'broken-
ness' (2014: 103; 104). Drawing on Melanie Klein's theory of object
relations and Laura U. Marks's ideas on how filmic bodies may be
involved in reparative processes, Quinlivan analyses a tension in the
film between its contribution to healing and its visual emphasis on
trauma, explaining that *Los abrazos* is 'not "healing"' by representing
or proposing 'an end to ... hidden suffering and unspeakable loss'
(2014: 104). In a comparable analysis, Katarzyna Olga Beilin interprets the film as 'a political parable of Spanish debates on historical
memory through stories of love, parenthood and broken bones' (2012:
35), focusing on how fatherhood is at the heart of the film; she stresses
the crucial role of Diego – the son – in eliciting and aiding in the
reconstruction of the past and, thus, the present. Diego, Beilin says,

> catalyses truth and reconciliation. His face on the photo fragment
> suggests that not only the past but also the present is a narrative con-
> struction in need of re-editing. Past and present fuse in the memory,
> or, perhaps more precisely, a reconstruction of the past's meaning
> accommodates present interests and prejudices. As well, the other way
> around, the present is the product of its past. (2012: 39)

Beilin is right in singling Diego out as the catalyst. He provides
the inquisitive 'grandchildren's gaze' described by Helen Graham

(2005: 143) and which recurs in Almodóvar's films from *Todo sobre*. Notwithstanding the importance of this gaze in the retrieval of fragmented history, the film's dramatic focus is on the reconstructed past and the production of 'replacement memories'. This is the case not only for Diego and the viewer, for whom all of Mateo's experiences are encountered through his storytelling/flashbacks, but also for Mateo himself, who cannot recollect the accident nor later see it so must rely on Diego's interpretation of Ernesto Jr's video recording.

The role of art (cinema and photography in this case) as supplying prosthetic memories is foregrounded in the use of photographs. If Mateo and, less so, Judit provide their own versions of the past, Diego is the character who attempts to put them together and whose life has been completely shaped by events he was not even aware of. After Harry/Mateo finishes telling Diego the story of his tragic relationship with Lena, Diego says to him: 'I'm trying to reconstruct some of your photos. I've got one that's almost complete.' This photograph 'refers back to the moment Lena and Mateo embrace on the sofa' (Virué Escalera, 2012: 141; my translation) but it is not quite it. Lena and Mateo face away from the camera in the scene in which the original photograph is taken, whereas in the torn photograph-object they gaze back at it, interrogating the viewer. This embrace between Lena and Mateo is also prominent in the film's still photography used in promotional materials. (Figure 14.1)

The 'almost complete' photograph can only be seen after a dolly zoom from Mateo's fingers on the fragments to the coffee table covered in them. A slight pan right reveals Diego's fingers also

14.1   Diego attempts to reconstruct Mateo's photographs (*Los abrazos rotos*, 2009)

hovering over the fragments. A variation on 'El sabor de tu boca' (The Taste of Your Mouth), the score for the crucial scene where Mateo touches the television screen as the video recording of his and Lena's final kiss plays frame by frame, plays throughout. Aurally the scene thus echoes the bittersweet moment of the lovers' final embrace before it breaks. It also links the photographic fragments to cinematic frames, emphasising how cinema, even when based on actual facts, is a composite of many stimuli absorbed at the same time.

The artificiality of all film, even documentary film, is further highlighted by Diego's explanation of how Ernesto Jr's 'car headlights and the illumination of the mobile sculpture' made filming possible: 'And he's retouched it digitally.' The use of video format also aids this metacinematic dimension. As Sanderson explains, 'the inclusion of sequences in video format' is 'common' to both *La mala educación* and *Los abrazos*: 'The heavy grain of this footage diffuses both color and definition since it does not render contrast and, consequently, conveys an impression of unofficial recording, the revelation of a secret we are not supposed to know' (2013: 484). In *Los abrazos*, this 'heavy grain' takes centre stage as it fills the screen on several occasions, most notably in the screening of the final kiss and, previously, during Lena's direct address to Martel in which she tells him that she loves Mateo and is leaving him. Ernesto Jr's recording is indeed unofficial as he spies on the couple, but Lena appropriates it (Kinder, 2010: 30).

Diego's description of the kiss prompts a recall effort by Mateo, who has no recollection of it, drawing on his perceptual memory (long-term memory for visual, auditory, and other perceptual information, which could include Mateo's memory of the flavour of Lena's mouth and her smell when kissing). Mateo's need for the footage to be embodied as biographical memory with a more solid corporeality is signalled by his attempt to read the screen with his fingers, just as he reads the young woman's face after her description of it at the beginning of the film.

Fingers, and touch more generally, are prominent in *Los abrazos*. Diego and Mateo's relationship is defined by their warm physical contact (Mateo holding hands with Diego as a child, for example) and the proximity of their hands without contact on numerous occasions. For example, in the above scene the photographic fragments act as intermediaries, as both men's fingers touch them at different times in the scene, which goes from Harry/Mateo's stretched fingers to Diego's. Without being aware of it, Diego is not only helping Mateo but also reconstructing his own family past. Like Esteban in *Todo sobre* and Benigno in *Hable con ella* (Talk to Her, 2002), Diego's life is marked by his mother's refusal to tell him about his father. Both Esteban and Benigno possess mutilated photographs where the father has been excised. In *Todo sobre*, the missing half of the photograph is seen by Esteban as a metaphor for his own missing half, both his father and his life story with that father. Diego does not possess such an object, but his life is missing the very same half as neither his mother nor Mateo have ever mentioned their past relationship to him. Similarly, neither Lola in *Todo sobre* nor Mateo in *Los abrazos* are aware of their paternity. Their lives, unbeknownst to them, are also missing something, although Harry/Mateo at least has a close (almost paternal) relationship with Diego. He does not need to be his biological father to act like a father to him. In a way, the revelation that they are father and son is an open secret neither of them should be that surprised by. The outstretched fingers that nevertheless do not touch are a visual clue of Mateo and Diego's closeness, which nevertheless has not been allowed to develop into a fully fledged family touch. They also show Diego as a representative of the grandchildren's gaze: he is not just delving into Mateo's past but also his own as they are intertwined. If Esteban voices the plight of young generations of Spaniards whose lives have been marked by censorship, Diego represents a generation even more removed from the Civil War and the dictatorship, one that is not even aware of their need to delve into history.

Mateo's ripped photographs are a sign of the disrupted 1994 present. They are an historical puzzle as well as a filmic one; who (and why) ripped them is a mystery as Mateo never goes back to the apartment and Judit discovers them in the bin. Herrera refers to photography as both shaping memory and mummifying time, relating it to 'a poetics of chance in a surrealist sense closely linked to the theory ... of photography as *punctum* indicating death, as frozen reality' (2012: 69; my translation). The fragmented photographs do just that, standing in for the couple's broken embraces, shaping our sense that those very same embraces are under threat from unknown forces. They are metonymies for death, both as photographic object and as objects that have been defaced. They are also the material sign of trauma from which art (in this case Diego's reconstruction and the film itself) emerges, much in the same way that Katerina speaks of

her ballet in *Talk to Her*: 'when a soldier dies from his body emerges
his soul, his ghost, and that's a ballerina. ... From death emerges
life. ... From the earthly emerges ... the ethereal, the impalpable, the
ghostly'.

The emergence of art from death and stillness is explicitly described
in *Los abrazos* as Mateo starts a new project called 'The Secret of Golfo
Beach' based on a photograph he has taken:

MATEO   When I took the photo I didn't see the couple kissing.
LENA   And what's the secret?
MATEO   I don't know. I have to write it to find out.
LENA   We're that couple.

Mateo uses the mystery of the couple in the photograph as a springboard to start a story, whereas Lena sees it as part of their own. Her
cryptic statement, 'We're that couple', verbalises the mythopoetic aesthetics at work. As in other Almodóvar films, images, patterns, and
music recur to create a mosaic of symbols that feed each other. Lena's
comments enable us to jump back to the moment the photograph
was taken, including a similar embrace by Mateo and Lena above the
beach, and to the future where their embrace is no longer. This photograph is also a contemporary equivalent to the Pompeii casts seen
in the scene of Rossellini's *Journey to Italy* quoted soon after. Both
photograph and cast represent an embrace and the absence of that
embrace, due to the passing of time which the photograph has frozen
or the decomposition of bodies which leaves only their empty shapes
on the solidified volcanic ash that had covered them.

The final images of the kiss are also a sign of both Mateo and
Lena's relationship and the end of it. Described by Smith as 'jerky
and snowy, endlessly extended' (2009: 19) because of the 'heavy
grain' of the video format, the footage reveals the secret of the final
kiss, as well as providing a final cast-like memento of the couple's
love. Herrera explores *Los abrazos*' intertextuality with *Viaggio in
Italia*, concluding that 'Lena identifies with Katherine and would
like to die [like the Pompeii couple] and be modelled' (2012: 72; my
translation). I am not so sure; after all it is Mateo who interrupts
their viewing of *Viaggio in Italia* to take a picture and it is Mateo who
tells Diego that they had dreamed of dying together. In fact, Lena
(like Katherine) is deeply moved and upset by the unearthing of the
Pompeii casts.

Whereas *Viaggio in Italia* has been linked to Mateo and Lena's personal story of trauma, its presence may have more to do with historical memory and contemporary calls to deal with Spain's own traumatic past during and after the Civil War. In *Viaggio in Italia*, Katherine visits numerous Neapolitan sites associated with death, not just Pompeii. One of the most chilling ones is the Fontanelle Cemetery Caves, an ossuary holding the bones and skulls of the anonymous dead (mostly from epidemics but also from WWII), which have been well cared for. The contrast with the numbers of unopened mass graves in Spain is stark but, as always, presented in an oblique way. As Almodóvar explains to Delgado, '*Broken Embraces* doesn't offer the analgesic experience; it doesn't deliver the big emotions that move audiences to tears. It's more commotion than emotion; more disturbance than thrill' (2009: 40). This may be what Carlos Boyero meant when he called the film 'tedious' and emotionally 'tepid' (2009; my translation). Almodóvar has been adept at working with heightened emotions throughout his career; the emotional restraint of the film is not unusual and even less so if one considers its closeness in time and sensibility to Spain's 2007 Law of Historical Memory. Delgado asks whether the 'processes of mourning' present in his films since *Todo sobre* relates to 'Spain's attempts to come to terms with its past'. Almodóvar replies thus:

> Absolutely. I collect all the cuttings from the press related to the Law of Historical Memory. ... There is a relationship between *Broken Embraces* and the Law of Historical Memory. There's a moment when Mateo has the accident, where in order to survive he has to deny the past. The past is so painful and such a negative influence that he doesn't know what to do with it. ... There comes a point, however, where he can no longer bury the memory and where he hears it knocking so loudly that he has to open the door and deal with the past. Just recognising it is the first step towards learning to live with it. This is actually what happened in Spain during the transition [to democracy]. We were all very pleased to move from a dictatorship to a democracy without the spilling of blood. It wasn't possible to look to the past, otherwise the feuds would have begun again; too many Spaniards had too much to throw back in the face of their compatriots. (2009: 44)

Like many of Almodóvar's films, *Los abrazos* presents a complex relationship between memory, historical fact, and fiction. It is not, as

Smith says, unconcerned 'with social conditions in Spain' (2013a: 28). On the contrary, it successfully comments on the need for passion to give way to painful archaeological work on Spain's traumatic past, even if we are doing so – as *Los abrazos'* iconic *copla* 'A Ciegas' (In the Dark) and Mateo mournfully state – 'in the dark'.

Like *La mala educación, Julieta*, and *Dolor y gloria*, the film engages profoundly with current debates about the need to deal with Spain's historical memory, showing how ignoring history and power structures as Mateo tries to do in the mid-1990s will lead to repetition of violence. Also like *La mala educación* and *Dolor y gloria*, it offers a tentative if imperfect healing method based on the power of cinema and prosthetic memory to build and grow a future upon the volcanic ashes of internicine conflict and social injustice. Lanzarote's improbable landscape, seen in numerous aerial shots, provides an image for this psychological recovery of the nation. The island is covered in a thick blanket of lapilli (small lava stones), but farmers are able to grow crops by digging the lapilli in search for the fertile soil and protecting the plants against the wind with small circular stone walls. *Los abrazos* replicates this technique, encouraging viewers to delve into past trauma in order to make a better future possible.

Note

1 Informe Abril (Informe y Recomendaciones de la Comisión de Análisis y Evaluación del Sistema Nacional de Salud) by a commission led by businessman Fernando Abril Martorell.

15

Visual seduction: *La piel que habito*

The title and photography of *La piel que habito* (The Skin I Live In, 2011) draws attention to appearance, surface, and form, something that reviewers highlighted (not always positively) on its release. Jenny McCartney calls Almodóvar the 'master of gleaming surfaces', explaining how she became tired 'of the dreary pornography of the surgery, the artily prurient close-ups of snipping and stitching' (2011). Peter Bradshaw, on the other hand, while acknowledging that the film is 'a tissue of surfaces, styles and images' embraces 'the extraordinary texture of the film: the colours and surfaces contrived by Almodóvar and José Luis Alcaine and art director Carlos Bodelón are delectable. The most casual scene or establishing shot looks as if it has been hand-painted in the subtlest detail' (2011). Xavier Aldana Reyes explains how *La piel* 'borrows directly from surgical horror and the closely related "torture porn" phenomenon, but also how it holds back at times by making certain visual choices' (2013: 820). Almodóvar has – to use Alejandro Yarza's term – cannibalised genres once again, recycling characters, plots, and tropes such as the mad scientist, the besieged heroine, and narratives of imprisonment to create a film that is neither repulsive nor frightening in the traditional sense. Carlos Boyero – in a reaction that exposes his preference for genre affirmation rather than cannibalisation or hybridity, as is characteristic of Almodóvar – says that he finds the 'grotesque' horror of *La piel* 'more comic than tragic' and considers that it is 'pathetic' that the film 'provokes laughter with situations, dialogue and characters that are meant to be tragic, complex, tortured and ferocious' (2011). The postmodern recycling widely identified is, nevertheless, used within a metamodern structure of feeling as discussed in previous chapters. It is precisely in the discordance between the plot's horrific events and its aesthetically pleasing form that the film's horror is to be found.

La piel is predominantly set in El Cigarral, a country house turned prison similar to Ernesto Martel's mansion in *Los abrazos rotos* (Broken Embraces, 2009). Both contain the stereotypically opulent décor of melodrama complete with winding staircase where violent scenes take place: domestic abuse in *Los abrazos*, rape and attempted suicide in *La piel*. El Cigarral is first seen as a beautiful weekend property doubling as a private plastic surgery clinic for the wealthy, comfortably furnished and serviced by a number of servants. Its inhabitants – a middle-aged doctor (Dr Robert Ledgard, Antonio Banderas) and a young woman (Vicente/Vera, Elena Anaya) – seem to lead the charmed life of the bourgeoisie. Yet all is not what it seems: the pleasant domestic setting turns out to be a site of imprisonment, torture and past trauma. The stasis conveyed by the visual representation of space is undermined by the fragmented personal history revealed therein. Ledgard's and Vicente/Vera's backstories are provided through flashbacks: Ledgard is a reputable plastic surgeon and researcher into skin and face transplants whose wife Gal and daughter Norma have committed suicide in separate incidents. Gal is severely burned in a car accident as she leaves him with her lover Zeca (who is also, unbeknownst to Ledgard and Zeca, his half-brother). Ledgard rescues Gal but she kills herself, witnessed by their young daughter Norma, who is left severely traumatised. Years later, as Norma is recovering, she is sexually assaulted by Vicente at a wedding. Ledgard kidnaps Vicente. Norma's mental health deteriorates and she also kills herself. Ledgard changes Vicente's sex and all his skin using transgenic experimentation. Vicente (now called Vera by Ledgard) is also given a face transplant and resembles Gal. As the film starts, Vicente/Vera is 'finished' but remains imprisoned and Ledgard is infatuated with him.[1] Following Vicente/Vera's rape by Zeca (who thinks he is having sex with Gal), Ledgard kills Zeca and Vicente/Vera becomes his lover/girlfriend, only to kill him and his mother/housekeeper Marilia two nights later in order to escape. Vicente/Vera returns to his mother and asks for help.

Alessandra Lemma links Ledgard's repression of 'suffering' to the film's use of 'seductive aesthetics':

> the real horror of this film lies in its seductive aesthetics. As our gaze is intoxicated with the beautiful physical surroundings of El Cigarral and

of its prisoner – the stunningly beautiful Vera whose skin is flawless – we are jolted by the reality that Vera's beautiful skin masks a body that has been brutally cut up and redesigned against her will. Beauty frames horror and the horror is all the more brutal against this surfeit of beauty, which is but a corruption of the reality it masks. (2012: 1299)

The film's use of characterisation, intertextuality, *mise-en-scène*, and narrative structure undermines this visual seduction, providing viewers with paths to uncover the characters' traumatic history and re-evaluate the initial seduction. For example, Almodóvar's use of *noir* elements, as in *Carne trémula* (Live Flesh, 1997) and *La mala educación* (Bad Education, 2004), tie *La piel* to a specific Spanish use of neo-*noir*, which explores the country's Francoist past. I share Ofelia Ferrán's view that 'it is important to recognize that, alongside the obvious important changes secured within Spanish politics during the transition, there were also certain elements of Spain's social reality that did not change enough' (2000: 194). In this chapter I argue that *La piel* uses 'gleaming surfaces' to explore how the ideological, political, and economic structures built during the dictatorship have remained hidden under a veneer of democracy, a veneer that became exposed during the 2008 global financial crash, which was exacerbated in Spain by economic mismanagement and political and institutional crises. The film, therefore, is not an abrogation of content in the pursuit of aesthetic mastery. On the contrary, it is a formal challenge to the use of these very same surfaces in social and political discourse about contemporary Spain.

La piel draws attention to its use of aesthetics as a trap, luring viewers into a position of comfort with stylised violence and encouraging them to look beyond appearances. In a key scene that has only been partly subtitled in the English version, viewers are explicitly warned not to confuse form as content. As is characteristic in Almodóvar's films, this self-reflective comment is displaced onto an apparent moment of relaxation for Vicente/Vera, as he flicks through television channels and discovers a programme about yoga, a discipline that he takes up and masters. Yoga is a source of strength for Vicente/Vera – together with his strong 'psychic skin', which allows him to retain a sense of self (Lemma, 2012: 1298), and his use of art as therapy in the manner of Louise Bourgeois (Jung, 2014: 630) – a discipline that allows him to retain his inner self whilst outwardly conforming to the identity that Ledgard wishes to impose upon him.

15.1   Vicente/Vera practises yoga (*La piel que habito*, 2011)

As the yoga instructor explains, 'there's a place where you can take refuge, a place inside you, a place to which no one else has access, a place that no one can destroy. To access that place there is yoga, an ancient technique.' The instructor continues (this time unsubtitled), 'one must be careful, however, not to confuse asana – form – with content' (my translation). (Figure 15.1)

In the film, Ledgard's confusion of Vicente/Vera's outward form with identity will cost him his life. In addition, viewers who cannot see beyond the film's cool beauty miss out on how its use of aesthetics challenges the power of appearances. The film's critique of contemporary Spain has also been largely overlooked, particularly in Spain, where Almodóvar was criticised for not offering 'a critical insight into his country's maladies' (Langue-Churion, 2016: 453). Whereas in *La mala educación* metacinematic elements are used to encourage mistrust of representations of the past, in *La piel* these – together with bodily manipulation and deceptively seamless formal mastery – encourage mistrust of representations of the present. The perceived 'emotional vacuum' of the film is, therefore, a deliberate formal reflection of contemporary Spain, a country whose democratic institutions have not been able to address the traumas of the past and which, as a result, has led to the continuation of historical trauma into the future.

The focus on form is thus used to great effect as a critique of contemporary Spain's confusion of (political, social, economic) form – which has changed substantially since the Transition – and the actual realities of a country that by 2011 was in the midst of a financial crisis and coming to terms with a second political and social disenchantment.[2] Whereas the first disenchantment was triggered by the 'death of a utopian fantasy of radical change' after Franco's death, which did not materialise after the Transition (Vilarós, 1994: 220), the second disenchantment was triggered by the 2008 financial crisis, numerous political corruption scandals, and the realisation that the advent of democracy had not dismantled social power structures, ended abuses of power, or dislodged the privileges of the establishment. There is no space here to mention all the factors in this disenchantment. The specific context of this film is social alarm at the discovery that the Francoist practice of removing children from 'undeserving parents' went on well into the late 1990s and had turned into the kidnap and sale of children in Spanish maternity hospitals with the alleged involvement of some doctors and Catholic nuns. This brought home the fact that the country was a democracy in name but one in which human rights abuses were still taking place. In addition to this, during the second decade of the 21st century tensions about the make-up of Spain (particularly between Catalan and Spanish nationalists) have further destabilised the fallacy of post-Transition Spain as a plural state where consensus reigns.

The film's stated location (the historic city of Toledo, not far from Madrid) confers on the story a national dimension linking historic and contemporary trauma, gender strictures, and Spain's ongoing denial of its national plurality. This can be seen in direct allusions to Luis Buñuel's *Tristana* (1970) – set in the same city – and intertextual dialogue with Icíar Bollaín's *Te doy mis ojos* (Take My Eyes, 2003), also set in Toledo, and Carlos Saura's *El jardín de las delicias* (The Garden of Delights, 1970). As Ralf Junkerjürgen explains:

> The image of Toledo in cinema is marked by the [Spanish] Civil War on the one hand, in particular the siege of the alcazar that was highly exploited in Francoist propaganda, and on the other by two films that focus on women's fate in the province, [*Tristana* and *I Give You My Eyes*] where Toledo symbolically represents the impossibility of escape women have in their dependence on men. (2018: 63–4; my translation)

The overt correlation between architectural (walled city and country house), geographical (provincial city in central Castille, Spain), and personal incarceration (subjection to socially defined limitations, particularly important for women) apparent in *Tristana* is present and challenged in *La piel*, which employs Toledo's filmic image as a site of gender oppression, conflating it with its problematic symbolic status as a site of heroic resistance and ultimate victory against the odds as seen in fascist propaganda films about the siege of the city and the resistance of those supporting the 1936 *coup d'etat*, including Italo-Spanish feature *Sin novedad en el alcázar* (The Siege of the Alcazar, Genina, 1940). As Gwynne Edwards explains, *Tristana* evokes 'the tensions that on a larger scale would erupt into the [Spanish Civil] war itself and then continue for many years during the Franco dictatorship' (2005: 14).

The use of the home as the site of (particularly gender-related) horror is a well-known Gothic trope and a staple of horror films. Big houses are also spaces where gendered psychic suffering is inscribed, as in melodrama and *noir*. There is a Spanish dimension to this; homes, Tatjana Pavlović states, can be labyrinthine, unpleasant, and violent, a bourgeois paradise fraught with danger (2006: 154). Ledgard's country house, El Cigarral, named after the common name for a country house with an orchard on the outskirts of Toledo with views of the city, is therefore a proxy for Spain's political façade, a 'bourgeois paradise' discovered to be the locus of unethical criminal behaviour associated with establishment figures. Ledgard's use of his contacts to obtain umbilical cord blood illegally from a maternity hospital to perform unethical experiments in his private laboratory/cellar is an example of how the house's spaces mirror complex social structures that enable those in positions of power to exercise it without restrictions so long as these activities are carried out under the guise of respectability.

The film's circular structure exposes the ideological contradictions inherent in its apparent blanc world of stylised realism. Viewers are placed in the role of detectives unpicking the initial situation, presented with information in the form of flashbacks in a borrowing from *noir*. Although the film is set in a future 2012, most of the action takes place in the past, between the years 2006 and 2012, through an almost continuous cinematic flashback lasting forty-eight minutes referring to events before the start of the narrative, with an embedded external analepses (narrative mostly combined with occasional visual flashbacks) as Marilia tells Vicente/Vera about Ledgard's and Zeca's pasts. The intertitle at the very beginning of the film,

'TOLEDO 2012', is constantly under assault by the pull of the past in the narrative itself, so much so that, as the film returns to 2012, there is a need for another intertitle, 'BACK TO THE PRESENT'. The attack on time unity is substantial and unravels filmic certainty and trust in visual perception. Circularity is reinforced using intertextual echoes, including films by Almodóvar.[3] This is evident even as the first intertitle appears over a postcard-like establishing shot of Toledo, which Almodóvar admits was a re-creation of the opening shot of *Tristana* (Delgado, 2011: 22). The allusion to Buñuel's classic emphasises *La piel*'s theme of façade versus history and hidden trauma. Toledo's outline has not changed much in more than forty years and neither have the social structures that enable Don Lope (Fernando Rey) to abuse Tristana (Catherine Deneuve) and Ledgard to torture Vicente/Vera, structures already present in the original novel, *Tristana*, by Benito Pérez Galdós (1892). In Buñuel's and Almodóvar's films, Toledo is depicted as beautiful and grand but hiding socially unacceptable abuse that is nevertheless silently condoned by its inhabitants. The victims of this abuse are first seen as fresh-faced *ingénues* (doubly in Vicente/Vera's case as Norma's face is transplanted to that of fresh-faced teenager Vicente[4]) who become heavily made-up *femme fatales* whose adoption of feminine codes of behaviour and appearance enable their revenge on their abusers. Lange-Churion explains how Vicente/Vera's killing of Ledgard is 'a symbolic manifestation of castration as performed by the proverbial *femme fatale*, along with all the insinuations of masculine fears towards feminine sexuality in patriarchy. If in *film noir* the *femme fatale* is decidedly a male fantasy, Vera is a paradoxical embodiment of this lethal trope' (2016: 451–2). The adopted façades of Tristana and Vicente/Vera hide their history of trauma and resistance in order to best enact their revenge.

This is replicated socially as the sleepy provincial city and big houses are revealed to hide breaches of social taboos (incest and child sexual abuse in *Tristana*, abuse in all its manifestations in *La piel*) perpetrated within the upper echelons of Spanish society with impunity. Because the film's present takes place in the near future, the 2011 spectators were aware that the film expected them to see Vicente/Vera's abuse and imprisonment as ongoing and the resolution at least a year away. This trick ensures that the sense of ongoing threat is present throughout. Unlike previous films such as *Volver*, which also focuses on trauma, *La piel* – like *Los abrazos* and *Julieta* (2016) – is not reparative, exploring instead what happens when trauma is allowed to reverberate.

Julián Daniel Gutiérrez-Albilla relates the film's violence to bodily trauma, arguing that 'in *La piel*, the imprisonment, mutilation and scientific manipulation of Vicente/Vera's body can be linked allegorically to historical events and traumatic experiences' (2013a: 71; my translation). Allegory is a far cry from the most valued realist tradition in Spanish national cinema. Gutiérrez-Albilla notes the 'fused time' of the first shot (2013a: 73; my translation) and the mansion-prison (2013a: 74; my translation). The fusion of time is replicated in the fusion of bodies (most notably in the use of dissolves to merge Vicente's and Vera's faces as well as the mannequin's and Vicente/Vera's body), spaces (through visual juxtaposition or use of glass walls), and people (particularly in Ledgard's mind as Vicente becomes Norma who in turn had taken Gal's place). These revenants and ghostly elements should in theory enhance the film's belonging to the genre of horror. However, as Aldana Reyes explains when discussing horror as a literary genre, horror 'actively, and predominantly, seeks to create a pervasive feeling of unease and which, consistently, although not necessarily always successfully, attempts to arouse the emotions and sensations we would normally ascribe to being under threat' (2016: 11). The fusion of characters and readers/viewers' perception of threat predominant in horror are not present in *La piel* as characters guard their emotions fiercely. As a result, viewers are not made aware of Vicente/Vera's feelings after his sex change is complete and are thus no longer prompted to feel Ledgard's actions as threatening.

The unfolding plot, however, undermines viewers' trust in their own perceptions as, for example, the gender ascribed to Vicente/Vera's body initially is seen to be culturally generated by cisgender logic. As Zachary Price explains, this

> uncanny backtracking required of the viewer exposes how viewers perceive and then inscribe gender onto bodies. After the reveal of Vera's sex reassignment surgery, the way viewers see Vera's captivity shifts; instead of the image of the helpless prisoner viewers traditionally attach to female bodies, the new information of Vera's previous life as a man transforms him into someone much more dangerous to Robert. (2015: 308)

Price highlights the normalised practice of 'inscribing gender onto bodies', how the film upends viewers who follow cisnormative premises, and ultimately how gender stereotypes are at play in the film's various interpretations and attribution of the roles of prey and predator to Vicente/Vera according to whether he is seen as a masculine agent (Zurián, 2013) or a feminine victim (Jung, 2014). As we will see, the body of Vicente/Vera is the aporia that unravels this and other gender-inflected dichotomies. As Price notes, however, this trans body is not visualised in the film (2015: 312), a decision that on the surface diminishes Vicente/Vera's body's potential to undermine sex's relationship to gender but could also be seen as an effort not to equate trans experience to genital status, avoiding the pitfall of focusing on bodies rather than lived experience. Vicente/Vera's insistence on his gender identity (by virtue of using the 'his' pronoun and identifying himself as 'Vicente') provides a limited insight from a cisgender point of view to a possible trans lived experience in a cisnormative society, as Vicente/Vera's self-determination is under attack by Ledgard and is forced to live as a male-identifying woman by the end of the film.

Darren Waldron and Ross Murray make a compelling case for Almodóvar's conservative politics in relation to transgender based on what they perceive as Almodóvar's view of identity as immutable and innate (2014: 70) and decry how 'the elision of self-determination, crucial to the material existences of transgender people' in *La piel* is a 'controversial form of provocation' (2014: 60):

> Whatever one does to the material body, according to Almodóvar, an immutable core or essence of subjectivity remains. Such a conceptualisation recurs in his films. While his characters are often read as queer because they are seen to figure gender as performative ... underneath their multiple disguises and consciously performed identities they are frequently depicted as having a certain fixity, presented as authenticity. (2014: 61)

Whereas the cisnormative 'elision of self-determination' is problematic, Vicente/Vera's treatment at Ledgard's hands is not ultimately endorsed by the film but refuted by its challenge to automatic cisnormative ascription of gender onto bodies. Although essentialism has been associated with cisnormative positions and Almodóvar may well be biased, there are trans contexts that also favour essentialism and suspect queer theory's use of transsexuality to destabilise gender binaries whilst erasing 'transsexual voices ... under the umbrella of transgender. Concentrating on the artificiality of gender can de-emphasise the need for transsexuals to change their sexed bodies, which is central to transsexual lived experiences' (Nagoshi and Brzuzy, 2010: 432). The double helix of the end credits should thus be read as at least double: a reminder of Ledgard's work in transgenesis (Olea Rosenbluth, 2016: 99) – which can be interpreted as indicating both the possibility of transformation, the role of DNA, and, ultimately, a questioning of not just gender but human nature – and the conundrum of identity as always in process rather than fixed. As Catalina Olea Rosenbluth notes, the title of Alberto Iglesias' score for this, 'La identidad inalcanzable' (Unattainable Identity), is significant. Olea Rosenbluth falls back on cisnormative views, however, arguing that this is because Vicente/Vera is a 'copy of the real, the truthful ... an imitation of Gal; imitation of woman' (2016: 101). It is more productive to relate the spiral to one of the film's intertexts Louise Bourgeois, particularly her use of the spiral to signal both control and unravelling in works such as *Spiral Woman* (1951–1952). The spiral is a perfect sign for the film's temporal circularity and elliptic nature, ellipses being crucial in trauma narratives and recurrent in Almodóvar's films.

The newness represented by Vicente/Vera's body and his subjectivity is ultimately affirmed in the film, as opposed to the cisnormative, heteronormative, and patriarchal impulses embodied by Ledgard and cannily exposed in the interpretive *faux pas* of viewers subjected to these discourses. *La piel* exposes how the prevailing social reading of bodies aligns with Ledgard's restrictive equation of appearance with personal identity. As Caron Harrang states: 'Robert represents a person for whom the outer appearance of the body – skin, at a concrete level – is synonymous with personal identity, something to be consciously manipulated without recognizing the distinction between internal and external reality' (2012: 1305). The ingrained 'inscription of gender' on to bodies is taken to extremes in Ledgard's fantasy that a change of body will result in a change of identity (Lemma, 2012: 1299). The removal of Vicente/Vera's self-determination is thus seen as a criminal and horrifying act, one that could well help the cisgender mainstream understand why this is also unacceptable in a trans context. Ledgard's attempts to annul Vicente's self-determination as he tries to convert him into an ideal partner and woman calls to mind ongoing debates about the nature of Spain and Spanishness that have come to the fore since the approval in 2006 of a new Catalan *estatut d'autonomia* (law of self-rule), which was later ruled to be unconstitutional, paving the way for current tensions.

Ledgard's belief in 'outer appearance' is undermined formally by the recurrent use of glass reflections in the film, most notably in his private laboratory and the entrance to Norma's psychiatric hospital. Ledgard is frequently represented as split, his polished behaviour contrasting with his illegal actions, his apparently confident and successful persona obscuring, as Lemma explains, his thin psychic skin, which prevents him from seeing his wrongdoings and leads him to blame others for his shortcomings. Significantly, Ledgard denies Vicente/Vera the chance to form a mental self based on his new body by removing the mirror from his room in an attempt to confine Vicente/Vera to being the object of his voyeuristic pleasure (like the paintings of Venus he owns). This, however, will in effect undermine Ledgard's plan to transform Vicente into a woman against his will by changing his sex.

The flashbacks give the impression that the backstory is fully revealed, hiding instead a number of narrative ellipses, most importantly Ledgard's relationship with Gal and Norma and the years between Gal's suicide and Norma's sexual assault by Vicente. This is particularly important given Vicente's sexual assault of Norma and her belief that it was her father who raped her. The lack of information about Ledgard's treatment of his wife and daughter other than from his and Marilia's point of view encourage us to interpret Ledgard's actions towards Vicente as motivated by grief. However, there are signs that Ledgard is not as loving a husband and father as Marilia says. Gal was leaving Ledgard for Zeca and Zeca is not surprised to see Vicente/Vera (whom he thinks is Gal) locked up by Ledgard. This normalisation of Ledgard's controlling attitude should ring alarm bells about domestic abuse. Similar clues are provided when Ledgard visits the neuropsychiatric institute where Norma is being treated: he enters Norma's room without knocking, approaches her from behind without speaking, and only identifies himself when she appears distraught. Ledgard stretches a hand to touch Norma, who becomes agitated and hides as medical staff intervene. Despite Norma clearly rejecting Ledgard's advances, he continues to approach her and stretch his hand towards her, even as he says 'I won't touch you'. Furthermore, it is clear from the medical staff's non-verbal communication that they have had to rescue Norma on other occasions. Norma's doctor gently rebukes Ledgard:

LEDGARD   Can't you put her in a dress? In that gown she looks worse
           than she is.
DOCTOR   We tried, but she can't stand any kind of fitted clothing.
           She rips it off. Dr Ledgard, I don't think you should visit
           her so often.
LEDGARD   She's my daughter.
DOCTOR   But she doesn't recognize you. And she gets worse when
           she sees you. In her mind, she's convinced you attacked
           her.
LEDGARD   I just found her lying there! Why can't you get that into
           her head?
DOCTOR   She identifies you with the rapist.

Ledgard seems more concerned about Norma's appearance than her
well-being. As in horror classic *Les yeux sans visage* (Eyes without a
Face, Franju, 1960), the surgeon/father literally imposes a patriarchal image of womanhood on his daughter. He asserts his ownership: 'She's my daughter.'

This exchange provides several clues to Ledgard's past and future
behaviour towards Norma and Vicente, as well as adding possible
factors to Norma's mental health problems other than Marilia's
explanation of trauma on seeing her mother's suicide. Marilia
already points out that Norma follows Gal in the form of their suicides. Norma shows other signs of identifying with the dead mother,
including her preference for loose-fitting white nightgowns similar to
Gal's. Her social phobia may also relate to this identification with the
mother. Ledgard's fixation with his daughter's looks and his desire
for Norma to appear 'normal' (meaning feminine and sexually attractive) can only make things worse.

Ledgard's remaking of Vicente to resemble both Norma and Gal
supports the theory that Norma's memory is correct, that Ledgard
has indeed abused her, making her a stand-in for her mother just
as Vicente is remade to stand in for both Norma and Gal. Vicente/
Vera becomes Ledgard's object of sexual desire, placed in the position of the sexual partner, Gal. He occupies this position by virtue
of his resemblance to Gal, which is achieved through the transplant
of Norma's face. When Marilia says to Ledgard, 'You shouldn't have
used her face', she is referring to Norma's face; Norma was buried
on the day that Ledgard performs vaginoplasty on Vicente, making
it conceivable that Ledgard envisages Vicente's transformation into

Vera as a way of replicating his lost daughter by using the body of the person who is, in his eyes, responsible for her loss. The use of Norma's face introduces an incestuous element to the plot, with Ledgard falling for a version of his daughter, whom he may have abused as a stand-in for his unavailable wife. The parallels between Vicente, Norma, and Gal are emphasised on the day of Norma's funeral. As Ledgard emerges from the second cellar where Vicente is imprisoned there is a hard cut from the cement ramp with bricks for steps to the cement path and tombstones at the cemetery. Norma is being laid to rest whilst Vicente is buried alive. Gal is also confined to her bedroom as Ledgard attempts to treat her burns. There is no escape for her except in death. This is visually conveyed by the curtains in Gal's room, which seem ablaze as sunlight pushes through them in a domestic and no doubt retraumatising replica of the burning car.

Marilia's memory of Gal's suicide is as suspect as Ledgard's and Vicente/Vera's dream-memories about the other garden scene, Norma's assault. They are united by location, lush private gardens, and the song 'I Need to Love'. Pedro Poyato Sánchez notes the song's importance to the narrative and its links to Gal's suicide: 'The notes sung by the child are interrupted, giving way to a piercing scream, inscribing in the image a hole that will not be sutured. This can be seen when, years later, a teenage Norma becomes uninterested in Vicente's sexual caresses on hearing the notes of the song ...: the scream is inscribed again in Norma's face and with it the hole of a definitive madness' (2015: 300). Poyato Sánchez attributes Norma's mental health crisis to the recurrence of the song and considers that Vicente, instead of being guilty of sexual assault or rape, was merely in the wrong place at the wrong time. The events leading up to Ledgard finding Norma in the garden are only told from Vicente/Vera's perspective, so this, in itself, ought to induce caution about judging his and Norma's actions. Nevertheless, Poyato Sánchez's use of Norma's disability to invalidate her experience is highly problematic. The film itself leaves open the possibility that Vicente assaults or rapes Norma, as well as that of an initially consensual encounter becoming assault. Ambiguity is visually dismantled as Vicente is seen to cover Norma's mouth in a silencing gesture similar to Zeca's during the unambiguous rape of Vicente/Vera. Later on we will see how Ledgard also covers Vicente's mouth with chloroform prior to what Lemma calls 'surgical rape' (2012: 1294).

There is another way of interpreting the garden scenes, which returns agency to the women in Ledgard's life and takes Norma's claims seriously. If, indeed, Ledgard has raped Norma, this prompts a rethinking of the earlier, childhood scene. Marilia's recounting of Gal's suicide resembles a screen memory: brightly lit, seeing the traumatised subject from the outside. She attributes to Gal thoughts and feelings that cannot be substantiated. The facts are: Norma is in the garden singing 'I Need to Love', a song associated with her mother. Gal goes to the window, screams, and throws herself out. Norma screams. What could Gal have possibly seen to kill herself, other than her reflection in the windowpane? What trauma does 'I Need to Love' trigger in Norma and why does she insist that her father raped her? Who in the film needs to love and feel loved repeatedly, even if it means violently remaking and coercing others into becoming what he wants them to be? 'I Need to Love' – together with a haptic memory prompted by Vicente's sexual advances – could function as the trigger for Norma's recovery of a traumatic memory of past sexual abuse.

The garden, as an extension of domestic space, is also a place where unpleasant and violent encounters can happen. Pavlović explores masculinity and the disabled male body in *Carne trémula* and *El jardín*, explaining that a 'bourgeois paradise' is 'suddenly fraught with danger' (2006: 154), analysing the masculine body out of context as a way of reflecting upon 'prevailing Spanish political models through the tropes of manhood and masculinity' (2006: 149). Whereas in *El jardín* the physical disability of the main character is used to explore the inherently violent social structures he once represented and upheld, in *La piel* we are presented with a young woman with mental health issues as well as a young man whose sex has been changed forcibly by the representative of patriarchal biopower. The garden scenes function as windows into traumatic past events, just as in *El jardín*. However, trauma in *La piel* is both shown and not shown, and idyllic garden landscapes are populated instead by taboo sexual fantasies, which in the case of Ledgard and Vicente have gone wrong. Ledgard's possible abuse of young Norma results in the loss of his wife and daughter and Vicente's in the loss of his freedom and body. Vicente's conversion into Vicente/Vera may thus respond to Ledgard's desire to enable his sadistic incestuous desires towards his dead wife and daughter, moving them into the socially acceptable domestic space (Vicente/Vera's movement from second cellar to the operating theatre in the first cellar, to a prison in the house, to Ledgard's own bedroom). Zeca cuts to the chase when he refuses Vicente/Vera's suggestion to 'fuck in the garden': 'I'm sick of screwing in the open air. This tiger wants a bed.' Ledgard's downfall is not his possible abuse of wife and daughter, or his kidnap and abuse of Vicente, but his desire for this abuse to acquire a socially acceptable face signified by heterosexual romantic love in the home.

Vera Dika shrewdly describes the film as a 'temporal and visual labyrinth' (2014: 44). The illusion of truth is constantly undermined by doubling and circularity, something that Gutiérrez-Albilla rightly associates with trauma: 'the superimposition of multiple and different temporalities seems to reproduce in cinematographic form the temporal structure and economy of trauma. If mutilation and surveillance are two crucial themes of this film, this thematic preoccupation with trauma is manifested in the film's narrative structure' (2013a: 77). The initial use of sleeping Ledgard and Vera as portals into flashbacks confers a degree of liminality to these flashbacks and casts doubt over their status as memories. Price, for example, interprets them as long dream sequences the 'authenticity' of which cannot be 'verified' (2015: 313) and proposes that the interpretation of the ending as a triumph for Vicente/Vera is undermined by 'the visual signifiers of the fade [to credits] that suggest Vera is only dreaming, and that he is physically back in bed with the sleeping Robert, wrapped by Robert's arms in a possessive and containing embrace. *The Skin I Live In* refuses to provide a straightforward ending where Vicente is able to escape from his captor' (2015: 315).

Whereas Price is right to temper triumphalist interpretations of the ending as Vicente's victory over Ledgard, noting that Vicente/Vera cannot be disentangled from each other, he is perhaps too keen for a plausible explanation for the story in the shape of the old dream trope. For most of the film to be Vicente/Vera's dream, including his killing of Ledgard and subsequent escape from El Cigarral, we must believe that the cut from Vicente/Vera's dream-memory of his abduction and abuse includes scenes to which he is not privy, such as Norma's funeral. The cut between Ledgard's visit to Vicente in the second cellar and the establishing shot of the cemetery for Norma's funeral indicates otherwise. The cross-cutting from this moment on shows the film moving away from the conceit of the sleeping characters to a more traditional way of providing backstory following a *noir* mode. This mingling of subjectivities replicates the entanglement of bodies noted by Price, only this time it concerns prey and predator, abuser and abused, in two different bodies. Just as Vicente/Vera's body is the product of forced transgenesis and transsexuality, and therefore his body is *both* male *and* female, *both* human *and* animal, Vicente/Vera is *both* prey *and* predator. What is more, Ledgard, who starts the film as a consummate predator, ends it as Vicente/Vera's kill.

In a departure from Thierry Jonquet's novella *Mygale* (Tarantula, 2002) from which the film is loosely adapted and where Richard is clearly the spider and Vincent transforms from male predator to female prey (Eve), the roles of prey and predator are not clearly allocated to Ledgard and Vicente/Vera. The latter wears a black bodysuit when he uses force to escape Ledgard and assert his self by trying to commit suicide. He also wears black lingerie in true *femme fatale* fashion on the night he kills Ledgard. Black is the colour associated with spiders, some of which (tarantulas among them) are known for occasionally eating their male sexual partners. Vicente/Vera, however, may be more suitably associated with the black widow because of his hourglass figure (paradoxically created by Ledgard). Whereas in *Tarantula* Eve falls for her captor, Vicente/Vera only pretends to, spinning a web of deceit that lures Ledgard to his trap. This is signalled visually in Ledgard's bedsheets (dark grey with a web-like pattern), among which he dies. To ensnare Ledgard, Vicente/Vera reconsiders his initial rejection of the trappings of femininity offered by Ledgard (make-up, dresses, high heels), complying with the form moulded by Ledgard.

Almodóvar takes Jonquet's use of entomological symbols further by extending the notion of regeneration and rebirth originally present in Jonquet's use of the spider shedding its skin through the use of another insect equally prevalent in Spain, the cicada. Spider and cicada merge in the character of Vera/Vicente in a way that develops the gender fluidity in Almodóvar's *Matador* (1986). Ledgard's property, El Cigarral, derives its name from the Spanish name for cicada (*cigarra*). The life cycle of cicadas is employed throughout the film: cicadas are born in trees and bury themselves underground to feed on roots, stay there for many years to surface as nymphs, shed their skin in metamorphosis, and begin a brief adult life. Freshly hatched nymphs are translucent white (like the silicone mask Vicente/Vera wears at first), then turn progressively beige until they take the black adult shape. Vicente/Vera's transformation follows closely the life cycle of the cicada, from imprisonment in the cellar to progressive metamorphosis and final transformation. The theme of burial and rebirth is also present in the doubling of Gal, Norma, and Vicente/Vera, who are forced to embody each other. In addition to this, Vicente/Vera's patience in waiting for the right moment to escape is linked to both the spider waiting for prey and the cicada, waiting underground, preparing until ready to metamorphose.

Vicente/Vera uses seduction to ensnare Ledgard into a romantic relationship, twisting Ledgard's actions and putting words into his mouth:

VICENTE/VERA   I'm yours. I'm made to measure for you. And you've just told me that you like me.

LEDGARD   Have I said that?

VICENTE/VERA   [Looking towards the security camera] I know you look at me. Since you brought me here we practically live in the same room.

Vicente/Vera plays the seductress, becoming a *femme fatale* as the action in the 2012 present develops. Ledgard is characterised as being in control of Vicente/Vera's body but not of his own feelings, which Vicente/Vera is probing as Ledgard retreats in haste.

For this reason, the 'splashes of red which have been noticed by reviewers', including a 'nod to Michael Haneke's *Caché* (Hidden, 2005), with a supremely orchestrated suicide attempt by kitchen knife', are not, as Aldana Reyes thinks, 'only used for cinematographic purposes' (2013: 822). Just as in *Caché* the suicide and accompanying 'splashes of red' are used as an indictment of Georges's role in the destruction of a young French Algerian boy's life, in *La piel* existential threat to life is self-inflicted but at the same time an indictment of Ledgard's less obvious attacks on Vicente's being and his controlling biopower. Price notes that *La piel*

forcefully screens out the figure of the male skin-ripper, instead making the victimized female the one most associated with puncturing skin. Scholars of the body horror genre ... locate the terror of breaking the skin as a moment of crisis in subjectivity. ... [H]owever, the cutting of the skin actually reaffirms Vera's subjectivity, because only by staging the destruction of the self is Vera able to establish that she has a self to destroy. In other words, Vera proves that she is still in control

of her own body, even if it is only her body's demise. For Robert, whose
wife and daughter both killed themselves, self-destruction is exactly the
power he wants to wrest away from women. (2015: 308)

In both films, extreme violence affirms and denounces attempts to
obliterate the self. The splashed blood is an embodied writ of *habeas
corpus* that affirms the right to one's own body. In *Caché* the French
Algerian man is not ostensibly imprisoned, but the film makes clear
that he is a victim of the racist 'structural violence' (also called social
injustice) that Georges embodies (cf. Galtung, 1969). Georges's
defence of his white French privilege removes the French Algerian
boy from the idealised home of Frenchness (Georges's parents' farm-
house) to an orphanage and, later, a life of social exclusion.[5] Similarly,
the treatment of Vicente/Vera at the hands of Ledgard can be interpreted as an affirmation of upper-class male privilege and an allegory
for the forceful and continued reshaping of Spain as beautiful and
compliant following a patriarchal Spanish nationalist idealisation of
the nation.

The fact that Galician Vicente, who is unhappy with the status quo,
is held in Toledo raises the spectre of how the myth of contemporary
Spain originating in the Transition continued the Spanish nationalist
Francoist project of homogenising the body politic of Spain, its plurality of nations, into a unified country, which was marketed abroad from
1948 with the slogan 'Spain is beautiful and different'. The creation
of an apparently seamless beauty that hides its artificiality therefore
links Ledgard's manipulation of Vicente's body and the ideological
transformation of Spain's body politic. The film's use of dissolves
to merge Vicente's and Vera's faces, as well as the mannequin's and
Vicente/Vera's torsos, draws attention to this cinematically. In the
context of Spain's second disenchantment, the dissolves also refer to
socio-political modelling. Just as Ledgard justifies his violence towards
Vicente by accusing him of raping Norma, Spain's political establishment on both the right and the left seeks to suppress and demonise
nationalisms other than Spanish nationalism within Spain to create a
model Spain of their mind (cf. Resina, 2000: 12). The contemporary
Spanish nation is, like Vicente/Vera, an artificial product shaped to
conform to the ideals of those empowered to describe it and suppress
that which is not considered 'Spanish' enough.

Despite the focus on horror, it is the *noir* elements that allow the
cynicism of the second disenchantment to be sown like a second

skin to this thriller. As Rob Stone explains, the first disenchantment brought about an interest in *noir*: 'True noir ... was not to appear until disillusionment with democracy took hold and a weary cynicism infected those who only a few years earlier had looked forward to the rebirth of Spain with optimism. But this is already neo-noir, a rebirth of something that never existed' (2007: 205). Almodóvar draws on this neo-*noir* tradition, linking national representation and 'rebirth' of a non-existent original. *La piel* embodies national representation as Vicente/Vera is modelled by Ledgard into what he considers an improved daughter/wife. However, neither Norma nor Gal existed as Ledgard reimagines them. Vicente/Vera – renamed 'Vera' (from the Italian meaning true or real) and who gives himself the surname of Cruz as a nod to Christian symbolism – is in fact a reproduction of Ledgard's ideal daughter–wife, part of his attempt to repress his failure to control both women. It is Ledgard who falls for surfaces, not the film as a whole, which, as heir to Spanish neo-*noir*, is aware that style may be used as a tool to recover lost historical meaning. *La piel* exposes manipulation of the body politic through a story about manipulation of the human body. Critical debates about Vicente/Vera's gender and Almodóvar's use of gender reassignment surgery omit this important though problematic use of the body as proxy for the nation. Just as Ledgard changes Vicente's form in order to change his identity, implanted memories via cultural representation as in 'prosthetic memory' may aim to change perceptions of the past and nation.

La piel offers spectators a celluloid version of Vicente/Vera's body stocking. Its emphasis on aesthetics moulds old and new material to fit artistic canons serving as a visual trap that can lead to complacent dismissal of its politics. Just as Gaultier's costumes in Almodóvar's cinema draw attention to and affirm normative standards of feminine beauty, as well as the sexual availability of those bodies assigned womanhood by mimicking and shaping skin, the film's own *pelicular* deception may divert spectators' attention towards its appearance. Almodóvar's perfect cobweb lies there, ready to trap the unsuspecting into abandoning critical reflection on gender, patriarchal and other forms of biopower, and the refashioning of old ideologies in democratic, modern outfits that nevertheless only partially hide their predatory and damaging nature.

Notes

1 I will use Vicente to refer to the pre-operative and post-operative Vicente who has not yet had a face transplant (played by Jan Cornet) and Vicente/Vera to refer to Vicente after the facial and skin transplants (played by Elena Anaya) to signal Ledgard's change of his name to Vera and the film's signalling of a change of sex and gender. However, I will use the masculine pronoun 'he' throughout as Vicente/Vera continues to identify as male.

2 I discuss Almodóvar's early films as a reaction to the first disenchantment (late 1970s–early 1980s) in Chapter 1.

3 Paul Julian Smith summarises many of these echoes to do with casting, scenes, staple characters, and so on (2011).

4 Vicente/Vera's face transplant will be discussed later on in this chapter.

5 The orphanage is linked to abuse through the scene where the boy is taken away and through a reference to Almodóvar's *La mala educación*, which is being shown in the cinema Georges visits after the man's suicide and may well be the film he watches.

16

'Crisis cinema':
Los amantes pasajeros and *Julieta*

After *La piel que habito* (The Skin I Live In, 2011), Almodóvar directed two very different films, a camp comedy inspired by American screwball comedy and both Spanish and American satire, *Los amantes pasajeros* (I'm So Excited!, 2013), followed by a full-blown drama, *Julieta* (2016). Ryan Gilbey's bewildered comments on Almodóvar's recent trajectory in his review of *Julieta* are typical: 'Pedro Almodóvar has entered a spell of late-period unpredictability. After scary (The Skin I Live In) and silly (I'm So Excited!) comes sad' (2016: 51). Mark Lawson also remarked on the tonal oscillation between films: 'Such is the shift in gravity from Almodóvar's last film, *I'm So Excited!* – a musical farce set on a jet – that it is as if the Zucker brothers had followed the success of *Airplane!* with an adaptation of Ibsen's *Hedda Gabler*' (2016: 50). Lawson's analogy is apt since *Airplane!* (Abrahams and Zucker, 1980) is a significant intertext for *Los amantes*.

Competing visions of Almodóvar as a serious art-house director (favouring his 1990s films) and provocative Spanish *enfant terrible* (more attached, perhaps, to his 1980s comedies and hybrid melodramas) frame how critics respond to these generic and tonal shifts films. Fionnuala Halligan, for example, praises *Julieta* by viewing *Los amantes* as an anomaly:

> All the visual elements which have made Pedro Almodóvar's work so consistently enticing are boldly represented in Julieta [*sic*], from strong colour tones to sculpted scenarios, to constant art-world nods ... alongside the infamous wallpaper collection of art director Antxon Gomez. This is a classic Almodóvar, at home in Madrid for the most part, throwing vibrant colour on the screen in silky reds, blues and

greens. It's as if 2014's I'm So Excited [*sic*] never existed in the director's thought-line. (2016)

Whereas Halligan considers stylised *mise-en-scène*, strong colours,
and intertextuality 'classic Almodóvar', thus favouring *Julieta*, Jorge
Marí describes *Los amantes* as 'one of his most luminous productions'
and 'a hilarious comedy that appears in the most sordid moment in
recent Spanish history' (2015: 627), concentrating on its function as
social and political satire more in line with his early work. Both Jordi
Costa (2013) in Spain and Paul Julian Smith (2013b: 52) in the UK
consider *I'm So Excited!* a 'minor' work; Almodóvar is, to their minds,
nostalgically returning to a *joie de vivre* associated with his 1980s films
without quite managing to recapture its freshness and spontaneity
(Costa, 2013) or reconcile 'the utopian hedonism ... reminiscent of the
1980s [with] current, sober concerns about equality and citizenship'
(Smith, 2013b: 51).

In this chapter, I argue that whereas there are clear generic, stylistic, and tonal differences between *Los amantes* and *Julieta*, these differences are not simply the result of 'late-period unpredictability' (an
unfortunate phrase that connotes randomness in relation to old age);
both films – and *La piel* – respond to a very similar socio-historical
context (after all, their releases are only a few years apart), but do
so in very different ways that are nevertheless completely within
Almodóvar's spectrum. The return to comedy, closely followed by
drama, is a very Almodovarian response to the deep financial and
institutional crisis that Spain has been immersed in for more than
ten years; the worldwide financial crisis that started in 2008 affected
Spain particularly intensely and was exacerbated by its concurrence
with a political and institutional crisis leading to a second political
and social disenchantment.[1] *Los amantes* and *Julieta* are products of
these social and historical crisis contexts.

Dean Allbritton identifies a specific tradition of 'Spanish "crisis
cinema"', the contemporary iteration of which responds to the financial crisis. Within crisis cinema he includes 'those Spanish films that
engage with or confront what it means to live in crisis', looking at
films made during Franco's dictatorship and afterwards, identifying 'physical vulnerability as a metaphor for vulnerability writ large'
(2014: 103). Allbritton's focus on how individual experience is organised 'into a communal one' (2014: 103) in certain contemporary
Spanish films fits *Los amantes*, a film he mentions briefly. The film,

however, makes it abundantly clear that, although the fate of all passengers is at stake, not all passengers are the same.

It is telling that the following disclaimer opens *Los amantes*:
'Everything that happens in this film is fiction and fantasy and bears
no relation to reality'. The disclaimer works both as a way to fend
off possible accusations of libel and to call attention to the film's
satirical 'relation to reality'. From the start, Almodóvar invites the
audience to escape into 'fiction' but keep an eye out for its satirical
targets, including the then king, Juan Carlos I.[2] The opening credits
use a cover of Beethoven's 'Für Elise' by the Peruvian band 'Los
Destellos', signalling comedy. As well as rhythm, which Almodóvar
identifies as key to comedy (2013), hyperbole is used to achieve
comic effect. Hyperbole produces both distance from and emphasis on 'reality', as seen in the initial exaggerated message sent by
the injured airport worker on being slightly hurt: 'I am bleeding
to death!!!!' The exaggeratedly comic opening functions as *mise-en-
abyme*, alerting viewers to the film's use of hyperbole throughout
as well as setting up the main themes of secrecy and the damaging
results of individualism.

Julieta does not overtly link the protagonists' experiences to 'communal ones', and it may thus sit outside Allbritton's narrower definition of contemporary Spanish 'crisis cinema'. It nevertheless uses
'physical vulnerability as a metaphor for vulnerability writ large'.
Its doubling of characters undergoing similar experiences and the
theme of parental–filial estrangement can be interpreted at the individual and collective levels in relation to Spain's wider crises. The
generational misunderstandings in *Julieta* between the eponymous
character and her father and daughter are also present in *Los amantes*,
which 'started off as a serious drama about a father, a corrupt financier on the run, who wanted to say farewell to his wife and daughter' (Arredondo, 2013). In the final cut of *Los amantes*, the financier's
daughter has disappeared due to her parents' conservatism. In *Julieta*
it is the daughters who adopt a conservative ideology and reject parental figures. In addition to this, both films address Spain's troubled
contemporary relationship with its former colonies. By considering
both films together, one can see that the return to camp comedy in
I'm So Excited! and *Julieta*'s relentless drama are a diptych resulting
from a Spain in crisis, the former responding to the circumstances
directly with 'merciless satire' (Delgado, 2013: 36) whilst the latter is
'a drama without screams' (Almodóvar, 2013; my translation). Both

are products of Almodóvar's often-voiced unhappiness with current Spanish social and political circumstances, a despair shared by many Spaniards. With its focus on how social groups (represented by character archetypes) interact with each other and with the political, financial, and social structures of the country, *Los amantes* undertakes an artistic form of prosopography. In contrast, *Julieta* adapts three short stories by Canadian writer Alice Munro – 'Chance', 'Soon', and 'Silence', from her collection *Runaway* – as a metaphor for the damage that silence can do to families and, by extension, societies, as well as the struggle of different generations to forge their destinies in a contradictory contemporary Spain.

A parody of the disaster plane film indebted to *Airplane!*, *Los amantes* uses the plot device of a plane whose landing gear is stuck and must find a safe way to perform an emergency landing. This situation has been caused by the comic carelessness of a ground staff member (Antonio Banderas), more concerned about his partner, a luggage handler (Penélope Cruz), than health and safety. While the pilots wait for an airport to be found, the plane – owned by a company tellingly called Peninsula (Spain is located in the Iberian peninsula and the national airline, one of whose planes we see taxiing in the background, is Iberia) – circles aimlessly above Toledo in central Spain, a city that was the setting for *La piel* and is associated with con-servatism. As first-class passengers and the crew are left to deal with the impending crash landing, some of their backstories are revealed to be linked, but, more importantly, a consciousness of themselves as a (temporary) community appears with small gestures of support for one another, culminating in a series of drug-induced sexual encoun-ters, one of which is undoubtedly rape. The film's Spanish title, *Los amantes pasajeros* (short-lived or passing lovers, with short-lived being a pun on passengers), points to the passing nature of these relation-ships and kinship between people more generally.

Although *Los amantes* was a huge success at the box office in Spain, Almodóvar did not return to comedy just to entertain. Nor is the film, as Smith believes, simply a bid to recover lost Spanish audiences (2013b: 49) undermined by the filmmaker's self-centred nostalgia: 'perhaps Almodóvar is more exercised by his own personal and pro-fessional history than by that of his country' (Smith, 2013b: 51). As I have argued throughout this book, Almodóvar frequently uses satire as a form of critique. As in *¿Qué he hecho?*, he employs Menippean satire with a loose narrative and representatives from various social groups, this time verging in Juvenalian satire in its direct criticism of contemporary institutions and persons. Instead of foregrounding indignation, however, comedy is used to provide a pessimist view of contemporary Spain. Resorting to playfulness and camp is a familiar strategy that harks back to his early films, when frivolity was used as a way of interrogating an impoverished national culture. Comedy helps make light of mistakes, social misdemeanours, and serious crimes, all of which appear flattened and may seem to be awarded equal importance. The film, however, balances intradiegetic humour – such as that employed by the crew among themselves to cement their social relations – with extradiegetic comedy and satire, which arise when the exchanges and situations generate a humorous response in the audience. An audience may, for example, respond humorously when characters have not, as in the flight attendants' failed attempt to distract the passengers from their plight by making them laugh with a performance of The Pointer Sisters' 1982 hit 'I'm So Excited',[3] and scenes where passengers break taboos such as having sex in public. Satire is also mainly extradiegetic. This helps distinguish, for example, between eschatological humour, comic mistakes and mis-understandings (those of the ground staff, for example), and premed-itated actions that are shown to be damaging to the community such as Mr Mas's (José Luis Torrijo) fraud.

Taboo-breaking (particularly sexual and bodily taboos) is essen-tial to comedy according to Almodóvar, who explains that 'taboo and humour are opposing concepts' (2013; my translation). The humour arising from taboo-breaking in *Los amantes* has been both praised and criticised, according to how effective it is considered to be. David Mermelstein criticises the film in *The Wall Street Journal* thus:

> the script is curiously lazy and flat, preferring inane sex talk and predict-able toilet humour to anything sustained or well considered. Almodovar [sic] toasts his country's ruin with a rainbow-coloured high-ball, self-consciously frivolous and determinedly fun – when a shot of something fiery might have achieved a better effect. (2013)

Mermelstein is right to identify the film as 'self-consciously frivo-lous', but fails to realise that the 'inane sex talk and predictable toilet humour' are satirical ways of critiquing not just Spain's 'ruin' but also its pretence of modernity. This strategy goes back to *Laberinto de Pasiones* (Labyrinth of Passion, 1982), a comedy that also ends with sex on a plane where all the other passengers are asleep and parodies the discourse of modernity prevalent during the Spanish Transition. Smith questions the effectiveness of *Los amantes* because of the progress made by Spanish society since the 1980s: 'Is Almodóvar still relevant? Where once his queer provocations were incendiary in a country that had only recently emerged from dictatorship, now they may seem like old news in a nation that legislated same-sex marriage rights without controversy eight years ago' (2013b: 49). Similarly, Costa considers the film to be a 'celebration of happily buried taboo' (2013). Almodóvar, however, differs in his assessment of contemporary Spain, blaming homophobia for *Los amantes*' negative press in Spain (Smith, 2013b: 49–50). The dialled-up campness of *Los amantes* thus corresponds to what Alberto Mira described in 2008 as a 'wilful act': 'For Almodóvar, *la pluma* [campness] is not a sign of pathology but a wilful act; it is not compulsive, but desired; it is the product of a search for pleasure that the transition had completely legitimised' (420; my translation and emphasis). This return to camp has been interpreted by D'Lugo as a 'serious effort to bring a Spanish audience to view their own current political and economic plight through the nostalgic filter of an Almodóvar sex farce' (2015: 76). D'Lugo discusses in detail how *Los amantes* revisits plotlines, characters, and motifs from Almodóvar's 1980s films, but considers this intertextuality self-indulgent.

To assess the relevance of the film's 'queer provocations', Marí highlights how advances in equality were actively unravelled by the conservative Partido Popular, which ruled Spain between 2011 and 2018, instead of past achievements during the socialist years (2004–2011):

> Is Spain today a more open, progressive, egalitarian, and free country than three decades ago? In the area of gender and sexuality, for example, reactionary measures such as the abortion law amendment proposed by Minister [of Justice Alberto] Ruiz Gallardón may lead us to think not. One could argue then that an unrestrained, impudent, antinormative film such as *I'm So Excited!* is not only relevant but necessary, and that its strident call for freedom is as powerful in 2013 as it was thirty years ago. (2015: 629; my translation)

Smith's assessment that Spanish society has become more liberal is true, but so are Marí's concerns about the resurfacing of extreme conservative ideology both in society and in mainstream politics. These positions refer us to one of the most important questions about the Transition to democracy and, by extension, about Spain's current institutions: did the Spanish Transition represent a continuation of or break from the dictatorship? (Moreiras Menor, 2002: 17–18). Whatever historians, sociologists, and political theorists conclude, it is clear that Almodóvar is part of a growing number of Spaniards who feel disillusioned with the Transition to democracy and desire a second, deeper Transition to fully move away from the dictatorship: 'we were undertaking a perfect Transition. Now we desperately need another Transition, but we do not know how this one will be achieved. Even worse, we should have gone through it already' (Almodóvar, quoted in Belinchón, 2015b; my translation). *Los amantes* responds to this affective crisis, a crisis that Cristina Moreiras Menor analyses in relation to Spanish film and literature until the 1990s and which has deepened in the second decade of the twenty-first century and thus is embedded in the 'contemporary cultural production [which] explores and questions the foundations upon which the Spanish modernity ushered by democracy rests' (2002: 18).

Los amantes is an example of what Almodóvar calls the 'Mediterranean school' of humour, which relies on the absurd to deflect emotion whilst commenting on difficult issues:

> In the Mediterranean school the passion of characters, carnality, and lack of modesty prevail, as if the characters did not respect themselves or each other. ... This earthiness allows the Mediterranean school to talk about social problems, with a lot of humour, laughing about the limitations and tragedies of life, and make light and laughter appear from within darkness. (Almodóvar, 2013; my translation)

Almodóvar sees satire as a social corrective tempered by taboo-breaking humour. As María Delgado explains, despite its billing as a camp comedy, '*I'm So Excited!* is anything but escapist entertainment. It ostensibly functions as a screwball comedy, ... but it is a feature grounded in the need for playful pleasure and excess at a time when politicians can only respond with the bland, uninspired discourses of austerity' (2013: 36). *Los amantes* blends this parodic impulse with an appropriation of nostalgic discourse about the potential Spain held during Transition years.

The passengers' backstories reveal past actions that range from clear crimes such as fraud, murder, accessory to murder, drug-trafficking, procuring, and blackmail to ethically suspect behaviour such as womanising and adultery. The only character who seems not to have a compromising backstory is Bruna (Lola Dueñas), a psychic. Delgado explains Bruna's relevance to the film's hidden themes: *I'm So Excited!* paints a society indelibly scarred by secrets and lies. Lola Dueñas's pensive psychic is en route to Mexico to try and locate the bodies of Spaniards who have disappeared in mysterious circumstances, a possible reference to the film's own "disappeared" from the Civil War and its aftermath, thought to number 100,000' (2013: 40). Bruna's amiable demeanour distracts from her actual behaviour. She uses her psychic powers as an excuse to harass men and is described by one of the characters, Joserra (Javier Cámara) thus: 'A crazy woman came in and said she's a psychic. Then she contacted the beyond through Álex and Benito's crotches.' Bruna subsequently rapes a sedated male passenger (Nasser Saleh) seated in Economy class in order to lose her virginity, attempting to start a relationship with him once he is awake without revealing what she has previously done. Bruna (whose name points to the darkness within her) acts as a personification of contemporary Spain's contradictions. She looks for the disappeared in Mexico for money when there are thousands of disappeared in Spain itself. The Mexican Infante self-identifies as a murderer when Bruna smells death. Interestingly, Bruna first associates the smell of death with the banker who has stolen money from thousands of Spanish citizens, a personification of the link between the financial crisis and an increase of suicides in Spain. The man Bruna rapes is also the only non-white character, likely to be read by Spanish audiences as North African. This gives a geopolitical dimension to Bruna's abuse.

The thematic ambivalence around the characters is replicated visually in the pastel shades of pop comedy dominant in the set and crew outfits (which are underscored by red curtains and motifs in their uniforms), as well as by the predominantly darker primary outfits of most passengers. The pastel tones, as Delgado explains, are markedly different, a 'more muted colour scheme than the primary shades that predominated Almodóvar's earlier comedies' (Delgado, 2013: 36). These, and the 'lengthy medium shots that allow performances to play out in the manner of a live television sketch' (Mintzer, 2013: 82), function as formal warnings about the film's awareness of its own use of nostalgic memorialising of the late 1970s and early 1980s, the years of both the Spanish Transition to democracy and the *movida* years.

Pastel tones give the film a fake, glossy, nostalgic look and the nods to the medium of television signal how *Los amantes* parodies a current Spanish trend in literature and television of re-creating Spain's recent past. The television series include *Cuéntame* (Televisión Española, 2001–), *Temps de silenci* (Televisió de Catalunya, 2001–2002), and *Amar en tiempos revueltos* (Televisión Española, 2005). They use 'the allure of nostalgic recollection ... as a main strategy to attract a loyal cross-generational audience' (Santana, 2015: 153). *Los amantes* also partakes of the 'nostalgic gesture that these TV series invite us to perform' which, as Mario Santana explains, 'is the desire to return to an imaginary past where competing interests and identities could be brought together and reconciled (and thus erased, ceasing to be recognized as a problem), a past where everybody, whether leftist or conservative, was above all the member of a homogeneous nation' (2015: 159).

The nostalgic warping of time is signalled at the beginning of the film, as D'Lugo explains: 'the established signature credit: "un film de Almodóvar" is replaced by the earlier, more modest "un film de Pedro Almodóvar" conspicuously recycling the same graphic used for the credits of' *What Have I Done to Deserve This?!*' (2015: 77). The interior of the plane is marked as a space both static and in flux, in and out of time. The plane circles above the Spanish plateau. It will never reach its destination. The events on board happen in a loop, where characters arrive back to their departing positions with some things having subtly changed. This time warping as circular movement is announced at the beginning in the image of a revolving turbine with a spiral in its centre, as the *huapango* (Mexican folk music) 'Malagueña Salerosa' begins to play and we hear the voice of the head steward Joserra start the safety procedure explanation for those on board. The cut to the bride and groom asleep in their seats is quickly followed by successive images of Joserra reading from a script and Fajas, Ulloa, and the Economy flight attendant looking utterly bored as they prepare to demonstrate the safety procedures. The experience of being on a plane is shown to be repetitive, its only point being to reach a destination that in this film is never reached.

The plane's fate is that of the Spain of the Transition, which thought it was going places but ended up in a protracted journey in 'limbo' (Gilbey, 2013: 51). The film tracks this thwarted journey: 'time has passed, and the country of the *movida* and design has become an abandoned no man's land, misty and spectral, from which the only thing left to do is run away' (Losilla, 2013: 97). The fictional La Mancha airport, 'an empty, ghostly space of pristine floors and mirrored surfaces that manifestly references the high-profile "white elephant" airports of Ciudad Real and Castellón' (Delgado, 2013: 40), is a fittingly sober setting for the end of the journey, appropriately filmed in linear takes (pans and podiums predominantly) as opposed to the sometimes dizzying camerawork inside the plane. Carlos Losilla analyses the airport scene as representative of Almodóvar's feelings about Spain's situation:

> Almodóvar sums up his feeling with disturbing takes of an empty airport, its deserted corridors, its motionless conveyor belts. These are the least glamorous images that Almodóvar has ever filmed and also the perfect metonyms for this imperfect, hobbling comedy – one that lacks real spark yet is at the same time moving in its involuntary vulnerability, in its meagre appetite for laughter at the shameful spectacle of a country in ruins. (2013: 97)

Losilla goes on to say that it is a 'failed film' (2013: 97), but I beg to disagree. A 'hobbling comedy' is the perfect form for a hobbling country, one that nostalgically dreams of national homogeneity and clings on to the idea of the 'perfect' Transition. As Losilla explains, the film 'may start out as a comedy but the apparently festive feeling soon translates into a melancholic tone–sometimes almost fiercely so–directed as much at the very persona the filmmaker has created for himself as at the surroundings that have allowed this character to flourish, and the country that has harboured him' (2013: 96). Delgado highlights how 'regression, infantilisation and play is evidently central to the director's handling of this skeletal plot' (2013: 38), but *Los amantes* makes clear that the high spirits and excessively optimistic narratives of the 1980s to which his early films were co-opted have given way to the prosaic realities of the continuity of the hegemonic structures in democratic Spain. As Almodóvar points out, the plane is a none-too-subtle metaphor for a directionless country: 'Spain, just like the plane in *I'm So Excited!* which goes round and round in the middle of a crisis and does not even know where it is going to land. ... This film is a metaphor of all this' (quoted in Arredondo, 2013; my translation). The sedation of Economy class passengers is clearly 'a wry metaphor for the way the ordinary people of Spain have been treated by their government' (Mermelstein, 2013). This state of

ignorance and apathy is shared by the only passengers clearly identified as average Spaniards travelling in Business class, the couple on
their honeymoon who spend the majority of the flight in self-induced
sleep after partying and taking drugs.

It is not the characters who lived through the Transition – Norma,
Mr Mas, and Diego Galán – who initiate the nostalgic appropriation
of the 1980s via the *Agua de Valencia* cocktail and lip-singing, but the
flight attendants, who are too young to remember the Transition in
detail. Mr Mas consents to taking the cocktail but is livid at the performance. Norma, on the other hand, becomes less disagreeable as
she remembers the 1980s. Infante's nostalgic memory of Norma as
his father's pin-up, which he inherited, is closer to the experience
of most of the characters; Norma is revered by the flight attendants
as a personification of the rebelliousness of the Transition years, but
it is clear that she has long given in to being an establishment play-
thing. As Delgado suggests, '[t]he phantoms of Madrid's *movida* may
run through *Los amantes*, but this promising generation is shown in
the film to have now either been put to sleep – like the passengers
in economy class – or been allowed to run riot without any sense
of social responsibility' (2013: 40). It is this contemporary update of
the *movida* generation (who have become blackmailers, fraudsters,
and pointless womanisers) that punctures any attempt at straightforward nostalgia. Even Infante, brought up in Mexico and thus not
strictly part of this generation, is a hired assassin and a liar. Although
he claims he does not kill women, he reads Roberto Bolaño's *2666*
(2004), a novel that centres on the unsolved murders of women, and
later on admits he is on the plane to kill Norma. On the other hand,
Diego Galán's former girlfriend Ruth (Blanca Suarez) represents a
way forward for contemporary Spain in her refusal to countenance
a resumption of her relationship with Galán. Ruth is a version of Pepa
in *Women on the Verge*, deciding to move on for self-preservation.

The Transition is also alluded to as Joserra explains how the pilots
and flight attendants are part of a 'Pact of Silence' to hush the past
murder of a passenger who was having a panic attack by the Business-
class passengers. This 'Pact of Silence' is a direct reference to the *pacto
del olvido* (Pact of Oblivion), the supposedly unwritten pact by all political parties to forget the past that was followed by a formal amnesty in
1977, granting immediate amnesty not just to those who had opposed
Franco's rule but also those guilty of crimes against humanity during
and after the Spanish Civil War (cf. Aguilar, 2002). Spain's Transition

to democracy was grounded in censorship and looking ahead rather than dealing with the country's traumatic past, just as the crew in *Los amantes* attempt to hide the plane's difficulties and then resort to distracting the passengers and each other. The 1980s is in this light revised both as a period of promise and as a time when distraction was chosen instead of in-depth reform and where new-found social freedom obscured the continuation of the structures of power.

Almodóvar's next film, *Julieta*, is a sombre study of personal crises that shows how silencing the past wreaks havoc in the present for two generations. Its working title was *Silencio* (Silence),[4] a title that Almodóvar chose because 'this element guides the worst things that happen to the protagonist' (quoted in Belinchón, 2015a; my translation). Whereas *Los amantes* wilfully uses camp in a parodic sending up of Spain's current affairs, satirising the country's complacent attitude to and nostalgic revision of its past, *Julieta* is an exhortation to confront the past and acknowledge how repression affects the present. As Delgado explains, '[t]he personal and the political interlock to potent effect in *Julieta*' (2016: 42). *Julieta* relies on structuring devices frequently used by Almodóvar in his exploration of trauma: analepsis, ellipsis, and repetition. Almodóvar 'set out to approach *Julieta* with as much sombreness as possible ... So it really was a matter of rejecting the habitual characteristics of my own cinema, the way I'm identified' (quoted in Lawson, 2016: 50). The camp sensibility prevalent in *Los amantes* is subdued here. What Susan Sontag describes as camp's 'love of the unnatural: of artifice and exaggeration' (1964: 515) is mostly conveyed through teenager Beatriz's (Sara Jiménez) love for the anachronistic 1970s décor in Julieta and Antía's rented apartment in Madrid.[5]

Peter Debruge thinks that *Julieta*'s visual style distracts from its serious subject: 'Even when working in earnest, Almodóvar can't hold back his own gaudiness, which threatens to overwhelm Julieta's emotions at all times' (2016: 125). A few set pieces stand out, including Julieta staring at the stormy landscape in a dressing gown reminiscent of Scarlett O'Hara's in *Gone with the Wind* (Fleming, 1939), her arrival in full mourning at the makeshift mortuary, the 'tableau in which Julieta dresses her bedridden mother and brings her outdoors', which, as Lawson states, 'is extraordinary' (2016: 51), and the bath scene when young Julieta becomes middle-aged Julieta. However, '[a]rtifice and exaggeration' of this kind rarely appear and, when they do, they are mostly contained within Julieta's flashbacks. The 'gaudiness' that Debruge complains about is absent from Julieta's current life. Her wardrobe, for example, is neutral (with the exception of her dressing gown and a red shirtdress), in contrast to the vibrant clothes she wore until she gave up on finding Antía. *Joie de vivre* has sapped away from her. One of the few times her outfit is foregrounded is during the opening credits. An extreme close-up of gathered red fabric becomes a close-up of Julieta's hands wrapping a sculpture of a naked male body in a sitting position. A piece by sculptor Miquel Navarro, it is supposed to be the work of Ava, Xoan and Julieta's artist friend, and it is visually suggested that the model for it is Xoan himself. The fabric of Julieta's dress is reminiscent of a flower and brings to mind the labia of a vulva. Jonathan Romney notes that 'it pulses like a human heart' (2016: 80) and Delgado perceptively notes how 'the close up suggests an intent to probe what lies within' (2016: 42). This initial image sets up the subject of motherhood and sexuality and the less apparent theme of covering up one's feelings. The red shirtdress is associated with the sculpture, which we later discover is made of bronze covered with a thin layer of terracotta. Unlike the sculpture, which projects vulnerability but contains a bronze core, Julieta's fabric covering hides her vulnerability. The film is the story of how Julieta's façade crumbles as she allows herself to reflect on her past and present circumstances. Delgado explains that the red fabric 'doesn't draw back like the framing curtains of *Talk to Her* or *I'm So Excited!*' (2016: 42), yet the image does suggest Julieta's life is a fiction.

We first meet Julieta in her middle age as she is planning to leave Madrid for Portugal with her partner Lorenzo (Darío Grandinetti). Julieta seems content, but a chance encounter with one of her daughter's former friends, adult Beatriz (Michelle Jenner), changes everything. Julieta decides to stay in Madrid alone, moves back to the apartment block where she once lived with her daughter, Antía, and starts haunting places associated with her, becoming increasingly depressed. Julieta remembers her past in the form of a long letter to Antía. It transpires that Antía left when she was eighteen and has not been in contact with her for twelve years. Julieta had been trying to move on by erasing any memory of Antía but seeing Beatriz (who told her she had seen Antía and her children recently) rekindles Julieta's hope of finding her, bringing back the past she has sought to forget. The film ends with a crisis followed by an optimistic denouement: Julieta meets Beatriz again, who explains to her that Antía was running away from her lesbian sexuality when she left. This revelation embeds Julieta's story of losing a daughter into the story of Antía's inability to cope with Beatriz's rejection and her suppression of her lesbian identity, rather than the other way around (Antía disappearing due to Julieta's role in Xoan's death) as Julieta believes. In shock, Julieta is run over by a car, a familiar device in Almodóvar's work. Lorenzo returns from Portugal and Julieta receives a letter from Antía, including her address, with news of her own son's drowning. The drowning of Antía's son opens up the possibility of reconciliation. At the end of the film, Lorenzo drives Julieta to see Antía, but even then Julieta resorts to old coping strategies: 'I'm not going to ask her for an explanation. I just want to be with her.' This ending feels as contrived and ambivalent as those of *Tie Me Up!* and *Kika*. The camera leaves the car with Julieta and Lorenzo to focus on the mountainous landscape they travel through, a reminder of Julieta's previous fruitless trip to fetch Antía and a sign of expanding horizons for the protagonist. Music returns, a reprieve in this unusually quiet film, acting as a reminder of the loss and grief that permeate it.

The film contains another, purely dramatic, ending, which could not be more different from the actual final scene: a memorable dolly zoom from Julieta at her desk towards a long, empty hallway as she finishes her letter to Antía. This scene represents Julieta's realisation that Antía's ghosting has destroyed her life, a psychological half life replicated in the scene by the lack of music as we plunge into Julieta's thoughts through voice-over. The empty corridor frames and traps her and the green *Vertigo*-like walls draw attention to her reimagining of Antía. This shot conveys Julieta's distance from her material through the writing process and the narrowing of her perspective as she becomes increasingly obsessed with Antía (Figure 16.1).

Julieta uses the language of addiction to explain her predicament: 'I abstained from you for years, but I made the mistake of relapsing into the hope of finding you or hearing about you. That absurd hope shattered the fragile base on which I'd built my new life. I have nothing left. Only you exist. Your absence fills my entire life and destroys it.' Erasure of the past is a 'fragile base' upon which to rebuild one's life. Like the life of characters in *Todo sobre mi madre* (All about My Mother, 1999), *Volver* (2006), and *Los abrazos rotos* (Broken Embraces, 2009), Julieta's new life is precarious. So was her life with Antía after Xoan's death. Silence disguises a growing sense of guilt, which, as Delgado points out, she 'passes ... on to her daughter'

16.1   Julieta completes her 'letter' to Antía (*Julieta*, 2016)

(2016: 41). As Almodóvar states, '*Julieta* might well have been called the return of the repressed' (quoted in Delgado, 2016: 42).

The ghosts of the past reappear easily, as seen in Julieta's two flashbacks on Antía's departure. First, the man on the train stares. Then Xoan appears at the doorway, replicating the moment Julieta left him after their final argument. Both men interpellate Julieta and spectators by looking straight at the camera, breaking the fourth wall. This is a visual instance of history – in this case Julieta's – 'becoming interrogative' through 'adjacency of past and present' (Lane and Tew, 2003: 12). The adjacency of Julieta's writing present, recent past, and historical past foregrounds Antía's disappearance, enhancing the film's symbolic plane in what I have identified in previous chapters as Almodóvar's use of the poetic function or cinematic excess.

These memories are traces of another elided traumatic event we are not privy to and which cannot be traced back. This is why Julieta writes 'Where do I begin?' She goes as far back as Antía's conception, unable or unwilling to make sense of anything before this time. Delgado links Julieta's question to Spain's inability to 'make sense of her past':

Antía's religious conversion may speak to the influence of the Church on civic life, and the narrative, although centred in Madrid, is crucially dependent on events that happen outside the capital – in Galicia,

Andalusia and the Pyrenees. At a time when calls for Catalan independence threaten the fragmentation of the Spanish state, this might be viewed as a comment on the interconnectivity of the nation. (Delgado, 2016: 41–2)

Delgado shows how *Julieta*'s very personal story is relevant to contemporary Spain's political situation. As Julián Daniel Gutiérrez-Albilla explains, Almodóvar's cinema 'mourns and witnesses the traces of trauma and fragments of memory' (2017: 1). The film is testament to Julieta's confrontation of the past, but in a way that replicates Julieta's own evasion in postponing showing the viewer what is currently making her unhappy and the source of her trauma. The epistolary form is not intended as a literal letter but as a way of making the absent Antía present in Julieta's mind. The narrative as a memorialising tool is apparent as Julieta starts writing:

Dear Antía,
I'm going to tell you everything I wasn't able to tell you, because you were a child, because it was too painful for me, or simply out of shame. But you're not a child any more. Beatriz told me that you have children of your own. Three, no less. You are a grown woman, and a mother.

The objects Julieta places on her writing table signal memorialisation: Antía's first communication, a message-less birthday card, and a ripped photograph of Julieta and Antía that she has reconstructed. The fragmented photograph recurs in Almodóvar's films as signs of censorship of the past; photographs are reconstructed in *Los abrazos* as a metaphor for the reparative reconstruction of the past through memory work, even if this work is partial and incomplete. This facing of the past, however, is not as productive as that in *Todo sobre* and *Los abrazos* because it is a solitary exercise, the sign of obsession rather than a genuine attempt at generating collective memory.

In *Julieta*, instead of the glossy pastel perfection of nostalgia we are mockingly offered in *Los amantes*, we encounter a fragmented narrative with a series of elisions at its heart and repetition as the past ripples into the present. As Delgado points out, 'in accordance with the rules of classical tragedy, the key acts – the stranger's suicide, Xoan's death, Antía's disappearance – take place off stage/screen. It is how Julieta responds to them that forms the narrative arc of the film' (2016: 40). Many other significant events are kept from us. We do not see the death of Julieta's mother (Susi Sánchez) or Antía's son or Antía's deteriorating relationship with Beatriz. Antía changes course only after her own son dies, unlike Julieta who has not been able to use Antía's disappearance to reconnect with her own father.

As Debruge explains, 'Almodóvar has constructed an extremely unconventional mystery, one in which there is no crime or culprit. Rather, his leading lady is herself a riddle' (2016: 125). If Julieta is a mystery for her family and spectators, Antía is no less so. Julieta is both the detective and the mystery as she writes down her memories to justify her actions to the missing Antía. Yet the film is not, as Debruge thinks, 'a sincere effort to understand her' (2016: 125). On the contrary, it performs the same function as Julieta's letter to Antía of conjuring up Julieta's presence whilst at the same time making us realise how little we know of her.

The technique of delayed disclosure is present in other Almodóvar films about memory and trauma. Additionally, behind Julieta's pain there is another, undisclosed source of pain, which is elided from the film and her narrative. This pain, not overtly referenced in the film, may well be the legacy of Franco, who Gutiérrez-Albilla refers to in a direct reference to Jacques Derrida's ideas on the trace as 'the "origin of the origin"' (2017: 2). Julieta's pain is not simply about Antía's absence but her failure to communicate with her, which relates to the traumatic loss of Julieta's mother to Alzheimer's and its symbolic link to censorship of the Spanish Civil War. Julieta and Antía suffer from survivors' guilt, but this guilt may be rooted further into the past than either Xoan's death or the suicide of the man on the train.

Lawson explains that the film tells 'the story of a character who is unable to communicate with her mother, because of Alzheimer's disease, or her daughter, from whom she is estranged' (2016: 50). The condition of Julieta's mother is similar to that of Rosa's father (Fernando Fernán Gómez) in *Todo sobre* and works as a personification of Spain's overwhelming historical silence, as a result of which children and grandchildren are not able to share their elders' memories. The mother acts as a symbol of Julieta and other characters' lack of communication, a product of repression that reverberates through the ages.

Julieta returns to the Transition, which is Julieta's repressed past and Antía's historical past. The film charts the development of its main character from the 1980s to the present day, from dynamic young woman to settled wife, depressed widow, and distraught mother. Julieta changes from transgressive presence (she raises eyebrows among older women in the train due to her punk outfit and thinks nothing of having sex on a train with Xoan, a married man whose wife is in a coma) to conservative accommodation (1990s Julieta has embraced married life and motherhood, berating her father for doing exactly the same she did as a young woman, starting a relationship with another woman as her mother succumbs to Alzheimer's). It cannot be coincidental that Xoan and Julieta live in Redes, near Franco's birthplace, or that the housekeeper (Rossy de Palma) voices opinions on the role of women more suited to the regime's fascist ideology. Xoan seems at first the best choice for Julieta, who snubs attempts to converse by the man who commits suicide, but Xoan's patina of modernity hides a hard, moulded interior like Ava's bronze sculptures. Xoan's surname is Feijóo, a surname most Spaniards would associate with conservative politician Alberto Núñez Feijóo, who has been the president of Galicia since 2009. Julieta chooses Xoan's red instead of the man's black clothes, life and sex rather than intellectualism that the man represents with his empty travel bag and self-immolation. This choice represents Transition Spain at the crossroads, choosing to leave 1970s left-wing intellectuals behind, with the promise of freedom, but ending up tied to the same old ways of doing things and burdened with repressed traumas. Julieta's journey is parallel to that of Spain, nodding to the nostalgic discourse about the potential of Spain during the Transition only to be disappointed in how things turn out and realising that confronting the past is essential for reconciliation at the personal and the national level. The final revelation about Antía also encourages consideration of how a younger generation of Spaniards, born in democratic Spain, can end up replicating their parents' silencing strategies. Julieta's and Antía's fates are a warning about the consequences of Spain's collective failure to confront the past and its turn to the right in the twenty-first century.

Julieta prompts consideration of the impact of censorship of the past on younger generations. Like Manuela (Cecilia Roth) in *Todo sobre*, Raimunda (Penélope Cruz) in *Volver*, and Mateo (Lluís Homar) and Judit (Blanca Portillo) in *Los abrazos*, Julieta chooses not to talk to her daughter about the past. Most of these characters realise too late the error of their ways and attempt to make amends but, whereas

Manuela, Raimunda, Mateo, and Judit opt for sharing their pain with others, Julieta commits her thoughts to paper, shutting herself away until her final breakdown. The lack of community makes Julieta one of Almodóvar's most vulnerable characters and brings to mind how many victims of the recent economic crisis in Spain are too ashamed to ask for help and suffer deprivation in silence. The film engages with this extreme vulnerability. Julieta, Almodóvar explains, 'isn't like the other mothers in my films, she isn't a fighter' (quoted in Delgado, 2016: 41). Julieta's crumbling body and mind, both as a young woman dealing with depression after losing her husband and as a middle-aged woman whose daughter has disappeared, fits Allbritton's description of the use of 'physical vulnerability as a metaphor for vulnerability writ large' (2014: 103). One could say that Julieta's vulnerable body stands in for contemporary Spain, a socio-political body built upon repression and silence.

Los amantes and *Julieta* are two sides of the same coin, one drawing on parodic camp aesthetics with clear socio-political satirical targets, the other employing the poetic function in the shape of analepsis, ellipses, and elisions that heighten the symbolic aspect of the metaphors. Although one is a comedy and the other a drama, they are products of the same point of crisis, responding to the country's concern with its past and how it affects its future, mirroring the crucial historical period of the Transition to which both films refer directly. Losilla's description of the contradictory feelings towards Spain displayed in *Los amantes* encapsulates perfectly the tension within Almodóvar's *oeuvre*: 'Spain, viewed with a mixture of attraction and rejection, a culture surrendered to its double vocation, both tragic and unconsciously hedonistic. ... [T]ime has passed, and the country of the *movida* and design has become an abandoned no man's land, misty and spectral, from which the only thing left is to run away' (2013: 97). It is this unease that lies at the heart of these two films' shift in tone and aesthetics and also to the competing versions of 'Almodóvar' the filmmaker. The 'tragic and [the] unconsciously hedonistic' are but aspects of Almodóvar's feelings of 'attraction and rejection' towards contemporary Spain and the outcome of his inconsolable awareness of the difficult circumstances Spain has been enduring for nearly a century and the probability that the country may be powerless to deal with them.

Notes

1 See Chapter 15 for a discussion of the second disenchantment.
2 There is an unspoken agreement not to publish compromising news about the monarchy that has partially broken down during the last decade. But artists still face censorship if they insult the king, as the prosecution of rapper Valtònyc (2018) demonstrates.
3 Fiona Noble analyses this performance in detail, arguing that *Los amantes* performs the past 'by revisiting camp aesthetics and screwball comedy genre preferences of Almodóvar's early works as well as through references to the Transition to democracy', performing 'the past to understand its legacies for both the present and the future' (2020: 58).
4 The title was changed to *Julieta* shortly before the film's release because Martin Scorsese was making a film with the same title in the same year.
5 Two actors play Julieta, Adriana Ugarte as the young woman and Emma Suárez as the middle-aged woman. Antía is played by Priscilla Delgado as the adolescent and Blanca Parés as the adult.

Afterword: *Dolor y gloria*

Although Almodóvar has expressed his wish to continue working, *Dolor y gloria* (Pain and Glory, 2019) feels like a last film in its condensation of 'themes present throughout the director's career' (Meseguer, 2019; my translation) and the culmination of a developing aesthetics that, despite continual change and a wide spectrum of styles, is recognisable in its use of recurring techniques. As Astrid Meseguer explains, the film 'drinks from the director's personal universe. The colourful aesthetic, the attention to dialogue, the figure of the mother, sexuality, drugs, and the movida of the 1980s are present in this story as a declaration of total love for cinema as an escape valve in childhood and also a dual element of torment-liberation' (2019; my translation). Sarah Bradbury also notes how the 'film is unmistakable "Almodóvar" in its exacting aesthetic that embraces artifice over naturalism, each scene a standalone composition filled with the bright hues of the Technicolor films he grew up watching' (2019: 32).

Dolor y gloria combines the bright colours of pop with more nostalgic (though always checked by metafictionality) scenes of everyday life. It uses flashbacks and narrative analepses, as well as an episodic structure that accommodates different time periods, genres, and narrative tones. Linked to this complex structure, as Pilar Roldán y Usó notes, is the use of 'different narrative points of view' and cinematic, painterly, literary, and musical *intertextual* allusions to Almodóvar's own work and the work of others (2019; my translation). Genre hybridity, another Almodóvar staple, is also present, in this case with references to autofiction and a blurring of the boundaries between traditional autobiography and fiction. The use of graphics to fast-forward the narrative has evolved from the comic intertitles present in his first feature film, *Pepi, Luci, Bom y otras chicas del montón* (Pepi, Luci, Bom, and Other Girls on the Heap, 1980), to two elegant animated graphic sequences (by graphic artist and long-term collaborator Juan Gatti) accompanied by the main character's voice-over narration, which could be stand-alone short pieces. This recurrence of features is a sign of Almodóvar's continuous work with long-standing collaborators such as cinematographer José Luis Alcaine, composer Alberto Iglesias, film editor Teresa Font, graphic designer Juan Gatti, and production designer Antxón Gómez, whose contributions cannot be underestimated.

As Luis Martínez states, '[f]ormally, the film reaches a level of perfection that is difficult to beat. ... everything flows without interruption or rupture' (2019; my translation). This level of formal accomplishment is remarkable given that Almodóvar continues to use complex plotting and genre hybridity, this time blurring the already slippery boundaries between autobiography and autofiction. This is reflected in how *Dolor y gloria* has been marketed. The film has been directly linked to Almodóvar's life, something that encourages thinking of it as 'confessional' (B. Martínez, 2019; my translation), even as the filmmaker tells the 'press that it is not biography' (Smith, 2019). As I explain in the introduction, personal experience is a powerful marketing tool for this media-minded director. Notwithstanding, the filmmaker is clear that: 'It is not autobiography. It is autofiction in its origins' (Almodóvar, quoted in Fernández-Santos, 2019; my translation). The film uses these genres to explore trauma in relation to the LGBTQ+ experience and as a way to muse on fiction and memory as productive, whether they become restorative or not.

Dolor y gloria tells the story of ageing filmmaker Salvador's struggle with chronic pain due to a number of physical ailments, anxiety, and depression. Salvador feels unable to work and spends most of the film under the effects of legal pain-relief drugs or heroin, to which he becomes addicted. During these slumbers, and also triggered by other stimuli such as water or music, we are presented with what seem to be memories of his childhood. These include (in chronological order) a night he spent on a train station with his mother Jacinta (Penélope Cruz) on their way to join his father (Raúl Arévalo) in the town of Paterna, near Valencia; their arrival in Paterna and discovery that they are to live in a cave; his mother's crafty way of making the cave habitable by agreeing with a local young construction worker and decorator, Eduardo (César Vicente), that Salvador will teach him to read and to write as well as basic maths in exchange for whitewashing the cave's walls and fitting a sink; Salvador and Eduardo's developing relationship during their lessons, culminating in Salvador's fainting on seeing Eduardo naked; Jacinta's machinations to secure Salvador a scholarship to study secondary education (just aged nine) at a seminary through the intervention of a pious old woman (Susi Sánchez); and his audition for the school choir. Many of these events are reminiscent of Almodóvar's biographical legend (mentioned in the introduction), particularly the filmmaker's health problems, his childhood experiences of moving, writing letters, and teaching labourers younger than himself, and his experiences as a scholarship boy and choir soloist in a seminary. Salvador's professional trajectory, his success in the mid-1980s, and his rift with one of his actors, Alberto (Asier Etxeandía), can also be mapped on to Almodóvar's career without corresponding completely.

Dolor y gloria contains ten flashbacks (eleven if we count the final, 'repeated', scene at the train station with its metacinematic twist) and six significant narrative analepses where either characters recount past events (for example, Salvador explains how his ill health followed his mother's death, Federico (Leonardo Sbaraglia) tells Salvador how he quit heroin, and Mercedes (Nora Navas) tells the doctor that the gastroenterologist thinks Salvador may have a tumour) or through reading and performing of life writing (as in Salvador's short story, 'Addiction', first read and then turned into a dramatic monologue by Alberto). There are two additional analepses that could stand alone as short films and take the form of voice-overs by Salvador with accompanying animated graphics.

These and other analepses comprise a good deal of the film; the present-day narrative frame is the story of how Salvador (a name that means saviour in Spanish) is literally saved from himself, returning to writing and filmmaking at the end of *Dolor y gloria* to make a new film, whether autobiographical or autofictional we cannot be sure. Whereas physical pain continues, Salvador's inimical state improves dramatically throughout the film as he meets with people from his past, a narrative strategy that (together with the analepses) confers on the film its episodic nature. The improvement of Salvador's mood starts with his reconciliation with Alberto, an actor Salvador had a major disagreement with during the filming of his classic film, *Sabor* (Taste), thirty-two years earlier. Salvador resented Alberto for taking heroin whilst filming and never forgave him for, in his opinion, destroying the tempo of the performance and lightness of the character that he had envisaged. After Salvador explains this in public and the actor and director nearly come to blows, he decides (by way of apology) to let Alberto turn his biographical short story, 'Addiction', into a dramatic monologue and gives advice on how to stage and perform it, explaining that he does not want to be credited.

'Addiction' dramatises Salvador's disintegrating relationship with his lover, Federico (named Marcelo in 'Addiction'), who was addicted to heroin around the time that *Sabor* was being made, and how cinema helped Salvador survive the break-up. 'Addiction' throws light on Salvador's fury at Alberto's drug-taking as displacement for the pent-up anger he must have felt at the time given Federico's addiction. It also provides the background as to why Salvador closes the door to human relationships because 'love is not enough to save the person you love'. 'Addiction' could be an example of the writing-as-therapy that Beatriz Martínez finds in *Dolor y gloria* (2019: 8), but it falls short of this since it enables Salvador to bury his past rather than deal with it. The narrator of 'Addiction' – Salvador's alter ego – relies on cinema and art to save himself; the monologue concludes: 'Cinema saved me.' Salvador attempts to forget the events depicted in 'Addiction' by writing the story, a memory that is retrieved in the present by Alberto's prying but which in effect is reopened by Salvador's own desire to seek and reconcile with Alberto, who becomes the embodiment of Salvador's 1980s past. Salvador's reconciliation with his past begins with Alberto, the staging of 'Addiction', and re-encounter with Federico. These reckonings prepare the ground for Salvador's even more difficult tackling of his relationship with his mother and his coming to terms with both her and society's rejection of his gay identity. The film also gestures towards a comparison between the carefree 1980s Spain (freedom that goes hand in hand with danger as seen in the theme of drug use) and a more regulated twenty-first-century Spain, which, like Salvador, is struggling to come to terms with both the recent past (the Transition) and the historical past (the dictatorship).

Whereas 'Addiction', as well as the characters of *Dolor y gloria* more widely, believes in the healing power of writing and cinema – something that is replicated in the critical views of the film as endorsing 'cinema as salvation for a creator who summons his past to settle scores with himself' (Fernández-Santos, 2019; my translation) – Salvador's predicament during most of the film shows that this is not necessarily so. He attempts to survive through his filmmaking and by collecting artwork, but these activities are shown to be insufficient. Salvador's assistant, Mercedes, and his doctor advocate for work and creativity (writing and filmmaking in particular) as a way to alleviate his depression, but it is his reconnection with Federico, who happens to see 'Addiction' and recognises himself in it, renewed friendship with Alberto, and acceptance of help from Mercedes (a replacement mother figure) that eventually give Salvador renewed impetus. This is followed by the discovery that Eduardo had sent him the painting of himself as a child, which prompts a return to writing and (potentially) filmmaking.

The structure of *Dolor y gloria* encourages a retrospective interpretation in which Salvador never stops creating in his mind, something that further unravels the idea that creativity leads to mental well-being. The final scene reprises an earlier scene from the film where the child Salvador and his mother have to spend the night in a train station on their way to join Salvador's father. Both these scenes stand out in their use of the star Penélope Cruz and the use of a warm colour palette. Both show the mother in an ambiguous way, devoted to her young child's physical needs (sewing a hole in his sock, feeding him bread and chocolate, allowing him to sleep on the bench while she takes the floor) but uncomprehending of his emotional needs. The first of these scenes happens early on in the film, as Salvador chases the dragon for the second time with Alberto. The child Salvador finds a novel in the bin. The scene closes as mother and son eat in the station and have the following exchange after Jacinta bemoans their situation:

SALVADOR   I like the station.
JACINTA   You are a dreamer. I don't know who you take after.

In the original, Jacinta calls Salvador 'muy novelero' (a fantasist), from 'novela' (novel). Here it is used pejoratively, the son being seen as an alien by his emotionally neglectful mother. The adult Salvador remembers, later on in the film, after he has acknowledged not getting over his mother's death, how Jacinta continued to be disappointed in him as an adult, even as he took care of her full time:

JACINTA   You haven't been a good son.
SALVADOR   No?
JACINTA   No

Immediately after this memory, Salvador jumps to another one, this time of himself recriminating Jacinta how, by saying 'I don't know who you take after', she made him feel that he was letting her down 'just by being who I am'. Salvador's sexuality is the taboo underneath this exchange. Paul Julian Smith explains that '[a]lthough Penélope Cruz as the beautiful beaten-down young mother is deeply moving, Julieta Serrano as the dying version of the same character is positively chilling' (2019: 36). The young Jacinta may fool spectators who cannot see past Cruz's persona, but her apparently innocuous comments are shown to be just as cutting for her child as those the character utters to the Salvador now grown up. The scene at the station becomes more painful and significant to the story with this later conversation in mind. It places the gay theme at the heart of *Dolor y gloria* and demonstrates how Salvador's inability to get over his mother's death is actually a displacement of his inability to get over her rejection of him.

Almodóvar told journalists that the scenes with old Jacinta were improvised the night before shooting and tried to distance them from straightforward correlation with his life whilst explaining that they are the creative expression of the very real pain of social rejection as he experienced it:

> this conversation never occurred. It is not real because it is not my life; I never had that kind of relationship with my mother. However, it is true that in this scene I am touching upon something I had not dealt with before. The sequence summarises deeply and painfully something that has more to do with my childhood and adolescence than with my mother. The astonishment I saw around me. (Fernández-Santos, 2019; my translation)

The continuation of the station scene at the end of *Dolor y gloria* shows more understanding of the mother by giving her the final words and focusing on how the mother's priorities were dictated by the context of post-Civil War Spain.

SALVADOR   Mum, do you think there will be a cinema in Paterna?
JACINTA   I'd be happy to have a house to live in, son.

Salvador can dream of cinemas because Jacinta focuses on their primary needs, but she is condemned to never understand her son, who nevertheless shows profound awareness of how his mother's limitations shaped her expressions of love. For example, Salvador treasures Jacinta's darning egg, which we see her using to mend his sock whilst they are at the station. As Smith states, the darning egg is a 'symbol of the material deprivations of post-Civil War Spain when the impoverished populace was obliged to make do and mend' (2019: 37). Jacinta does not realise how important the egg is to Salvador as the only physical sign of her love for him.

The final scene at the train station ends with what Smith calls 'a brilliant sleight of hand' as the camera pans back to reveal a sound assistant holding a boom and Salvador instructing his team to cut; the exchanges between the child Salvador and Jacinta are thus discovered to be scenes from Salvador's new film and 'the film that [Almodóvar's] character constantly complains he can never make becomes the very film that we have just had the intense and complex pleasure of seeing' (Smith, 2019: 37). Of course, there is a further twist as this scene is part of Salvador's reveries triggered by general anaesthetic. It is therefore unclear whether he is dreaming of film-making or making the film he has previously dreamt of.

Salvador's reveries are revealed to be scenes from a new film, *El primer deseo* (First Desire). This film-within-the-film may qualify as the type of creative work that can become restorative, as opposed to Salvador's writing of 'Addiction', a short story that he wrote, he says to Alberto, 'to forget its content'. Whereas 'Addiction' is a dramatisation of repression, *El primer deseo* represents Salvador's attempt to work through past traumas in relation to his sexuality and how this affected his relationship with this mother. *Dolor y gloria*, in turn, represents Almodóvar's own attempt at creatively tackling the issue of his sexuality and how LGBTQ+ individuals were perceived and treated in Spain during his formative years. Whereas *El primer deseo* may be autobiography or autofiction for Salvador, *Dolor y gloria* is not strictly autobiography or autofiction in relation to Almodóvar. Nevertheless, Salvador's use of 'deseo' in his film echoes Almodóvar's own use of the term early on in his career, in the name of his and brother Agustín's production company, El Deseo, S.A., and of the first film it produced, *La ley del deseo* (1987), his first feature film to place same-sex desire centre stage.

Despite the relevance of *mise-en-abyme* and the constant metacinematic references, myriad links to Almodóvar's life and career in *Dolor y gloria*, many of which were used in promotion materials and

highlighted by journalists, have encouraged some biographical readings that ignore the film's warnings about its own fictionality and
possibly the fictionality of all memory and biography. Paratextual promotion materials such as the Pressbook draw attention to the film's
links to Almodóvar's persona, encouraging viewers to become biographers. For example, Beatriz Martínez writes that 'through its images'
the film reveals 'the essence of an artist who for the first time appears
naked, with no need to hide beneath artifice, generously opening the
doors to his intimate life' (2019; my translation). Even if *Dolor y gloria*
were straight autofiction, which it is not, such confessional readings
of the film miss the point. The blurring of the character of Salvador
with some of Almodóvar's own life experiences is emphasised by paratextual information, such as the news that 'the filmmaker deemed
necessary that his own furniture, objects, books and paintings, the
ones he owns in his own home, be used to shoot the film' (Roldán
Usó, 2019). Such information reinforces what the great theorist of
autobiography, Philippe Lejeune, called the autobiographical pact,
which assumes that the author, narrator, and protagonist are iden-
tical, something which is not the case in *Dolor y gloria* as there is
no such strong correspondence between Almodóvar and Salvador.
The desire to ascertain how firm the autobiographical pact is drives
questions by the press on, for example, whether Almodóvar has ever
taking heroin, to which he replies: 'No, never. It all started when
my back problems kept me at home. One day I thought of myself
as a character. Since painkillers were not working, I dreamt that my
character would consume smack to withstand the pain' (Almodóvar,
quoted in Fernández-Santos, 2019).

Almodóvar uses some genre conventions of autofiction – a genre
'inaugurated by queer and women writers in the 1990s' (Sturgeon,
2014) – to play with the idea of authenticity in cinema, biography,
and memory more widely. Whereas Salvador may be making autobiographical or autofictional cinema, *Dolor y gloria* manages to explore
these through Salvador *and* affirm the role of cinema as fiction that
explores emotional truths which, in departing from factual detail,
may achieve a closer portrayal of experience as situated. This is what
Almodóvar refers to when he says, 'There's an element of profundity,
an element of sincerity. I wanted to avoid these shadows of rhetoric' (quoted in Bradbury, 2019: 32). This is in line with Almodóvar's
frequent use of 'prosthetic memory' (Landsberg, 1995; Cook, 2005)
and films as memory texts and offers an alternative form for the

exploration of situated identity to artists, an alternative that may be particularly important for LGBTQ+ artists whose work is frequently pegged to their identity.

Generic differences between *Dolor y gloria* and *El primer deseo* are marked by style and content. Jonathan Sturgeon contrasts postmodern writing to autofiction, the latter described as 'a new class of memoristic, autobiographical, and metafictional novels ... that jettison the logic of postmodernism in favour of a new position' (2014). *Dolor y gloria* is partially memoristic and autobiographical, and very metacinematic. *El primer deseo* seems highly memoristic and autobiographical but not necessarily metafictional unless we believe that the use of *mise-en-abyme* during the filming of the final scene at the train station is part of it. Almodóvar is having his cake and eating it, conveying through the metacinematic *Dolor y gloria* some of the insights that autofiction has highlighted such as, as autofictional writer Ben Lerner explains, 'how we live fictions, how fictions have real effects, become facts in that sense, and how our experience of the world changes depending on its arrangement into one narrative or another' (quoted in Sturgeon, 2014). Drawing on Lerner, Jonathan Sturgeon explains that in autofictional narratives 'the self is considered a *living thing* composed of fictions. ... Fiction is no longer seen as "false" or "lies" or "make-believe." Instead it is more like Kenneth Burke's definition of literature as "equipment for living." Fiction includes the narratives we tell ourselves, and the stories we're told, on the path between birth and death' (2014). Salvador's journey from incapacity to functioning revolves around changing his narrative about himself, learning to live with his past, and accepting his present.

Dolor y gloria is a memory text that encourages collective and individual remembering whilst at the same time exposing how remembering is both active and dynamic. As Peter Bradshaw states, 'Almodóvar does not see the act of remembering as passive, as a kind of submission to a wave of involuntary images, but rather as a positive, creative act' (2019: 60). The allusions to autofiction and the use of prosthetic memory achieve just that. As in his other films, camerawork pausing over objects and people in close-ups encourage such memory formation within the film. Repetition is also used, in camerawork (dolly and tilt, for example), scenes, and memory objects such as water, music, soap, and the all-important watercolour. Memory work is seen, as I explained in previous chapters, as 'a conscious and purposeful performance of memory' (Kuhn, 2002: 157), most notably in the second iteration of the train station scene. The credits' allusion to watercolour painting with its changing patterns and colours convey both the dynamism and creativity involved in making both cinema and the self.

In addition to this, *Dolor y gloria* can be interpreted, as Luis Martínez proposes, as

a reading of the time we live in and even an opportunity, or invitation, for collective healing. For sanity. I speak, to be clear, of politics. Almodóvar asks loudly how is it possible to emerge from a crisis, whether personal or collective. And he proposes not so much an answer as a daring illumination. It is not about humiliating each memory or letting oneself be humiliated by it; the idea is not to turn each wound or pain into an excuse for rancor. On the contrary, it is possible ... to articulate an orderly tale where without renouncing pain there is space for the only type of glory: the grace of gracefulness. (2019; my translation, bold in original)

Martínez points to the film's important socio-historical dimension. In the context of the ongoing financial crisis that Spain has endured since 2008, Martínez's reading of the film as an exhortation to move on is an elegant solution to the despair that has engulfed many Spaniards, including Almodóvar himself (see previous chapters). As a recipe for 'collective healing' in response to repressed historical trauma, it is both painful (particularly as there has never been a truth and reconciliation commission in Spain dealing with the Civil War and the dictatorship) and difficult. Salvador's healing through confronting and accepting his painful past in relation to family (and social) rejection, and how this shaped his life and present, is an allegory for the pressing need for Spain to confront and accept its painful past and, more importantly, how this past and the narratives about it shape the country today.

The conclusion to 'Addiction' is very close to what Almodóvar says about 'the important role that cinema plays in [his] life': 'Cinema is my life and my life is cinema' (quoted in Delgado, 2019: 38). The allusion to Pedro Calderón de la Barca's classic play, *La vida es sueño* (*Life is a Dream*, 1635), introduces the belief in a person's ability to shape their destiny (as Salvador does towards the end in shaking off his ennui, seeking help for his physical ailments and depression, and seizing hold of his past through narrative). It also draws attention to the film's use of the Platonic allegory of the cave, of a life in shadows that humans can only leave by moving towards good (and light). Salvador journeys from a nostalgically remembered childhood bathed in light (the first memory of watching his mother and other women do laundry by the river) to living in a literal cave in Paterna (albeit one that is still bathed in the light of family and friendship with Eduardo), to a self-imposed dark 'cave' as a recluse in his dark apartment (ostensibly because of headaches but also as a metaphor for his depressive state after the death of his mother), and back to the light in his renewed friendships and resumption of work.

Cinema, Almodóvar once said, is literally made up of light (Iñaki, 2011). This is clearly signalled in the film's multiple references to Salvador's predilection for sunlit windows and skylights and his photosensitivity during migraine episodes (Almodóvar suffers from photosensitivity, which triggers migraines; Salvador's migraines trigger photosensitivity), which result in his having to live in the dark. The well-known trope of the window as cinema screen recurs in *Dolor y gloria* mostly through Salvador's point of view, for example, as a child on first entering the cave and discovering the skylight, a space that will be strongly associated with Salvador's survival of deprivation through fantasy aided by cinema, his love of reading as shown in his portrait painted by Eduardo, and his discovery of same-sex sexual desire.

The wonder expressed by Salvador the child at the cave's skylight, cinema, novels, and Eduardo's body resonates later on in the film, as the adult Salvador rebels against his circumstances and begins to tackle his illnesses, acknowledging depression (ostensibly due to his mother's death four years earlier). Whilst at the pain clinic, he looks up at a contemporary skylight, which frames blossoming trees against a blue sky in a seemingly obvious use of pathetic fallacy. The gesture is reminiscent of young Jacinta's looking up at the cave's skylight and it brings back his childhood predilection for the skylight. So is the composition of his view. The Crittall-style glass (partitioned as a grid) echoes a similar effect created by iron rods criss-crossing the cave's open skylight, which in this case are there to provide stability rather than for aesthetic reasons. The composition of these two low-angle shots provides relief from the depressing darkness that viewers (and adult Salvador) have been plunged in for most of the film. The hospital shot returns Salvador and viewers to his childhood state of wonder about the outside world and the world of aesthetic pleasure.

Just as looking out to the world through windows and grids transforms perception into composition, the cinema screen can be seen as a window to other worlds, in the case of the child Salvador to Hollywood Technicolor and melodrama and in the case of Salvador the filmmaker into fictionalisation (and possibly amelioration) of his past through autofictional narratives. The child Salvador distracts himself from his poverty and having to sleep rough at a train station by looking at the rectangular film trade cards he collects. He also resorts to reading (books are also rectangular windows into other worlds). Almodóvar reports similar hobbies as a child. As Alejandro Varderi explains,

> For Francoist Spain, intent on hiding under black religious processions that 'purified the streets', the colours of Art Nouveau architects Gaudí and Domènech i Montaner, Hollywood's Technicolor, seen in neighbourhood cinemas, was the only possibility to escape misery and fear. This is why Spaniards lived modernity as a simulacrum until the death of the dictator. (Varderi, 1996: 66)

Salvador's memories of neighbourhood cinemas in 'Addiction' (borrowed from Almodóvar's own writings) reflect the escapist function of Hollywood's cinema. So do both train station scenes. Opposing attitudes towards cinema are expressed in the film, most notably by the choir headmaster, a Catholic priest who on hearing Salvador express his love for The Beatles and cinema says: 'Here we will widen and redirect your tastes towards less pagan themes.' This is not peculiar in a country where it used to be a mortal sin to watch a film that had been rated 'highly dangerous' by official religious censors. Whilst not openly condemnatory, Salvador's mother Jacinta sees cinema as a distraction from more pressing needs.

Salvador's apartment replicates the grid as a decorative motif using quadrilateral shapes, from the kitchen partition doors to the book cases and other furniture and furnishings. Accompanying – and sometimes breaking – the lines, we encounter a series of allusions to flight and the natural world, such as the butterflies that decorate Salvador's cabinet. The recurrence of the grid combined with less structured lines also harks back to his childhood home, with its irregular walls, circular holes, and vanishing point at the end of the corridor as well as to the colourful off-cut tiles that Eduardo uses to make a splashback.

The cave's skylight not only provides a frame for daydreams, the light also works as a natural spotlight for Salvador on his arrival and as Eduardo sketches him. It is also used during the pivotal moment of sexual awakening for Salvador, his intense desire and shock on seeing Eduardo naked as he washes in full sun. The light sculpts Eduardo's muscular male body. This moment of scopophilic pleasure for the main character and the audience is a development from numerous instances in Almodóvar's filmography when gazes have signalled same-sex desire.

Salvador's sexual awakening is marked by physical discomfort (a sunstroke) and a retreat into the depths of the cave. The metaphor is clear and becomes even more so when Jacinta arrives to find Salvador in bed, attended by Eduardo; Salvador has been exposed to too much sunlight *and* (in Jacinta's opinion) spent too much time alone with Eduardo. The implication is that the budding relationship between Eduardo and Salvador must be relegated to the shadows, not displayed in public. Towards the end of the film Salvador discovers that Eduardo tried to send him the finished watercolour, speculating that Jacinta must have received it and disposed of it. The mother can thus be regarded as the gatekeeper of patriarchal heteronormativity, a development of what Marsha Kinder describes as 'the Spanish Oedipal narrative', where 'mothers frequently stand in for the missing father as the embodiment of patriarchal law and thereby become an obstacle both to the erotic desire of the daughter and to the mimetic desire of the son' (1993: 198–9). Here, the mother embodies the fascist 'patriarchal law', which used heteronormativity as a unifying principle and thus became an obstacle to the erotic same-sex desire of the son.

Commenting on a previous scene when Salvador is guiding Eduardo's hand to show him how to hold a pencil, Elisa Fernández-Santos explains that the relationship between the young mother, construction worker, and child becomes a triangle and that 'the mother senses something she does not like' (2019; my translation). This scene codes same-sex desire and shows Jacinta's realisation that Salvador and Eduardo's relationship is straying from Spain's established heteronormativity. Like other Almodóvar films such as *¡Átame!* and *La flor de mi secreto*, the scene heavily signals the links between state discourse – as seen both in the reading set by Salvador and the oilcloth depicting a map of Spain that covers the table upon which the lesson takes place – and the traditional family represented in the photograph of Salvador's parents that hangs behind Salvador and Eduardo. The photograph is particularly important as it is a re-creation of an actual photograph of Almodóvar's parents (which will appear later on in the film in Jacinta's room), an early indication that the scenes with young Jacinta and the child Salvador are not necessarily standard flashbacks but re-creations of the past by Salvador the filmmaker. Almodóvar has talked about this photograph of his parents as unusual in that they display affection in public. The unusual touch of the parents can be used to read Salvador and Eduardo's holding of hands (even if this is for a reason) as transgressive. Salvador sets Eduardo a reading task that includes a well-known phrase used to describe Spain during the dictatorship:

> EDUARDO   *reading* A holy, Catholic, apostolic ... *Looks at Salvador.* And who is this woman?
> SALVADOR   Spain. Who else could it be?

The content of the lesson follows the precepts of the dictatorship, a formal adherence that is also revealed in the *mise-en-scène*, as Eduardo and Salvador are working on a table covered with an oilcloth depicting the map of Spain. The characters' dialogue and actions, however, depart from the prevailing ideology, although they do not know it yet.

One wonders if some of Salvador's ailments may stem from his awareness of past social rejection and realisation that, after Jacinta's death, there is no possibility of acceptance. Significantly, old Jacinta is not played by glamorous Cruz but by Serrano, an actor who has played dangerously controlling mothers to characters played by Banderas twice in Almodóvar's filmography. Even the eyes of the young and old Jacinta are of a different colour as *mise-en-abyme* trumps continuity, as in *La mala educación* (Bad Education, 2004), and in contrast with Almodóvar's use of two actors for the same character in *Julieta* (2016). *Mise-en-abyme* lends credence to the idea that all of the scenes depicting Salvador's childhood are fictional re-creations that form part of *El primer deseo* (First Desire), the film that Salvador is seen to be making at the very end of *Dolor y gloria*.

The reduplication of images is most clearly seen in the metacinematic station scene, but the recurrent trope of Salvador's reveries, together with the doubling of the mother, unattainable erotic object (Eduardo, Federico, Marcelo), and constant references to filmmaking, also lead to semantic instability in *Dolor y gloria*, particularly in relation to the mother figure and Salvador's childhood memories.

The importance of dreams and the link between unattainable maternal love (reminiscent of *Tacones Lejanos*) and the lost erotic object is foregrounded in the official trailer's use of Mina's song, 'Come Sinfonia' (1961), which provides a soundtrack to the juxtaposition of Salvador's metaphorical return to the mother's womb whilst in the pool at the start of the film and the erotic images of Eduardo washing in full sun. Salvador has been unable to save any of his love objects; he can only dream about them.

The doubling of the mother points to Salvador's awareness of his role in re-creating his childhood and relationship with his mother as a purely nostalgic love object in the first instance, a nostalgia channelled through the golden light that bathes the laundry scene in the river, which is nevertheless cleverly undermined by Almodóvar in his use of Cruz's and the world famous singer Rosalía's star personas. The *flamenco bolero* they sing, 'A tu vera' (1962), is about unrequited heterosexual romantic love, where the woman speaker resolves to profess eternal love despite the man's indifference, but here it is appropriated to describe Salvador's relationship with his mother.

Salvador is not the only filmmaker revisiting representation. As Almodóvar's alter ego, his strife is bound to suggest Almodóvar's own treatment of memory and autobiographical material. Luis Martínez explains that 'the director fights against his memories, but he also fights against the reveries that moved him in the past. It is not so much nostalgia as the certainty that art, in general, does not improve anything. ... Fabulation seems in Almodóvar's thinking a bastard form, perhaps even impossible, to improve reality, but also necessary' (2019; my translation). The ending of *Dolor y gloria* is deliciously ambiguous in relation to this issue. Like Federico Fellini's *8½* (1963), *Dolor y gloria* offers a reflection on creativity as a means to survive crises but also a gift that can provide both titular feelings: pain *and* glory. Its complex emotional relationship to filmmaking echoes Truman Capote on writing as quoted in *Todo sobre mi madre* (All about My Mother, 1999): 'a noble but merciless master. When God hands you a gift, it also hands you a whip and the whip is intended solely for self-flagellation.' Salvador's journey from the initial Arcadian La Mancha riverside scene centred on the mother to his potential story about how this very mother thwarted his relationship with Eduardo turns *El primer deseo* into both a story of sexual awakening and a painful revision of his first love, Jacinta. Both loves are linked through the presence of soap.

Dolor y gloria also undertakes a revision of 'the reveries that moved' Almodóvar 'in the past'. As Smith explains: 'Where once he celebrated an idealised motherhood, now Almodóvar lays bare maternity's bitterness and disappointments. In pain, but perhaps also with hard-won defiance, Salvador acknowledges that he let her down "just by being who I am"' (Smith, 2019: 37). Smith mentions Almodóvar describing *Dolor y gloria* as the last of an unplanned trilogy following *La ley del deseo* and *La mala educación*. These are not, however, the only films in his career to establish a link between same-sex desire and filmmaking; his first feature film, *Pepi, Luci, Bom y otras chicas del montón*, features a gay director. These four films potentially offer 'links between cinema and homosexuality' and crucially chart a fascinating journey through Almodóvar's increased openness about social alienation and the exclusion of those who do not fit the heteronormative mould. Whereas Almodóvar's films have always included LGBTQ+ characters and issues, they have increasingly moved away from the presentation of an alternative social reality where the effects of social stigma are minimal to placing these characters' varying ways of dealing with the past centre stage. The LGBTQ+ experience thus becomes central to the wider national search for a way to interpellate past historical trauma, accepting the past without glossing over or wilfully ignoring its positive and negative aspects. Roldán Usó misses the centrality of the LGBTQ+ experience to what she sees as the film's central theme, how 'pain and bitterness lead to acceptance of the past', going as far as positively noting how the film leaves aside 'infrequent relationships such as transsexuality with sex and body changes' (2019).

In fact, as Acevedo-Muñoz notes, Almodóvar 'returns to the recurring motif of the human body as symbolic of the national trauma, and eventually of the possibility of reconstruction' (2007: 240). Salvador Mallo's body represents the body politic of the substantial part of the nation battered by history and struggling to deal with the physical and psychological consequences of having to mould their selves to the expectations of others. Salvador's sexuality and his class (Mallo means mallet) meant adapting to what others thought appropriate in post-Civil War Spain. But Salvador's is not only a victim's story but also the story of a perpetrator. He has to learn to live with a past of rejection and understand that he has behaved similarly towards others who did not adjust to his requirements, such as Alberto, and make amends. Only by unlearning the painful lessons Jacinta taught him can he overcome his physical and mental paralysis.

In *Dolor y gloria*, Almodóvar continues to use cinematic excess to foreground the mythopoetic function, disrupting time through paused or slow-motion takes to show Salvador's engagement with memory work as he slumbers and encourages viewers to do likewise. Memory is presented as dynamic, not fixed. Salvador must use creativity to confront his past and engage in self-definition and reimagination whereas in the past he has used it (to use Paul Ricoeur's idea) to structure forgetfulness (2006: 450). Salvador's penchant for nostalgia is clear in the visual style of *El primer deseo*, which is a companion to Enrique's *La visita* in *La mala educación*. However, as is usual in Almodóvar's cinema, the use of techniques that undermine comforting transparency such as *mise-en-abyme*, self-referentiality, circularity, fragmentation, and so on encourages the formation of multiple memories and construction of personal and collective pasts, which open a critique of the creation of these comforting memories. *Dolor y gloria* is an outstanding example of Almodóvar's magnificent obsession with mothers and motherlands, bodies and trauma, the past and its hold on the present. His cinema both uses and exposes fantasy as 'wish fulfilment, as a way of journeying back in time and conquering the demons of the past, and the present' (Bradshaw, 2004: 14). Almodóvar's 'postNostalgia', his use of postmodern strategies to encourage scepticism about representations of the past, seeks to both scratch the scabs that form over (sometimes unacknowledged or unknown) past trauma and ponder the uncertain role of art – cinema in particular – in the repression and reproduction of that past as well as the reconstruction of personal and collective selves in the present through acknowledgement of its painful history.

Filmography

This is a filmography of Pedro Almodóvar as director. I have indicated where he has also written the script. Data are from the IMDB and Filmoteca Española (www.culturaydeporte.gob.es/cultura/areas/cine/mc/fe/portada.html).

Short films

Film político (1974)
Dos putas, o historia de amor que termina en boda (1974)
La caída de Sodoma (1975)
Homenaje (1975)
El sueño, o la estrella (1975)
Blancor (1975)
Tráiler de 'Who's Afraid of Virginia Woolf?' (1976)
Sea caritativo (1976)
Muerte en la carretera (1976)
Sexo va, sexo viene (1977)
Salomé (1978)
Folle ... folle ... fólleme Tim! (1978)
Tráiler para amantes de lo prohibido (TV, 1985)
Pastas Ardilla (TV, 1996)
La concejala antropófaga (The Cannibalistic Councillor, as Mateo Blanco, 2009)
La voz humana (The Human Voice, 2020)

Feature films

Pepi, Luci, Bom y otras chicas del montón (Pepi, Luci, Bom and Other Girls on the Heap/Pepi, Luci, Bom and Other Girls like Mom, 1980) (Spain), 82 mins
Production company: Figaro Films
Producer: Pepón Coromina, Pastora Delgado

Writers: Pedro Almodóvar (screenplay), Pedro Almodóvar (story)
Cinematography: Paco Femenia
Editing: José (Pepe) Salcedo
Sound: Miguel Ángel Polo

Laberinto de pasiones (Labyrinth of Passion, 1982) (Spain), 100 mins
Production company: Alphaville
Writers: Pedro Almodóvar
Cinematography: Ángel Luis Fernández
Music: Bernardo Bonezzi and Fabio de Miguel (as Fanny MacNamara)
Editing: Miguel Fernández, Pablo Pérez Mínguez, José Salcedo

Entre tinieblas (Dark Habits, 1983) (Spain), 114 mins
Production company: Tesauro
Screenplay: Pedro Almodóvar
Cinematography: Angel Luis Fernández
Editing: José Salcedo

¿Qué he hecho yo para merecer esto? (What Have I Done to Deserve This?,
    1984) (Spain), 101 mins
Production company: Tesauro
Screenplay: Pedro Almodóvar
Cinematography: Ángel Luis Fernández
Editing: José Salcedo
Music: Bernardo Bonezzi

Matador (1986) (Spain), 110 mins
Production company: Iberoamericana, with TVE
Screenplay: Pedro Almodóvar, Jesús Ferrero
Cinematography: Ángel Luis Fernández
Editing: José Salcedo
Music: Bernardo Bonezzi

La ley del deseo (The Law of Desire, 1987) (Spain), 102 mins
Production company: El Deseo, with Laurenfilm
Screenplay: Pedro Almodóvar
Cinematography: Ángel Luis Fernández
Editing: José Salcedo

Mujeres al borde de un ataque de nervios (Women on the Verge of a Nervous
    Breakdown, 1988) (Spain), 88 mins
Production company: El Deseo, with Laurenfilm
Screenplay: Pedro Almodóvar
Cinematography: José Luis Alcaine
Editing: José Salcedo
Music: Bernardo Bonezzi

¡Átame! (Tie Me Up! Tie Me Down!, 1989) (Spain), 101 mins
Production company: El Deseo
Screenplay: Pedro Almodóvar
Cinematography: José Luis Alcaine
Editing: José Salcedo
Music: Ennio Morricone

Tacones lejanos (High Heels, 1991) (Spain/France), 112 mins
Production company: El Deseo, with Canal+ and CiBy 2000
Screenplay: Pedro Almodóvar
Cinematography: Alfredo Mayo
Editing: José Salcedo
Music: Ryuichi Sakamoto

Kika (1993) (Spain/France), 114 mins
Production company: El Deseo, CiBy 2000
Screenplay: Pedro Almodóvar
Cinematography: Alfredo Mayo
Editing: José Salcedo

La flor de mi secreto (The Flower of My Secret, 1995) (Spain/France), 103 mins
Production company: El Deseo, CiBy 2000
Screenplay: Pedro Almodóvar
Cinematography: Affonso Beato and Alfredo Mayo
Editing: José Salcedo
Music: Alberto Iglesias

Carne trémula (Live Flesh, 1997) (Spain/France), 100 mins
Production company: El Deseo, Ciby 2000, France 3 Cinéma
Screenplay: Pedro Almodóvar
Cinematography: Affonso Beato
Editing: José Salcedo
Music: Alberto Iglesias
Art Direction: Antxón Gómez

Todo sobre mi madre (All about My Mother, 1999) (Spain/France), 101 mins
Production company: El Deseo, Renn Productions, France 2 Cinéma
Screenplay: Pedro Almodóvar
Cinematography: Affonso Beato
Editing: José Salcedo
Music: Alberto Iglesias
Art Direction: Antxón Gómez

Hable con ella (Talk to Her, 2002) (Spain), 112 mins
Production company: El Deseo, Antena 3 Televisión
Screenplay: Pedro Almodóvar

Cinematography: Javier Aguirresarobe
Editing: José Salcedo
Music: Alberto Iglesias
Art Direction: Antxón Gómez

La mala educación (Bad Education, 2004) (Spain), 106 mins
Production company: El Deseo, Canal+ España, Instituto de la Cinematografía y de las Artes Visuales
Screenplay: Pedro Almodóvar
Cinematography: José Luis Alcaine
Editing: José Salcedo
Music: Alberto Iglesias
Art Direction: Antxón Gómez

Volver (2006) (Spain), 121 mins
Production company: El Deseo, Canal+ España, Ministerio de Cultura
Screenplay: Pedro Almodóvar
Cinematography: José Luis Alcaine
Editing: José Salcedo
Music: Alberto Iglesias

Los abrazos rotos (Broken Embraces, 2009) (Spain), 127 mins
Production company: El Deseo, Universal Pictures International, Canal+ España
Screenplay: Pedro Almodóvar
Cinematography: Rodrigo Prieto
Editing: José Salcedo
Music: Alberto Iglesias
Art Direction: Víctor Moreno

La piel que habito (The Skin I Live In, 2011) (Spain), 120 mins
Production company: El Deseo, Blue Haze Entertainment, Canal+ España
Screenplay: Pedro Almodóvar
Cinematography: José Luis Alcaine
Editing: José Salcedo
Music: Alberto Iglesias
Art Direction: Antxón Gómez

Los amantes pasajeros (I'm So Excited!, 2013) (Spain), 90 mins
Production company: El Deseo
Screenplay: Pedro Almodóvar
Cinematography: José Luis Alcaine
Editing: José Salcedo
Music: Alberto Iglesias
Art Direction: Federico García Cambero

Julieta (2016) (Spain), 99 mins
Production company: El Deseo, Echo Lake Entertainment, Canal+ France
Screenplay: Pedro Almodóvar
Cinematography: Jean-Claude Larrieu
Editing: José Salcedo
Music: Alberto Iglesias
Art Direction: Carlos Bodelón

Dolor y gloria (Pain and Glory, 2019) (Spain/France), 113 mins
Production company: El Deseo, Gobierno de España, Radio Televisión Española
Screenplay: Pedro Almodóvar
Cinematography: José Luis Alcaine
Editing: Teresa Font
Music: Alberto Iglesias

References

Abeel, E. (2004) 'School for scandal: Almodóvar turns his memories into movie masterpieces'. *Film Journal International*, 107(11), 14–16.

Acevedo-Muñoz, E. R. (2004) 'The body and Spain: Pedro Almodóvar's *All about My Mother*'. *Quarterly Review of Film and Video*, 21(1), 25–38.

Acevedo-Muñoz, E. R. (2007) *Pedro Almodóvar*. London: BFI.

Aguilar, P. (2002) *Memory and Amnesia: The Role of the Spanish Civil War in the Transition to Democracy*. New York and London: Berghahn Books.

Aguilar, P. (2003) 'Hable con ella (pero solo si ella no responde). Punto de Vista 2'. *Mujeres Hoy*, 20 January, www.mujereshoy.com/secciones/181.shtml [accessed 20/02/2005].

Alcover, N. (1998) '*Carne Trémula*'. In A. Pérez Gómez (ed.), *Cine para leer 1997* (pp. 187–90). Bilbao: Mensajero.

Aldana Reyes, X. (2013) 'Skin deep? Surgical horror and the impossibility of becoming woman in Almodóvar's *The Skin I Live In*'. *Bulletin of Hispanic Studies*, 90(7), 819–34.

Aldana Reyes, X. (2016) 'Introduction: What, why and when is horror fiction?'. In X. Aldana Reyes (ed.), *Horror: A Literary History* (pp. 7–17). London: British Library Publishing.

All about Desire: The Passionate Cinema of Pedro Almodóvar (2001) [TV documentary]. N. C. Wright, 22 December.

Allbritton, D. (2014) 'Prime risks: the politics of pain and suffering in Spanish crisis cinema'. *Journal of Spanish Cultural Studies*, 15(1–2), 101–15.

Allinson, M. (2001) *A Spanish Labyrinth: The Films of Pedro Almodóvar*. London and New York: I.B.Tauris.

Allinson, M. (2005) 'Todo sobre mi madre'. In A. Mira (ed.), *The Cinema of Spain and Portugal* (pp. 229–37). London and New York: Wallflower Press.

Allinson, M. (2009) 'Mimesis and diegesis: Almodóvar and the limits of melodrama'. In B. Epps and D. Kakoudaki (eds), *All about Almodóvar. A Passion for Cinema* (pp. 141–65). Minneapolis and London: University of Minnesota Press.

Almodóvar, P. (1990) 'Industria e hipocresía'. *El País*, 22 April. https://elpais.com/diario/1990/04/22/opinion/640735206_850215.html [accessed 24/11/2020].

Almodóvar, P. (2004) '*La mala educación*. Autoentrevista'. Pedro Almodóvar Official Website. www.clubcultura.com [accessed 19/04/2004].

Almodóvar, P. (2009) '*Volver*: A filmmaker's diary'. In B. Epps and D. Kakoudaki (eds), *All about Almodóvar. A Passion for Cinema* (pp. 446–63). Minneapolis and London: University of Minnesota Press.

Almodóvar, P. (2013) 'The rhythm of comedy'. *Sight & Sound*, 23(5), 39.

Amiguet, T. (2016) 'Cristina Sánchez, una mujer en el ruedo'. *La Vanguardia* Hemeroteca, 10 April, www.lavanguardia.com/hemeroteca/20160502/401511685702/cristina-sanchez-toreras-tauromaquia-mujeres.html [accessed 18/05/2018].

Anon. (1991) 'The Flower of My Secret'. *The Washington Post*, 31 May, 51–2.

Arredondo, C. (2013) 'Pedro Almodóvar regresa a la comedia con "I'm So Excited!"', *La Opinión*, 23 June, https://laopinion.com/2013/06/23/pedro-almodovar-regresa-a-la-comedia-con-im-so-excited/ [accessed 02/02/2019].

Arribas, J. (1985) '¿Qué he hecho yo para merecer esto?'. In A. Pérez Gómez (ed.), *Cine para leer 1984* (pp. 268–70). Bilbao: Mensajero.

Arroyo, J. (1992) '*La ley del deseo*: A gay seduction'. In R. Dyer and G. Vincendeau (eds), *Popular European Culture* (pp. 31–46). London and New York: Routledge.

Arroyo, J. (1998) 'Live Flesh/*Carne trémula*'. *Sight & Sound*, 8(5), 50–1.

Arroyo, J. (2002) 'Pedro Almodóvar'. Transcript of interview at the NFT, *The Guardian*, 31 July, www.theguardian.com/film/2002/jul/31/features.pedroalmodovar [accessed 23/09/2002].

Backstein, K. (2003) '*Talk to Her*'. *Cineaste*, 28(2), 41–2.

Ballesteros, I. (2009) 'Performing identities in the cinema of Pedro Almodóvar'. In B. Epps and D. Kakoudaki (eds), *All about Almodóvar. A Passion for Cinema* (pp. 71–100). Minneapolis and London: University of Minnesota Press.

Beilin, K. O. (2012) '*Broken Embraces*' "unearthing the dead": on *amour fou*, fatherhood and memory'. *Studies in Hispanic Cinemas*, 9(1), 35–47.

Belinchón, G. (2015a) 'Pedro Almodóvar anuncia su siguiente película: "Silencio"', *El País*, 3 January, https://elpais.com/cultura/2015/01/03/actualidad/1420299744_818175.html [accessed 12/01/2015].

Belinchón, G. (2015b) 'Almodóvar: "El tiempo es devastador con todo: cine, memoria y cuerpos"'. *El País*, 12 January, https://elpais.com/cultura/2015/01/11/actualidad/1421008820_095933.html [accessed 12/01/2015].

Bersani, L. and Dutoit, U. (2009) 'Almodóvar's girls'. In B. Epps and D. Kakoudaki (eds), *All about Almodóvar. A Passion for Cinema* (pp. 193–266). Minneapolis and London: University of Minnesota Press.

Blandford, S., Grant, B., and Hillier, J. (2001) *The Film Studies Dictionary*. London: Edward Arnold.

Boquerini (as F. M. Blanco) (1989) *Pedro Almodóvar*. Madrid: Ediciones JC.

Bourdieu, P. (1993) *The Field of Cultural Production: Essays on Art and Literature*. London: Polity and Columbia University Press.

Bourdieu, P. (2013 [1984]) *Distinction: A Social Critique of the Judgement of Taste*. London and New York: Routledge.

Boyero, C. (2009) '¿Qué he hecho yo para merecer esto?'. *El País*, 18 March, https://elpais.com/diario/2009/03/18/cine/1237330802_850215.html [accessed 12/01/2016].

Boyero, C. (2011) 'Horror frío? No, horror grotesco'. *El País*, 2 September, https://elpais.com/diario/2011/09/02/cine/1314914404_850215.html [accessed 08/06/2012].

Bradbury, S. (2019) 'There's a new restraint to my work'. *The i*, 16 August, 31–2.

Bradshaw, P. (2004) 'When we were boys'. *The Guardian Friday Review*, 21 May, 14–15.

Bradshaw, P. (2011) 'The Skin I Live In – review'. *The Guardian*, 25 August, http://guardian.co.uk/film/2011/aug/25/the-skin-i-live-in-review/print [accessed 08/06/2012].

Bradshaw, P. (2019) 'Life meets art in a wistful fantasia from Almodóvar'. *The Guardian Saturday*, 24 August, 60.

Brooks, P. (1995) *The Melodramatic Imagination: Balzac, Henry James, Melodrama, and the Mode of Excess*. New Haven and London: Yale University Press.

Buse, P., Triana Toribio, N., and Willis, A. (2007) *The Cinema of Álex de la Iglesia*. Manchester: Manchester University Press.

Cardús i Ros, S. (2000) 'Politics and the invention of memory. For a sociology of the transition to democracy in Spain'. In J. R. Resina (ed.), *Disremembering the Dictatorship: The Politics of Memory in the Spanish Transition* (pp. 17–42). Amsterdam and Atlanta: Rodopi.

Cerdán, J. and Fernández Labayen, M. (2013) 'Almodóvar and Spanish patterns of film reception'. In M. D'Lugo and K. M. Vernon (eds), *A Companion to Pedro Almodóvar* (pp. 129–52). Chichester: Wiley-Blackwell.

Cervantes, V. D. (2014) 'Drag acts of transitional performance: sex, religion and memory in Pedro Almodóvar's *La mala educación* and Ventura Pons's *Ocaña, retrat intermitent*'. *Journal of Spanish Cultural Studies*, 15(4), 419–36.

Colmenero Salgado, S. (2001) *Todo sobre mi madre: Estudio Crítico*. Barcelona and Buenos Aires: Ediciones Paidós.

Cook, P. (2005) *Screening the Past. Memory and Nostalgia in Cinema*. London and New York: Routledge.

Cook, P. and Bernink, M. (eds) (2004) *The Cinema Book*. London: BFI.

Correa Ulloa, J. D. (2005) *Pedro Almodóvar: Alguien del montón*. Bogotá: Panamericana Editorial.

Costa, J. (2013) 'Los amantes pasajeros: Para Almodovarianos con lujuria de after'. *Fotogramas*, 10 July, www.fotogramas.es/peliculas-criticas/a48 5649/los-amantes-pasajeros/ [accessed 17/02/2019].

Davies A. (2004) 'The Spanish femme fatale and the cinematic negotiation of Spanishness'. *Studies in Hispanic Cinemas*, 1(1), 5–16.

Davies A. (2007) *Pedro Almodóvar*. London: Grant & Cutler.

Debruge, P. (2016) 'Julieta'. *Variety*, 331(12), 124–5.

Delgado, M. (2009) 'Sensory perception'. *Sight & Sound*, 19(9), 40–4.

Delgado, M. (2011) 'Flesh and the devil'. *Sight & Sound*, 21(9), 18–22.

Delgado, M. (2013) 'Wings of desire'. *Sight & Sound*, 23(5), 36–40.

Delgado, M. (2016) 'Open secrets'. *Sight & Sound*, 26(9), 38–42.

Delgado, M. (2019) 'Cinema is my life'. *Sight & Sound*, 29(9), 38–40.

Dentith, S. (1995) *Bakhtinian Thought. An Introductory Reader*. London and New York: Routledge.

Dika, V. (2014) 'The remake of memory: Martin Scorsese's *Shutter Island* and Pedro Almodóvar's *The Skin I Live In*'. *L'Atalante*, July–December, 43–51.

D'Lugo, M. (1995) 'Almodóvar's city of desire'. In K. M. Vernon and B. Morris (eds), *Post-Franco, Postmodern: The Films of Pedro Almodóvar* (pp. 125–44). Westport and London: Greenwood Press.

D'Lugo, M. (2006) *Pedro Almodóvar*. Urbana and Chicago: University of Illinois Press.

D'Lugo, M. (2009) 'Postnostalgia in *Bad Education*: written on the body of Sara Montiel'. In B. Epps and D. Kakoudaki (eds), *All about Almodóvar: A Passion for Cinema* (pp. 357–85). Minneapolis and London: University of Minnesota Press.

D'Lugo, M. (2013a) 'Almodóvar and Latin America: The making of a transnational aesthetic in *Volver*'. In M. D'Lugo and K. M. Vernon (eds), *A Companion to Pedro Almodóvar* (pp. 412–31). Chichester: Wiley-Blackwell.

D'Lugo, M. (2013b) '*Los abrazos rotos/Broken Embraces* (Pedro Almodóvar, 2009). Talking cures'. In M. M. Delgado and R. Fiddian (eds), *Spanish Cinema 1973–2010: Auteurism, Politics, Landscape and Memory* (pp. 212–25). Manchester: Manchester University Press.

D'Lugo, M. (2015) '*Los amantes pasajeros*: An update on Almodóvar's trans-border cinema'. *Rebeca: Revista Brasileira de Estudos de Cinema e Audiovisual*, 4(7), 73–90.

D'Lugo, M. and Vernon, K. M. (2013) 'Introduction: The Skin He Lives In'. In M. D'Lugo and K. M. Vernon (eds), *A Companion to Pedro Almodóvar* (pp. 1–17). Chichester: Wiley-Blackwell.

D'Lugo, M. and Vernon, K. M. (eds) (2013) *A Companion to Pedro Almodóvar*. Chichester: Wiley-Blackwell.

Domingo, C. (2007) *Coser y cantar. Las Mujeres bajo la dictadura franquista.* Barcelona: Lumen.

Donnell, S. (2001) 'If the shoe fits: Buñuel, Almodóvar, and the modernist/ postmodernist question'. *Bucknell Review*, 45(1), 52–64.

Edwards, G. (1995) *Indecent Exposures. Buñuel, Saura, Erice & Almodóvar.* London and New York: Marion Boyars.

Edwards, G. (2001) *Almodóvar: Labyrinths of Passion.* London and Chester Springs: Peter Owen.

Edwards, G. (2005) *A Companion to Luis Buñuel.* Woodbridge: Tamesis.

Ellis, J. and Sánchez-Arce, A. M. (2011) '"The unquiet dead": memories of the Spanish Civil War in Guillermo del Toro's *Pan's Labyrinth*'. In A. Sinha and T. McSweeney (eds), *Millennial Cinema: Memory in Global Film* (pp. 173–91). London and New York: Wallflower Press.

Elsaesser, T. (1987) 'Tales of sound and fury: observations on the family melodrama'. In C. Gledhill (ed.), *Home Is Where the Heart Is: Studies in Melodrama and the Woman's Film* (pp. 43–69). London: BFI.

Epps, B. (1995) 'Figuring hysteria: disorder and desire in three films of Pedro Almodóvar'. In K. M. Vernon and B. Morris (eds), *Post-Franco, Postmodern: The Films of Pedro Almodóvar* (pp. 99–124). Westport and London: Greenwood Press.

Epps, B. (2005) 'Entre la efusividad multicolor y la desaparición mono-cromática: melodrama, pornografía y abstracción en *Hable con ella*'. In F. A. Zurián Hernández and C. Vázquez Varela (eds), *Almodóvar: el cine como pasión. Actas del Congreso Internacional 'Pedro Almodóvar'* (pp. 269–86). Cuenca: Ediciones de la Universidad de Castilla-La Mancha.

Epps, B. and Kakoudaki, D. (eds) (2009) *All About Almodóvar: A Passion for Cinema.* Minneapolis and London: University of Minnesota Press.

Evans, P. W. (1996). *Women on the Verge of a Nervous Breakdown.* London: BFI.

Faulkner, S. (2013). *A History of Spanish Film: Cinema and Society 1910–2010.* London: Bloomsbury.

Fernández-Santos, E. (2019) 'Banderas interpreta al "alter ego" de Almodóvar en su nueva película'. *El País*, 20 February, https://elpais.com/ elpais/2019/02/18/eps/1550513030_369310.html [accessed 23/08/2019].

Ferrán, O. (2000) 'Memory and forgetting, resistance and noise in the Spanish transition: Semprún and Vázquez Montalbán'. In J. R. Resina (ed.), *Disremembering the Dictatorship: The Politics of Memory in the Spanish Transition* (pp. 191–222). Amsterdam and Atlanta: Rodopi.

Flores, F. (1990) 'Almodóvar topó con el muro'. *La Vanguardia*, 12 February, 31.

Fouz-Hernández, S. and Martínez-Expósito, A. (2007) *Live Flesh: The Male Body in Contemporary Spanish Cinema.* London and New York: I.B.Tauris.

French, P. (2002) 'Coma versus coma'. *The Observer Review*, 25 August, 6.

French, P. (2006) 'Shall I carve, dear?' *The Observer Review*, 27 June, 14.

Fuentes, V. (2009) 'Bad Education: fictional autobiography and meta-film noir'. In B. Epps and D. Kakoudaki (eds), All about Almodóvar: A Passion for Cinema (pp. 429–45). Minneapolis and London: University of Minnesota Press.

Galán, D. (1984) 'Proyecto de esperpento fragmentado'. El País, 26 October, https://elpais.com/diario/1984/10/26/cultura/467593209_850215.html [accessed 05/08/2008].

Gallero, J. L. (ed.) (1991) Sólo se vive una vez. Esplendor y ruina de la movida madrileña. Madrid: Ediciones Ardora.

Galtung, J. (1969) 'Violence, peace, and peace research'. Journal of Peace Research, 6(3), 167–91.

García Alcázar, S. (2011) 'The romantic influence on the nineteenth-century architectural restoration in Spain'. Anales de Historia del Arte, supl. Volumen Extraordinario, 197–210.

García de León, M. A. (1989) 'Sociología del cine de Pedro Almodóvar'. In M. A. García de León and T. Maldonado, Pedro Almodóvar, la otra España cañí (sociología y crítica cinematográficas) (pp. 23–139). Ciudad Real: Diputación de Ciudad Real – Área de Cultura.

Geyskens, T. (2010) 'Literature as symptomatology: Gilles Deleuze on Sacher-Masoch'. In L. De Bolle (ed.), Deleuze and Psychoanalysis: Philosophical Essays on Deleuze's Debate with Psychoanalysis (pp. 103–16). Leuven: Leuven University Press.

Gilbey, R. (2004) 'Bad Education'. Sight & Sound, 14(6), 44–6.

Gilbey, R. (2013) 'Great Spanish take-off'. New Statesman, 3–9 May, 51.

González Requena, J. (2015) '3. La estructura del film y su pesadilla: Hable con ella, Bodas de Sangre, Yerma'. http://gonzalezrequena.com/la-estructura-del-film-y-su-pesadilla-hable-con-ella-bodas-de-sangre-yerma/ [accessed 22/02/2017].

Graham, H. (2005). The Spanish Civil War. Oxford: Oxford University Press.

Guarner, J. L. (1986) 'Matador'. La Vanguardia, 15 March, 30.

Guarner, J. L. (1990) '"Átame": después de la expectación llega la polémica'. La Vanguardia, 12 February, 31.

Gutiérrez-Albilla, J. D. (2005) 'Body, silence and movement: Pina Bausch's Café Müller in Almodóvar's Hable con ella'. Studies in Hispanic Cinemas, 2(1), 47–58.

Gutiérrez-Albilla, J. D. (2011) 'Returning to and from the maternal rural space: traumatic memory, late modernity and nostalgic utopia in Almodóvar's Volver'. Bulletin of Hispanic Studies, 88(3), 321–38.

Gutiérrez-Albilla, J. D. (2013a) 'La piel del horror, el horror de la piel. Poder, violencia y trauma en el cuerpo (post)humano en La piel que habito'. Journal of Spanish Cultural Studies, 14(1), 70–85.

Gutiérrez-Albilla, J. D. (2013b) 'Scratching the past on the surface of the skin: embodied intersubjectivity, prosthetic memory, and witnessing in

Almodóvar's *La mala educación*'. In M. D'Lugo and K. M. Vernon (eds), *A Companion to Pedro Almodóvar* (pp. 322–44). Chichester: Wiley-Blackwell.

Gutiérrez-Albilla, J. D. (2017) *Aesthetics, Ethics and Trauma in the Cinema of Pedro Almodóvar*. Edinburgh: Edinburgh University Press.

Halligan, F. (2016) '"Julieta": review'. *Screen International*, 8 April, www.screen daily.com/reviews/julieta-review/5102234.article [accessed 28/11/2018].

Harrang, C. (2012) 'Psychic skin and narcissistic rage: reflections on Almodóvar's *The Skin I Live In*'. *The International Journal of Psychoanalysis*, 93, 1301–8.

Hernández Vicente, A. (2003) 'Cómo la aprendiz superó al maestro'. In J. Gorostiza (ed.), *Pedro Almodóvar* (pp. 25–31). Las Palmas de Gran Canaria: Filmoteca Canaria.

Herrera, J. (2012) 'Tiempo momificado y coqueteo con la muerte en *Los abrazos rotos* de Pedro Almodóvar. A propósito de la cita de *Viaggio in Italia* de Roberto Rossellini'. *Fotocinema*, 5, 62–75.

Higginbotham, V. (1988) *Spanish Film under Franco*. Austin: University of Texas Press.

Hutcheon, L. (1988) *A Poetics of Postmodernism. History, Theory, Fiction*. New York and London: Routledge.

Hutcheon, L. (2006) *A Theory of Adaptation*. London and New York: Routledge.

Ibáñez, J. C. (2013) 'Memory, politics, and the post-transition in Almodóvar's cinema'. In M. D'Lugo and K. M. Vernon (eds), *A Companion to Pedro Almodóvar* (pp. 153–75). Chichester: Wiley-Blackwell.

Informe Semanal (2016), *Almodóvar entre los muertos*, TVE (Spain), 11 February.

Iñaki (2011), *Con Pedro Almodóvar*, Canal+ (Spain), 25 August.

Jessup, F. R. (1994) '*Women on the Verge of a Nervous Breakdown*: sexism or emancipation from machismo?'. In G. Finney (ed.), *Look Who's Laughing: Gender and Comedy* (pp. 299–314). Amsterdam, Reading, and Langhorne: Gordon and Breach.

Jones, K. (2002) 'Pedro Almodóvar creates another lush, bittersweet object of beauty'. *Film Comment*, 38(3), 15.

Jordan, B. and Morgan-Tamosunas, R. (1998) *Contemporary Spanish Cinema*. Manchester and New York: Manchester University Press.

Jung, D. (2014) 'Yuxtaposición artística en *La piel que habito* de Pedro Almodóvar: en torno a las obras de Tiziano, Louise Bourgeois, Guillermo Pérez Villalta y Juan Gatti'. *Neophilologus*, 98(4), 617–35.

Junkerjürgen, R. (2018) '*La peli que habito*: Intermedialidad entre el arte, la auto-reflexión y el *product placement* en la obra de Almodóvar'. *Bulletin of Hispanic Studies*, 95(1), 61–74.

Kakoudaki, D. (2009) 'Intimate strangers: Melodrama and coincidence in *Talk to Her*'. In B. Epps and D. Kakoudaki (eds), *All about Almodóvar: A*

Passion for Cinema (pp. 193–238). Minneapolis and London: University of Minnesota Press.

Keown, D. (1996) 'The critique of reification: a subversive current within the cinema of contemporary Spain'. In W. Everett (ed.), *European Identity in Cinema* (pp. 61–73). Exeter: Intellect Books.

Kinder, M. (1987) 'Pleasure and the New Spanish mentality: a conversation with Pedro Almodóvar'. *Film Quarterly*, XLI(1), 33–43.

Kinder, M. (1992) '*High Heels*'. *Film Quarterly*, 45(3), 39–44.

Kinder, M. (1993) *Blood Cinema: The Reconstruction of National Identity in Spain*. Berkeley, Los Angeles, and London: University of California Press.

Kinder, M. (2004). 'Reinventing the motherland: Almodóvar's brain-dead trilogy'. *Film Quarterly*, 58(2), 9–25.

Kinder, M. (2007) '*Volver*'. *Film Quarterly*, 60(3), 4–9.

Kinder, M. (2009) 'All about the brothers: retroseriality in Almodóvar's cinema'. In B. Epps and D. Kakoudaki (eds), *All about Almodóvar: A Passion for Cinema* (pp. 267–94). Minneapolis and London: University of Minnesota Press.

Kinder, M. (2010) '*Broken Embraces*'. *Film Quarterly*, 63(3), 28–34.

Kuhn, A. (2002) *Family Secrets: Acts of Memory and Imagination*. London and New York: Verso.

Landsberg, A. (1995) 'Prosthetic memory: *Total Recall* and *Blade Runner*'. *Body & Society*, 1(3–4), 175–89.

Lane, R. and Tew, P. (2003) 'Introduction' to Myth and History Section. In R. Lane, R. Mengham, and P. Tew (eds), *Contemporary British Fiction* (pp. 11–12). Cambridge: Polity.

Lange-Churion, P. (2016) 'Pedro Almodóvar's *La piel que habito*: of late style and erotic conservatism'. *Bulletin of Hispanic Studies*, 93(3), 441–53.

Lawson, M. (2016) 'No chance of Spexit'. *New Statesman*, 26 August–1 September, 50–1.

Lemma, A. (2012) 'A perfectly modern Frankenstein: Almodóvar's *The Skin I Live In* (2011, Sony Pictures Classics)'. *The International Journal of Psychoanalysis*, 93(5), 1291–300.

Lev, L. (1995) 'Tauromachy as spectacle of gender revision in *Matador*'. In K. M. Vernon and B. Morris (eds), *Post-Franco, Postmodern: The Films of Pedro Almodóvar* (pp. 73–86). Westport and London: Greenwood Press.

Llopart, S. (1993) 'Entrevista a Pedro Almodóvar, director de cine. "*Las uñas del asesino* es un filme duro y creará mucha polémica"'. *La Vanguardia*, 14 March, 2–3.

Losilla, C. (2013) 'I'm So Excited!'. *Sight & Sound*, 23(5), 96–7.

McCartney, J. (2011) 'The Skin I Live In: Seven magazine review'. *Sunday Telegraph*. 25 August, www.telegraph.co.uk/culture/film/filmreviews/8723179/The-Skin-I-Live-In-review.html [accessed 05/05/2019].

McDaniel, D. (1994) 'Children of Almodóvar: an imagined past and the collective present'. *The Spectator*, https://search.proquest.com/docview/1 461379178?accountid=13828 [accessed 25/11/2013].

Maddison, S. (2000) 'All about women: Pedro Almodóvar and the heterosocial dynamic'. *Textual Practice*, 14(2), 265–84.

Maldonado, T. (1989) 'Crítica cinematográfica'. In M. A. García de León and T. Maldonado, *Pedro Almodóvar, la otra España cañí (sociología y crítica cinematográficas)* (pp. 141–233). Ciudad Real: Diputación de Ciudad Real – Área de Cultura.

Marí, J. (2015) 'Los amantes "pasajeros" by Pedro Almodóvar'. *Hispania*, 98(3), 627–9.

Markuš, S. (2001 [1998]). *La poética de Pedro Almodóvar*. Trans. Maja Andreivié. Barcelona: Littera.

Marsh, S. (2004) 'Masculinity, monuments and movement: gender and the city of Madrid in Pedro Almodóvar's *Carne trémula* (1997)'. In S. Marsh and P. Nair (eds), *Gender and Spanish Cinema* (pp. 53–70). Oxford and New York: Berg.

Martínez, B. (2019) 'Dolor y gloria: para quienes quieran disfrutar del autor en la cúspide de su carrera'. *Fotogramas*, 18 March, www.fotogramas. es/peliculas-criticas/a26851028/dolor-y-gloria-critica-pelicula/ [accessed 28/03/2019].

Martínez, L. (2019) 'Dolor y gloria: la fiebre del cine perfecto'. *El Mundo*, 21 March, www.elmundo.es/metropoli/cine/2019/03/21/5c9112bfc6c837f11 48b4719.html [accessed 23/08/2019].

Martínez-Vasseur (2005) 'La España de las 80 en *Mujeres al boarde de un ataque de nervios*'. In F. A. Zurián Hernández and C. Vázquez Varela (eds), *Almodóvar: el cine como pasión. Actas del Congreso Internacional 'Pedro Almodóvar'* (pp. 107–31). Cuenca: Ediciones de la Universidad de Castilla-La Mancha.

Méjean, J. M. (2007). *Pedro Almodóvar*. Barcelona: Ma non troppo.

Mermelstein, D. (2013) 'On a plane in Spain'. *The Wall Street Journal*, 20 June, D.4., www.wsj.com/articles/SB10001424127887324021104578 5533 73495005616 [accessed 02/02/2019].

Mercer, J. and Shingler, M. (2004) *Melodrama: Genre, Style, Sensibility*. London: Wallflower Press.

Meseguer, A. (2019) 'Almodóvar desnuda su alma (con pudor) en "Dolor y gloria"'. *La Vanguardia Cine*, 23 August, www.lavanguardia.com/ cine/20190322/461153081685/almodovar-desnuda-alma-pudor-dolor-y-gloria-estrenos-cine.html [accessed 23/08/2019].

Mildren, C. (2013) 'Spectator strategies, satire and European identity in the cinema of Roy Andersson via the paintings of Pieter Bruegel the Elder'. *Studies in European Cinema*, 10(2–3), 147–55.

Mintzer, J. (2013) 'I'm So Excited!'. *Hollywood Reporter*, 419(11), 22–29 March, 82.

Mira, A. (2008) *Miradas insumisas: gays y lesbianas en el cine*. Barcelona and Madrid: Editorial Egales.

Mira, A. (2013) 'A life, imagined and otherwise: the limits and uses of autobiography in Almodóvar's films'. In M. D'Lugo and K. M. Vernon (eds), *A Companion to Pedro Almodóvar* (pp. 88–104). Chichester: Wiley-Blackwell.

Moreiras Menor, C. (2002) *Cultura herida: Literatura y cine en la España democrática*. Madrid: Ediciones Libertarias.

Morgan-Tamosunas, R. (2000) 'Screening the past: history and nostalgia in contemporary Spanish cinema'. In B. Jordan and R. Morgan-Tamosunas (eds), *Contemporary Spanish Cultural Studies* (pp. 111–22). London: Arnold.

Morgan-Tamosunas, R. (2002) 'Narrative, desire and critical discourse in Pedro Almodóvar's *Carne trémula* (1997)'. *Journal of Iberian and Latin American Studies*, 8(2), 185–99.

Morris, P. (1994) 'Introduction'. In P. Morris (ed.), *The Bakhtin Reader: Selected Writings of Bakhtin, Medvedev and Voloshinov* (pp. 1–24). London: Arnold.

Mulvey, L. (1997) 'Visual pleasure and narrative cinema'. In R. R. Warhol and D. Price Herndl (eds), *Feminisms* (pp. 438–48). New Brunswick: Rutgers University Press.

Mulvey, L. (2012) *Fetishism and Curiosity*. London: British Film Institute.

Nagoshi, J. L. and Brzuzy, S. (2010) 'Transgender theory: embodying research and practice'. *Affilia: Journal of Women and Social Work*, 25(4), 431–43.

Naughten, R. (2006) 'Comatose women in "El bosque": sleeping beauty and other literary motifs in Pedro Almodóvar's *Hable con ella*'. *Studies in Hispanic Cinemas*, 3(2), 77–88.

Noble, F. (2020) *Subversive Spanish Cinema: The Politics of Performance*. London: I.B.Tauris.

Nora, P. (1989) 'Between Memory and History: Les Lieux de Mémoire'. *Representations*, 26, Special Issue: Memory and Counter Memory, 7–24.

Novoa, A. (2005) 'Whose talk is it? Almodóvar and the fairy tale in *Talk to Her*'. *Marvels & Tales*, 19(2), 224–48.

Ohi, K. (2009) 'Voyeurism and annunciation in Almodóvar's *Talk to Her*'. *Criticism*, 51(4), 521–57.

Olea Rosenbluth, C. (2016) 'La chica Almodóvar: Algunas reflexiones sobre la construcción de género a partir de *La piel que habito* de Pedro Almodóvar'. *Revista Nomadías*, 21, 99–116.

Pastor, B. M. (2005) 'Sexualidad, género y "alteridad": Pedro Almodóvar – el deseo como ley'. In F. A. Zurián Hernández and C. Vázquez Varela (eds), *Almodóvar: el cine como pasión. Actas del Congreso Internacional 'Pedro Almodóvar'* (pp. 441–9). Cuenca: Ediciones de la Universidad de Castilla-La Mancha.

Pastor, B. M. (2006) 'Screening sexual and gendered otherness in Almodóvar's *Law of Desire* (1987) – the real "sexual revolution"'. *Studies in European Cinema*, 3(1), 7–23.

Pavlović, T. (2006) 'Allegorising the body politic: masculinity and history in Saura's *El jardín de las delicias* (1970) and Almodóvar's *Carne trémula* (1997)'. *Studies in Hispanic Cinemas*, 3(3), 149–67.

Pingree, G. (2004) 'Pedro Almodóvar and the new politics of Spain'. *Cineaste*, 30(1), 4–8.

Place, J. A. and Peterson, L. S. (1974) 'Some visual motifs of *film noir*'. *Film Comment*, 10(1), 30–5.

Poyato Sánchez, P. (2015) 'Programas iconográficos en *La piel que habito* (Almodóvar, 2011)'. *Anales de Historia del Arte*, 25, 283–302.

Price, Z. (2015) 'Skin gazing: queer bodies in Almodóvar's *The Skin I Live In*'. *Horror Studies*, 6(2), 305–17.

Prout, R. (2004) 'All about Spain: transplant and identity in *La flor de mi secreto* and *Todo sobre mi madre*'. *Studies in Hispanic Cinemas*, 1(1), 43–62.

Quinlivan, D. (2014) 'Film, healing and the body in crisis: a twenty-first century aesthetics of hope and reparation'. *Screen*, 55(1), 103–17.

Resina, J. R. (2000) 'Introduction'. In J. R. Resina (ed.), *Disremembering the Dictatorship: The Politics of Memory in the Spanish Transition to Democracy* (pp. 1–16). Amsterdam and Atlanta: Rodopi.

Ricoeur, P. (2006) *Memory, History, Forgetting*. Chicago and London: The University of Chicago Press.

Rodríguez, H. J. (2004) 'Nunca volveremos a casa'. *Dirigido por ...*, March, 32–4.

Roldán Usó, P. (2019) 'Emoción: Dolor y gloria'. *El Espectador imaginario*, 101, April, www.elespectadorimaginario.com/dolor-y-gloria/ [accessed 23/08/2019].

Romney, J. (2016) 'Julieta'. *Sight & Sound*, 26(3), 80.

Rothberg, M. (2009) *Multidirectional Memory: Remembering the Holocaust in the Age of Decolonization*. Stanford: Stanford University Press.

Saenz, N. (2013) 'Domesticating violence in the films of Pedro Almodóvar'. In M. D'Lugo and K. M. Vernon (eds), *A Companion to Pedro Almodóvar* (pp. 244–61). Chichester: Wiley-Blackwell.

Sánchez Noriega, J. L. (1996) 'La flor de mi secreto'. In A. Pérez Gómez (ed.), *Cine para leer 1995* (pp. 273–5). Bilbao: Mensajero.

Sanderson, J. D. (2013) 'To the health of the author: art direction in *Los abrazos rotos*'. In M. D'Lugo and K. M. Vernon (eds), *A Companion to Pedro Almodóvar* (pp. 471–94). Chichester: Wiley-Blackwell.

Santana, M. (2015) 'Screening history: television, memory, and the nostalgia of national community in *Cuéntame* and *Temps de silenci*'. *Journal of Iberian and Latin American Studies*, 21(2), 147–64.

Schatz, T. (1981) *Hollywood Genres: Formulas, Filmmaking, and the Studio System.* New York: Random House.

Schrader, P. (1972) 'Notes on *Film Noir'. Film Comment,* 8(1), 8–13.

Smith, J. L. (1996) 'Sex? Kitsch? That's over now'. *The Times,* 19 January, 31.

Smith, P. J. (1992) *Laws of Desire: Questions of Homosexuality in Spanish Writing and Film 1960–1990.* Oxford: Clarendon Press.

Smith, P. J. (1999) 'Silicone and sentiment'. *Sight & Sound,* 9(9), 28–30.

Smith, P. J. (2002) 'Only connect'. *Sight & Sound,* 12(7), 24–7.

Smith, P. J. (2004a) 'All I desire'. *Sight & Sound,* 14(6), 15–18.

Smith, P. J. (2004b) 'The emotional imperative: Almodóvar's *Hable con ella* and Televisión Española's *Cuentame como pasó'. MLN,* 119(2), 263–375.

Smith, P. J. (2006) 'Women, windmills and wedge heels'. *Sight & Sound,* 14(6), 16–18.

Smith, P. J. (2009) 'Airless love'. *Sight & Sound,* 19(6), 18–20.

Smith, P. J. (2013a) 'Almodóvar's self-fashioning: The economics and aesthetics of deconstructive autobiography'. In M. D'Lugo and K. M. Vernon (eds), *A Companion to Pedro Almodóvar* (pp. 21–38). Chichester: Wiley-Blackwell.

Smith, P. J. (2013b) 'Los Amantes Pasajeros (I'm So Excited)'. *Film Quarterly,* 66(3), 49–52.

Smith, P. J. (2014) *Desire Unlimited: The Cinema of Pedro Almodóvar.* London and New York: Verso.

Smith, P. J. (2019) 'Stardust memories'. *Sight & Sound,* 29(9), 34–7.

Sontag, S. (1964) 'Notes on "Camp"'. *Partisan Review,* 31(4), 515–30.

Sotinel, T. (2010) *Pedro Almodóvar.* Paris: Cahiers du cinéma Sarl.

Spain (1969) 'Real Decreto 1/1969, de 24 de enero por el que se declara el estado de excepción en todo el territorio nacional'. *Boletín Oficial del Estado,* 25 January, 22, 1175, www.boe.es/diario_boe/txt.php?id=BOE-A-1969-98 [accessed 26/08/2015].

Spain (1984) 'Real Decreto 3304/1983, de 28 de diciembre sobre protección de la cinematografía'. *Boletín Oficial del Estado,* 10, 12 January, 806–9, www.boe.es/eli/es/rd/1983/12/28/3304 [accessed 05/05/2019].

Stone, R. (2007) 'Spanish film noir'. In A. Spicer (ed.), *European Film Noir* (pp. 185–209). Manchester: Manchester University Press.

Strauss, F. (2006) *Almodóvar on Almodóvar.* London: Faber.

Sturgeon, J. (2014) '2014: The death of the postmodern novel and the rise of autofiction'. *Flavorwire,* 31 December, http://flavorwire. com/496570/2014-the-death-of-the-postmodern-novel-and-the-rise-of-autofiction [accessed 23/08/2019].

Thompson, K. (1977) 'The concept of cinematic excess'. *Ciné-Tracts: A Journal of Film, Communications, Culture, and Politics,* 1(2), 54–63.

Tirard, L. (2002) *Moviemakers' Master Class. Private Lessons from the World's Foremost Directors.* London and New York: Faber and Faber.

Triana Toribio, N. (1995) 'Hollywood melodrama in the films of Pedro Almodóvar'. In A. Horner and J. Wigmore (eds), *Working Papers in Literary and Cultural Studies*. European Studies Research Institute, University of Salford.

Triana Toribio, N. (2003a) '*¿Qué he hecho yo para merecer esto?* Almodóvar (1984)'. In P. W. Evans (ed.), *Spanish Cinema. The Auteurist Tradition* (pp. 226–41). Oxford: Oxford University Press.

Triana Toribio, N. (2003b) *Spanish National Cinema*. London and New York: Routledge.

Triana Toribio, N. (2008) 'Auteurism and commerce in contemporary Spanish cinema: *directores mediáticos*'. *Screen*, 49(3), 259–76.

Ueda, C. and Smith, M. (1996) 'The Flower of My Secret'. *Cinema Papers*, 109, 39–40.

Van den Akker, R., Gibbons, A., and Vermeulen, T. (eds) (2017) *Metamodernism: Historicity, Affect, and Depth after Postmodernism*. London: Rowman & Littlefield International.

Varderi, A. (1996). *Severo Sarduy y Pedro Almodóvar: del barroco al kitsch en la narrativa y el cine postmodernos*. Madrid: Pliegos.

Vázquez Montalbán, M. (2000) '*Autobiografía del General Franco*: Un problema lingüístico'. In J. R. Resina (ed.), *Disremembering the Dictatorship: The Politics of Memory in the Spanish Transition to Democracy* (pp. 223–44). Amsterdam and Atlanta: Rodopi.

Vegas, V. (2016) 'Todos los chicos Almodóvar, ordenados de peor a mejor'. *Vanity Fair*, www.revistavanityfair.es/actualidad/cine/articulos/chicos-pedro-almodovar-ranking-peor-a-mejor/22383 [accessed 23/02/2017].

Vermeulen, T. and van den Akker, R. (2010) 'Notes on metamodernism'. *Journal of Aesthetics & Culture*, 2(1), 1–14.

Vernon, K. M. (1993) 'Melodrama against itself: Pedro Almodóvar's *What Have I Done to Deserve This?*'. *Film Quarterly*, 46(3), 28–40.

Vernon, K. M. (2009) 'Queer sound: musical otherness in three films by Pedro Almodóvar'. In B. Epps and D. Kakoudaki (eds), *All about Almodóvar: A Passion for Cinema* (pp. 51–70). Minneapolis and London: Minneapolis University Press.

Vernon, K. M. and Morris B. (1995) 'Introduction: Pedro Almodóvar, Postmodern *Auteur*'. In K. M. Vernon and B. Morris (eds), *Post-Franco, Postmodern: The Films of Pedro Almodóvar* (pp. 1–23). Westport and London: Greenwood Press.

Vidal, N. (1989) *El cine de Pedro Almodóvar*. Barcelona: Ediciones Destino.

Vilarós, T. M. (1994) 'Los Monos del Desencanto Español'. *Modern Language Notes*, 109(2), 217–35.

Virué Escalera, L. (2012) 'La fotografía fija en los abrazos rotos: categorías y uso en la construcción de la marca Almodóvar'. *Fotocinema: Revista científica de cine y fotografía*, 5, 112–45.

Waldron, D. and Murray, R. (2014) 'Troubling transformations: Pedro Almodóvar's *La piel que habito/The Skin I Live In* (2011) and its reception'. *Transnational Cinemas*, 5(1), 57–71.

Walters, M. (1989). 'Kitsch and make up'. *The Listener*, 121(3118), 15, 31.

Walters, M. (1990) 'Hit or kiss: can love be battery-powered?'. *The Listener*, 124(3173), 40.

Watney, S. (1994) *Practices of Freedom: Selected Writings on HIV/AIDS*. London: Rivers Oram Press.

Watney, S. (1997) *Policing Desire: Pornography, AIDS and the Media*. London: Cassell.

Willem, L. M. (1998) 'Almodóvar on the verge of Cocteau's *La Voix Humaine*'. *Literature/Film Quarterly*, 26(2), 142–7.

Willem, L. M. (2002) 'Rewriting Rendell: Pedro Almodóvar's *Carne trémula*'. *Literature/Film Quarterly*, 30(2), 115–18.

Wilson, E. (2003) *Cinema's Missing Children*. London and New York: Wallflower Press.

Yarza, A. (1999) *Un caníbal en Madrid: La sensibilidad camp y el reciclaje de la historia en el cine de Pedro Almodóvar*. Madrid: Ediciones Libertarias.

Zurián, F. A. (2013) '*La piel que habito*: A story of imposed gender and the struggle for identity'. In M. D'Lugo and K. M. Vernon (eds), *A Companion to Pedro Almodóvar* (pp. 262–78). Chichester: Wiley-Blackwell.

Index

Page numbers in italics refer to figures.

Lightning Source UK Ltd.
Milton Keynes UK
UKHW021320231122
412709UK00028B/319